D0913910

The Rise and Fall of the Paraguayan Republic,
1800–1870

Latin American Monographs, No. 48
Institute of Latin American Studies
The University of Texas at Austin

The Rise and Fall of the Paraguayan Republic, 1800-1870

by John Hoyt Williams

Institute of Latin American Studies
The University of Texas at Austin

International Standard Book Number 0-292-77017-0 (paper)
0-292-77016-2 (cloth)
Library of Congress Catalog Card Number 78-620052

The Latin American Monographs Series
is distributed for the Institute of
Latin American Studies by:
University of Texas Press
P. O. Box 7819
Austin, Texas 78712

Contents

Preface   ix

Chapters

1. The "Provincia Gigante" in the Eighteenth Century   3
2. José Gaspar de Francia and the Paraguayan Revolution   19
3. Perpetual Means Forever: Francia and the Remodeling of Paraguayan Society   43
4. The Diplomacy of Isolation, 1820-1840   63
5. The Supreme Dictatorship, 1820-1840   81
6. The Old Order Changeth?   101
7. A New Paraguay is Stirring   113
8. The Economic Pulse Quickens   129
9. The Diplomacy of Frustration   139
10. Threat and Counter-Threat: The 1850s   157
11. Foreigners and the Modernization of Paraguay   177
12. "Francisco Solano's Error: The War"   195
13. The Immolation of Paraguay   211

Notes   229

Bibliography   263

Index   273

Maps

1. Northern Paraguay   45

2. Southern Paraguay   47

3. Paraguayan Offensives, 1864-1865   207

4. Allied Offensives, 1866-1870   213

Plates

1. José Gaspar de Francia   18

2. Carlos Antonio López   112

3. Elisa Alicia Lynch   176

4. Francisco Solano López   194

Preface

I have been interested in Paraguay and its history for a decade and have been privileged to spend three years in that country and its archives. The Paraguayan past is etched in acid, all sharp line and high relief, few rounded, softened curves.

Paraguay, today hardly a super-power, was for a while, a century ago, a major regional force. During the 1800-1870 era, it changed from an imperial backwater, half forgotten by Madrid, to a dynamic, dictator-directed, semi-industrialized, semi-militarized, financially sound nation. Unfortunately, the last five years of that period witnessed the virtual destruction of Paraguay and its relegation to almost colonial status vis-à-vis Argentina and Brazil.

No one to date has attempted to deal with this critical period of Paraguayan history as a period. There are specialized monographs in Spanish and a variety of biographies of the major dictators, but almost all of what has been written is either polemic or comes from the pens of philosophers rather than historians.

To prepare this manuscript it was necessary to literally return to the documents in Asunción, Corrientes, Buenos Aires, Rio de Janeiro, London, Madrid, and the United States. For the opportunity to do that, I am very deeply in the debt of the Indiana State University Research Committee, the American Philosophical Society, and the National Endowment for the Humanities for their generous financial aid, without which this study would have been impossible, and to a large number of individuals, both in the United States and in South America, for their encouragement and other help along the way. Among these I should like to single out Dr. Harris Gaylord Warren, "father" of Paraguayan studies in the United States, and Dr. Lyle N. McAlister. In Paraguay, I am indebted to Dr. Hipólito Sánchez Quell, director of the Archivo Nacional, Dr. Miguel Angel González Erico, of the Centro Paraguayo de Estudios Sociológicos, and the late Dr. Efraím Cardozo, most thoughtful of Paraguayan scholars.

Finally, and not at all due to mere convention, I must recognize the wanderlust of my family. Elisabeth and Owen not only learned Spanish, Portuguese, and Guaraní and adapted chameleon-like to a great variety of environments but also brought me cold beer when I needed it. My wife, Martha Marie, was always in my corner, provided me with many ideas, and kept up my sometimes flagging spirits. Without her active support, no amount of patience would have enabled me to finish this book.

The Rise and Fall of the Paraguayan Republic,
1800–1870

1. The "Provincia Gigante" in the Eighteenth Century

Paraguay: Giant Province of the Indies

As the colonial era drew toward its end, few in Madrid would have been able to locate Paraguay on a map of the empire. Once bearing the majestic legend "Provincia Gigante de Indias," between 1537 and 1800 the map of Paraguay had shrunk in the scorching sun as if it had been painted on wet hide.

The last governor, Brigadier General Bernardo de Velasco y Huidobro, had little to report of his province in 1807 save "that blind obedience and great esteem and respect shown me by every class." Describing the riverbank behind Government House in Asunción, Velasco wrote fondly that "I order a chair to be carried there in the afternoon when I do not ride, from which, with the greatest ease, I throw the line and catch monstrous fishes."[1]

Throughout a full century, from 1750 to 1850, there were two salient characteristics, noted by both foreigners and Paraguayans, that appear in writings about Paraguay—the natural richness of the country and consequent ease of life there, and the continual military threat under which most Paraguayans lived out their lives. The two are not contradictory characteristics.

There can be no doubt that nature paraded all its bounty in Paraguay. From the jungles of the north to the rolling savannahs in the south, nature smothered Paraguay in a true riot of vegetation and fruits. Although at times barbarously hot, Paraguay is never truly cold, and the people could live well from nature's profuse gifts with minimum effort. Throughout the period indicated, most Paraguayans did just that, only adding to nature's generosity the domesticated cow. Paraguayans were rural folk almost in their entirety, and made as few demands on nature as it did on them. Eschewing regimented agriculture, Paraguayans maintained no imposing plantations, preferring instead simpler lives lived out on small, virtually self-sufficient farms and ranches scattered throughout the more pleasant sections of their land. Even in the case of yerba mate, the province's one genuine export, the tea was harvested wild in the forest, not cultivated in a systematic manner. Within this essentially "gathering" society most Paraguayans lived, and quite well at that, having an impact on the environment as minimal as that of their pre-Columbian ancestors.

Foreigners, impressed by the natural potential of Paraguay, were generally appalled by the laissez-faire attitude of its inhabitants. As one Scotsman who knew Paraguay intimately wrote to describe a "typical" Paraguayan:

> The abundance and richness of his own native soil, together with the paucity of his wants, permit his idleness at home. Stretched out in his hammock, which is slung in the porchway of his cottage, his delight is to be there in listlessness the live-long day, and, in the course of it, to smoke a succession of cigars, and sip some twenty or thirty cups of his favorite mate.[2]

A famous compatriot wrote just a few years later, in prose more blunt and arrogant, that "they are a rude people; lead a drowsy life of ease and sluttish abundance," not at all concerned with what tomorrow might bring.[3] The Europeans' disdain, of course, is related to their perception of an immense gap between the actual and what they saw as the vast potential of a rationally exploited Paraguay. As one traveler noted in 1825, "So many are the resources of this fine country, that it comprises in itself all that is necessary for its wants . . . . the sugar, yuca (yam), and other mealy and nutritious roots, and the cattle and fish with which their lands abound."[4]

The second major characteristic was also a dominant factor in Paraguayan life and life-style. The land of the Guaraní was a paranoid's paradise, severely threatened by enemies from 1537 until 1870 and beyond. One can forgive a Paraguayan in the year 1793, for instance, who felt that "they are after me," for all too frequently he was right. Paraguay in the colonial epoch was a marcher province of the Spanish empire, and a continually threatened one. Enemies were potentially everywhere, and the frontier began only blocks away from Government House in Asunción.

Paraguay's two main enemies had been and were the nomadic Indian tribes of the Chaco and far north and the Portuguese. Either was serious enough to threaten the actual existence of the province. As constant and reliable as death and taxes, and causally related to both, the activities of the Chaco nomads required most Paraguayans to live in a virtual state of siege. Operating from the uncharted Chaco, a land inhabited only by themselves and a variety of insects and reptiles that beggars description, the Guaicurú, M'Bayá, Abipón, Payaguá, Mocobí, and other related tribes routinely swept through eastern Paraguay in a continual carnival of rapine and death. Satisfied with their booty, the painted, self-mutilated warriors would then slip across the river and disappear once more into their sanctuary, almost immune to pursuit and retaliation. An eighteenth-century priest, one who knew the area perhaps better than any other white man of his time, wrote of it simply that "such is the aspect of the Province of the Chaco! The Spaniards consider it the theater of misery; the savages, in turn, their Palestine." The cleric went on to note that Paraguay, if "judged by its extension, is immensely large, [but] because of the dangerous proximity of the barbarians on the one side and the Portuguese on the other it is enclosed in limits too tight for its number of inhabitants. The fear of its people impedes their utilization of extensive and fertile lands."[5]

This prolonged struggle with the Indians placed severe strains on Paraguayan resources, both material and human, and did much to define life in the province. Even the capital itself was open to attack from the Chaco: in 1747, Asunción was ravaged by a large daylight raid.[6] The yerba-rich north was almost destroyed in the eighteenth century as M'Bayá and Guaicurú slaughtered yerba gatherers with such regularity that agricultural life stagnated. Hundreds of gatherers died in the forests of the north, their last screams absorbed by the verdant foliage, and the potential of the area was unrealizeable.

In the south, mounted Abipones and Mocobís swept into the missions clustered around the Río Tebicuari on massive raids that could last for years and amount to virtual occupations. In 1799, Santiago, one of the largest missions, was all but wiped out by an Abipón attack. For nearly a century before that large raid, the Abipones had regularly traveled the "highway" through northern Corrientes Province, across the Alto Paraná and into southeastern Paraguay's fertile cattle regions, "killing and robbing as much as they could."[7]

The far east of Paraguay was a no-man's land, with an undefined border with Brazil, inhabited largely by Tapé and Monteses Indians, who were only slightly less hostile than their Chaco counterparts.

If Paraguay was surrounded and vulnerable, so were her lines of communication and commerce seriously threatened and often interrupted. The Payaguá, a canoe-borne tribe of remarkably fierce warriors, specialized in attacking vessels on the rivers and ravaging the score of small ports along the Paraguay and Tebicuari Rivers and a host of smaller waterways to the north. Our awed missionary, Martín Dobrizhoffer, who had worked among the Payaguá and barely lived to tell the tale, graphically reported their activities:

For four hundred leagues to the south of Asunción, they navigate with their canoes in expeditions against the merchant and colonial ships of the Spanish. . . . Mountains of corpses, boys and girls carried off, houses in ashes, merchandise and provisions stolen, and devastated Churches are monuments . . . to the ferocity of these fluvial Pirates.[8]

The erection of scores of small forts and guard posts, the constant patrolling of river fords, and the mobilization of the entire population into militia units did no more than slow down the rhythm of attacks from time to time. Paraguay was as sorely pressed in 1800 as it had been a century earlier, and even in 1867 the Guaicurú would snuff out, like candles in a tropical rain, the lives of hundreds of Paraguayans in the north.

The Portuguese threat also lasted the entire colonial period and beyond, disappearing only gradually after the War of the Triple Alliance. Expanding from São Paulo in search of precious metals and gems, large raiding expeditions stumbled across unmarked borders in the early seventeenth century and encountered another valuable commodity: Indian slaves. By 1650 the new Jesuit mission provinces of Guairá and Itatín were attacked, savaged, and destroyed by these bandeirantes, and thousands of Guaraní neophytes were led from their smoldering pueblos in chains to be sold to the slave-starved plantations of the Brazilian northeast.[9] Due to this unofficial aggression, large chunks of Paraguay (including almost the whole of today's Mato Grosso) fell to the expanding Portuguese empire.

Guaraní survivors of the Guairá and Itatín disasters were led south by their Jesuit mentors and merged into the system of missions clustered around the Alto Paraná and Uruguay rivers. Spain, unable to provide Paraguay with a professional defense, and aware of the secular Paraguayan's nonchalance about the fate of the Jesuit "empire," did provide the Paraná missions with some modern weapons and training, and when the bandeirantes belatedly followed the missionary trail to the south, they suffered grievous losses at the hands of the priest-led Guaraní. Before 1700, the Portuguese threat to the Paraguayan southeast had been stifled.[10]

This, however, did not mean that the threat of Brazilian expansion at Paraguay's expense had been terminated. In the eighteenth century, a new focal point emerged as Brazilians discovered gold at Cuiabá in the Mato Grosso, and large numbers of Portuguese settled the area, pushing ever southwards, decade after decade, across land long claimed by Paraguay. The land between the Juarú and Apa rivers, unoccupied by Paraguay because of the many hostile Indians there and lack of evident economic worth, was absorbed by Brazil. Only by hastily constructing a line of forts along the Apa did Paraguay at last manage to detain the gradual march south of the Luso-Brazilians.

Brazilians also moved to fill the void in the far east of Paraguay. In the eighteenth century thousands of Portuguese immigrants were sent to the present-day states of Paraná, Santa Catarina, and Rio Grande do Sul as colonists. Some of these, often with imperial military support, spilled into what clearly was Paraguay, and had to be expelled by force from lands near Igatimí, San Estanislao, and Caraguatay. Wrote one high official in 1809 to the viceroy in Buenos Aires, "On one frontier 100 leagues from this capital occur continual incidents, now with the Portuguese, now with various races and distinct Nations of Indians."[11]

Only a series of treaties signed after imperial clashes of major proportions in 1750 and 1777 finally clarified the eastern (but not the northern) Paraguayan boundary with Brazil. Paraguay then was a province under pressure, continually shrinking and unable to effectively settle and exploit much of what land remained to it. This environment goes far to explain the defensive nationalism displayed after 1810.

A Growing World of Problems

If Paraguay was being nibbled by the Portuguese territorially, she was also being gouged by Madrid through Buenos Aires. The Provincia Gigante had early proved a disappointment to the Spanish monarchy. No precious metals or stones had been discovered, no major export crop save yerba arose, and the Chaco was an effective barrier to plans for transporting the silver ingots of Peru to Europe by what was, in miles, the shortest route.

Within fifty years of its foundation, Asunción was a rustic backwater of the Spanish empire, moldering in the sun, a tropical village of poorly constructed huts squatting on the banks of the Río Paraguay. By 1570 most of the footloose conquistadores had moved on to what they hoped would be greener fields or nobler deaths, leaving a few score of their compatriots as a thin European patina atop Guaraní society. Those who remained went native, marrying or living with comely Guaraní women, siring biblical numbers of offspring, and living on and from their farms and ranches. Their large mestizo progeny, who spoke Spanish poorly, if at all, but Guaraní well, lived in pueblos whose names underlined the province's isolation: Caacupé, Quiquió, Ybitimí, and Ytá. A thousand miles from the sea, Paraguayans lived in rustic plenty, and in the late sixteenth century, all but forgotten by Spain, sent small expeditions to found or refound such villages as Santa Cruz de la Sierra, Corrientes, and Buenos Aires.

Although Asunción remained for several more decades titular capital of the entire subcontinent, its position eroded steadily in predominance in inverse proportion to the rise of Buenos Aires. Asunción was simply too far in the interior to retain an important official position. Imperial edicts and viceregal commands whittled away Paraguayan jurisdiction and limited its access to Europe and other parts of America. In 1620, an audiencia, or administrative high court, was established at Buenos Aires, and through that organ, political control over the vast La Plata would be exercised. In 1662, Paraguayan commerce was restricted to the port of Santa Fe on the Paraná, relegating most commercial profits to Porteño, or Buenos Aires, middlemen established there. High taxes were levied by the crown on Paraguayan exports to raise money for imperial defense in other quarters, and due to this, yerba mate was almost priced out of the markets of Chile and Peru by 1750.[12]

Due in part to the anti-Jesuit and at times anti-crown Comuneros revolt (1717-1735), half of the thirty Jesuit missions (those south of Candelaria) were detached from the jurisdiction of Asunción and made subject to Buenos Aires, and in 1768, a year after the expulsion of the order from the empire, a further seven missions were placed under Porteño authority, leaving only those eight within the bounds of modern Paraguay subject to Asunción. In 1802, as a logical conclusion, the crown created a separate administration for all thirty missions of the ex-Jesuit "empire," but then changed its royal mind when in 1806 Candelaria and the missions north of the Paraná were placed under control of the Paraguayan governor.[13] Despite its repeated truncation, Paraguay remained an important border province, albeit one almost always left to solve its own problems in splendid isolation.

The Jesuit Arcadia and the Paraguayan Church

The colonial era was notable in Paraguay for the achievements of the Society of Jesus. After the destruction of its Guairá and Itatín mission complexes by the bandeirantes, the order concentrated its energies in creating a veritable "empire within an empire" in their thirty Paraná missions. In these reducciones, each of which had its own ranches, yerbales (yerba forests), and farms, the Jesuits supervised by 1730 the labor of almost 150,000 neophytes.[14]

Through dedication, linguistic ability, shrewd business organization, and good bargaining, the Jesuits managed to place in their control the majority of the sedentary Guaraní. This virtual monopoly by the blackrobes of the Paraguayan labor pool, along with their exemption from most taxation on produce, made it very difficult for secular Paraguayans to compete with them in the economic sphere. The resultant lack of economic incentive helps explain the peculiar Paraguayan isolation in the colonial era.[15]

Each of the Jesuit reducciones was overseen by two friars, although the number of their charges normally exceeded four thousand. All business was conducted in Guaraní, a language reduced to written form by the priests. There were cabildos, or municipal boards, in each mission and Indian officials

who exercised routine powers. Each reducción maintained its own militia and
its own rudimentary schools, and most neophytes dwelt in the pueblo center,
in large, stonework barracks. The missions were segregated: non-Indians were
not allowed to contaminate the religious simplicity and purity in which the
Indians lived, and property was communal rather than private. The two priests
oversaw labor division, planting schedules, and the schools and militia, and
acted as final arbiters in petty squabbles. Divorced from the society at large,
the Indians of the missions lived a highly regimented life, their schedules set by
the paternalistic priests and their activities announced by the tolling of bells at
set times of the day.[16]

Paraguayan mestizos and many crown officials distrusted and disliked the
Jesuits for their seeming domination of the province and their physical and
psychological aloofness, and the serious revolt of the Comuneros can be seen
largely as an attempt by secular Paraguayans to break the Jesuits' iron grip on
their province—especially its labor resources. Although the revolt was a failure,
the Jesuits did not long outlast their detractors. In 1754, Indians of seven of
the Jesuit missions revolted rather than accept a boundary shift that would re-
locate them within Brazil. This "War of the Seven Missions" dragged on spora-
dically for several years, and although not a major affair, and definitely not
fomented by the Jesuits, the unhappy little war discredited the order in the
eyes of Spanish officialdom.[17] Due to the war, repeated and often exaggerated
complaints from Asunción, and a growing regalism in Spanish religious thought,
Charles III in 1767 became the third monarch to expel the Jesuits from his
domains. In that year the missions contained at least ninety thousand Guaraní,
administered by eighty-nine Jesuit priests, who also oversaw a network of detached farms, ranches, yerbales, and schools.[18]

Once the Jesuits had decamped, the tightly administered mission system
seemed to fall apart, as corrupt and inept management by other clerics and
civil authorities (many of whom spoke only Spanish), measles, smallpox, and
renewed threat from hostile Indians, as well as the rapacious behavior of mestizo settlers, destroyed the paternal organization so carefully built by the
Jesuits. By 1801, the population of the missions had decreased to forty-two
thousand, with a corresponding diminution of herds and plantings, prompting
the viceroy in Buenos Aires to write despairingly of the missions, observing
the "decadence . . . that, if not halted, will reduce the occupied lands to a
desert."[19]

The salient position of the Jesuit order was in part responsible for the rather
unhealthy general state of the Paraguayan Church, for the Jesuits' domination
discouraged missionary zeal on the part of the other orders and secular clergy.
The prompt post-1767 decay of the missions (and of other Jesuit properties
and schools) signaled the end of any major ecclesiastical influence in Paraguay,

as no other order emerged to fill the void.[20]

Before the opening of the seminary in Asunción in 1783, most of Paraguay's few native secular priests received their training at distant Córdoba, where, as one writer commented morbidly, "the sign of Torquemada presided."[21] The score or so Paraguayans who entered the religious vocation were in no way sufficient, even with their foreign-born reinforcements, to meet the spiritual needs of their widespread flock. Indeed, the number of curacies vacant at the turn of the century, especially in the interior, was termed by the bishop "embarrassing."[22]

Nor was the ecclesiastical shortage restricted to humble parish priests. Perhaps unique in Latin America, Paraguay had always suffered a chronic want of prelates. In fact, in almost three hundred years of Spanish rule, although thirty-one bishops had been named to the diocese of Asunción, sixteen never arrived. The Paraguayan prelacy was occupied for only 92 years, remaining vacant for 170. As the bishop of Buenos Aires wrote after making a tour of Paraguay in 1765, the Church in that province, "where scarcely a Bishop has been seen," was in dire need of ecclesiastical succor. He sadly noted that in the Guaraní province, the Church "I have found both headless and footless."[23]

Nor were all the clergy paragons of probity and models of morality. An angry viceroy wrote the Paraguayan governor in 1790 concerning various "irregularities" in priestly comportment: "I understand that there are some vagabond religious . . . outside their monasteries without proper license." It was time, the viceroy fumed, to get tough: these errant clergy should be rounded up immediately, and, he concluded, "arrest them if necessary."[24]

At the close of the colonial era, there were perhaps 140 clergy of all types in Paraguay and the missions. Of these, about half were members of the orders. The latter maintained a Dominican, a Mercedarian, and two Franciscan monasteries in Asunción. The Franciscans, largest of the orders, also had a small monastery at Villa Rica and a textile workshop at Tapúa, and they administered seven large Indian pueblos. Its personnel included 47 friars and 18 clergy of minor orders. The Paraguayan Church was headed by a bishop, a vicar, and a 5-man ecclesiastical cabildo.[25] Many interior pueblos would continue, as in previous generations, "without benefit of clergy." It would get worse.

The State of the Nation

Not all in Paraguay was in perpetual crisis. For most Paraguayans, life in 1800 carried on in the same rhythm that had marked it for past generations. No longer merely "a land of priest-craft," as one European insinuated,[26]

Paraguay experienced generally good government and limited economic prosperity.

The Spanish bureaucracy in Paraguay was minimal, a mere skeleton crew that little altered the daily life of the people. The governor, as Velasco no doubt pondered as he hauled his "monstrous fishes" from the river, was like a general with no army, a basically ceremonial figure. By 1800, there was also a teniente asesor letrado (lieutenant governor), often an American from another province, who handled the routine chores of administration. There was also in this period a lieutenant governor for Misiones. In addition, in Asunción were two administrators of the royal treasury, a postmaster with a few employees, a tax overseer, officials of the hospital and militia funds, and a few bureaucrats of the royal tobacco monopoly. With the exception of a treasury official each at Villa Rica, Pilar, Concepción, and Curuguatí, there were no other royal servants in a Paraguay whose population was in excess of 100,000.

In addition to the royal bureaucracy, beyond the capital, highest authority was in the hands of a few subdelegados located in what amounted to regional capitals. These men were occasionally Spaniards but often Paraguayans locally recruited. Subdelegados, whose vague powers were essentially military and political, were usually found at Santiago, capital of the northern missions, Villa Rica, Ytapúa, and Concepción, and were often described as super militia chiefs. Below the subdelegados ranked the comandantes políticos y militares, men of limited authority found in the chief centers of the various partidos into which the province was subdivided, and largely absorbed in military duties. Lesser in prestige were the sixty or so commissioned judges spread throughout the province. These men, responsible for local justice, were often local citizens unadorned by legal training.[27]

On the municipal level was the cabildo. Each of Paraguay's twenty-seven segregated Indian pueblos had its own cabildo, aided by a resident priest and a few other Indian officials, to govern the town. Aside from these pueblos de indios, only centers of some size and importance were permitted cabildos. Asunción, the province's only "city," had an influential cabildo that often governed the entire province in the absence of the governor, and the villas of Pilar, Villa Rica, and Curuguatí maintained independent municipal corporations. Hardly democratic, the cabildos tended to be dominated by local elites, Spanish and Creole.

Paraguay was an overwhelmingly rural province, and its isolation within the Spanish empire was matched by the isolation of most Paraguayans within their own province. Asunción, the capital, was a "city" in name only, with perhaps 5,000 inhabitants in 1782, of whom 1,625 were Blacks, slave and free.[28] The only other relatively large centers of population were Villa Rica, with an "urban" core of perhaps a thousand people, and Pilar and Curuguatí, with considerably fewer. The northern administrative center of Concepción was a collection of tumbled shacks almost falling into the river, and Pilar was but little more impressive, while Cuarepotí and Ycuamandiyú, important yerba centers, were considered rural even by those in Villa Rica. Beyond these few nuclei were a few score villages composed of thirty to fifty huts surrounded by farms.

The poor state of the few roads and the almost utter absence of bridges made travel and the transport of goods and ideas a torturous process. Travel, even at the pace of an oxcart, became impossible during the frequent rains, and a Paraguayan living more than fifty miles from the capital was locked in dismal isolation. In such circumstances, what change came to Paraguay came creeping on all fours. As one observer wrote: "Jealous of their provincial usages and customs, they have varied little, if at all, from what they learned from their fathers."[29]

This isolation, internal and external, permitted, among other things, the encomienda system's endurance until shortly after independence. The encomienda, extinguished in the early eighteenth century by imperial edict, was a system for allocating to meritorious individuals the labor or other tribute of specified groups of Indians. Mutated in Paraguay, the encomienda came to represent a form of personal service—a mild and paternalistic type of slavery. As such, it outlived the institution in every other part of the empire. In 1772, a crown official wrote that "although the King has prohibited" the encomienda, it was alive and well in Paraguay, with seventy-one of "the most distinguished inhabitants" still beneficiaries.[30]   Charles IV himself wrote the viceroy at Buenos Aires in 1803 about the problem, noting that despite royal orders of 1778, 1795, 1798, and 1800, some 6,212 Paraguayan Indians still served in encomienda. "So I have come to order the immediate incorporation into my Royal Crown of as many encomiendas as exist in Paraguay in contravention of my" law."[31]   As late as December, 1812, the revolutionary junta of the new Paraguay was still wrestling with the problem of this anachronistic institution.

Many of the interior pueblos, including some of the ex-Jesuit missions, were quietly prosperous at the turn of the century. In fact, the estancias of Santa María de Fe had recovered since the Jesuit expulsion and were running almost as many head of livestock in 1790 as they had fifty years before, despite a significant decline in population.[32]   The same might be said for the smaller pueblo of San Cosme, another ex-Jesuit mission, which in 1797, with a population of only 1,020, counted five estancias with over 35,000 animals. The people of San Cosme themselves consumed some 4,000 head of cattle annually, a homeric intake of beef even in cattle-rich Paraguay.[33]

Some of the Indian pueblos, however, were poorly managed, as a series of letters denouncing the administrator of Yaguarón attest. That official, García Rodríguez de Francia, father of the future El Supremo, was himself far from supreme. Perhaps attempting to expand his fortunes through fringe benefits, he had assumed the post at the large and prosperous pueblo in 1787, on leave from the semi-professional (and poorly paid) militia, in which he was a lieutenant of artillery. Within two years, his corrupt stewardship elicited screams of outrage from his wards, who alleged that his mismanagement "threatened the ultimate desolation of the afflicted pueblo by such cruel domination." A few months later, two Yaguarón Indians petitioned the viceroy himself "that he . . . remove the present Administrator because of the despotism of his rule."[34]

The Indians, however, suffered the fate of all imperial litigants: delay. Rodríguez de Francia was not removed until 1796, rejoining his old unit, perhaps considerably enriched. El Supremo's father was lucky, for Paraguayans, while recognizing the principle of authority, have often acted against it. Such was the case in 1766, when, wrote the viceroy at Lima in somewhat laconic style, the people of Curuguatí, angry at inept government, "committed the serious crime of submerging the Lt. Governor and two officials, drowning them in the river."[35] This ultimate, participatory democracy, rather than a defined system of checks and balances, had been a hallmark of the Paraguayan body politic since the deposition of Governor Cabeza de Vaca in 1544.

Near the turn of the century, Paraguay's population of perhaps a hundred and twenty thousand was composed of about two hundred peninsular Spaniards, fifty thousand mestizos, forty thousand settled Indians, twenty thousand nomadic Indians, and ten thousand pardos, or Blacks.[36] The people were largely concentrated within a radius of fifty miles of Asunción, where over half dwelt. Thin bands of settlement wandered north and south of the capital for perhaps a hundred miles along the river, and there were foci of population around Villa Rica and the Jesuit missions, but very few in the north or east.

The number of Blacks had grown during the latter part of the eighteenth century, in part due to runaway slaves from Brazil and in part to the new "rage" of solid citizens for acquiring bond servants for prestige. Also, the Blacks in Paraguay soon evidenced the zest for miscegenation shown by the rest of the population, and procreated not only within their race but with the entire available color spectrum. This accounts for the growth of the pardo community, as resultant children, even if genetically defined as Indian, were officially noted as pardo if they showed the slightest negroid features.

So common did this cross-racial fraternization become that the crown was forced to call attention to it and order it halted, informing Paraguayan authorities "about the disorders that have been noted from the marriage of Indians with Blacks . . . slave and free."[37]

Asunción at the Turn of the Century

Asunción was hardly an impressive city in 1800, even by regional standards. With its three barrios and closest suburbs, it counted fewer than ten thousand inhabitants. Only the cabildo building had two stories, and the large Government House, a rectangular structure enclosing a sizeable courtyard, was so unobtrusive as to be invisible a mere block away. The Cathedral's spires poked through the tops of myriad orange trees, but the four monastery buildings were all but buried in foliage, which also kindly cloaked many a crumbling adobe hut in vines and creepers.

One observer noted that "it was always a poor, disorderly city, with horrible, unpaved streets, which inundating rains filled with deep holes and thick sandbanks."[38] With its one main street, potholed and mosaicked by oxcarts, twisting like a worm gone mad on its way from the bay to the countryside, the city clustered on the low hills flanking the bay, attempting to resist debilitating, almost visible heat, torrential rains, and a rising river. Both of the latter caused frequent flooding and such atrocious damage to the streets that a trip of a few blocks on foot was a major undertaking.

Interim governor Gutiérrez looked at his city in 1808 and described it as a depressingly squalid river town at the mercy of cruel elements. "The streets are canals," he wrote; "the old Cathedral and Monastery of San Francisco are submerged, along with a part of the City." The official noted of the jail that it was "almost in the air; a great part of its base destroyed by the River," and this building was merely typical of "the current ruinous state of the City."[39] Gutiérrez was kinder than some in this mordant description of the "Mother of Cities," forgotten by all save its own inhabitants.

Asunceños, however, liked their town, and, unaccustomed to travel in more advanced areas, they had a certain pride in its verdant clutter, its five pulperías, or taverns, forty shops, silversmiths, and various churches.[40] Unlike the rest of the province, Asunción could also offer an education to at least some of its people. There was a public primary school, several Franciscan schools of various levels, and private schools as well as tutoring to be had for the fortunate. There was also the Royal Colegio Seminario of San Carlos, opened in 1783, which provided both secondary and clerical education leading to the priesthood. By 1800, the seminary maintained chairs of theology, philosophy and arts, and Latin and grammar, and it was licensed to grant the doctorate, although it never did so. Many of Paraguay's future elite received their education within its walls, and many, such as Dr. Francia and Carlos Antonio López, taught there.[41]

For those with the money and inclination, the nearest bastion of intellectual renown was the University of Córdoba in today's Argentine province of that name. That institution, one of the better universities in Spanish America, between 1760 and 1800 provided a superior education for perhaps a score or more Paraguayans, including José Gaspar de Francia, who received his doctorate in theology there.[42] Córdoba, in fact, was the chief intellectual battery for Paraguay's elite, introducing a chosen few to the influential youth of other provinces and to stimulating ideas from abroad.

According to a 1790 census entitled "List of Pure Spaniards without mixture of caste," a charming genealogical impossibility in Paraguay, Asunción contained in its barrios 597 families of pure whites, with a total of 2,719 "Spaniards." These families were masters of 617 slaves (most owned by families residing in the Cathedral barrio), and a large number of other servants. Militia lists in the same census reveal that the semi-professional officer ranks were dominated by the capital's elite, for the 16 officers of the city's infantry unit owned a total of 103 slaves, and 3 artillery officers admitted 21 (Capt. Francia owned 5), while the cavalry detachment, most prestigious of all, reported 16 officers and 140 slaves.[43]

A Nation of Farmer-Warriors

If Paraguayan institutions were uncommonly weak, so too was the provincial military, which was barely able to hold the province together as the new century brought in its wake greater pressure from both Portuguese and Indian. The Paraguayan militia system until the governorship of Pedro Melo de Portugal (1778-1782) was composed of small, local urbano units, whose training was non-existent and whose arms were on a par with those of their Indian enemies. Almost all males between sixteen and forty-five years of age were, by routine, urbanos, and served their turns in the local guard posts.

Melo de Portugal, in part because of the utter absence of imperial aid, reorganized the militia, creating the filiado system, composed of elite units of a semi-professional nature, supposedly available for more than purely local defense. In 1790, the filiados counted four cavalry regiments (2,884 men), a battalion of infantry (568 men), and a company of artillery (70 men); but in reality, when the tocsin sounded, less than half the paper strength could or would appear. At the same time, the province boasted a total of twenty-eight small cannon, almost museum pieces, spread throughout twenty-seven forts and guard posts.[44]

An earlier report on the militia available from the Jesuit missions was even more disenchanting. Of a total of 8,721 enrolled, only a handful possessed firearms, most of which were truly antiquated. The pueblo of San Ygnacio Miní reported no muskets or shotguns but a few deteriorated cannon, which "serve only for fiestas," and other authorities reported men "capable of

bearing arms but without arms," or "with weapons corresponding to their
poverty." In the eighteenth century the militia fought its enemies with lance,
machete, and garrot.[45]

As a part of a viceregal militia reform in 1800, the filiados were reduced to
two volunteer cavalry regiments of 1,200 men each and two artillery companies. These units were kept at full strength, trained and officered by creoles
on permanent salary who would enjoy the fuero militar, or Spanish corporate
military privileges. This "ready reserve" was soon commanded by sons of the
elite families, who now saw the career of arms as a respected and recognized
profession: the Yegros, Montiel, Cavañas, and Iturbe.[46]

Despite the acquisition of a few professional advisors and a small number
of modern weapons, the militia was hardly competent to pacify the frontiers.
A disastrous 1801 expedition to drive the Portuguese from the southern Mato
Grosso was a sobering experience that merely underlined the genuine threat
to the north, prompting Portuguese retaliation that resulted in the taking of
Paraguay's most important Río Apa fort, San Carlos. Some 400 Portuguese
and M'Bayá slaughtered most of the garrison and looted the fort before disappearing again into the jungle.[47] One of the few Paraguayan survivors was
young Lt. Fulgencio Yegros, who had a more important role to play later.

Tardy pay for troops on active service and generally atrocious garrison
conditions further reduced militia morale and effectiveness. The governor
had to write Viceroy Santiago Liniers in 1803 about "the general clamor and
discontent" evident among the ranks of the filiados, and a few years later an
inspection tour revealed that the fort at Lambaré "does not have any rifles
or munitions," and that at San Antonio was "found with no arms" or horses.
Inspections turned up a variety of horrors. At Remolinos, "the troops find
themselves without anything to eat," and at Arroyos y Esteros "the Sixth
Company, as I informed you verbally, is abandoned because of the desertion
of its Officer."[48] With an appallingly incomplete and poverty-striken defensive
system, complicated by a host of enemies, Paraguay was called upon in 1806
and 1807 to send immediate aid downriver to help repel successive attacks by
British armies against Buenos Aires and Montevideo. Governor Velasco, a
brigadier general of wide military experience, was ordered to proceed to
Buenos Aires, with as many filiados as possible, to assume the rank of major
general and sub-inspector of the combined provincial hosts. In that city,
with his small Paraguayan contingent merged into the larger Porteño levies,
Velasco helped oversee the destruction of the invaders.[49]

Flushed with a victory achieved with few losses, the governor and the Río
de la Plata army, augmented by new drafts and now counting 1,000 Paraguayans (the First Filiado Regiment), took part in the siege of Montevideo.
There, Paraguayan units distinguished themselves in action and suffered

horrendous losses—a casualty rate of about 70 percent—but they again triumphed over their vaunted British enemy.[50] Many of them wounded, the older, wiser filiados returned to Paraguay in 1808, bringing with them wider perspectives, new, more radical friendships, and a new sense of worth.

Perhaps as they disembarked from their creaking, noisome river boats in the heat of an Asunción summer, the young filiado officers were being observed by a frail, dark-visaged man in somber dress, habitual cigar in hand. Doctor of Theology José Gaspar Rodríguez de Francia, a few years short of destiny, would later have most of them killed.

Plate 1. José Gaspar de Francia

2. José Gaspar de Francia and the Paraguayan Revolution

Francia and the Provincia Gigante

A damp chill wafted off the Río Paraguay that day in June, 1785, when Dr. José Gaspar de Francia landed from his overcrowded riverboat at Asunción. Standing on his native soil again for the first time in several years, he perhaps let his gaze wander to the low but imposing Government House, which sat on a small promontory at the edge of the bay. As he rode with his baggage past dark-eyed men sipping their yerba mate as they crouched against a penetrating winter cold to which Paraguayans have never grown accustomed, past Government House, he had no way of knowing that he would occupy its rooms longer than any man in his nation's history.

As with so many things about Dr. Francia, there is much debate as to his family tree. His father, García Rodríguez de Francia, probably born in Brazil, migrated to Paraguay from the Captaincy of Rio de Janeiro in 1750. After working for some years in tobacco commerce, García Rodríguez entered the provincial militia in 1758. Five years later, he was promoted to sub-lieutenant and stationed in Asunción, where he was soon transferred to the small artillery unit. He later became its captain and commander.[1] As one of the leading provincial militares, he was frequently employed in important and arduous inspection tours of the threatened frontiers. His military career was a varied one. He was for a while chief of the Asunción gunpowder factory, and founded the important fort of San Carlos on the Río Apa frontier. He also served a tour as commander of the fort at Remolinos, and then was put in charge of Fort Borbón in the northern Chaco, Paraguay's most distant and crucial bastion. For years he collaborated with various demarcation expeditions that set and mapped the Paraguay-Brazil border in the 1780s and 1790s. He was, in short, one of the most experienced and valued of Paraguayan officers.[2]

In 1796, after his disastrous employ as administrator of the Indian pueblo of Yaguarón, he re-entered military service,[3] at his old rank and post, serving Paraguay for another decade. In 1806, however, Charles IV ruled that all artillery officers must be regular army (Spanish) rather than militia (creole), and García Rodríguez retired in disgust, dying the following year.

José Gaspar, future El Supremo, was born on the Day of the Kings, January 6, 1766, to the officer and his aristocratic Asunceña wife, Doña María Josefa de Yegros y Ledesma, who was related by blood to most of the province's finest families. He was the third child and first son of a five-child family. It is notable that nowhere is there the slightest trace of his having been close to any member of his family, either in early or later life.[4]

The future theologian learned his "first letters" at the Asunción monastery school of San Francisco, completing his secondary education in the city as well.[5] In 1781, he packed his bags and headed downriver for the College of Monserrat at the University of Córdoba, finest seat of higher education in the viceroyalty. He was aided in his quest for knowledge and a superior education not only by his quick and enquiring mind but also by the fact that two uncles were on the teaching staff at Córdoba. Financial aid, not easily come by, was provided by a wealthy Asunción merchant, Martín José de Aramburu, chief treasury official of Paraguay at the time.[6]

The intellectual atmosphere at Córdoba in this era is the subject of much debate, as are the effects of this atmosphere on the formative period of Francia's intellectual growth. Some see Córdoba as a center of medieval reaction, whereas others maintain that the monkish cells in which the students lived produced nothing save "larvae of madness." According to one of South America's first psychoanalysts, the curriculum and general environment were so barren and frustrating that they could only prepare one for "a life of eternal intellectual masturbation."[7]

More accurate seems the judgement of Prudencio de la C. Mendoza, who claimed that in the 1780s there was great intellectual ferment at Córdoba, a center of regalist religious thought rife with anger at the pretensions of an arrogant papacy. Córdoba was, for its epoch, a liberal school.[8] Another author states unequivocally of Córdoba that "its republican organization, the constant exercise of the ballot, made of the university . . . a permanent school of liberty."[9] Along the same lines, yet another scholar has concluded that Francia's basically Rousseauan view of life was shaped by the free-thinking atmosphere at Córdoba.[10]

In July, 1782, young José Gaspar was awarded his licentiate and immediately began work toward his doctorate in theology. The following year he was expelled from Monserrat as punishment for his refusal to submit to discipline, but he merely moved himself and his books to another private residence and continued his studies undeterred.[11]

The study of theology in the late eighteenth century was in large part a study of canon law, and the doctorate in theology enabled one to practice law as a profession.[12] Francia developed at Córdoba an interest in the law that would shape his career until he ruled a nation. His fellow students, many of whom became close acquaintances ("friends" is too strong a word), would later become a virtual pantheon of the revolutionary movements in the Río de la Plata. Porteños Juan José Paso, Antonio de Ezquerrenea, Juan José Castelli, and others, and fellow Paraguayans Marcos Valdovinos and Francisco Bogarín were just a few of Francia's colleagues destined to be prime movers in the coming revolutions and early patriot governments. Among them, only Francia would create a nation.[13]

On April 13, 1785, José Gaspar became Doctor of Theology in an impressive ceremony and prepared to return to his native land. Some two months later he disembarked at Asunción, which lay, quiet as always, "sleeping in a perennial colonial siesta."[14]

Dr. Francia and the "Creole Problem"

Once again in Asunción, Francia, who now held minor orders in the Church, decided not to complete the process and enter the religious vocation, a common decision in that period. He opted to teach his specialty, theology, at the seminary. In 1786, he temporarily obtained the chair in Latin at the school, and settled down to await an opening in his own field. For half a year he taught without pay, a sort of apprenticeship, and when at last a vacancy occurred in theology, Francia prepared to compete for it in the traditional concourse against any challengers.[15] To his surprise and chagrin, no competition was permitted (a breach of tradition), perhaps because Francia had the reputation of being rather anti-clerical. The post was given, without a test of his skills, to Dr. Francisco Xavier Bogarín, an ex-Córdoba colleague.[16]

Dr. Francia interpreted the manner of Bogarín's selection as a personal insult, and realizing that it might be many years before another such post fell vacant, he decided to protest the affair, writing several times to the governor to demand an open competition. The governor, vacillating in the midst of what was becoming a factional, local quarrel, referred the matter all the way to the viceroy. Soon Asunción was divided into two camps around the figures of Francia and Bogarín, and the former's enemies renewed old rumors that José Gaspar was the son of a Brazilian mullato. Francia reacted bitterly to these attacks and called together various witnesses who formally swore to the "purity" of his blood and honorable conduct. With such legal documents in hand, the theologian answered the slurs of his critics.[17]

In 1789, Francia had his vengeance when it was finally decided that a

competition would have to be staged. In that academic clash with his now
bitter enemy, Francia easily won, and in March of that year was named to the
chair by Governor Alós. It had taken two long, bitter years, but Francia had
won.[18]

In spite of all the work and humiliation suffered in order to gain the teaching
post and vindicate his honor, Dr. Francia freely renounced his position in 1792.
He did so at least in part owing to the hostility between him and the ecclesiastical hierarchy stemming from his unorthodox and liberal thought and teaching.[19]

Having left the seminary, Francia dedicated himself to the study and practice of law. With his university experience, excellent library, and keen mind,
he was soon prominent among lawyers in Asunción, always an extremely liti-
gious city. He did not, however, show a strong interest in earning money,
unlike most of his colleagues, and he soon had a reputation for rigorous
honesty and compassion for the less wealthy among his clients. In the future,
this reputation would be very useful to him, as it gained him much support as
a supposed "man of the people." He never, we are told, accepted unjust
causes, and chose to defend the humble against the powerful. While he always
took substantial fees from his wealthier clients, he would often "forget" to
collect from the less fortunate. It would seem that, for the epoch, he was
something of a social activist, and he often served people as legal advisor for
free.[20]

During the most active period of his career as lawyer, 1790-1800, Dr.
Francia abandoned his normally monkish life-style and became something of
a *bon vivant,* healthy proof indeed that he had some passions in a life that did
little to betray their presence. He frequented card parties and was known as
a bit of a ladies' man. About 1800, however, when his health deteriorated as
a result of his erratic nocturnal life, he purchased a small chacra, or farm, at
Ybiraí, in the suburbs, and sought a more tranquil life.[21]

In 1798, Francia for the first time attempted to enter politics. The only
positions to which a Creole could aspire within his own province were those
on the cabildos, and that of Asunción was virtually a closed shop, long
dominated by a small group of Peninsular merchants and aristocratic Creole
families. Francia, never intimidated by tradition, ran for election to the
cabildo, with the expected result. His failure stung his pride and perhaps
activated his conscience as well.[22]   The foreigners who dominated both
cabildo and province were not disposed to accept a Creole such as Francia,
no matter his recognized qualities.

Perhaps due in part to this frustration, Dr. Francia centered his ire and
attention on Governor Lázaro de Ribera and his equally rapacious intimate,
Col. José de Espínola. Ribera, during whose government it was said some 260
Paraguayans were arbitrarily shot, was as close to a despot as Paraguayans had

known.[23] He had mounted many costly expeditions against both Indian and Portuguese, and worse yet, had ended the exemption from military service enjoyed by those working in the crown tobacco monopoly in order to refill his decimated units. Francia became one of the leaders of an underground resistance to Ribera that was growing in Asunción.

Tempted to join a budding conspiracy against the governor, Francia intelligently decided to write a forceful denunciation of Ribera, which was smuggled out of Paraguay to Viceroy Aviles at Buenos Aires. In September, 1805, a year after Francia's memorial, Ribera was relieved of his post and replaced by the previous governor of Misiones, Brigadier General Velasco. It is not possible to calculate what contribution, if any, the theologian's written protest had on the change of governors, but it certainly increased his stature within Asunción.[24]

With the new governor also came his lieutenant governor, Porteño Pedro Alcántara Somellera. Educated at Córdoba, Somellera soon became a friend of Francia's, one of the very few people who could claim to have penetrated the distant, aloof shell within which José Gaspar existed. Through a combination of this friendship and the liberal policies of the jovial Velasco, Francia was successful when he again turned to the political arena. In 1807 he was named to his first official, if minor, post on the cabildo. The following year he rose to the position of fiscal officer of the municipal body, and later to that of Alcalde of First Vote. As alcalde, he served almost two years, and for several months he simultaneously had the charge of procurator as well. Thus, in a very brief period, Francia had occupied almost every one of the political positions permitted to Creoles within their own province: an imperial tragedy.[25]

By 1809, Francia had gone as far as he could go. In August of that year, the viceroy instructed the Paraguayan governor to elect a special deputy to represent the province before the Central Junta in Seville. Such was Dr. Francia's stature that he was selected by a special assembly. An objection was raised by a Dr. Manuel José Báez, however, based on what Báez still considered Francia's questionable lineage. The objection was overruled, but it marred the moment for Francia. Events moved so rapidly in both Europe and America in 1809 that the theologian never left for Spain on his special mission. He remained and changed Paraguay.

The rapidity of his political ascension and his evident capacity make Dr. Francia a fine example of the frustrated Creole. It could not be expected that throughout the colonies men like Francia, in growing numbers, would consent to live their "lives of quiet desperation." The world revolutionary scene, 1789-1825, would have its effects on these ambitious men, so bitter about a system that offered them no escape. From Mexico through Peru and Argentina, such men, by the thousands, would seize the opportunity offered by chaos in Spain and bureaucratic uncertainty in America and would act to control their own destinies.

Espínola, Belgrano, and the Awakening of Paraguay

The internal tranquility of Paraguay, so often noted by complacent Governor Velasco, did not shatter overnight: it slowly dissolved under foreign pressure. In 1809, Velasco was warned by the viceroy to "take care with foreigners" wandering about Paraguay, for they might have more than clothing in their baggage. The governor promptly arrested all foreigners in his province under suspicion of sedition.[26]   A few months later, the nervous Asunción cabildo created a committee of vigilance to guard against a dreaded "French Party," which might attempt to topple the royalist government.[27]

When the stunning news reached Paraguay in June that the viceroy had been deposed and replaced by a revolutionary Porteño junta, royalist fears took on shape and form. Francia, busy settling his father's estate, must have soon learned that three of the seven members of the Buenos Aires junta, Juan José Paso, Manuel Alberti, and Juan José Castelli, were old Córdoba classmates.[28] Circular letters from the new junta soon reached Asunción, explaining recent events in the capital and calling for recognition of the authority of the new government over the old viceregal domains.[29]   Few Paraguayans, however, were prepared to accept Porteño dictation in such questionable circumstances, and local royalists merely increased their internal vigilance while ignoring the Porteño missives.

In Buenos Aires it was decided to speed things up by sending an envoy to Asunción, but the junta chose the wrong man for this delicate task: Col. José de Espínola. Described by an acquaintance as "ordinary, violent, arrogant, ambitious, and ignorant," Espínola was perhaps the most hated Paraguayan of his era, having served too enthusiastically the detested Governor Ribera.[30]

Arriving at Pilar, Espínola promptly alienated the populace as well as the authorities by forcing the cabildo there to swear fealty to the Porteño junta and by distributing clumsy propaganda. When he arrived at Asunción, Velasco ordered him north into exile, and Espínola fled, battling a troop of pursuers and compounding his vile reputation by kidnapping the sons of the comandante of Pilar. Though Velasco published a bando, or proclamation, to refute all that Espínola had said, this was hardly necessary, for the colonel had convinced but few in Paraguay.[31] All in all, no one man, by accident or design, could have done more to harm the Porteño cause, yet his encore was yet to come. Safely in Buenos Aires, Espínola managed to convince the junta that most Paraguayans, given the chance, would leap to support the revolution and accept Porteño leadership. In September the colonel died, blissfully unaware of his crucial role in sundering the viceroyalty.[32]

Velasco, sensing that the sword might follow the dove, called an open assembly of the prominent men of Asunción to gain a mandate for action. On July 24, some 200 men, after little debate, swore allegiance to the Spanish Regency Council, denied any subordination to Buenos Aires, and created a war board of leading royalists.[33] The board, composed mainly of Peninsulares, set about mobilizing the province and circulating preventive propaganda throughout the interior pueblos.[34] The mobilization was swift and effective: thousands of Paraguayans flocked to defend their province against the Porteño threat. Velasco moved to Yaguarón with his hosts, leaving war board chief Col. Pedro Gracia and a triumvirate of the Asunción cabildo to rule in his stead.

The Porteños were also busy. They ordered officials at Corrientes to seal off Paraguay, and in September chose Manuel Belgrano to lead an army to the Banda Oriental and Paraguay to guarantee the adhesion of those two provinces to the revolution.[35] It thus fell to Belgrano and his troops to convince Paraguay that Buenos Aires sought union and peace. As he moved north, gathering men and supplies in the Litoral provinces, Belgrano learned of Paraguayan offensives against Corrientes, where a flotilla had forced the release of detained Paraguayan ships and coerced the cabildo into acknowledging the Spanish Regency Council, before withdrawing temporarily to the north.[36]

Belgrano hoped to gain Paraguay without bloodshed and then proceed to the Banda Oriental with massive Paraguayan aid. To this end, from Corrientes, he waged a propaganda battle, sending spies and bandos into Misiones and Paraguay, promising "to protect the Pueblos, restore to them their Rights, end the oppression of their Bosses, and give them Liberty."[37] Soon aware that Espínola had miscalculated, Belgrano crossed the Paraná at Ytapúa in late December at the head of some 1,500 well-armed men.

Velasco also turned on the tap of propaganda. At the head of 6,000 ill-armed but well-mounted militia, he told Paraguayans that the Port wanted the province chiefly as a manpower pool for its own, illegal wars. This struck a responsive chord, as for too long Paraguay had been just that. The bones of its sons lay scattered all over the sub-continent.[38] Belgrano drew scant support from the populace as he marched toward Asunción, and the inhabitants melted away, leaving behind few cattle or foodstuffs. The invader, short on provisions, decided to press the issue, and on January 15, 1811, he attacked the Paraguayan levies at Paraguarí. After initial success, the Porteños were routed, leaving a few dead and some hundred and thirty prisoners on the field. When the Paraguayan center began to crack, Velasco and most of his peninsular staff fled in panic, galloping into Asunción with tales of utter defeat and triggering a frantic evacuation of the city by much of the elite, whose barges laden with movable wealth soon filled the harbor.[39] The governor regained his compo-

sure when he learned that Creole officers had rallied the militia to win the day, but he had lost the respect of his army, his people, and his province.

Slowly, Belgrano retreated south, chased at a leisurely pace by some two thousand cavalry led by Creoles Manuel Atanacio Cavañas and Juan Manuel Gamarra, both filiado colonels. The two forces exchanged missives and gifts rather than bullets, and fraternization was the rule, even after the Porteños took up defensive positions along the shallow Río Tacuarí, just north of the Paraná.[40] Only on March 9, prodded by Velasco's orders from Yaguarón, did Cavañas order a general assault. In short order, Belgrano sued for peace, and was given such generous terms by Cavañas that he and his army slipped across the Paraná, armed and unmolested, a few days later, to avoid the imminent arrival of Velasco.[41]

The governor, arriving at Tacuarí on March 19 and expecting to preside over Belgrano's capitulation, was irate at Cavañas's behavior. The Asunción cabildo, suspicious of the colonel's usurpation of authority, demanded an explanation. The resistance of Paraguay to the Belgrano invasion, it seems clear, was no act of servility to the distant and captive Spanish crown, but "an affirmation of localism" that would soon mature into nationalism. The governor, his authority broken and almost mocked, turned more and more to the ultra-royalist cabildo for support, progressively alienating the Creole officer corps who represented the Paraguayan aristocracy.[42]

Stirrings of Disaffection

The province had rallied to the defense of its own soil against a hereditary foe, but some Paraguayans were in favor of the new order, and while Velasco was in the field they surfaced behind the lines. Provocateurs, some sent directly from Buenos Aires, were active in spreading propaganda in both Asunción and Pilar, and though many were arrested, others continued the war of nerves. As Belgrano entered Paraguay, royalists acted to stamp out rumormongers and the suspected "Trojan horse" of Porteñistas within the province.[43] In September, a conspiracy was detected in Asunción, and when this Trojan horse was pried open, a large number of people tumbled out. With epistolary support from the Porteño junta, the plotters planned to take over the barracks and, armed, arrest and summarily execute Velasco and other leading royalists. For some six months testimony was taken from prisoners and informants, and suspects were sent in chains to Fort Borbón.[44]

As this conspiracy was unfolding, news came in of others. In Ycuamandiyú, Porteño merchant José de María was arrested for peddling subversion, and an investigation of his activities uncovered a web of Porteño sympathizers spread throughout the north. Fellow conspirators José Fermín (chief cleric of the entire north), Dr. Manuel José Báez, and several other priests and businessmen were soon headed toward inhospitable Fort Borbón. At Velasco's own headquarters, the administrator of Yaguarón was arrested for having "attempted to seduce various Individuals, inclining them to join the Insurgent Party," and just before the battle of Paraguarí another plot was discovered, at Itá, one that ominously included a militia officer who had hoped to facilitate Belgrano's march to Asunción.[45]

Porteñistas were indeed at work in Paraguay, but they failed because they were identified with Porteño coercion, so well exemplified by Belgrano's "Liberating Army." The governor, skillfully playing on old Paraguayan resentments, clung to power. In some of his bandos he pointed to Corrientes, where, supporting the revolution, many had been dragooned to fight for Buenos Aires in the Banda Oriental. Warning that this would be the fate of Paraguayans if the Porteños won out, he wrote his people that "you are not my Slaves . . . you are my sons, companions and Friends. They are the true Slaves, of an arbitrary, tyrannical and despotic Government."[46]

The Cuartelazo of May 14 and 15

Astute as Velasco and his supporters were, they did not discover all the plots in a very conspiratorial province. By April, 1811, there were still two operative conspiracies. These complementary, non-Porteñista plots were composed of Creole officers on the one hand and the civilian elite of the capital on the other. The officers were geographically diffused from Ytapúa to the capital to Corrientes, for the Creole heroes of Paraguarí and Tacuarí had either been demobilized or sent to the various frontiers. The governor was taking no chances. He had been suspicious of the officers ever since Cavañas allowed Belgrano to escape and had determined to give them little opportunity to combine. The civilian plotters, led by Pedro Somellera, were in contact with certain of the disaffected officers and with Somellera's friends Belgrano and Castelli in Buenos Aires as well.[47]

The plan called for an uprising of various garrisons on May 25, anniversary of the Porteño coup. Fulgencio Yegros, titular leader of the revolution, was to march on the capital from Ytapúa, gathering support on the way. Blas Rojas was to rise in occupied Corrientes, and Col. Cavañas was to revolt in the Cordillera. Captain Pedro Juan Caballero was to bring the Asunción garrisons into the streets at the last moment, and the Velasco government would collapse. This complicated plan was coordinated with Somellera's civilian conspiracy, and although the actual rising would be a military affair, civilians would be entrusted with the provisional government.[48]

The plotters, however, fearing Portuguese occupation of Paraguay, were forced to act prematurely. The governor, worried about the loyalty of his officers and the proximity of large Porteño forces, had in early 1811 approached commanders in Brazilian Misiones concerning possible aid they might tender the royalist cause.[49] The Portuguese response had been overly generous: to offer a sizeable army to be put at Velasco's disposition. Many Creole officers, fearing that the governor was about to betray Paraguay, hardened in their resolve to oust him before it was too late.[50]

When the Portuguese captain general of Rio Grande do Sul sent Lt. José de Abreu to Paraguay to formalize joint defense plans, the Creole officers were spurred to action. While Abreu was informing Velasco and cabildo that the price of Portuguese aid was recognition of the claim of Carlota Joaquina to the throne of Spain, the officers frantically completed their organization in mid-May.[51] It seems today that the officers were getting excited about nothing, for although the cabildo accepted the proffered aid, Velasco had second thoughts and refused it. A standing order of the crown forbade the entrance of foreign troops on the soil of homeland or empire. The governor had not received permission from the new viceroy (now at Montevideo) to violate this rule, and there is little doubt that he became suspicious of Portuguese military generosity at a time when the Porteño threat was receding. He may also have guessed that his officers would not permit Portuguese aid on any terms.[52] In a hurried note of May 13, Velasco informed the captain general that he no longer needed Portuguese soldiers, but instead "25,000 pesos, which is what I now need to maintain the constant fidelity" of the province. It appears that the money was needed to pay the large arrears in salary of the officer corps.[53]

The next evening, however, before Abreu or the governor's note could be dispatched, Pedro Juan Caballero, leading the officers and men of the Asunción garrisons, produced his smooth, bloodless coup, claiming that blood had not been shed at Paraguarí and Tacuarí merely that Paraguay "be delivered to a foreign Power."[54]

The governor was to be permitted titular but no genuine power, which would be exercised by two "associates" to be chosen by the barracks chiefs and civilian plotters. The men selected were, ironically, Peninsular Col. Juan Valeriano de Zevallos and Dr. Francia, who had not been actively involved in the plotting but whose experience, training, and reputation for honesty made him a natural choice.[55] Of the actual conspirators, only Somellera had extensive political experience, but he was a Porteño. The real power in the government remained in the hands of the barracks, especially after the arrival of Fulgencio Yegros from Ytapúa on May 21.

A congress was called, to meet in mid-June, to decide what form of government to follow in the future and how best to regulate relations with Buenos Aires. Before it was convened, Velasco was deposed and jailed for allegedly being part of a shadowy royalist conspiracy.[56] Somellera was confined against his will before and during the congress, probably on Francia's orders, to keep him from dominating the assembly and presenting his Porteñista views.

On June 17, 1811, 251 delegates from all parts of Paraguay met in Asunción, presided over by Dr. Francia, who impressed and perhaps confused them with his learned, Enlightenment rhetoric. The following day, Francia's friend, Mariano Antonio Molas, presented a well-thought-out plan calling for the creating of a five-member junta, composed of Yegros (as chief), Francia, Caballero, Dr. Juan Bogarín, and Fernando de la Mora. A delegate would be sent to Buenos Aires to work out plans for a confederation of equals, and the Regency Council of Spain would no longer be recognized.[57]

The Molas plan was immediately accepted by the congress, perhaps because no one else espoused an alternative, and the junta began operating on June 22. A month later, an official note was sent to Buenos Aires, explaining events in Paraguay and expressing a strong desire for union, so long as it be one of equals—a warning of sorts to the pretensions of the Port. Drafted by Dr. Francia, the note made it clear that Paraguay would not exchange one metropolis for another and that she would be cautious in considering any form of union.[58] There would be no reconstruction of the old viceroyalty, and Francia, named special delegate to Buenos Aires, would make sure of that.

On August 1, before he was to leave, however, Francia retired in anger to his chacra at Yriraí. Frantic letters from the cabildo, the barracks chiefs, and junta members eloquently indicate the theologian's importance in and to the government.[59] The leaders of the coup, untutored in politics and diplomacy begged the doctor to return, for without his guidance, wrote the junta, "the Fatherland and all is lost."[60] Dr. Francia answered by denouncing the influence of the barracks in the political field, noting that he was "horrified" by the officers' interference and had decided to retire "and care for my own security."[61]

After a period of silence designed to fray the nerve ends of his suitors, Francia took his first major risk and named his terms: Bogarín was to be dismissed from the junta. He, member of the family most hated by Francia for its slurs concerning his racial origins, was removed from his post a few days later, and the barracks chiefs, through their leader Antonio Tomás Yegros, informed Francia that his will had been done, admitting that "even in the countryside it is known that there is disgust" at his absence.[62] The doctor understood that it was the barracks and not the junta that had recalled him and met his terms, and the lesson was not lost. It was clear that Antonio Tomás was the Yegros in power and not Fulgencio. It was equally apparent that Francia himself was regarded as indispensable to the government and tranquility of Paraguay. This would only increase with the ousting of the only other learned civilian, Dr. Bogarín. Francia had won his gamble and in so doing he had proven the veracity of his charges of military intervention in politics.

Once again in the junta, he concentrated on winning the support of the cabildo against further military interference, writing that influential body that the officers, by nature of their profession, "should be the first who give an example of subordination and fidelity" to the government. He painted a grim picture of Paraguay "become a Camp of discord and uprisings, a Theater of Revolution, of ruin and weeping," if the officers persisted in their ways. Only the junta and the cabildo in concert could preserve Paraguay from anarchy and chaos.[63]   Francia was to parlay this bit of political pap into total victory, redefining it by dropping the junta and cabildo out of the equation and leaving only himself as the bastion behind which Paraguay might survive. That he got away with this myth of indispensability is a measure of the political immaturity of the Paraguayan people.

How Don José Gaspar Rose to Power

The Porteño junta, worried by Paraguay's lethargy in embracing union, and needing more troops to defend and expand its revolution, reassured the up-river province by writing of its commitment to equality, its desire for union, and its pleasure with recent events in Asunción.[64]   The junta named Manuel Belgrano and Dr. Vicente Anastacio Echevarría to travel to Asunción as special emissaries. These men were instructed to stress the common danger from Spain and Portugal and to secure the best relations possible with Paraguay. "You will insinuate with sagacity and skill the great necessity of removing some dangers" through union and subordination to Buenos Aires. Such subjection should be shown as necessary for survival, and "this subjection," said the junta, "will always leave the Rights of the Province intact." Federation, the junta explained, was not a strong enough bond in the face of extreme danger: "The general will of all the Provinces should be the Superior Law that obliges Paraguay to lend itself to Subordination." At the least, the envoys were to gain a defensive-offensive alliance against all enemies.[65]

The Porteños had made their choice. There would be no union of equals but either a centralist government on their terms or a mere military alliance. This choice cost them Paraguay. As Efraím Cardozo wrote, although Richard III may have cried, "My kingdom for a horse," in the winter of 1811 Buenos Aires whispered, "A province for some soldiers."[66]

While Belgrano and Echevarría traveled north, a royalist plot was denounced in Asunción in September, a plot whose aim was to restore Velasco to power.

A number of men, including the governor's good friends, were arrested and sent north to exile at Fort Borbón, a broiling outpost that was almost becoming a hostel for political losers. At the same time, the government lashed out at local Porteñistas, shipping Somellera downriver and arresting several men of similar persuasion.[67] In a matter of days, the Francia-led junta had crippled both royalist and Porteñista parties, removing their principal figures from circulation. When Francia faced the Porteño diplomats, he would do so without interference.

The negotiations, which began on October 4, were swiftly completed. Disabused of his hope for a confederation of equals, Francia, chief Paraguayan negotiator, opted for the loosest possible link with the Port. On October 12, a treaty was signed that contained commercial and military clauses and that also allowed Paraguay to retain disputed Candelaria until a future commission could sort out conflicting claims to the area. More important was the mutual pledge to aid one another against all enemies for "the sacred end of annihilating and destroying" any threat to either party, "according to what the circumstances of each one permit."[68]

The treaty was a victory for Francia, who had gained unofficial recognition of Paraguayan independence, the status quo in Candelaria, and lower duties on Paraguayan trade—all in return for a vague promise about unspecified military aid at some uncertain date, if "circumstances" permitted. For this parody of an alliance, the Porteños lost Paraguay politically, and would soon lose it economically as well. And to think that the Porteño envoys were considered sophisticated! Behind the rhetoric of the treaty, Francia had effectively separated Paraguay from Buenos Aires. Now that confederation on the basis of equality was out of the question, he began working for true independence. Only the barracks, the cabildo, and his junta colleagues stood in his way.

After this brief period of harmony, which would represent the high-water mark of Paraguayan-Porteño relations for some forty years, the situation rapidly deteriorated, within the Paraguayan government as well as without. The military, realizing that Francia's sagacity was needed in the negotiations with the polished Porteños, had been on their good behavior, but they soon returned to their imperious ways, openly influencing the course of government and exciting Francia's ire.

On December 15, Dr. Francia again rode quietly through the city streets to Ybiraí and retirement. He informed both junta and cabildo that he alone had carried the entire burden of government, and though he did not regret that great personal sacrifice, he found intolerable "the extortion and violence of some few who prevail by arms." The military must be curbed, wrote Francia, and since the junta, now minus both its educated civilians, was

understaffed, a new congress should be called. Confident of his popularity
with "the people," Francia no doubt expected to be buttressed by them with
additional powers. He claimed that only frequent congresses could prevent
small cliques of ambitious men from dominating the government, implying that
this had already come to pass.[69] With consummate skill, Francia made his
plight a warning to all who favored civilian government.

The truncated junta, composed now of officers, angrily retorted, damning
the exile's own exalted ambitions, his "arbitrariness" and "irregularity," and
urging him to subordinate his ego to the will of the province. Blaming Francia
for the governmental atrophy that could result from his absence, the junta
fought him with his own weapons, even while acknowledging his importance.[70]

For months, Francia sat at Ybiraí in relative ease, sending notes to both
friend and foe and assiduously attempting to seduce the cabildo to his view
that the present junta was a mere tool of the barracks. He soon began to see
results, and it is clear that most cabildo members favored his position and
were suspicious of the growing pretensions of the junta.[71] He failed utterly,
however, in his desire for a new congress, for which he would have to wait
almost two years. Lacking this forum, he turned to active propaganda among
the clergy, ranchers, and townspeople, chipping away at the junta's authority
and awaiting an opportunity to act.

The incipient split between cabildo and junta widened in 1812, the two
organs driven wider apart by questions of foreign policy and jurisdiction, the
junta wanting to reserve for itself all broad matters of policy. In an atmosphere
of secrecy, the junta angered both Francia and cabildo by extending limited
aid to Uruguayan rebel José Artigas and refusing to discuss the issue with the
latter body. Questions also arose over worsening relations with Buenos Aires,
as the junta, claiming scarcity of arms, denied the Port succor in its need, and
Buenos Aires reciprocated in kind.[72] The October treaty was soon ignored
by both parties, who chose to insult one another for violating its nebulous
provisions. Porteño suspicions of a possible union of Paraguay and the anti-
Buenos Aires Artigas led to bitterness and recriminations.

Encouraged by deteriorating relations, authorities in the Litoral did their
share to anger Paraguay, overtaxing Paraguayan river commerce, detaining and
even confiscating Paraguayan vessels, and effectively cutting off Paraguay
from access to the outer world.[73] These tactics, later called the "guerra
aduanera," or customs tax war, Paraguay blamed on Buenos Aires.

Into this charged situation in 1812 came threats from Portugal in both
north and south and from Spain on the rivers. In May, strong Portuguese
forces entered Candelaria. After a brief skirmish with Paraguayan troops they
retreated, but the presence of large Portuguese units at São Borja was a
constant worry for Paraguay.[74] Worse news came that month from the north.

Fort Borbón, lynchpin of the frontier, fell to the M'Bayá, who soon turned it over to a Portuguese garrison. Only the rapid mounting of a large expedition from Asunción prevented permanent occupation of this vital bastion by the Portuguese.[75] A sense of imminent doom pervaded the halls of Paraguayan officialdom, compounded by the presence of Spanish corsairs on the Paraná. This enemy, preying on merchant vessels, was felt to be a threat to Paraná and Paraguay river ports as well.[76]

By late 1812, relations with Buenos Aires had reached crisis levels. In response to Paraguayan complaints of high commercial duties, which violated the October treaty and effected a virtual blockade, the Porteños blandly replied that "you have looked with icy indifference on our dangers, and . . . have not attempted to cooperate in the common defense." In such a situation, asked Buenos Aires, "who then has the right to complain?"[77]

Aware in the last months of 1812 that Buenos Aires intended to force Paraguay into its orbit through economic sanctions, the abbreviated Paraguayan junta more and more felt the absence of Dr. Francia. A desperate move to have Scottish merchant John Parish Robertson carry goods downriver and return armed with a safe conduct from the commodore of the British Río de la Plata flotilla failed.[78] Even the hope of cloaking Paraguayan commerce in the British flag proved unable to pry open the constricted Paraná.

The Politics of Progress: Life without Francia

If Francia's absence was marked by worsening relations with neighbor states, it was also a time of considerable internal progress, in large part fomented by the junta. In 1812, that body published an education code, attempting to provide Paraguayan youth "all the instruction they need to be good Christians and Citizens, useful to God and Fatherland."[79] The seminary was reopened after a year's closure, and a Patriotic Literary Society was founded to provide an outlet for adult intellectual interests. There were also plans to expand education on all levels, and schools were built by the junta in the interior as well as in the larger towns. A military academy was founded in name, and the junta even funded a public school in Asunción directed by a woman.[80]

Other worthwhile projects occupied the junta's attention. Plans were made "to make the rivers navigable" and to aid internal commerce in the largely trackless interior by the "widening and opening of roads." An arsenal was built, and attention was to be paid to the "conservation of the yerbales, which are being senselessly exhausted" by careless harvesting. In addition, the junta promised to finally end the encomienda, correct abuses of forced labor, and provide full legal equality for all save slaves.[81] Another task the junta implemented was the resettlement of the 648 free Blacks of Tabapí on free lands in the north. These settlers would help develop the frontier and guard it against Indian and Portuguese alike. The wheels began to turn in 1812, and the colony, though never successful, was established at Tevegó in 1813.[82]

All this was undertaken by the junta in an atmosphere of external crisis and internal bickering, as the cabildo and partisans of Francia filled the air with denunciations of junta rule. To establish domestic peace, barracks commander Antonio Tomás Yegros arranged to meet with Dr. Francia in May of 1812, but nothing came of the conference, Francia returning to his rustic chacra. If he had named terms for his re-entry into the government, the junta and barracks were not yet desperate enough to accede, and, in fact, several supporters of Francia were soon deposed from the cabildo for "having worked against the respect and public confidence" that the junta demanded. Even the cabildo chief, Juan Valeriano de Zevallos, was arrested by order of the junta on trumped up charges—he had not placed a cushion on the church stool of Pedro Juan Caballero on All Saints' Day![83]

Dr. Francia Invicta: Exile's End

At Ybiraí, Francia continued his propaganda and lobbying, telling all who would listen that the junta's foreign policy would involve Paraguay in war and grief. He claimed that conspiracies of Porteñistas and royalists were rife and that the junta itself was both illegal and incompetent in its abbreviated form. He emerged in his retirement as a staunch defender of honest government and Paraguayan sovereignty, and his austere, scholarly retreat compared favorably with the ostentatious and hedonistic lives of Fulgencio Yegros and Pedro Juan Caballero, who "dedicated the great part of their time to fiestas and diversions."[84]

It was at this time that Francia began to construct his efficient espionage service, which, in the words of one contemporary observer, turned the land into "a great whispering gallery." That observer also recalled a conversation with one of Francia's agents, a man called Orrego: "He has many others employed besides myself, and *I do not know who they are* . . . whined Orrego, in cringing testimony that the Doctor was well along on the road to make Paraguay subject to his will."[85]

In late 1812, the junta's veneer of self-sufficiency cracked when it was learned that the Porteños were sending another diplomat, Nicolás de Herrera, to Asunción. Realizing that Francia alone was competent to deal with the worldly Porteño lawyer, the junta permitted patriotism to override personal concerns and wrote the exile in November that the new circumstances "imperiously necessitate your swift reunion" in the government.[86] Junta and barracks had capitulated, and the extent of their surrender became known on November 16, when Francia and the junta members signed an accord spelling out the former's terms. The most important concession granted the doctor was the creation of a new infantry battalion that was to be directly under his command. This unit would "be also freed from the junta," officered by Francia appointees, and have at its disposal half of all arms and munitions in the city. Francia would at last be free of the caprices of the military: he would have one of his own. This arrangement would endure until the convening of a new congress in 1813. News of Francia's return was forwarded to the cabildo as "new proof" that the junta had the welfare of the nation at heart. Many in Paraguay were relieved.[87]

Dr. Francia had won another challenge, returning on his own, elevated terms. He was now clearly in control of the government. Protected by his own army, he could now use militarism as a tool for his own ends. He was almost ready to create the Republic of Paraguay and assume its undisputed rule.

Nicolás de Herrera: Present at the Creation

Although domestic troubles had been an important factor in stimulating Francia's recall, far more crucial had been the multiple foreign threats. In the year of his retirement, bloody clashes with the Portuguese occurred on both the southern and northern frontiers. José Artigas, who had hoped for Paraguayan aid against both Porteño and Portuguese, was becoming disenchanted and was fomenting violence in Candelaria. Finally, relations with the Port had reached a dangerous impasse: the October treaty was moribund, Paraguayan commerce was increasingly harassed, and the junta was being pressured to send a delegate to the upcoming 1813 Congress of the Provinces of the Río de la Plata. In such an atmosphere, Francia seemed literally indispensable, for his astute handling of the Belgrano-Echevarría mission had demonstrated his skill as a negotiator who put freedom of action for his nation above all else.

On May 20, Herrera disembarked at Asunción. His instructions were very explicit. He must persuade Paraguay to attend the Congress of the Provinces, stress the impossibility of the province's surviving alone in the world, and press Paraguay for "aid in arms and recruits." He was also to inquire concerning "the intrigues of Artigas," but nowhere in his instructions is noted anything that Buenos Aires was willing to offer Paraguay in return for the concessions sought—save the supposed safety of union under the Porteño aegis.[88]

The day after his arrival, Herrera met with the junta, and to his shock learned that no substantive decisions could be made until October, when a Paraguayan congress would meet. Francia gained from the meeting the impression that Herrera was a mere messenger with no latitude of negotiation. There was little, it seemed, that Paraguay could wring from the Port at this stage.[89]

Herrera agreed to remain in Asunción, but was disheartened. The delay indicated that the junta itself would not act: a poor portent for union. He at least planned to put his time to good use, counteracting the evident anti-Porteño sentiment in Asunción, but he was prevented from doing this. The envoy was lodged in the old customs shed, carefully watched by authorities and allowed few visitors. In fact, he was under polite house arrest. Nor, despite his diplomatic standing, was he permitted free access to government officials. In isolation, Herrera caught what rumors he could, passing them on to his government in frequent letters, often "written in secret ink at the bottom of innocent letters to his family."[90]

Artigas, worried by Herrera's presence in Asunción, wrote the junta, waving the flag of a confederation of equals and claiming that Paraguay and the Banda Oriental alone could guarantee equality in such a union, and could force their will on Buenos Aires if they acted in concert. He wrote several frantic letters to the junta, but received only the most laconic of replies, which indicated little desire for union of any type.[91] Aware that Paraguayan abstention would make a true confederation all but impossible, Artigas's bitterness at rejection shortly turned to hostility.

Herrera, soon aware of Artigas's correspondence with the junta, if not its content, and growing daily more irritated by his enforced inactivity, wrote his government, warning about a Paraguay-Artigas alliance. He advised that "in these circumstances it is necessary to treat this Province as Neutral or Enemy." Perhaps a show of force, wrote the envoy from his cramped quarters, might bring Paraguay to its senses.[92]

The Porteño diplomat knew by rumor, observation, and perhaps instinct who held power in Asunción. He assured his leaders that it was Francia "who carries the voice in these affairs" of statecraft. He had several interviews with the doctor, who told him to bide his time, for the people of Paraguay had to be informed of the issues before a congress was convoked. Noting a strong distrust bordering on paranoia on the part of many Paraguayans toward Buenos Aires, Herrera even attempted some bribery: "Some of the hundred coins which you have sent . . . have been distributed among the individuals of the Government." He was "reserving the rest to divide among the most important persons of the Congress . . . who will know how to communicate" his desire for "eternal union" to the gathering as a whole.[93]

In August, the thousand delegates to the congress were chosen throughout Paraguay, and, bearing election proofs and certificates of good character, they journeyed to the capital.[94] While they were on the road, Dr. Francia moved to insure his authority. In mid-August, he, Caballero, and Yegros announced that Fernando de la Mora had been sacked for unspecified suspicious activities. Several days later, Gregorio de la Cerda, who had been unofficially attached to the junta during Francia's second absence, was also removed. In September, the junta, now a triumvirate, presented formal charges against de la Mora, alluding to his supposed "desire to submit this Province to the government and command of another"—he was, in short, a Porteñista. He was further charged with conducting secret negotiations with Portuguese officials and with belonging to "a suspicious faction." Thus branded with the myriad sins of having colluded with various "suspicious" types, de la Mora was arrested, being given no opportunity to defend himself. De la Cerda was exiled downriver, accused of being "a character fatal to society."[95]

On the eve of the congress, Francia was the only civilian on the junta. He had just decapitated the Porteñista party, or, more realistically, eliminated potential civilian rivals. With half the army at his call, he was now free to exercise his vaunted influence on the people as the patriotic defender of Paraguay.

As the delegates flocked into the capital, Herrera was even more restricted in his movements and unable to communicate with them. Francia, however, was busy spreading his ideas among the delegates, holding court at Ybiraí and at Government House as the "Caraí-guazú" (great señor). At the customs shed, Herrera furiously drew up a speech he planned to read to the assembled delegates. Wrote the envoy, "Liberty is a phantasm worthy of exciting the ambition of the throne of Despotism," unless carefully protected through unity.[96] He had just finished his powerful speech when he was bluntly informed that he would not be able to read it, for he was forbidden to attend the congress. Nor could the message be read by any other person.[97]

With Pedro Juan Caballero presiding, the congress convened on September 30, 1813, in the Temple of Mercy. It was described by one sarcastic witness as "a motley group, to which the pencil of a Hogarth alone could do justice."[98] The Caraí had prepared documents illustrating Porteño perfidy, and these were read aloud on the first day, accompanied by patriotic oratory. The result was impressive. Within hours the congress voted to the effect that Buenos Aires had violated the 1812 treaty and had acted in bad faith. The treaty and its vague alliance were declared null and void by acclamation. It was then decided that Paraguay would not attend the Congress of the Provinces, and, as the first day ended, many of the more rustic members of congress started home, leaving committees to draft other crucial decisions.[99]

On October 12, the decisions of the congress, in thirteen articles, were proclaimed. This proto-constitution, written by Francia himself, changed the course of Platine history. Paraguay was declared an independent republic, to be ruled by two consuls, Fulgencio Yegros and Francia, who were to alternate in power for four months at a time. Each consul would be given exactly half of the military and its materiel, and a flag and coat of arms were adopted. A new congress would meet in twelve months to review the success of the government and decide on any changes to be implemented.[100]

This victory of Paraguayan nationalism, so much the work of Francia, was matched by his personal triumph. His foreign policy of aloofness was accepted, and he now personally outranked all officers in the republic save Yegros, a man already dependent upon him in the subtle realms of diplomacy and politics.

On October 13, Herrera, at last free to move about, spoke with Dr. Francia (who, having managed to assume the first period of rule, would also have the last, or eight months out of twelve). Following this conference, the Porteño wrote his government that, according to the consul, Paraguay would at some future date indeed join the other provinces in union. As for the October treaty, Herrera quoted Francia as remarking that "Paraguay did not need treaties in order to conserve fraternity."[101]

Herrera should have realized that Buenos Aires would have to offer something grand to attract Paraguay to union and alliance. This it could not or would not do. The only deal that might have interested Francia was an advantageous trade treaty, but the Port needed Paraguayan soldiers more than her yerba, and would not give Paraguay the benefits of union without its responsibilities. Porteño control of the rivers gave them the only leverage they had with Paraguay, and it was soon put to the test. If Paraguay desired trade with the outside world it would have to come to terms with the Port. After another fruitless talk with Francia, Herrera dejectedly set out for Buenos Aires, writing ahead that Francia "has persuaded the Paraguayans that the province alone is an Empire without equal: that Buenos Aires . . . desires it because of need."[102] He may well have been correct. What he did not admit and what Porteños would only learn over the years, is that they grossly underestimated both Francia and his new nation. They could and did go it alone.

José Gaspar in Control: 1813 and 1814

Dr. Francia faced two major tasks late in 1813. He had to rule his infant republic and, at the same time, augment his personal power. He was remarkably successful in both endeavors. Having weakened the Porteñistas, he turned his attention to the haughty Peninsulares, many of whom were vocally royalist. The last of these were divested of government posts, and it was ordered that all who were not legal citizens of Paraguay must register with the government immediately, "with the penalty that those who fail to comply will be shot."[103] The time for soft talk had ended. Plans, never implemented, were drawn up for the exile of all foreigners downriver, and in March, 1814, a bando appeared that made it illegal for a Peninsular to marry another of that station, the choice being reduced to Indian, mestizo, or "known mulatto" mates.[104] Enforced with rigor for twenty-six years, the law virtually completed the Paraguayan genetic revolution, guaranteeing completion of the intermixture of races begun centuries before. Spaniards were also forbidden to act as religious witnesses or godparents. The Spanish social structure was to be uprooted; the network of social bonds that had unified that stratum, against which Francia had personally struggled for years, was to be torn asunder.

In 1814, a large proportion of government monies was spent to enlarge and equip the army. Arms were purchased, and gradually officers known to be partisans of Yegros and Caballero found themselves ducking arrows at small forts on the dangerous frontier.[105] Officers chosen by Francia became more numerous and prominent in and around the capital, and centralized control over the interior militia was established and enforced. Renewed Indian war in the north and fear of Portuguese in the south was the justification for the general buildup, but at least in part it was politically inspired. Francia, whose "grenadier company was his great hobby," personally supervised the training, arming, and supply of the units under his control. As one observer wrote: "I never saw a little girl dress out her doll with more self-importance and delight than did Dr. Francia with his own hands, dress and fit out each individual grenadier of his guard."[106] No matter what the Caraí chose to call his military establishment, it was, in fact, his guard. No rival could seriously threaten Francia again.

The year of the consulate saw few changes save the anti-Spanish laws and the growth of the army. In 1814, a state prison system was inaugurated, with cells beneath the two largest Asunción barracks. From this humble beginning would evolve the grim "Francia system." The year was marked by a house-cleaning of corrupt and inefficient civil servants and the making of a generally clean government. Dr. Francia, "conspicuous for his rectitude," gained yet more respect.[107]

In the international sphere, there was more pressure from Buenos Aires and renewed supplication from Artigas, but the consuls gave in to neither, even though one ranking officer, Vicente Antonio Matiauda, took his troops south of the Paraná, joined Artigas, and began killing Porteños. Disavowed by the consuls, Matiauda and most of his men remained with Artigas, disappearing in the smoky civil wars to the south. A crisis with Buenos Aires was narrowly averted.[108]

As the consulate neared its end, the pace of political activity again increased.

Francia, his eyes fixed on the coming congress, did not idly rest on his excellent record. He openly propagandized for a change to a one-man executive, to streamline and simplify the governing of Paraguay. In this work of political propaganda, he had influential friends who were pleased at the course and tenor of Francia's rule to date. Mariano Antonio Molas and José Tomás Ysasi, among others, made it clear to many Paraguayans that it had been Francia and not Yegros who had guided Paraguay through the last year, despite the inherently clumsy government structure. Francia's picked officers were also busy extolling his virtues, and for the first and only time the doctor became known for his frequent parties and get-togethers. He was careful to include on his guest lists men of influence from Asunción and the interior.[109]

The opposition was also gathering, primarily in the capital, led by many of the social elite—the 1811 revolutionaries who had seen their influence, power, and social position eroded as Francia's grew. This group attempted to stall Francia's drive for power, turning to Fulgencio Yegros, who had retired for several weeks to his ranch at Quiquió to await events in tranquility.[110]

As Francia learned of the growing opposition to his continuance in power he convinced his co-consul that such opposition was dangerous to the nation. A week before the new congress met, both he and Yegros signed orders exiling Pedro Juan Caballero, Juan Manuel Gamarra, and several others to their family estates in the interior. These men were told to absent themselves from the capital for an indefinite period.[111] The list of Francia's outmaneuvered rivals was coming to resemble a who's who of Paraguay. Of all the revolutionary leaders, only Yegros, a man of no political ambition, remained. The Caraí had identified opposition to himself as either incompetence or treason, and he had decapitated another rival group on the eve of its testing.

The Supreme Dictator of the Republic

In late September, the delegates began riding into Asunción, guttural Guaraní clashing in the streets with Asunceño Castilian tones. On October 3, again in the Temple of Mercy, the assembly convened, many members clutching broadsides written in praise of the Caraí. The garrison's arms were stacked and the soldiers themselves confined to barracks, to guarantee the "tranquility" of the elections.

A decision was immediately reached: the form of government would be changed to a one-man executive. On October 4, Francia was named assembly president, and from this position completed his domination of the sessions.[112] He gave a long speech, stressing the need to invest the man chosen to rule alone with sufficient powers to do so effectively. A vote was then taken to see which of the consuls would rule Paraguay, since no other names were put forward.

In a one-sided contest, perhaps influenced by Francia's company of *armed grenadiers*, who were conspicuously lounging around the Temple, the doctor won handily.[113]

Announced publicly that afternoon, rule "would be united in Citizen José Gaspar de Francia, with the title of Supreme Dictator of the Republic," for a term not to exceed five years. A Superior Tribunal of Justice was created (it never functioned), and a committee (composed of Molas, Ysasi, and other friends of the Caraí) was named to finish the work of the congress. That august body promptly dissolved itself. Its deputies, hastening to return home to Yhú, Belén, and Itá, strode proudly from the Temple between the ranks of grenadiers, mounted, and left the city en masse.[114]

The committee and Dr. Francia met again. It was decided that there would be no congress until May, 1816, permitting the Dictator eighteen months without supervision. Congresses would hence number 250 delegates rather than 1,000, for the most part drawn from the interior. At the end of the meeting, Francia took the oath of office, administered by his friend José Miguel Ibáñez, at "which ceremony at the same time the baton of command was given to him."[115]

On October 6, El Supremo, as he came to be called, sent form letters to all officials in Paraguay, informing them that the congress had

> resolved to reunite and congregate in my Person the Supreme Government of the Republic, in which charge I have been received and recognized generally by the Illustrious Cabildo and Military Corps of this City. . . . I am afflicted when I consider the great weight which has been put upon my shoulders at such a difficult time [but] . . . I have the satisfaction of counting you who will help me carry such an enormous burden.[116]

That same day, news reached the Caraí of serious disaffection in the barracks, perhaps due to anger over the eclipse of the last of the revolutionary heroes and the doctor's elevation of personal friends to high commands. This was evident when Lt. Manuel Iturbe, one of the 1811 rebels, broke his sword in protest over the outcome of the congress. At the request of Fulgencio Yegros, Pedro Juan Caballero rode in from exile and persuaded unruly officers to remain calm and accept the decisions of the assembly. Caballero, a figure who commanded respect from the officers and who would have been a logical choice to lead them, removed the last obstacle to Francia's total power. It is quite possible that, in so doing, he spared Paraguay a civil war.[117] The military missed their last major chance to influence the course of their nation's formation. Perhaps this was best.

Francia had shunted aside the last vestige of rival power, as he had earlier disposed of Bogarín, de la Cerda, de la Mora, Caballero, Gamarra, and Yegros. He slowly whittled away the opposition. If, as Mussolini was reported to have said, "violence is moral when sudden as a storm," Francia proved that disposing of one's political rivals was, if not moral, at least acceptable when gradual and inconspicuous. He had become Supreme Dictator, and he had done so not by fiat but by the imposition of a people.

3. Perpetual Means Forever: Francia and the Paraguayan Society

The Theologian Takes Power, 1814 and 1815

The Franciata, initiated with the overwhelming approval, if not the understanding, of the Paraguayan people, had begun. Francia, behind the ornate grillwork of Government House, faced a number of grave problems, both personal and national. Perhaps the most salient characteristic of his long rule was his conviction that both types of problems were really one: his intense and honest identification of himself with his nation.

Francia was described at this time by a European visitor:

He is a man of middle stature, with regular features, and those fine black eyes which characterise the Creoles of South America. He has a most penetrating look, with a strong expression of distrust. On this occasion he wore the Official Costume, which consisted of a blue laced coat . . . waistcoat, breeches, stockings of white silk, and shoes with gold buckles. The Dictator was then sixty-two years of age, though he did not appear to be more than fifty.

The same observer also noted that "he had also the misfortune to be subject to fits of hypochondria, which sometimes degenerated into madness. His father was known to have been a man of very singular habits; his brother was a lunatic; and one of his sisters was out of her mind for several years."[1] From this description one would scarcely expect a remarkably successful twenty-six year rule for the Caraí.

In 1814, Francia was dictator-elect of an interior nation still considered by Buenos Aires to be a subject province. Isolated a thousand miles up a river easily controlled by the Porteños, surrounded by the ancient enemy, royalist Brazil, and a newer enemy, the revolutionary provinces under the direction of Buenos Aires, Paraguay had to face hostile Indians, bandit gangs, and gaucho armies spawned by the civil wars to the south as well. Dr. Francia also had to treat domestic unrest, both real and potential, that might involve his new nation in the growing regional strife.

His policy was extremely cogent and simple. To preserve Paraguay and his own position, he dedicated himself to a course of rigid non-intervention in the affairs of his neighbors, an abstention that evolved into an official and general isolation. Aside from various individuals opposed to such a policy, he would face major obstacles in the Church, the merchant community, and the Creole elite. His solution, devoid of ideology and sophistication, was to disarm and render powerless any group or institution capable of posing a threat to him or his policy—in short (by his definition) to Paraguay.

No sooner had Francia become El Supremo than the crisis year of 1815 opened. He was almost immediately confronted with a renewal of the northern Indian wars, as the M'Bayá virtually besieged Concepción. Francia sent men and supplies north, and in May ordered an expedition of 500 soldiers to chastise the hostiles. That force, after hacking through the jungle for months, reported success, but in reality it had done little save scatter the M'Bayá before it. Hostilities continued throughout the year, a major drain on the exchequer.[2]

The north continued to be a chief preoccupation for the Caraí, for with its very scant population, almost continual Indian war, and aggressive Brazilian neighbor, the area was effectively lost to Paraguay. Yet, weaving between roaming M'Bayá and suspicious Paraguayan militia, intrepid Portuguese officers from the Mato Grosso still came to Fort Borbón to trade arms and powder taken from their own garrisons for yerba and tobacco.[3] There was precious little else to be had at beleaguered Borbón (soon to be called Olimpo), for the Dictator in 1815 found it necessary to ration the garrison, cutting the meat allowance to a meager seven ounces daily per man. In a nation addicted to massive consumption of beef, this was a true belt-tightening. Such conditions go far to explain the high desertion rate at Borbón.[4]

Perhaps because of the unpredictability of life in the verdant north and Francia's desire to hold it for Paraguay, he began sending prisoners there in 1815. For the following decade, hundreds of murderers, thieves, rustlers, and immigrants from surrounding states were sent north in chains.[5] The Tevegó colony, situated between Concepción and the Río Apa, was so harassed by nature and Indians that its reputation put a halt to the voluntary migration of Tabapí Blacks, and the Caraí had to fill its ranks with hardened brigands and soldiers. These men and women, hard cases all, could barely hold their own against the still harder M'Bayá, and the envisioned community of armed farmers was unrealizable. When Francia finally ordered Tevegó abandoned in 1823, there were more criminals and armed guards there than settlers. Most

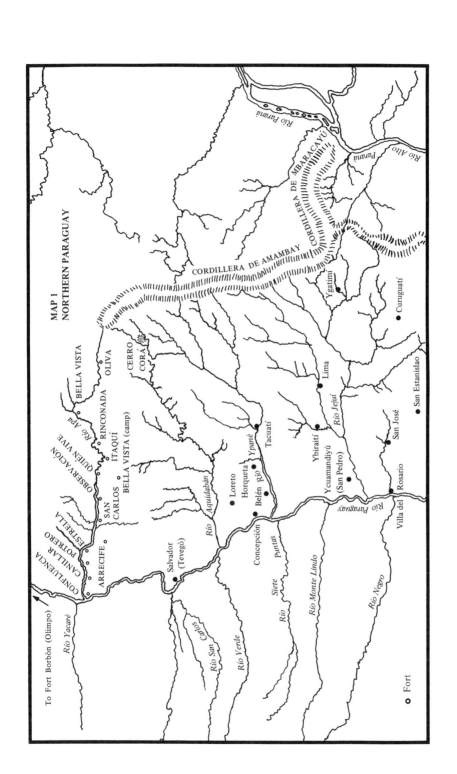

MAP 1
NORTHERN PARAGUAY

of these were forced to resettle around Concepción. Their presence did much to lessen the threat to that villa.[6]

If there were crises in the north, Francia faced the greatest foreign threat of his career in the south. In 1815, José Artigas, open enemy of centralist Buenos Aires, invaded the Litoral provinces, and it appeared that the United Provinces were to be torn apart. In such circumstances, the Port viewed Paraguayan military cooperation as crucial, and, in March, Porteño authorities urged Francia to come to their aid and forget the old disputes. Buenos Aires noted that the Río de la Plata also faced royalist and expansionist threats from Portuguese forces then operating in parts of the Banda Oriental and from the "imminent" arrival of "a huge expedition" being prepared by Spain. Offering to send arms, the Porteños requested Paraguayan support in yerba, tobacco, and recruits. These pleas, repeated in April and May, were not responded to by the Caraí.[7]

Dr. Francia, worried by the same issues, had more immediate problems, for Corrientes fell to the gaucho armies of Artigas and a load of vital arms being conducted by John Parish Robertson was confiscated by Artigueños. Writing an official at Pilar, Francia exploded, damning Artigas and his "brutes and thieves who have neither Law nor Religion," who "propose to live by cheating, disturbing and robbing everyone" with "the careless license of Savages."[8] Mobilizing his militia, El Supremo soon learned that the gauchos had imposed a general blockade of the river and were not permitting goods or communications in or out of Paraguay.[9]

In August, Artigas sent a strong force of cavalry into Candelaria, and Francia's subdelegado in the south wrote Asunción warning of an invasion of Paraguay proper—an invasion that his scattered troops could do little to oppose. Before reinforcements could be sped south, Paraguayan forces in Candelaria had been trounced, and the subdelegado informed Francia that "we were so destroyed" that "we are lost, with no recourse, not even a knife," with which to defend Paraguay.[10]

The gauchos had inflicted a major defeat on Paraguayans in Candelaria, perhaps, but it would take a massive invasion across the broad, easily defended Paraná to seriously threaten Paraguay, and soon the north bank of that river was swarming with Paraguayan militia. To further safeguard the border, Francia decided "to prepare an expedition of at least five thousand men" to evict the invaders from Candelaria and "sustain the sacred Rights, Dignity, and Sovereignty of the Republic."[11]

The Artigueños, however, had problems of their own, and abandoned Candelaria in the face of Porteño attacks in Corrientes. While the Porteños were taking the initiative, Paraguayan troops reentered Candelaria to take up their old positions in those pueblos nearest the Paraná. The bulk of the

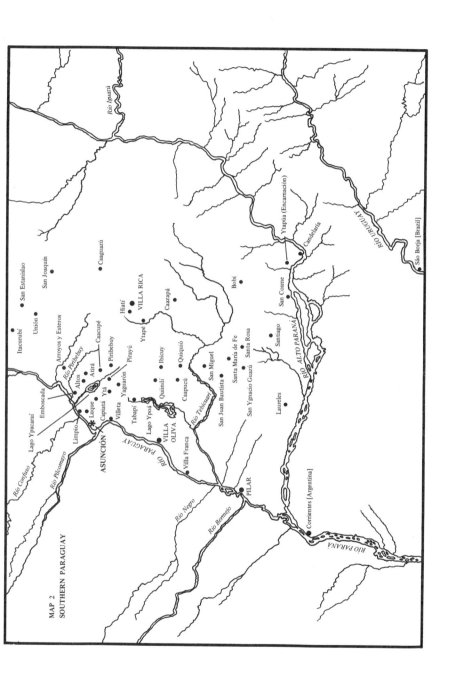

MAP 2
SOUTHERN PARAGUAY

Paraguayan forces remained north of the river, awaiting events. It is well that Francia showed such caution, for in 1816 a death struggle between Artigueños and a Portuguese army broke out in Candelaria in which the latter eventually triumphed. Paraguayan troops remained aloof spectators and the Guaraní Republic maintained its neutrality.[12]

Perpetual Means Forever

Much of 1815 and 1816, amidst the various frontier crises, Francia used to prepare for the upcoming congress. He wanted to use the congress to insure his continuance in power without supervision. As foreign crises mounted, he became yet more assured that he alone could guide Paraguay through the dangerous corridors of its destiny. He sought unchecked power not from ego or megalomania but from his deep commitment to Paraguayan nationalism. He saw himself as a sophisticated, dedicated man in a nation composed of well-meaning yet untutored rustics who did not grasp the magnitude of the dangers facing them. As he himself observed, it was his effort alone that protected the republic. He had obtained the arms "that until now no one had done, because I alone have been the only one who, since the revolution, has striven, worked, and procured arms . . . due only to my diligence, industry and labors . . . for these are things that no one thinks of, nor has thought about."[13]

As before the previous congress, El Supremo waged an effective propaganda campaign aimed at explaining to the people his indispensability in these times of crisis. He pointed out his fruitful abilities as diplomat and his unquestioned patriotism, stressing, with some truth, that domestic peace, clean government, and relative prosperity were due to his sagacity. Nothing was possible without internal peace, he argued, and a glance at the provinces to the south bore out his point. Chaos, civil war, and subsequent famine were impelling hundreds of Correntinos to flee to Paraguay.[14]

Nor was Francia alone in advertisements for himself. His friend, Comandante of the North José Miguel Ibáñez (also a deputy to the congress), stumped the streets of Asunción for his benefactor, arguing in favor of a lifetime mandate for the Caraí.[15]

Some, of course, seeing the Dictator's goal, argued against it. Most of Francia's opposition, like erstwhile friend Mariano Antonio Molas and Father Marco Antonio Maíz, were Asunceños, and their cogent arguments fell without impact on the rural majority of the delegates, whose perception of the Caraí verged on the idolatrous.[16]

On May 31, the congress convened, and on the following day votes were cast for proposals presented by Francia and Ibáñez. Within a few hours, the deputies approved (perhaps unanimously) five basic resolutions. By late afternoon, copies of these were being read by criers as fast riders sped the news into the interior. The first resolution was very much to the point: Due to "the full confidence which the Citizen José Gaspar de Francia has justly merited from the People, he is declared and established Perpetual Dictator of the Republic during his life." The second noted that Francia had declined an annual salary of 12,000 pesos in favor of a less ostentatious 7,000. The third resolution stated that "the Republic will have a general Congress whenever the Dictator deems it necessary," and the fourth informed all clerics that they must refer to Francia in masses as *Dictatorem nostrum populo sive comiso et exercitu suo* and should praise from the pulpit both patriotism and "love and respect for the orders of our Supreme Government." The final resolution merely noted that "the present Congress has resolved to dissolve itself, not having other points to resolve nor other materials to deliberate," and called for a solemn mass to be celebrated the following night.[17]

This incredible document, which marks the abdication of a people, gave Francia his perpetual mandate and unregulated authority. He would use it.

The Bases of Power

As if to demonstrate his new mandate, and perhaps to forestall actions opposed to it, Francia prohibited all assemblies in the streets and plazas of the city, excepting only those traditional ones of a religious nature.[18] He also ordered the arrest of a Villa Rica cleric. The priest, Francisco del Valle, was incarcerated for having celebrated a midnight marriage in which a Peninsular was both witness and godfather. All the principals were jailed, the newlyweds suffered confiscation of all their property, and del Valle was sent into northern exile.[19] It was only rarely in the future that Francia would again be forced to prove that his decrees were not to be ignored.

He spent much attention in 1816 and 1817 on matters of defense. In addition to dispersing officers not in his confidence to remote frontiers, he allocated money for the construction of new warships, decreed the free importation of arms by the state (for which alone cash would be paid), and donated most of his salary to the Asunción garrisons.[20] He was well aware of the potential of the barracks for foul play and he would take no chances.

In 1817, one of the last important figures of the 1811 coup resigned the army in disgust. Writing Francia that his honor and patriotism were being subjected to a vicious smear campaign, Capt. Vicente Iturbe noted that "it is not my intention to abandon the Fatherland in its greatest urgencies," but begged the Caraí to be released from service. El Supremo, whose people may well have been behind the slander, graciously acceded,[21] and the last of the founding fathers was removed from the army.

In 1817, he also began to appoint all members of the Asunción cabildo, choosing annually the men he most favored from nomination lists presented by the outgoing cabildo.[22] He would do so until 1825, when he dispensed entirely with that corporate body and simply chose the men he wanted without benefit of nomination. Between those two dates he reversed cabildo decisions and removed members at will. The Franciata was truly beginning, but there were some among the Paraguayans who did not like it.

The Repression: Destruction of the Elite

Some Paraguayans, and a few foreign residents as well, were not happy—and were becoming less so—with Francia's absolute power and his penchant for using it. Some suffered from the stagnation of commerce; others desired union with Buenos Aires, accord with Artigas, restoration of royal rule, more liberty within Paraguay, or political power commensurate with elite social and economic status. It is also clear that by 1817 some were making their displeasure known and that the Caraí was carefully watching the malcontents.

It is not as clear just when Francia's counter-measures began, but in January, 1818, one José Ignacio Almagro was arrested "for having proffered certain expressions of a tendency directly contrary to the Most Excellent Dictator."[23] This is the first "political" arrest of which we have record—the first of many hundreds. Later that year, recently retired Vicente Iturbe was imprisoned by Francia, to remain in his underground cell for almost twenty years before being executed by one of the last firing squads of the Franciata.[24] He was the first prócer arrested and the last executed.

In 1819, the tempo of repression increased. Two Spaniards were arrested at Santiago for sedition and were brought to Asunción and executed for their indiscretion.[25] Francia had little patience with the elite, homegrown or imported. At the same time, Francia ordered the incarceration of former friend and confidant José Miguel Ibáñez, who was accused of speaking ill of the government in public. He rotted away the rest of his life in a dungeon.[26] The annual review of the jails in 1819 turned up at least three other political prisoners, including one who had argued publicly that Francia "would have to be deposed from his position, being replaced with D. Fulgencio Yegros . . . with other threats."[27] The disaffected had begun to surface, and when their open criticisms were supplemented with caricatures and scrawled epithets on the walls of Asunción, the Caraí decided on an ounce of prevention.

Fulgencio Yegros, natural (though uninterested) focus of discontent and the only viable replacement for Dr. Francia, was in retirement at his Quiquió estancia. Learning that Yegros was hosting frequent meetings at his isolated ranch, the Dictator ordered him to take up residence in Asunción, where he could be more closely watched. Yegros moved into one of his huge family's town houses late in 1819.[28]

In February, 1820, after a stakeout indicated something unusual was afoot, police crashed through the doors of the house of Dr. Marcos Baldovinos and arrested the group of men present, save for Juan Bogarín, who managed to slip away. Bogarín, in panic, made a confession the next day to a priest, who convinced the shaken penitent to repeat the story to El Supremo. Docilely, Bogarín did just that, admitting in Francia's presence that he and a large number of friends had been plotting to assassinate the Dictator on Holy Friday as he took his habitual ride through the city. Capt. Vicente Montiel, a leading prócer, and Pedro Juan Caballero were to take over the city garrisons, while Fulgencio Yegros was to assume civil authority.[29] Although it has always been assumed that the plotters planned to shoot the Caraí, or capture him for later disposal, there are indications that the plot was technologically more sophisticated. The November 30, 1821, edition of *El Argos de Buenos Aires* reported that many Paraguayans had been arrested, and although it was not known exactly why, "it is normally inferred that an explosion was planned."[30] The same article noted with more optimism than accuracy that the arrests ordered by Francia would permit at best "one year more of life for the perpetual dictatorship." Other evidence for the explosion theory comes from Francia's own funeral oration, given almost twenty years later. This document notes that "dangerous assemblages were taking place" and that "we are aware that a mine was in preparation that, had it exploded, would have produced all the dire effects of anarchy."[31] Whether the plotters hoped to blow Francia into the air as he rode through the streets or as he relaxed in his hammock at Government House we shall perhaps never know.

Immediately after hearing Bogarín's confession, the Caraí ordered his personal guard to arrest those implicated or suspected by Francia. Orders went out for arrests beyond the city as well, and for weeks men in chains filed into the city, silent beneath the stoic gaze of their guards. The prisons became so overcrowded that private homes had to be requisitioned to hold the overflow. Within a week, the prisoners numbered well over 100, and included men of virtually all of the nation's elite families: the Yegros, Caballero, Montiel, Iturbe, Machaín, Acosta, Noceda, Bogarín, Arístegui, and others. All nine adult male Montiel were arrested, as were most of the 1811 heroes.[32]

The entire nation entered what may be aptly called a "terror pánico" as Francia, frantic to learn the true dimensions of the conspiracy, subjected the aristocrats to interrogation and judicial torture, the latter activity performed by the Caraí's two Guaicurú specialists, who practiced their calling with grim skill. Many broke under the pain, producing a spiderweb of connections indicating that the plot was a very large one, fed by diverse currents of dissatisfaction. For more than a year the investigation continued, turning up new names and causing a widening circle of arrests. All was made infinitely more complicated and confused by the fall of Artigas and the rise of caudillo Francisco Ramírez.

On September 5, 1820, Artigas was ousted from power by his ambitious lieutenant, Ramírez, and fled with some 200 followers across the Paraná into Paraguay, seeking asylum.[33] After having the gaucho questioned, the Caraí surprisingly granted the request of his old nemesis, settling him on a farm in distant Curuguatí with a small pension.

Ramírez, however, was unhappy. A live Artigas posed a problem for him, and he sent messengers to Francia asking for the gaucho's extradition. When these messengers were thrown into teeming dungeons, Ramírez's requests became orders and then threats, and the caudillo began to assemble an army with the avowed aim of invading Paraguay.[34] The Caraí responded by sending the bulk of his army to the southern frontier and stepping up his efforts to learn if Ramírez, and perhaps even Artigas, had been party to the conspiracy within Paraguay. In November, 1820, a priest was arrested at Pilar for favoring a Ramírez invasion, and the Caraí seemed to link the several currents of unrest into one vast plot.[35] It may well be that his ultimate destruction of the elite was made easier to justify by divulging its supposed links with foreign powers.

Just as tensions in Asunción were reaching the almost unbearable stage, Ramírez had to order his army south to deal with other, more immediate enemies, and almost on receipt of this information the Caraí acted against another suspected enemy. On June 9, he decreed that all Peninsulares gather in the main plaza within a space of two hours. Decrying the "perverse influence, opposition, and incessant, insidious suggestions and seductions of the European Spaniards," Francia warned them that failure to comply with the decree would result in executions. Spaniards dwelling outside the city were given six hours to reach the plaza.[36]

Once assembled, the Spaniards were treated to a vicious harangue by a minor official and told that they were suspected of being involved in the plot of the Creole elite. They were then led off to jail. Only months later were they informed that on payment of a huge, collective fine they would be released. With the notable exceptions of Velasco, who soon died, and Bishop Panés, who was quickly released, the more than three hundred Spaniards spent a full eighteen months in prison. Most were then released after more than 100,000 pesos was paid by wives, daughters, and mothers into the state treasury.[37] The long, unproductive stay in jail and the heavy fine were ruinous to the Peninsulares as a group, removing most of them from the turgid commercial life of the nation that they had for so long dominated.

A week after the arrest of the Spaniards, Francia passed judgement and sentence on the Creole conspirators, a few of whom had already died. On June 17, 1821, Fulgencio Yegros, Capt. Montiel, Dr. Juan Arístegui, and five others were shot before an old, gnarled orange tree in the patio of Government House, probably under the direct gaze of El Supremo. Those not killed by the initial volley were dispatched by machete or bayonet, for the executioners, three in number, were permitted but one ball each per victim. If their aim was poor, they had to finish their work with the blade. Rather than face such an end, Pedro Juan Caballero committed suicide in his cell. Each day through June 24, a further eight men were executed, and on June 25, the last day, four more died. In all, sixty-eight or sixty-nine were killed in the courtyard, and scores more rotted in vegetal silence for many years in jail. Beneath a list of the names of the dead, El Supremo wrote suggestively and supremely, "Pax Francia."[38]   One of the very few próceres to escape extinction, although perhaps at the cost of nineteen years in a dungeon, was, surprisingly, military meddler Antonio Tomás Yegros, who appears in 1846 living peacefully on a family ranch at Quiquió with his progeny.[39]

Most of the próceres were now dead and the remainder safely out of circulation, yet Francia's fears were far from stilled. The repression, again confused by exterior events, continued.

From Terror Pánico to Paranoia

In December, 1821, the Dictator sent troops into Candelaria to kidnap French scientist Aimé Bonpland and destroy his botanical camp, dragging the renowned intellectual into a loose Paraguayan captivity that would last a decade. Bonpland had made the mistake of setting up his camp, without the Caraí's consent, along the main trade route between Ytapúa and São Borja in Brazilian Misiones. At this critical juncture in time, El Supremo was prone to interpret any unusual movements on Paraguay's borders as potentially dangerous.[40]

In 1822 and 1823, more arrests linked to the 1820 conspiracy were made within Paraguay, and a few men were shot in both Asunción and Pilar.[41] Virtually everyone named by any of the actual conspirators found himself in jail in this epoch, and in 1823, the Dictator took yet another step by arresting all natives of Santa Fe in Paraguay. These unfortunates, who were not informed of the reason for their imprisonment until 1834 (and then by accident), were the objects of the Caraí's wrath because Governor Estanislao López of Santa Fe had confiscated a load of arms the Dictator had purchased in Buenos Aires. Many died, and none were released until after Francia's death in 1840, but two of them left us a unique, if myopic, view of the

Franciata entitled, with only slight exaggeration, *Veinte años en un calabozo* (Twenty years in a dungeon).[42]

By late 1823, the terror pánico was over, and with it an epoch of Paraguayan history that had begun in 1537. Whereas the change of government in 1811 was a mere barracks coup, the repression following the 1820 conspiracy and events linked to it was the true Paraguayan revolution. During the repression, the population of the capital declined, perhaps by one-third, and Paraguayan society was permanently changed.[43] Gone was the relative opulence and power of the Peninsular merchants. That haughty group ceased to be an influence, social, economic, or political. Gone also was the major part of the old Creole elite, the adult males of the finest families. A few of the local elite, or those who aspired to such status, such as Carlos Antonio López and Mariano Antonio Molas, managed to leave Asunción and disappear into quiet, removed pastoral existences deep in the interior. Even some of these, however, such as Molas himself, were later arrested. Not only were many of the aristocrats dead but their survivors were left destitute, for the state confiscated all the properties of the convicted. The wealth added in this way to the national patrimony was enormous, comprising most of the finest ranches in the nation and many of the best houses in the capital. Two estancias of Manuel Cavañas alone accounted for twenty-three slaves and over five thousand head of livestock.[44] So, too, were confiscated the properties of those merely jailed. In short, Francia had ruined the traditional families of Paraguay, and had done so in the name of the law and the concept of nationalism. He had rendered them both impecunious and leaderless. After this, as one observer at Corrientes noted, "he rules them with a rod of iron without their showing or perhaps feeling the slightest discontent."[45]

Dr. Francia's World of Enemies: Pilar and Beyond

The mass executions of 1821 and the repression that ended in 1823 have long been supposed to have ended any further desire among Paraguayans for conspiracy. New documents, however, indicate otherwise. In 1825, the Pilar trade was flourishing and a number of foreign merchants were based at that entrepôt, including at least ten Peninsulares. In June of that year, Francia abruptly ordered the arrest of a number of foreign and local merchants at Pilar, including Artigas's henchman Peter Campbell, French citizen Luis Escoffier, a Correntino, and several Spaniards. "Seven prisoners in chains" were sent to the capital, and the first act of a confusing new conspiracy was about to open.[46]

In July, José Tomás Gill, subdelegado at Pilar, wrote the Caraí that several merchants at his port were "talking about the introduction of weapons and the surprise conquest of this Villa." These, wrote Gill, were now festooned with chains in the local calabozo.[47] The following May, Francia wrote Gill, ordering that all Europeans be evacuated from the port and adjoining border area. This order was swiftly and zealously carried out, and seven Peninsulares were ejected from Pilar after their merchandise was confiscated.[48]

A few months later, Gill mentioned in a letter to the Caraí that "two months after the four traitors were shot here," a mysterious rider appeared at the villa, and the subdelegado suspected that "he is paid, perhaps by some of the discontented here," to foment trouble.[49] Tied in with the Pilar plot, which must have been serious to result in several executions beyond the supervision and interrogation of Francia, was the strange case of Manuel Cavañas. That gentleman, one of the few próceres to escape arrest in 1821, had been living quietly at his ranch in the Cordillera. In November, 1826, however, he was implicated in the Pilar-based conspiracy by an informant who quoted a subversive conversation at Arroyos:

> Since Francia has governed our Fatherland, we have not been able to meet our own needs, because since then there have not been commerce nor dynamic men, because he has killed them all. But Francia is not *gente* like Don Manuel Cavañas. . . . As soon as Don Manuel Cavañas receives the word from Ysasi, we have to kill

Francia. All of this was said "heatedly, and with blows on the table."[50]

Cavañas was arrested, dying in prison in 1833, labeled one of "the plotters against the State" and denounced for his "infamous treason."[51]

Ysasi (José Tomás), trusted commercial agent of Francia's, had just left Asunción in 1826 for Buenos Aires, taking with him, or, in the words of El Supremo, "furtively extracting" some "100,000 pesos in gold or stamped silver" and a load of government trade goods. Francia only later learned that Ysasi had long been illegally exporting specie and duty-evaded goods to Buenos Aires—he had installed, according to Francia, a false deck on his vessel in order to hide his illegal cargo.[52] The incensed Caraí, calling the crime treason, confiscated all of Ysasi's known property within Paraguay.

A number of other arrests were made at this time, including that of Manuel Pedro de Peña, who spent fourteen years in jail, a great deal of which he devoted to memorizing the entire dictionary of the Spanish Academy of Language.[53] The following year, several Pilar merchants were assessed huge fines for their clandestine operations, and Francia wrote of the affair in terms implying that more was involved than contraband: "This treason has been very great."[54]

Precisely at this touchy moment, an unbidden vessel appeared at Pilar, having navigated the uncharted Río Bermejo from Salta. Its commander, Pablo Soria, claimed to have acted on orders of his provincial government, to which El Supremo responded that such was "a shameless act" of aggression.[55] The Dictator confiscated the weapons and papers aboard and sent Soria, his English and Italian friends (Lucas Crecer and Nicolás Descalzi), and the crew north, fearing that they were perhaps part of the Pilar disturbances. They would spend five years, unhappy, astride the Tropic of Capricorn at Concepción.

Into this chaotic web of events should be tossed the unusual demise of Bernardino Villamayor in 1825, a man later accused by the Dictator of "being an accomplice in this treason and iniquity." It is difficult to ascertain just which treason and iniquity the Caraí refers to, but there is no doubt that Villamayor, once influential Government Secretary, suffered terminal immersion in the Río Paraguay. It is also worth speculating on Francia's charges that Swiss physician Johann R. Rengger was at this time attempting to poison various government authorities, including the Caraí himself, and the fact that Government Secretary Juan Decoud died mysteriously in either 1825 or 1826.[56] Clearly something was amiss.

The Caraí and the Church

Both before and during the repressions, Dr. Francia was actively reducing the prerogatives of other sectors and institutions of Paraguayan society. Virtually any thing or group that stood between El Supremo and his exercise of supreme authority was limited, bound, or emasculated. One such force within the nation that might have survived as a vehicle for discontent or rival authority was the Church. Although not numerous, the clerics were not without their influence in schools and parishes throughout the land, and they were both relatively well educated and possessed of foreign contacts and commitments.

As early as 1815, Francia had begun to extend his control over the ecclesiastical corporation, assuming the right to routinely approve or deny priestly appointments or transfers. In July, he ordered the severance of all contact between the Paraguayan Church and superiors in other lands, including the Vatican, declaring the national Church "exempt from all interference or exercise of jurisdiction of the prelates or authorities of other countries: I prohibit . . . all use of the authority and supremacy of the said authorities."[57] Bulls emanating from Rome and all other religious correspondence would have to be cleared through El Supremo's office prior to dissemination within Paraguay, and he further declared that friars would henceforth "remain free of all obedience and entirely independent of the authority" of the hierarchies of their respective orders. To prove his point, he soon exiled the provisor of the Franciscans, a Spaniard.[58]

    As 1815 drew to a close, Francia confirmed his personal friend, Father Roque Antonio Céspedes Xeria, as vicar-general of the Paraguayan Church. Céspedes, recommended by ailing Bishop Panés himself, assumed his duties and exercised many of the routine functions of the bishop, becoming a very strong and loyal influence within the Church.[59]

    Céspedes was soon in actual control of the clerical corporation, for Panés, perhaps suffering under the strains of leading a Church hobbled by growing governmental restrictions, became "lost in melancholy" and almost totally ignored his duties. By 1817 he had stopped officiating at confirmations and was not available for the ordination of new priests. The following year he declined to appoint clerics to the posts where they were so urgently needed, yet failed to delegate authority to Céspedes to do so. In 1819 his condition worsened, and growing signs of senility, plus rumors of a conspicuous consumption of alcohol, made him an object of derision.[60]

    It is common to ascribe the notable decay of the prelate to the odium and harassment of Dr. Francia, much being made of the fact that Panés was both priest and foreigner.[61] There is no evidence, however, that El Supremo badgered the bishop, and it is more probable that the many strains of witnessing a dictator usurp direction of the Church took their toll. It was said that Panés began to pay more attention to the bottle than to the Bible, snapping back only briefly in his old age, just before dying in 1838, with a display of infirm dignity.

    In 1816, the government assumed financial stewardship over the Church, collecting tithes and other Church monies and putting all clerics on a regular salary. In that year, fiscal records indicate that the treasury collected some 32,655 pesos in the name of the Church (20 percent of all central government ingress), and paid out to the clerics only 5,141 pesos in quarterly payments—a tidy profit for the civil sector.[62]

    In May, 1817, a Franciscan inspector wrote the Caraí from Buenos Aires, begging him to relax his various decrees isolating the Paraguayan Church and permit the resumption of ties between Paraguayan Franciscans and those abroad.[63] As was usual in such cases, Francia declined to honor the request or acknowledge the query.

    Dr. Francia's control of the Church went an unprecedented step further in 1819, when he personally ordered the convocation of a church council in order to clarify Church/state issues. While we have no record of what was discussed, later the same year El Supremo abolished the customary Church levies of "Jerusalem" and the "Alms," labeling them unimportant to the Church and an imposition on the populace.[64]

    Although Francia thus gradually usurped direction of the national Church, it would be an error to ascribe to him any Draconian repression of the priest-hood. Those few clerics who disobeyed or affronted him were not flogged to bloody shreds or shot, but were, for the most part, sent to the frontiers to suffer for the faith in the scattered garrisons. Francia had no more desire to waste clerical talent than other resources, and was quick to find uses for errant members of society.

Eloquent testimony of Francia's domination of the weak national Church is contained in a letter of 1822 in which the curate of Villeta asks the Dictator's permission to take up a collection in his parish to help finance Holy Week cele-brations. Wrote the priest: "The parishioners have always voluntarily contributed," and "I humbly beseech Your Excellency to concede me the Supreme Permission that I may receive the alms which they offer."[65] Few leaders in this hemisphere have possessed such control of the Catholic Church, and Francia, unlike many other despots, never professed to be its servant.

Despite El Supremo's domination, the Paraguayan Church was still the only non-government economic and social power in the land. Perhaps because in the Dictator's perception it was vaguely connected to the 1820 conspiracy, the seminary was closed in 1823. He wrote the relevant decree on the reverse of a plea from one of its teachers for back pay, excoriating the supplicant for his "irregular, uncivil, and rustic style" of writing. He ordered the seminary's buildings abandoned and, "to avoid the useless continuance of its growing costs," the delivery to the state of "all furniture or effects" of the school and its farm at Campo Grande. Somewhat surprisingly, the chastened supplicant soon received his overdue pay.[66]

With this action, Francia seriously affected the functioning and the future of the Church, for not only was the seminary the only institution of higher education in Paraguay, and a forum for learned members of the clergy, but it was also the only national mechanism for the production and ordination of native priests. To the Church, the closure of the seminary was a telling blow, a wound that grew more serious with every year that the Caraí ruled.

As if on a timetable, Francia next turned his attention to the task of dis-solving the nation's few monasteries and decreed the secularization of all monks. The new "secular" priests were then sent to interior parishes where need for religious solace was most pronounced. Among the various orders, there were only fifty-three friars in Paraguay at the time of the 1824 decree. All but five foreign-born were eventually secularized,[67] and the state added all monastery property to its already immense patrimony. The one small conventual house of San José in the capital delivered to the government several buildings in Asunción, tracts of land in other partidos, forty-three slaves, large herds of livestock, and rents from ninety families who were tilling its lands. It is obvious that even the truncated Paraguayan Church had managed to retain considerable wealth. The main monastic buildings in Asunción, four in number, and the one in Villa Rica were soon converted to barracks for the growing military establishment.[68]

With his secularization decree, Francia caused the collapse of the economic independence of the Church and did away with the small orders, whose foreign connections undoubtedly worried him. By 1825, the Church was entirely composed of individual clerics thinly spread throughout the nation, dependent on El Supremo and not the ecclesiastical hierarchy for their pay and assignments.

The last, somewhat gratuitous blow at the Church was struck in 1828, almost as an afterthought. The Dictator suppressed the ecclesiastical cabildo, berating that body for the advanced age of its members and its utter lack of relevance. The cabildo was not abolished, however, and for some reason Francia left the door open for its eventual reestablishment.[69]

With the Spanish minority, the Creole elite, the merchant community, education, and the Church eviscerated and rendered harmless, the Caraí had few quarters from which to fear domestic threat. Yet he decided to seek further insurance of rivalless rule. In 1824 he decreed the abolition of the cabildos of Asunción and Villa Rica, the most influential vehicles in the past for the important families of the nation. In his decree, the Dictator expressed his "gratitude for and recognition of" the "zeal and love of order" shown by the outgoing cabildantes, but noted that, in the future, municipal affairs would be handled only by "those employees necessary for the Administration of Justice and other indispensable tasks: that is, the two Alcaldes." Significantly, he added that the alcalde of first vote would be primarily responsible for the "upkeep and other expenses of the penal system."[70]

In abolishing the two cabildos, Francia did not intend to end municipal government. He soon named from among his loyal followers men to assume individual municipal posts such as that of alcalde. What he did destroy was the corporation, the organized institution, much as he had ended the monastic orders but not the work of the monks. Few writers have noted that he made no such move against the dozens of cabildos in the rustic towns of the interior, cabildos that represented no corporate or class interests and hence no threat to his security or that of the nation.[71] Thus it would be an exaggeration to claim, as some have, that El Supremo ended local government in Paraguay. Decisions in Yhú or San Miguel were carried out after 1824 as they had been for centuries.

The New Centurions: Dr. Francia's Army

Given El Supremo's zeal to end the existence of institutions other than the Supreme Government itself, it might seem paradoxical that he would foster the rise of a new and potentially dangerous one. Between 1814 and 1820 the Paraguayan army was born, with the Dictator's star over its manger.

Until Francia became El Supremo, Paraguay had no army, certainly not as an identifiable institution. Instead there were the urbano and filiado militia, poorly armed, poorly organized, and led by a score or more semi-professional officers drawn from the upper ranks of society. In power, Francia showed himself uncommonly interested in things military and took personal charge of the training, arming, and supply of his soldiers. As one European present in 1814 reported: "The Dictator himself became general, colonel, paymaster, quartermaster and head tailor" to the military, devoting much time to his grenadiers, which "he pampered, flattered, paid and caressed."[72] Nor was this gentleman fantasizing, for another European wrote a decade later, also from personal experience, that "he is generally present at the cavalry exercises; sometimes takes command, and putting himself sword in hand at the head of a squadron, leads a charge with boyish pleasure."[73]

In the years 1814-1816, Francia scattered the officer elite throughout the interior, where they could not combine against him, and appointed his own followers—men of both loyalty and patriotism—to the major commands. At the same time, using his grenadier unit as a base, he began creating new, salaried professional units, normally of company size, perhaps as a counter-balance to the filiado drafts, which might still feel loyalty to the aristocrats. He assumed the power to nominate all militia officers as well, thus gaining some control over the dispersed structure.[74]

By 1819, with a considerable body of paid professionals officered by men in his trust and armed with recently-purchased, modern arms, El Supremo ended the "antiquated filiado system, disbanding its units and ordering its integration into the local, urbano defense forces." With the stroke of a pen, he replaced a traditional, somewhat elitist organization with one of his own creation. Henceforth, only regular troops would be entrusted with the defense of the more important frontier forts and the capital itself.[75]

Garrisoning the city turned out to be the regular troops' main duty: from 1819 through 1838, the urban garrison gradually grew, both in absolute numbers and in proportion to the capital's civilian population. By 1822 there were sixteen companies of regulars—two of artillery, eight of infantry, three of hussars, and three of mounted grenadiers (Francia's elite and guard units)—quartered in three main barracks.[76]

The Asunción garrison comprised as much as 70 percent of the regular soldiers, with much smaller garrisons at Pilar, Ytapúa, and Concepción. The best units were kept at Asunción, acting as a sort of bodyguard for El Supremo and as insurance against coup or revolution. Perhaps more important, Francia, in making the capital an armed camp, was easily able to keep his jealous eyes on the bulk of his army and its officers. Only in times of severe border threat did Francia permit his officers to command large bodies of troops beyond his eyesight, and then for only short periods. Officers were rendered harmless by being given relatively small corps of regulars, by frequent rotation in command, and by being held to a maximum rank of captain, followed by early, mandatory retirement. His own institution would not be permitted to devour its master.[77]

An unexcelled practitioner of the "divide and conquer" school, José Gaspar was in undisputed, unrivaled control of his nation by 1824, and, although feared by his people, he was also, by most, revered.

The average Paraguayan had little if anything to complain about in Dr. Francia's Paraguay. Should he complain about a professional army that took much of the burden of defense from his shoulders? Would he be sympathetic to the plight of the once haughty europeos, now brought down to his level? Would he protest the end of the elite seminary, which had always been beyond his means and hopes, or should he show anger that there were more priests in the villages than before? Could he become angry at the end of the two major cabildos when his own still functioned? Would he be disheartened that the national patrimony had doubled or tripled and he was now paying a lower rent to the government for pasture rights? Would he weep at news of the destruction of the elite or the incarceration of foreign merchants? Would he be seriously affected by the stagnation of international commerce, when he had never been able to enjoy its fruits?

Virtually all of El Supremo's repressions affected the aristocracy, both Creole and Peninsular. If they affected the common man at all, it was often for the better. Seen from the village level, Francia's domestic policies were populist— a forced leveling and homogenization of a largely rural society. Herein lie the seeds of Paraguayan unity in later decades: a unity and sense of purpose and national cohesion fostered by the Caraí. Under his sway began a retreat from the city to the countryside, a surge of self-sufficiency, a certain pride in self and nation, a resurgence of Guaraní over Spanish, and a near deification of the leader. El Supremo's title was a reflection of reality as 1824 ushered in a new age.

4. The Diplomacy of Isolation, 1820–1840

The Dearth of Diplomacy

The Paraguay of Dr. Francia must be painted in rather somber hues. It was a quietly prosperous nation almost totally predictable and empty of great, noteworthy events. After 1824, Francia's revolution moved slowly on and the forging of the republic was a silent process unmarked by upheaval and chaos. The nation followed cart tracks into the interior and it learned itself and its worth.

Properly speaking, there was no diplomacy during the Franciata—no give and take according to mutually understood, internationally standardized norms. This is not to say that there was no contact between Paraguay and the outside world, but that the contact that did take place was almost entirely unsought by Paraguay and can scarcely be considered diplomacy.

Only two interests entered the arena of foreign contact: commerce and Francia's detention of foreigners. This was so because the long-term goals of recognition and free navigation were simply unattainable. From 1814 until about 1822, the Caraí's major international preoccupations logically centered around relations with two large, hostile neighbors. Brazil, still a colony, tended to view Paraguay as a stumbling block to further territorial expansion and as a potentially dangerous republican state. The province and city of Buenos Aires and its allies, on the other hand, never ceased to regard Paraguay as a rightful political appendage.

Dr. Francia's cautious policy of announced neutrality, coupled with other, more critical worries of his neighbors, prevented open conflict, and Paraguay was spared the fate of the Banda Oriental, which underwent invasion, civil war, mass migrations, emigration, banditry, and rule by caprice, and finally served as a battlefield for Brazil and Argentina in the 1825-1828 Cisplatine War. Ignoring the threats and supplications alike of all parties who sought to use Paraguay for their own ends, Francia maintained peace and guaranteed the survival of his nation.

Perhaps the most notable cause célèbre of the Franciata was the abduction of French scientist Aimé Bonpland, personal friend of Simón Bolívar, traveling companion of Alexander von Humboldt, and leading botanist of his day. Bonpland suffered from a classic run of bad luck, camping in Candelaria just as the terror pánico was reaching its peak across the river. The Paraguayan army, in full strength on the border in anticipation of the Ramírez invasion, followed the Caraí's orders and kidnapped Bonpland in late 1821, bringing him across the river into the loosest of arrests.

Hardly an irrational act, as it is often depicted, the removal of Bonpland was merely the first in a series of steps to renew and guarantee Paraguayan control over Candelaria.[1] In the next three years, Paraguayan forces firmly reestablished their nation's claim to the region, and did so without large-scale hostilities.

Bonpland, who spent the next decade in various parts of southern Paraguay, was not at all mistreated. He was initially settled near the pueblo of Santa María de Fe, and there he went to work, practising medicine, collecting botanical specimens, and constructing a rum distillery, a blacksmithy, and a carpentry business. As he himself admitted, he "acquired the means to live in great comfort."[2] Busily content with creating his miniature botanical-industrial complex, the scientist was blissfully unaware of the international furor over his abduction.

Bonpland's fate was to focus a great deal of international attention and ire on Francia, though it must be said that he utterly failed to respond to it. Bolívar, at the height of his considerable powers, begged for his friend's release in 1823, and even threatened to use his "Liberating Army," then in Bolivia, to pry him loose if necessary.[3] Less than awed, Francia ignored the Great Liberator.

The next year, French diplomat Richard de Grandsire and an Admiral Grivel both took up the botanist's cause, one in the name of the French Institute, the other in that of the King. Both were also studiously ignored.[4] British minister Woodbine Parish had no better luck from Buenos Aires—his letters were returned to him unopened, "a rude intimation that from now on our correspondence was ended."[5]

It was later learned that an increasingly angry Bolívar, anxious to use "his troops to bring about a change" in Paraguay's government as well as to free his friend, had been rebuffed in his attempt to gain Buenos Aires's adhesion to his plan—the Cisplatine War was absorbing all of his potential ally's attentions and energy.[6]

Staunchly resisting outside pressure, Francia surprised everyone in 1829 when he gave Bonpland permission to leave, unrealistically noting that he had just learned that the botanist was a family man. Despite the permission, Bonpland was detained a further twenty months at Ytapúa, "a true punishment for me," before actually crossing the border.[7] Long after El Supremo became El Difunto, Aimé Bonpland, then aged Director of the Corrientes Museum of Natural History, reentered Paraguay, to be welcomed by Carlos Antonio López and allowed to gather plants. He died at São Borja in 1858 at the age of eighty-five on the eve of another trip to Asunción as guest of the Paraguayan government.[8]

The botanist was merely the most celebrated of the Caraí's foreign detainees. Two Swiss physicians, Johann R. Rengger and Marcel Longchamp, who arrived unbidden at Asunción in 1819, were forced to remain for six years, becoming, to pass the time, salaried surgeons for the Asunción garrisons. The account they have left us of their Paraguayan interlude, although often bitter, is one of the very few printed sources on the Franciata.[9] If in their book they presented Francia in a harsh light, so too did the Dictator denounce them later in an uncharacteristically emotional letter, which found its way (on purpose) to the Buenos Aires press. In this missive, the Caraí struck out especially at Rengger, the "Swiss European atheist" who had "been intimately involved with the European Spaniards" in a subversive plot. Not content with mere plotting, continued Francia, Rengger had poisoned many of his personal guard while pretending to administer medicine: "Almost all who were sick infallibly died when he administered his drugs to them . . . the deaths ceasing when he was expelled from said Barracks."[10] According to the Caraí, Rengger also hoped to poison him. One may probably attribute this surprising letter to Francia's desire to counteract the effects of the Rengger and Longchamp book, which had appeared in 1827.

As the Dictator gathered unwilling French and Swiss into his realm from time to time, so did he detain a sizeable number of Britons who passed within his borders, and by 1823 the influential British merchant community at Buenos Aires insisted that its home government work for their release. Woodbine Parish, His Majesty's first resident consul to the United Provinces, arrived in the city in 1824 and was immediately presented with demands for action against the Paraguayan government for "its arbitrary detention of men, ships and cargo" of British origin.[11]

Parish began writing Francia in mid-July, soothingly opening each note with phrases such as, "The British people desire to cultivate relations" of a commercial nature with Paraguay. Then followed protestations of the diplomat's "confidence in the well-known talents and wisdom" of the Caraí, and expressions of faith that Francia would prove that wisdom by releasing the Britons.[12] Parish also wrote the Foreign Office, suggesting that a British steamship (a technological rarity in 1824) visit Paraguay, for "the novelty of the undertaking might attract the notice of Don Gaspar de Francia" and favorably dispose him on the issue at hand.[13]

Steamship diplomacy, however, was unnecessary, for early in 1825, Parish proudly reported that "I have this day had the great satisfaction of hearing that all the British Property and Detenies [sic] have been released."[14] In April, the men in question arrived at Buenos Aires, and with them came that rarest of all things, a formal note from the Dictator as well, albeit signed by Government Secretary Bernardino Villamayor. In this missive, El Supremo evinced strong interest in the commerce and recognition hinted at so astutely by Parish, and he noted that he had released the detainees only because "they are Individuals of a magnanimous and wise Nation," which must recognize interior Paraguay's claims to free navigation of the Paraná.[15]

Twelve British subjects had been repatriated: five merchants, three carpenters, three sailors, and a shoemaker. Three more soon arrived at Buenos Aires. Flushed with his victory in opening the Paraguayan "box," Parish again wrote the Dictator, explaining that British trade, recognition, and support for free navigation would all depend on Paraguay's initiating formal relations with the feared and hated southern neighbor.[16]

Parish's reply effectively terminated further communication with Francia. The Caraí, wary of Argentine political goals, also feared commercial discrimination and high taxes within the Porteño system, and was obsessed by the lesson of the current war in the Banda Oriental. Also, any serious negotiations with Buenos Aires might threaten the major trade with Brazil carried on through Ytapúa. This would be too uncertain and high a price to pay for the "probable" presence of a few British vessels in Asunción Bay. Although the superficial issue was commerce, the basis was seen by El Supremo as something more profound: survival as an independent nation. His response was to terminate diplomacy while maintaining both the Brazilian trade at Ytapúa and the unofficial commerce with the United Provinces through Pilar. Both of these interchanges were conducted on his terms alone.

While Parish and his successors at Buenos Aires continued to watch Paraguay for signs of a thaw, or a change that might open the country to British trade, there was no further communication from the landlocked nation. Even the subsequent detention of several more overly-ambitious Britons failed to bring about renewed correspondence.[17]

Parish alone of all supplicants had succeeded in at least his immediate objective in 1824 and 1825, but he failed to open Paraguay to British commercial interests because he tempted Francia with an inherently unrealistic vision. If Britain would not move unilaterally toward Paraguay for fear of risking its thriving connection with the United Provinces, neither could the Caraí attract British trade without endangering his nation's neutrality.

Other foreigners became unwilling participants in daily life in Paraguay. In 1826, the Soria party was arrested and treated as enemy agents, for being, in the inimitable words of El Supremo, "atrocious, daring, insolent, despotic, and shameless."[18] Shipped to loose imprisonment at Concepción, Soria, Italian astronomer Descalzi, and Englishman Crecer, feeling "like lead statues," began an exile steeped in sheer tedium. Descalzi's only excitement was keeping a diary, and that document makes superb reading. As the astronomer, who described the local official's daughters as "ugly and whorish," reported, Crecer in only partly facetious style begged a soldier one day for his gun, with which "to kill myself: I am so bored with your Paraguay."[19]

In July, 1831, with no warning, the three were ordered to settle their affairs and leave. Given no explanation, they were permitted to purchase yerba at Pilar and take their ship south to Buenos Aires.[20] With their release, no captive foreigners of note remained in Paraguay.

Portuguese, Brazilians, and the Ytapúa Connection

After decades of sporadic commercial contact between the Paraguayan north and the Mato Grosso, the Dictator ordered that border sealed in 1817, partly to cut down the contraband trade, partly because of his anger at the involvement of Brazilian authorities with the hostile M'Bayá who so routinely raided the area. The M'Bayá, habituated to attacking Paraguayan farms and settlements, brought their loot north to exchange for firearms and firewater. The cycle complete, they descended on Paraguay with more modern arms to repeat the process. Since the Mato Grosso garrisons obtained much-needed beef, yerba, and tobacco in this manner, officials there did little to halt the vicious spiral of raids.

In the south, the situation before 1820 was chaotic at best, with Artigas, the Portuguese, Correntinos, assorted caudillos, bandits, and stray Indians hacking their way through Candelaria in a carnival of destruction, making the land bridge between Paraguay and Brazil one of the most hazardous terrains in the hemisphere.

Even the sound of guns and the clash of cane lances, however, could not stay the hand of some Brazilian merchants, and by 1819 a heavily armed few were making the dangerous trip from São Borja to Ytapúa. What appears on paper a minor interchange soon became a vital matter to El Supremo because of the virtual blockade of the Paraná.[21] Candelaria was thus recognized by Francia as a highway, and, if it were to be profitably traveled, it would have to be controlled by Paraguay. In 1820, with Artigas in exile, such control appeared possible. The following year, troops were ordered into Candelaria to establish a large fort at San Miguel, and Bonpland

was kidnapped. In 1822, a new fort was constructed at Tranquera de Loreto (Posadas), and within months a crucial section of Candelaria was in Paraguayan hands.[22]
While the Caraí was planting the Paraguayan standard in the red soil of Candelaria, Pablo Machado, a Brazilian envoy, arrived at Asunción to discuss the opening of formal commercial ties. Francia, impressed by this de facto recognition of Paraguayan sovereignty, agreed to a trial period of commerce, to be restricted on the Paraguayan side to Ytapúa.[23]
Because Brazil soon opened São Borja to Paraguayan merchants, the Dictator allowed the trade to survive and thrive—subject, of course, to his rigid supervision. In Rio de Janeiro, interest in this nascent trade increased in direct proportion to the growth of war clouds in the Banda Oriental. With the threat of war, commercial and other agreements with Paraguay took on a new urgency, as Rio desired to guarantee at least the Caraí's neutrality.
In May, 1824, the Brazilian Court named Antônio Manuel Correa da Cámara "Consul and Commercial Agent of the Empire to the Government of Paraguay." This act constituted recognition of Paraguayan independence, although such would not be stated in an official document for several decades.[24] Woodbine Parish, always alert, wrote that this "opening" of Paraguay was "an object of very great importance to British interests here" in Buenos Aires.[25] Also named Comandante of the Mato Grosso in order to give him authority to settle the problems of the northern frontier, Correa was sent off to Paraguay with instructions to halt any possible rapprochment between that country and the United Provinces.[26]
In late August, 1825, the Brazilian commercial agent reached Asunción, becoming the first diplomat received by the Paraguayan government since Herrera in 1813. Although his powers were vague, Correa's haste to win favor with El Supremo led him to promise far more than he could ever fulfill. His failure to make good on his rash promises doomed the potential relationship between the two nations. Before he left Asunción to return to Rio and try to convince his government to formally recognize Paraguayan independence and appoint him ambassador,[27] Correa pulled out all the stops in a note to his Foreign Ministry, describing in detail the beauty, prosperity, tranquility, and military potential of Paraguay. "Brazil," he wrote, "united in alliance with Paraguay and there is no one to fear," adding that even without a written accord the Dictator's "word of honor is worth a thousand treaties." Unfortunately, his appreciation of Paraguayan reality was not shared by his more jaded colleagues in Rio de Janeiro.[28]
Designating a Brazilian merchant to represent imperial interests at Ytapúa, Correa rode out of Asunción in December, 1825. As he wended his way south, his path must have crossed that of a courier with messages from Rio instructing

him to gain some sort of formal alliance with Paraguay, an issue crucial since the outbreak of war with the United Provinces. This Paraguayan commitment was to be gained even at the cost of offering Paraguay full trade facilities at Montevideo.[29]

Correa was almost entirely unsuccessful in Rio as he attempted to fulfill his promises of recognition, peace in the north, and creation of an embassy in Asunción. The imperial government, its energies devoted to war, appointed him commercial chargé (not ambassador) in 1826.[30] A very disappointed would-be ambassador departed Rio for his post in November, arriving after war-related delays at Ytapúa only in September, 1827. There, the diplomat was shocked to learn that El Supremo denied his travel to Asunción and refused him permission to make a written memorial concerning his mission. Obviously Francia had already learned of Correa's inability to make good on what he had so rashly offered. Correa remained at unattractive little Ytapúa for nearly a year, hoping that Francia would relent, busying himself with supervising the growing trade. He left only in mid-1828, thoroughly disillusioned. As he departed, he now warned Rio against a dangerous and aggressive Paraguay that, he predicted, would one day be a threat to Brazil—an interesting presentiment, considered irrelevant at the time.[31]

Commerce and the Conquest of Candelaria

Despite the lack of diplomatic sanction after 1828, the Ytapúa trade continued to grow. As long as Brazilian merchants behaved themselves and dealt in "useful goods," the Dictator protected the interchange. By 1828, Ytapúa was a bustling little port with a small foreign community, and heavily guarded cart and pack trains were in constant movement across Candelaria. Although the trade flourished, it was at times harassed, and the danger from bandits (often encouraged by Litoral authorities) and Indians grew in direct proportion to the value of the goods hauled. The long caravans were tempting targets, and in 1830 the Caraí was forced to extend and tighten his control over the disputed territory. He sent more troops and ordered more aggressive patrolling, for, as he noted in a letter, the bandits were "becoming overconfident."[32]

In 1831, El Supremo's normal calm was shaken by news that a large part of Candelaria was about to be sold to a group of English investors. Angered over a possible loss of territory and interruption of the vital Ytapúa trade, the Dictator warned that "the English should drop such a project and retire."[33] Although not because of the Dictator's protests, the English colonization never materialized. Instead, pressure from Corrientes mounted, with an increasing frequency of armed clashes. Never apathetic, the Caraí quickly reinforced the region, and in 1832 a Correntino settlement at San Miguel, west of Candelaria, was destroyed. Of this incident, El Supremo laconically noted that "Paraguayan troops, as always, will move through their own territory."[34] New garrisons and forts were soon established, and huge, regular patrols of 400 cavalry were sweeping through Candelaria all the way to the Río Uruguay. Francia, as always the realist, reproached his verbose and patriotic subdelegado at Ytapúa, instructing him to cease his prattling about "dying in defense of Liberty, which is now irrelevant," and maintain his aggressive patrolling, which was of far greater value to the nation.[35]

Armed clashes with Correntinos continued and tension vibrated in the region, yet no wider conflict erupted. Francia made it clear that he sought no territory save the heart of Candelaria, which was necessary for the Brazil trade. Corrientes, with little support from the other, supposedly "united" provinces, was simply too weak to challenge Paraguay. In 1833, the Dictator provided cavalry escorts for Brazilian caravans on a round-trip basis, and the trade may be said to have become truly official.[36]

"513 Little Wooden Dolls": The Ytapúa Trade

Although commerce increased, the Caraí's penchant for minutiae and his inherently suspicious nature caused an occasional problem. In 1829, he wrote an official, claiming that some sample boxes of cloth were not in order. He had unrolled each bolt of cloth and had found one seven and a half yards short.[37] Always wary of being cheated, he wrote in 1831 that the sabers offered for sale at Ytapúa were two inches too short to be effective. He refused their purchase at any price and ordered the Brazilians informed that "they are morons for coming here with this trick . . . they should not accustom themselves to bring trash" for sale in Paraguay.[38] The same year, he further complained about a load of hats, samples of which he had just inspected. "Of the fine Portuguese hats, only two fit normal heads." He explained that "the rest are very small, and cannot be sold."[39]

His constant perusal of trade goods was all too often rewarded by the discovery of shoddy material. He once told his subdelegado to inform a merchant that all of his goods were "defectuosos," his cloth was "weak," and his yellow cotton faded. He complained most bitterly about faulty rifles and other defective arms, for one of the principal reasons for the commerce was the arming of Paraguay. In a letter, he told his chief official in the south that "it is necessary to talk frankly with those people so that they do not think we are stupid about weapons, and do not get into the habit of bringing and dumping in Paraguay defective goods or those worn out elsewhere."[40]

Merchants with licenses from El Supremo appeared at Ytapúa from all sections of Paraguay, even from the far north. Contrary to myth, Paraguayans were permitted to market not only what they themselves had produced but whatever they could accumulate in the interior partidos. One man, in fact, Manuel Flota, recorded profits of 12,000 pesos in 1824 from selling to the Brazilians at Ytapúa.[41]

Much of what was sold at Ytapúa came from the area of Yutí, north of the port, and from nearby ex-Jesuit missions. Both areas were exceptionally fertile and contained state ranches whose produce accounted for the large government share in the commerce. The one state estancia at San Cosme delivered 1,334 hides, 224 bales of tobacco, 6,400 pounds of yerba, 10 boxes of salt, 4 boxes of hats, and 2 "high-backed benches" for the state trade in 1840.[42]

The commerce boomed. By 1840, sales tax (alcabala) receipts remitted to the capital reached 25,000 pesos; even more was retained at Ytapúa. Export taxes, lowered in 1829 due to phenomenally good harvests, amounted to 12 reales per hundred pounds of yerba, 5 reales per arroba of tobacco, 10 per arroba of cigars, and a scale of from 1 real to 1 peso for hides or skins, depending on type and size.[43] Other goods were taxed at previous (unknown) rates.

Contraband also existed. A convicted smuggler found his goods confiscated and was forced to pay a fine equal to the exact market value of those goods. In 1838, fourteen Paraguayans were fined a total of 10,184 pesos, indicating a rather sizeable "invisible" commerce.[44] Income from such fines was used to subsidize Paraguayan caravan escorts.

Not all the trade at Ytapúa was in "useful goods." In 1837 a shipment of "513 little wooden dolls, painted in all colors for childrens' toys," arrived, a pleasant reminder that even in Francia's Paraguay not everything operated according to reasons of state.[45] Also on the human side was the Caraí's admonition to his southern subdelegado to ignore the "loose women" accompanying some Brazilian merchants. That official was not to concern himself with Brazilian morals:

> These merchants and the women they bring are not Subjects of this State. . . . It is not right that the Government or anyone else bother to enquire about their friendships or their private lives . . . nor judge if the women some bring are legitimate or concubine. . . . What is it to you that a poor woman, through inclination or passion for the merchant . . . be his woman, or, according to your language, a false woman? [46]

Despite defective goods and minor moral issues, the trade functioned smoothly, providing the nation with what it could not itself produce and the state with the arms with which to maintain its independence.

Pilar: Unknown Trade with Unacknowledged Partners

A serious commerce also existed between Paraguay and the United Provinces, despite official hostility. This trade, overlooked by most historians, was based at Pilar (del Ñeembucú), and became very important.

Even during the most chaotic period, 1817-1820, with a succession of caudillos ravaging the Litoral, some trade with Paraguay was conducted, and in 1818 the Porteño customs house levied duties on yerba, tobacco, sweets, and other items noted as Paraguayan.[47] The following year, at least thirteen Porteño vessels sailed from Buenos Aires to Paraguay. One, the *Santa Fe y Animas,* brought to Buenos Aires 70 tons of yerba, 351 bales of tobacco, 500 hides, and 8 boxes of sweets, a substantial cargo for the era.[48]

This unofficial trade increased yearly despite official Porteño views on Paraguayan sovereignty, and was limited only by the violence of the caudillos along the route. Incomplete customs records at Asunción and Buenos Aires are misleading, for many of the cargos carried from Corrientes south were of Paraguayan origin. It is very doubtful that underpopulated, civil-war-wracked Corrientes could have been much more than a way station, as it later clearly was, between Paraguay and Buenos Aires.[49]

It is also clear that in the early 1820s Porteño authorities attempted to seek at least a partial detente with Paraguay. In 1821, the governor of Buenos Aires Province, Martín Rodríguez, wrote Francia, noting that, with Artigas and Ramírez out of the way, it might be time to consider "the great object of liberally freeing the commerce of our ports." Two years later, the president of the United Provinces, Bernardino Rivadavia, also directed himself to the Caraí, flattering him by claiming to be "an addict to your Person and the nobility of your Sentiments." Rivadavia sought economic and political cooperation with Paraguay, and even sent an envoy to speak with Francia, but he was not permitted, of course, to enter Paraguay.[50]

On New Year's Day, 1821, a cargo of 200 modern rifles reached Pilar, sent by the Dictator's factor José Tomás Ysasi from Buenos Aires—a remarkable event, considering Ramírez's projected invasion.[51] Precisely one year later, true isolation for Paraguay ended as Governor Juan José Blanco of Corrientes wrote the Caraí expressing his desire "to maintain and foment the strictest friendship . . . and openness of our Commerce."[52] Proof of the official thaw was soon at hand. Later in the month, the subdelegado at Pilar wrote Francia in amazement that a Paraguayan vessel had just reached Pilar from Buenos Aires, and "no one collected any duty in any port" on the long voyage. This news marked a great upsurge of the Pilar trade and greater freedom for Paraguayan goods and merchants. Perhaps greater in volume than that of Ytapúa, the Pilar commerce would long outlast Francia himself.[53]

As with the Ytapúa trade, the Pilar interchange was very closely supervised. Pilar was declared the only entrepôt for the downriver commerce. All vessels, after clearing Corrientes, were met at the border post of Curupaití by a Paraguayan naval escort that conducted them to Pilar. There, the merchandise was checked against the merchants' invoices and given a quick quality control check, and samples were sent on to Francia for his perusal. It was not unusual for El Supremo to declare an item useless[54] or to arbitrarily lower retail and wholesale prices on imported goods, leaving the vendor the choice of selling at lower prices or hauling his goods downriver in search of less rigorous markets. In any case, only with Francia's written approval could a merchant sell his wares at Pilar, a fact noted by an observer from Corrientes: "Francia keeps the trade wholly in his own hands and acts with the greatest caprice."[55]

Some preferred goods were selected by the Caraí for government purchase. The government alone was permitted to buy arms and munitions, and only rarely was a private citizen allowed to acquire books and periodicals from the outside. The state also eagerly sought specie, some of which it was itself obliged to pay out for weapons. For the most part, the government financed its purchases through the sale of produce from its own estancias and internal taxes paid in produce.[56] A government monopoly of the export of fine "construction"-quality lumber also figured substantially in the official trade.

A detailed 1831 report indicates that the Paraguayan merchant was most interested in acquiring wide bolts of cloth, women's stockings, thread, needles, hats, shoes, iron, wine, coffee, olive oil, vinegar, and salt.[57] In return, they sold yerba, tobacco, hides, sweets, cigars, and oranges. The Pilar connection met what the Caraí considered the chief needs of his government. In 1822, several shipments of English rifles, bronze cannon, and other heavy arms arrived, sent by Ysasi aboard Argentine ships.[58] This was indeed an open and useful trade. Throughout the Franciata the bulk of the Pilar commerce was carried on Porteño or Correntino bottoms, although Paraguayans were from time to time licensed to carry goods to Corrientes or beyond.[59]

Smuggling, of course, also existed at Pilar, and in 1826 and 1827 it seems to have reached momentous proportions. Many arrests were made and seven Peninsular merchants were stripped of all their goods. The Caraí, always suspicious of foreigners, denounced the smugglers as subversives, accusing Government Secretary Bernardino Villamayor of "being an accomplice in this treason and iniquity."[60] That official, however, was beyond Francia's vengeance, for, as Parish wrote from Buenos Aires, he "threw himself into the River and was drowned."[61] Whether Villamayor jumped or was pushed into the muddy waters, there was probably some connection between him and the smugglers, and perhaps between the latter and an anti-Francia movement. Coincidence was a rare thing in the Caraí's Paraguay.

Smuggling was never eradicated at Pilar, for the illegal trade simply paid too handsomely. In 1827, yerba sold for four times its Asunción price on the wharves of Buenos Aires,[62] and the differential widened almost yearly, while Brazilian merchants wanted to buy yerba at Ytapúa even though their own nation produced huge amounts of its own. Paraguayan yerba had a deservedly high reputation for quality.

Where a lucrative trade existed, so did a foreign community. In addition to a number of Peninsulares who traded at Pilar, one finds semi-resident Correntinos and other provincial Argentines, Porteños, and an occasional Englishman or Italian. A strange isolation indeed.[63]

Government revenue from the Pilar trade was substantial. The treasury collected 29,000 pesos duty on yerba and tobacco sold there in one day in 1827, and a few weeks later levied fines of 41,200 pesos on smugglers. The fines alone increased state ingress as reported by the treasury by almost 50 percent that year. The subdelegado at Pilar wrote Francia at that time, enthusiastically noting that foreign merchants had told him that when the Cisplatine War ended and regional stability permitted, "All Nations will come to Paraguay to trade."[64]

In 1834, Brazilian merchants were given free access to Pilar as well as Ytapúa, Francia announcing that "Paraguay will trade there with any entity that does not trouble Paraguay's commerce." By 1834, then, this was the Dictator's only qualification on the trade in "useful" articles with the rest of the world.[65] The Pilar commerce was flourishing when the Caraí died in 1840.

Isolation?

Given the sizeable commercial interchange at Pilar and Ytapúa during most of the Franciata, it is difficult to conceive of Paraguay as truly isolated, the "American China" so often pictured. The trade is a mark of the political genius of the Caraí, who found himself and his nation surrounded by hostile forces that threatened the survival of the Paraguayan state. At the two entrepôts Francia took advantage of his neighbors' need for fine yerba and crude black tobacco, needs that impelled them to ignore official decrees, blockades, and the other salient dangers of the trade. El Supremo derived what he sought from the connection: arms, munitions, and coin, all vital elements in Paraguay's survival. And he did so with minimal risk to himself and his nation's domestic peace. By restricting trade to the two small ports, far from centers of population, and by carefully supervising movement of both goods and merchants, he effectively isolated the virus of foreign ideas and influences from his people. To the Caraí this was the true danger of foreign contact—the possibility that foreign ideologies and ideas might communicate the very real political chaos that surrounded his nation to the body politic of his people. One may well view this as merely one major part of El Supremo's general goal of non-intervention in the affairs of other states, a non-intervention aimed at maintaining his nation's independence through limiting the exposure of his people as well as through lack of offensive measures that might antagonize other nations. He sought and gained a low profile for his nation abroad together with a low profile for foreign nations and foreigners within Paraguay. He was very successful.

The Meaning of Paranoia

Lest we picture the frail man in the black frock coat as a certifiable paranoid, it should be noted that Francia actually did face severe threats both to his rule (as in the 1820 plot) and, by natural identification, to the independence of Paraguay. If he perhaps distorted and magnified the extent of these external threats, it was a magnification of something that existed.

One must remember that Buenos Aires never gave up hopes of reintegrating Paraguay, by force if necessary, into its orbit. Not only did the Porteño government refuse to recognize Paraguayan sovereignty until 1852, it also exercised its stranglehold over the Paraná to overtax and then virtually seal off Paraguay— a policy that backfired by isolating the inland nation yet more from foreign contact, thus fostering self-sufficiency and heightening defensive nationalism.[66] It is a valid judgement that had not Buenos Aires been preoccupied with Artigas, the Spanish, the Portuguese, and the taming of its own interior caudillos, Paraguay would probably have been subjected by brute force to Porteño rule.

If Buenos Aires's hostility presented genuine problems and threats, the Portuguese and Brazilians were also carefully watched by the Caraí. Since its foundation, Paraguay had been a wedge driven north from the Plata estuary behind the coastal claims of Brazil. The Luso-Brazilians had been hereditary enemies since the days of the bandeirantes, and the Provincia Gigante had withered under Portuguese expansion. From 1811 to 1822 Brazil was royalist and Paraguay was vulnerable. The Portuguese invasion of the Banda Oriental in 1816 was an object lesson.

Border problems in the north were an added danger, as Luso-Brazilians settled in the contested lower Mato Grosso, stirring up the volatile Indians to fracture the very fragile Paraguayan frontier. As the Dictator himself explained in 1820: "I have not wanted to help the caudillo Artigas against them because of my pacific spirit and my desire to live in peace with everyone. . . . Their response has been to agitate, aid, and favor the barbarous Nations . . . in making invasions of our frontiers." He went on that they "continue to buy from the M'Bayá the horses, mules, and cattle stolen from us, giving them in exchange

firearms, sabers, munitions, and whisky." Francia characterized this activity on the part of the Portuguese as "contrary to peace and harmony," adding that the Indian attacks were designed to denude the Río Apa frontier to permit later Portuguese penetration. Before we let that occur, finished the Caraí, "we are all resolved and determined to die."[67] With the coming of Brazilian independence in 1822, tensions eased a trifle, but Brazilian reluctance to help tranquilize the northern frontier resulted in purely commercial contact at Ytapúa.

To the unfriendly giant neighbors must be added a gaggle of bellicose caudillos in the Litoral. Not only did some of these harass and assault Paraguayan commerce, but others threatened the existence of the nation itself. Artigas raided Candelaria, conquered Corrientes, molested Paraguayan commerce, and provoked many a border incident. Ramírez threatened to invade Paraguay with a gaucho host just as internal conspiracies (with vague foreign links) were being unearthed.[68]

While these events were transpiring, complications arose in Candelaria, beginning with Bonpland's retinue camping on the trade routes, and widening into serious military clashes in the contested area as Paraguay moved in to guard the crucial commercial artery. Aside from Bolívar's attempt to convince Porteño authorities to cooperate in the invasion of Paraguay, a new threat was soon to appear in the south that was, potentially, among the most serious to confront the new nation.

With the war in the Banda Oriental concluded, several gaucho armies and the attention of Buenos Aires were free to turn on Paraguay. Woodbine Parish wrote the Earl of Aberdeen late in 1828 to announce that momentous events were in the offing. He theorized that the Paraguayan people were restless and were ready "to throw off the yoke the moment a favorable opportunity presents itself." He went on to say that the army of gaucho Fructuoso Rivera would soon be used against the tyrant and that the Buenos Aires "Gov^t were projecting to employ him in an attack upon Paraguay, which would serve the double purpose of gratifying his cupidity with the prospect of a rich Plunder, and of attaining perhaps the more satisfactory object of" assuring the integration of Paraguay into the United Provinces and the subsequent opening of that area to world (read British) trade.[69]

Parish was not alone in his hopes for prising open Paraguay. Rivera himself considered the option, but, at least in 1828, turned it down—not for lack of interest, but because, as he explained to a friend, "this Paraguayan business, Julian, is not so simple as some suppose; this Country has a numerous population, superabundant resources and a government of action and power, and what have we? Horrible desolation, extreme misery . . . disunion and no national spirit."[70]

Despite his caveats, however, Rivera was ordered to proceed by Porteño leaders, the goal being "the organization . . . of a military expedition destined for the conquest of Paraguay so that it be reintegrated to the breast of the United Provinces."[71] Although Rivera was not destined to actually put the plan into effect, El Supremo was kept busy with other ominous warnings. In 1829, Miguel Castro, subdelegado at Pilar, wrote the Caraí that he had just learned that "the Government of Salta had written to that of Corrientes, proposing that they start moving by river or by land to take this Villa; that the Government was disposed to send sufficient people through the Chaco for the same purpose." Castro noted, however, with some relief, that the governor of Corrientes replied that "he found himself very pleased with the Government of Paraguay," and so refused to cooperate in the scheme.[72]

In 1832, a new wave of crises began to batter the shores of the south. The previous year the Dictator had written his Ytapúa subdelegado concerning growing tensions with Corrientes, ordering increased vigilance and the removal of local Peninsulares away from the river, into the interior, because "they are a perverse people and . . . conduct secret communications . . . with those of Corrientes."[73]

The latest southern problem was caused by a revival of interest in Candelaria by the government of Corrientes. The Pilar subdelegado warned Francia early in 1832 that Rivera "is gathering the Indians and may try an attack on Ytapúa" to destroy the Brazil trade.[74] Although Rivera did not enter the scene as feared, large units of Correntino troops did, and as Francia shunted more troops to that frontier, hostilities erupted. In September, the Caraí wrote his subdelegado at Ytapúa in high dunder, brutally tongue-lashing him for permitting "a few Correntino bandits" to push him around. He offered that timid official 2,000 more soldiers to help pacify the area.[75] The Ytapúa chief, stung by the insulting tone of the communication, overreacted, ambushing a caravan of Correntino settlers a few weeks later. Proudly reporting his "victory," the official was astounded when the Dictator responded: "You always do things backwards. I ordered no such ambush. . . . To confuse things is very stupid and rude. . . . You have committed a barbarity . . . and you will bear the blame for the outcome."[76] The cowering subdelegado withdrew his troops, as he was so irately bid, but hostilities did not abate for years.

In the United Provinces, war fever was gaining ground as Correntino Governor Pedro Ferré, fearing invasion of his province, ordered a general mobilization. He also sought and gained what turned out to be a paper alliance with Santa Fe and Entre Ríos to ward off the Paraguayans. Later that month, Ferré learned that the Caraí's troops had taken over the large and strategically important Paraná island of Apipé, long considered Correntino.[77] Many Correntinos encountered there were shipped north to Concepción in chains, where they were "divided up to live inland, away from the Frontier."[78]

In 1833 and 1834, with large Paraguayan forces in Candelaria, armed clashes occurred frequently, and Correntino irregulars began to harass Brazilian caravans on the way to Ytapúa, for, as one Correntino general wrote, the "Portuguese are always our enemies, inclined to sustain the opinions of the Dictator of Paraguay."[79] The threat was averted by Dr. Francia's decision to provide a strong escort for each caravan and build a string of forts across the region. His show of force, although at the risk of war, won the day, for the Correntinos, unable alone to challenge Paraguay, and receiving no aid from their allied provinces, backed down. Paraguay would remain in control of the relatively narrow land bridge between the Paraná and the Uruguay, and so long as the Caraí refrained from expanding into Corrientes proper, war could be averted.

Dr. Francia, then, had ample cause to remain vigilant, poised to strike down foes at home and repel enemies abroad. It was for this that he closely limited contact with the outside world, reducing that interaction to two narrow, intensely scrutinized commercial avenues. Domestic subversion might feed on foreign ideas, and foreigners themselves might attempt subversion within Paraguay. Given the nature of Paraguay's neighbors, it is highly probable that Francia equated both domestic unrest and foreign intrigue as destructive of Paraguayan sovereignty. As a British observer wrote in 1824, "the people are, however, kept in ignorance of what is going on in the world around them and thus they remain in a state of passive ignorance little better than servility."[80] As the Caraí himself liked to explain it: "You know what my policy has been with respect to Paraguay: that I have kept it on a system of non-intercourse with the other Provinces of South America, and from contamination by that foul and restless spirit of anarchy and revolution that has more or less desolated and disgraced them all."[81]

The Dictator was successful. While other states and provinces were experiencing chronic upheaval, with consequent economic dislocation and famine, Paraguay remained stable, tranquil and productive, all at minimal cost in human lives. For this reason foreigners sought refuge in Paraguay in growing numbers. Right of asylum was by 1820 a Paraguayan hallmark, given international credence that year by the humane treatment afforded Artigas and his loyal followers. Among the latter was the hated and exceedingly cruel Peter Campbell, a notorious cutthroat. Francisco Ramírez, who had handed Campbell over to Francia for speedy execution, was aghast to find the renegade settled at Pilar working as a barber.[82]

Francia ordered his officials to assist in the resettlement of all Brazilian emigrés in 1824, even military deserters, and in 1837 we find him writing the subdelegado at Ytapúa, "You have your orders to admit all Brazilians who come for refuge, just as yesterday one passed over with his family."[83]

The same year, the subdelegado noted in a letter to the Caraí that "I put at liberty the Negro who came in flight from San Borja upon receipt of your orders" to do so.[84] Two years later, an entire company of Brazilian soldiers was admitted when they deserted en masse from Brazilian Misiones.[85] Free or slave, Correntino or Brazilian, people were attracted to Paraguay and were permitted to function as free within the nation: a side of the Franciata too long ignored.

The international scene, in short, was complex and potentially very dangerous for Paraguay. The Dictator, with policy goals very simple in nature, steered his craft through the shallows with consummate skill. His clearly defined objectives and his neighbors' constant and severe internal and external problems allowed him to maintain Paraguayan independence and create a nation. If his performance in the realm of foreign affairs was redoubtable, the internal organization of his state is unique and has long outlived him.

5. The Supreme Dictatorship, 1820–1840

The quiet night continues,
sepulchral silence reigns,
the cocks no longer crow
nor do dogs bark.[1]

Father Manuel Antonio Pérez, speaking a month after Francia's demise to a large crowd gathered to hear his belated funeral eulogy, hardly exaggerated when he said:

It might be surmised that so many and so weighty cares which require the attention of several men, would divert him from the other exigencies of the State. But no—his greatness and activity extended to everything and provided for everything as if each one exclusively occupied his individual attention.[2]

The Burdens of Indispensability

If there was one single, salient characteristic of the Franciata it was the Dictator's *personal* control over virtually the entirety of state business, from deciding the beef ration for each fort on the frontier to taking the calculated risk of war in Candelaria. The bureaucracy of the central government was all but non-existent. It consisted of a treasury minister (for many years José Gabriel Benítez) and his assistant, and a government secretary who doubled as scribe and messenger boy. Even the latter post was downgraded by 1830 as Policarpo Patiño became merely Francia's record-keeper and general helper. There was no supreme court, no congress, no other ministers with or without portfolio. Every avenue led directly to the Caraí, who daily and nightly pored over reams of reports, denunciations, pleas, treasury drafts, licenses, invoices, and state estancia inventories. His decisions he normally jotted down (in rather poor handwriting) on the margins or backs of the various documents, and these in turn, the trivial and the crucial, were communicated to officials elsewhere to be translated into action.

Francia thus kept his fingers on the many pulses of his nation and met the requirements incumbent on the indispensable man. But even El Supremo had his weak moments and gave in to an occasional fit of self-pity. In 1830, he whiningly wrote the Ytapúa subdelegado, telling him to prepare concise and not verbose, confusing reports: "I find myself here drowning, unable to breathe, in the immense accumulation of attentions and cares that fall upon me alone, for in the Nation, due to a lack of worthy men, the Government finds itself without the helpers and functionaries it should have."[3]

Most contemporaries, even those hostile to Francia and his rule, agreed with his assessment. Pedro Somellera, who knew Francia well and had little reason to love him, put it simply: "He was the only Paraguayan who could lead them."[4] The Porteño press also recognized the lonely nature of Francia's mandate, although perhaps not the reason for it: "The Paraguay tyrant on the contrary stands alone, trusting or depending upon no created being but himself. . . . He seems to have thought further reliance on subordinate agents unnecessary."[5]

El Supremo personally trained his cavalry in the use of the saber, granted permission for an Indian of Atirá to marry a white woman, ascertained the exact number of nails in the inventory of Fort Orange, awarded 102 pesos to a French resident whose anchor had been melted down by the state, sent wine to churches near Concepción, tested a repeating pistol and found it too complicated for his troops, lowered the price of salt in the capital, donated state yerba to the people of Saladillo, and denied permission for a "quatroon" to marry in Villa Rica. It would not be surprising if he handled these actual problems all in the space of a few minutes on a Monday morning.

Scarcely a decision was made in Paraguay by anyone but the Caraí, and his monastic habits and life-style were dictated by his own strongly felt need to attend to all affairs of state personally, no matter their minute nature. From dawn until late evening he worked in Government House, resting briefly during the siesta period with his cup of yerba and a strong black cigar, perhaps discussing affairs with his record keeper or strolling the large patio in his formal black frock coat. Each day, after his brief siesta, Francia would ride through the streets of Asunción, normally accompanied by a single watchful sergeant of grenadiers. The people of the capital, aware of this ritual, and also addicted to their own, much longer siestas, were rarely to be seen at midday, and he often rode through deserted streets, his horse's hooves echoing as if in a corridor.[6]

No doubt it was during one of these rides through the irregular Asunción streets that the idea came to him to make the city "orderly" and more respectable by widening and straightening the streets, to better conform to the traditional Ibero-American grid design. Within hours orders were issued and several score families were informed that they would have to raze their houses, which were now considered impediments to the city's regularity.

Work began immediately, with gangs of prisoners helping to level private dwellings, cut down old and plant new trees, and construct new, cosmetic walls. For months, this dream occupied a large part of the Dictator's attention. As the labor progressed, his vision widened along with the boulevards: "He marks out the squares; he raises some public buildings . . . he orders the erection of walls to connect the town; and thus he entirely remodels the city."[7] In so doing, Francia much improved the physical aspect of Asunción, for, as Rengger described Asunción before the remodeling, it could only be bettered: "The capital of Paraguay presented the aspect of a city that had been bombarded for several months." Some forty new houses were constructed by the state itself, which subsequently profited from their rents. Tenants included Rengger and Longchamp themselves.[8]

At times after his daily rides, he did not return to Government House but went instead to his special quarters at the Hospital Barracks in the suburbs, or, more rarely, to his own chacra at Ybiraí. He did this randomly, and would perhaps spend an average of two nights per week away from Government House. This habit was acquired after discovery of the 1820 plot, which may well have centered on a tunnel being dug under his official quarters for placing a mine. In both alternative locations he had books and writing materials and so could pursue his work late into the night.[9]

Nor was security forgotten at Government House, where the heavy doors were closely guarded and the adjoining plaza constantly watched. Two fine-quality dueling pistols lay near at hand on the Caraí's desk. He gave fewer audiences after 1821, and his residence was kept nearly empty of people. No one, not even Patiño himself, was allowed armed in El Supremo's presence, even officers being required to check their swords at the main door. The Swiss doctor Rengger had a typical experience on his first meeting with Francia:

> As I was not acquainted with this etiquette, it happened that my hands were not in the position required by the Dictator, when he gruffly asked me if I was endeavoring to draw a poignard from my pocket. On my replying that such was not the custom amongst the Swiss, he became appeased and continued the conversation.[10]

All of the Caraí's meals were prepared by his elder, unmarried sister,

Petrona Regalada, who personally served them directly from the kitchen to her brother's table. It seems that his favorite dish was roasted partridge, accompanied by a single glass of wine. Perhaps because of his accusations that Rengger had planned to poison him, the Caraí carefully checked each of his many cigars before lighting them, despite the fact that they had been hand-rolled by Petrona.[11] An indispensable man carries a great burden.

Aside from his sister, and a brother who was relegated to the interior as a ranch foreman, Francia seems to have had no contact with his family. In addition to Petrona, the actual household was composed of two mulatto women (maids and perhaps casual bedmates), a young Negro barber, Pilar, who served as confidant and butler, and three armed guards.[12] Pilar was for many years a valued advisor and source of information and rumor, until one day, as one source guesses, "the north wind, dry and molesting, blew viciously, and the nerves of the Satrap" broke—for some reason, he had Pilar shot.[13] Whatever the cause of Pilar's exit, Patiño was assigned his duties in addition to his own regular tasks.

El Supremo also had problems with another servant, the mulatto José María, a man of incredible gall. José María joined Francia's household after Pilar's demise, and late in the Franciata was arrested for "the robberies that I know my servant the Mulatto José María has made from me." Found guilty of having indeed stolen many things from Francia's personal effects, José María was severely flogged and perhaps later shot.[14]

The Dictator, on at least a few occasions, proved himself a suave host, chatting with guests such as Rengger about European affairs and indicating that he managed to keep abreast of important international developments. He would often proudly display his private library, which included works by "the best Spanish authors," Voltaire, Rollin, Rousseau, Raynal, and La Place, as well as mathematical treatises and a multi-volume history of Napoleon. As Rengger noted in spite of his personal antipathy, "You perceive him to be a man of great talent; he turns the conversation upon the most varied subjects, evinces considerable powers of mind, great penetration, and very extensive acquirements for one who, it may be said, has never quitted Paraguay."[15]

In a previously undiscovered document, yet another facet of the Caraí is hinted at. In 1824, he wrote "Mi Señora Juana Ysabel Francisca de Torres" in very undictatorial style, requesting that "you employ me in your services as your most affectionate and affected servant." Before signing off with a hand-kiss, he admitted that "I singularly esteem you." Perhaps Dr. Francia was not entirely a slave to the state, for even by the flowery epistolary conventions of the epoch, this was a very warm note.[16]

About 1826, El Supremo attached Dr. Vicente Estigarribia to Government House and his own person. Estigarribia was the only genuine Paraguayan physician in the nation and former surgeon to the army. While he still attended the medical needs of the barracks, he clung to the Caraí like a Parisian cloak, and there is some indication that they may have become friends. Of all Paraguayans, only Estigarribia was allowed free run of Government House and entrance to the rooms of El Supremo. No man was with the Dictator more than was his physician in the last decade of his life.[17]

It was a lonely, dedicated life that Francia led, and although he could converse in English and French and was an amateur scientist whose office was filled with books, maps, astrolabes, and botanical drawings, he chose to refuse to meet with botanist Aimé Bonpland.[18] Nor would he accede to the many requests of José Artigas for an interview. Except for brief early chats with John Parish Robertson, whom he hoped to use as a commercial link with Great Britain, the only foreigners with whom he personally treated were Rengger and Longchamp, and to these he probably spoke more in the line of practical duty than for personal pleasure or enlightenment.

The Supreme Government: Personae Non-Dramatis

The minister of the treasury was one of the few men to meet with the Caraí on a regular basis. That functionary tendered his account books daily for Francia's scrutiny, and those same books, today in the Asunción archives, show that page by page the Dictator placed his rubric to certify the accuracy and probity of the data.

There were but four treasury ministers during the Franciata, one of whom, Pedro Miguel Decoud, died mysteriously (Francia wrote that he was one of Rengger's victims).[19] Of the others, José Gabriel Benítez served several times for a total of at least twelve years, Francisco de Bedoya retired gracefully around 1822, and Juan Manuel Alvarez, who assumed the position in the mid-1830s, was still checking accounts when Francia died. The treasury minister was reasonably well-paid, at a rate of 600 pesos per annum, a salary equal to that of government secretary and lower only than El Supremo's own, frequently uncollected pay.[20] As far as can be determined, no military salary exceeded 540 pesos, and that was subject to a variety of official deductions.

Little is known of the men who acted as government secretary, the position closest to the Caraí in the chain of command. Bernardino Villamayor, who rose from a minor treasury job, held the post from 1821 to 1825, when he died in the Río Paraguay. According to the Swiss medicoes, Villamayor had been a confidant of the Caraí. "The Dictator, who, no doubt, began to perceive how heavily his yoke bore, even upon those persons who were most devoted to him, could not hear of this death without emotion."[21]

We know more about Policarpo Patiño. He rose through the ranks, as it were, from scribe to treasury assistant in 1824.[22] Within a sort time of Villa-mayor's death, Patiño, an efficient and loyal servant, became government secretary, serving Francia in that capacity until the Caraí's death. A jack of all trades, Patiño arranged audiences, transcribed documents, visited the jails, and conferred with the Dictator on most routine matters. Toward the end of Francia's life, and presumably with his knowledge, Patiño began signing some official documents that did not bear his master's signature. Drafting and often personally announcing El Supremo's decisions, decrees, and orders, he became the focus of much popular wrath, and even today his name is a hated one in Paraguay, while that of Francia is respected, if not universally loved. This animus, directed at the servant rather than the master, presents us with a picture of Patiño that is no more than a gross caricature, yet there is little concrete data by which to judge the man.

One striking feature of the secretary, indicating that perhaps corruption was not entirely absent from the Francia regime, can be seen in records that show a large number of land purchases in and around the capital and Villa Rica made by him and his immediate family between 1820 and 1836. A perusal of the testament of cleric Roque Antonio Céspedes shows another remarkable accretion of wealth, as neither he nor Patiño came from wealthy, elite families. One is tempted to ask if it did not, after all, pay to be a major figure in the Francia government.[23]

Patiño also pops up in a fascinating legal action. In 1835, he denounced a slave for attempting to induce an abortion in his daughter and to poison him. A close investigation by a concerned Caraí, however, turned up a different tale: the daughter had requested the abortion, and Patiño had lied about the attempted murder.[24] It is a measure of his influence with the Dictator that Patiño was not jailed or worse, but instead retained his power-ful position.

The only other man to get close to the Dictator also had his flaws—José Tomás Ysasi, a foreign merchant long a resident of Asunción. As early as 1818, Ysasi was sent to Buenos Aires by Francia to act, perhaps sub rosa at first, as Paraguayan commercial agent. He was quite successful, making contracts with British and Porteño merchants to supply Paraguay with certain essentials, notably arms. Especially after the 1822 "thaw," Ysasi handled a large business, selling Paraguayan yerba at Buenos Aires and sending cargo north. His absconding in 1827 with a huge load of produce and a chest filled with government cash was a rude blow to the Caraí, who had trusted few men.[25]

Government in the Interior: A Little Less Supreme

Beyond Dr. Francia, the national government was skeletal. The highest-ranking political figures outside the capital were the "military-political comandantes," stationed in the larger population centers and often responsible for administering up to ten or more rural partidos. A few of the comandantes, those who oversaw vital frontier regions and commercial entrepôts, held the prestigious title of subdelegado. Normally there were three subdelegados, one each at Concepción, Pilar, and Ytapúa. At times of crisis there was also a sub-delegado at Santiago. The Ytapúa subdelegado not only monitored the commerce of that port but also ruled in El Supremo's name over most of Candelaria, the mission pueblos and partidos of Jesús, Trinidad, San Cosme, and Carmen, and as far north as Yutí on the Tebicuari-Guazú. The Concepción official oversaw government and defense for the entire northern frontier, from the Río Apa south to the Jejuy. The Pilar subdelegado had jurisdiction south to the confluence of the Paraguay and the Paraná, north to Villa Franca, and east to Tacuarás. When Santiago was the seat of a subdelegado rather than a simple comandante, all the Tebicuari mission partidos south to the Paraná were subject to his control.

These officials had three major functions—a sort of general supervisory capacity over government in their areas, close scrutiny and protection of commerce, and, most important, coordination of defense. This last task was complicated by the wide dispersion of the rather slight population. Most sub-delegados were military men, selected from the officer corps and usually captains (the highest military rank). They had already proven themselves loyal to Francia and the nation as well as at least somewhat efficient. In their ascent they had acquired considerable experience in things civil, for most had served as comandante or jefe político y militar of a partido before their promotion. The Caraí's constant and habitual shifting of tried and trusted men between the political and military spheres not only provided them with diverse experience but also insured that no man would remain long in an important position, building up an independent base of support or a web of corruption. In all his voluminous correspondence, the only occasions when El Supremo used the familiar "tu" form of address were with certain subdelegados.

Despite the familiarity, Francia never dropped his habit of suspicion, and rarely would a subdelegado cling to his post for more than four years before being retired to a minor, terminal sinecure. A case in point is the career of Romualdo Agüero, subdelegado at Concepción, who ended his service to Francia as foreman of a state estancia at isolated San Estanislao, far removed from temptation.[26] At least one Francia favorite, however, Norberto Ortellado, held rank for a longer period, serving as subdelegado at Ytapúa (1821-1824),

Santiago (1825-1826), and Pilar (1826-1828) before gentle exile to a minor post.

Although the Dictator maintained generally good relations with his subdelegados, the position was not for the emotionally insecure, for Francia in his letters was every bit as powerful as he was in person. Criticizing his chief officials for everything from "writing vaguely and without due specifics" to their "stupidity and rusticity," the Caraí often ended his tirades (which make some of the best reading in the archives) with "I know that which I order," or "You will bear the responsibility"—phrases that made many a strong man wince. Reports from Pilar and Ytapúa subdelegados reached Asunción on almost a daily basis, ridden north or northwest by special couriers, and the Caraí wrote each official an average of three times weekly, his letters spelling out instructions in such minute detail as to appear today insulting.

The capital itself had no subdelegado save Francia, and Villa Rica made do with a comandante in spite of its size and economic importance. Comandantes were also found at Piribebuy, Santiago, Ycuamandiyú (San Pedro), Curuguatí, Caraguatay, San Estanislao, and a few other centers. In powers, the comandantes were similar to the subdelegados, but restricted to smaller areas and instructed to pay especial attention to matters of taxation and militia organization.

Most day to day government in Francia's Paraguay was carried on by judges, of whom there were several types. Jueces ordinarios were common citizens without legal training, selected by the Caraí to exercise minor judicial functions. Often they were alcaldes of the local cabildo. Jueces comisionados, however, were higher officials. Perhaps eighty in number by 1825, these men were expected to be somewhat versed in the law and were entrusted with both judicial and administrative power. There were also judges with more specialized roles, such as those for appeals and for commerce. Although Francia rarely concerned himself with the daily activities of his judges, he was in all cases supreme arbiter, and appeals could be and were made directly to him. Such was the case when a soldier of the Asunción garrison wrote, asking him to reverse a decision of a local judge who had fined him three pesos for disorderly conduct.[27]

For the rural areas where El Supremo did not personally name the jueces ordinarios, cabildos or local officials would tender nomination lists to the Caraí, and he would soon communicate his choice. Jueces comisionados were rotated from partido to partido on an almost annual basis. As he instructed a new juez comisionado, he must be sure to reside at his post in Quiquió "so that the inhabitants may come with their complaints and demands" to him in person. He described the duties of the new appointee as transmitter and enforcer of "the decrees and orders of the Government, and that equally he care for the development of agriculture and the establishment of schools." Furthermore, he should vigorously enforce the peace, arrest troublemakers, clear the land of vagabonds and suspicious characters, and represent the Dictator in his area. All judicial decisions should be based on the Spanish colonial *Recopilación* of laws of the Indies.[28]

In 1820, Francia, noting growing confusion of jurisdictions and sheer meddling in the legal sphere, decreed some changes. He angrily denounced interference by military officers in the judicial process, for they were "purely restricted to military service and are not judges." Each official, judge or comandante, had a "duty to limit himself to that which is his particular task." Even alcaldes must abstain from contesting or reversing decisions made by other judges, for that prerogative, wrote the Caraí, was his alone.[29]

The same year, Francia clarified the problem, creating a small new category of judges, the jueces de recursos, who were to function as appeals judges in both criminal and civil cases. Although they disposed of most categories of crime, they were not permitted to impose death, exile, or corporal punishment without the Dictator's approval. The government reserved to itself the right to decide cases involving conspiracy, treason, and "infamous thieves." The judges were to receive "a good and regular" salary, and their tenures would last as long as Francia's pleasure.[30] Only rarely again would Francia feel compelled to hear a three-peso appeal.

Although El Supremo often had to send instructions to his judges more closely defining their duties, normally injunctions "to arrest and contain vagabonds, card players, and bad actors,"[31] he allowed them a great deal of freedom in routine matters. He also felt called upon to defend them from time to time, for they were, after all, representatives of his government. In the case of a man who insulted a judge after losing a suit at Capiatá, Francia had him arrested and sent to public works, remarking that the sore loser must have "wandered among idiots and ignoramuses" to have picked up such bad manners.[32]

By 1840, Francia's control, based on personal appointees who were spread throughout the nation, reached into every corner of Paraguay. The flow of reports, briefs, synopses, testimony, denunciations, and rumors of sedition reached the Caraí at virtual flood stage. His "feedback" was notable perhaps more for its sheer volume than for any responses it elicited from him. This system of placing his own men in the countryside probably does much to explain the much-vaunted "secret service" of spies he had at his beck and call. So effective was this feedback that one Bartolomé José Galiano of Atirá wrote the Dictator in the following vein: "Most Excellent Sir: I have felt the fear and shame caused by my disgrace for a long time . . . but now, Sir, with respect, fear, and shame, and hope in your pity, I agitate myself to beg, as I beg You now, that You permit me to throw myself at Your benign feet to receive Your pleasure and the reprehension worthy of my crime." It is a shame that we do not know the nature of his "crime," but the approach tells a good deal about life in Francia's Paraguay.[33]

Violence and Crime in the Tranquil Nation

A logical assumption drawn from the above and from the very strict, and at times ruthless nature of Francia's rule would be that Paraguay enjoyed a sort of "Octavian Peace." Thinking that crime was all but nonexistent, most observers have agreed with one who stated that the tranquility of the population was due to the fact that it "was reduced to the lowest state of servile subjection." Francia's Draconian rule was supposedly an inhibitor of antisocial behavior. According to this amateur psychologist, the people were docile because of the smothering effects of dictatorship and the "Apathy which a burning Climate and the greatest natural abundance" reputedly produced.[34] Continuing this mosaic of the docility of the Paraguayan people, an Italian described Asunción in 1826 as a city "where men with tongues do not speak and never are two people seen together." According to yet another observer, if "there was a national isolation, there was an individual isolation as well."[35]

Although one might at first glance agree with the last statement, a perusal of the documents suggests that man's normal inclination towards mayhem and larceny was scarcely absent from the Franciata. The commercial history of the epoch discloses both considerable smuggling and lenient punishment. Further, it should be remembered that Francia himself encountered (despite his fearsome reputation) a thieving servant, an embezzling commercial agent, and a perjuring government secretary.

Annual reports on the public jails reveal a wide spectrum of immorality, including murder, shootings, stabbings, beatings (with a variety of blunt instruments), matricide, wife-killings, infanticide, rustling, mandioca theft, vagrancy, subversion, bigamy, debt, rape, and running berserk.[36] One even finds that *summun malum* of all dictatorships: one Pedro Nolasco González, "arrested for having wounded the policeman at Tembetarí . . . and the murder of a soldier."[37] Assaulting (and killing) the uniformed agents of a dictator has always and everywhere been frowned on.

Dr. Francia's "total" rule, despite its often harsh nature, could not curb his people's passions nor their violent self-expression, and his quite lenient treatment of most criminals is no doubt part of the reason. Far from executing such dangerous criminals, Francia preferred to put them to work on behalf of the state. A sentence on public works, often of indeterminate length, was the common judgement for serious crimes such as murder, the killer literally paying his debt to society with constructive labor. The social nature of the Paraguayan penal system may perhaps best be viewed in the requirement that each prisoner be self-supporting. One acute, if bitter, observer noted that the best artisans during the Franciata were prisoners, most of whom were required "to bide their time by making small, fancy articles." These handicrafts, then as now, were sold to the public, the proceeds being devoted to meet the food and clothing needs of the incarcerated.[38] The memoirs of the prisoners from Santa Fe who spent the last seventeen years of the Francia period staring at Asunción through bars also repeatedly mention that political prisoners were expected to be productive if they desired to eat.[39]

Only rarely did cases of public morality engage the Caraí's attention or ire, for he tended to regard such as matters of conscience. Yet at times his officials exercised their own brand of puritanism. Such an instance occurred in 1825 when a judge arrested a man for openly living with a woman not his wife, "setting a bad example for the inhabitants with their loose lives." The culprit was fined 25 pesos, but instead of paying he fled to Asunción, where he was located only after a long search. The judge later reported that "he maintained himself for six months with no other occupation than that of following after card games . . . living in libertinage and hooliganism." The man, with El Supremo's blessing, was put on public works, while the woman was placed in the custody of "a man of good conduct" whose stewardship, it was hoped, would curb "her disordered appetites."[40]

The traditional picture of Paraguay as a bulwark of puritanical morality reinforced by steel bayonets is a gross distortion. Perhaps in the area of public morality and crime the Dictator changed things least. Somehow, it is pleasant to discover that Asunción itself had its own underworld, in which a bad actor could exist for months.

The Internal Economy of Dictatorship

The economy of Paraguay was changed during the Franciata far more than was its international commerce. The major changes followed two mutually reinforcing paths, self-sufficiency and state socialism—paths along which Carlos Antonio López would push Paraguay at a more accelerated pace after 1840.

Two observers from Buenos Aires judged that "their object is to husband their resources," and "in men and money [these] are said to be considerable, and no Country is more independent of foreign supplies."[41] Certainly with the eclipse of the small Peninsular and Creole elites, there was little that Paraguayans wanted or needed to import.

Rengger and Longchamp, alone of the various visitors to Francia's Paraguay, paid some attention to economic detail. They noted with interest that late in 1819 a plague of locusts visited destruction on much of the nation's newly-sown crops. Dr. Francia, unwilling to face a year of famine and expensive food imports, decided on a novel concept—"to compel the proprietors to sow a second time, a considerable portion of the land which had been thus laid waste." The experiment was a success, "and the year 1820 was one of the most abundant that had been remembered . . . to the surprise of the old farmers." The discovery that the Paraguayan soil could produce two annual crops, plus the Caraí's efforts to tell farmers in each area what as well as when to plant, "produced a complete revolution in the system of the rural economy,"[42] and produced an abundance of staple foods from that year on.

No doubt due in part to a lessening of the yerba and tobacco trade, more effort and manpower could be utilized to cultivate other crops, and the semi-nomadic, migratory way of life characteristic of the yerba-gatherer ("The herb of Paraguay, which grows without any aid of art") tended to disappear as gatherers became sedentary farmers.[43]

Not only were mandioca and corn planted in increased acreage, but rice and cotton became major crops in their own right, freeing Paraguay of dependence on outside sources of supply. Sugarcane was also made more abundant, suf-ficing by 1825 to meet local needs for molasses and sugar. So too was wheat introduced as an important crop in the Tebicuari zone, and "vegetables, which were hitherto unknown in Paraguay, began now to cover the plains."[44] In addition, the pastoral economy was officially encouraged, and the herds, especially of cattle, multiplied to the point where cattle products were exported in large amounts, whereas before 1820 they were imported.[45] Internal com-merce in agricultural goods was regulated and regularized. Farmers traveling to Asunción to sell their produce had to carry licenses, permisos, and detailed lists of their goods.

If agriculture and livestock production increased notably, so too did manufacturing of most basics. This was especially true of clothing, which was now almost entirely made within Paraguay of domestic materials. Only "fine" ponchos, hats, and handkerchiefs were imported in their finished state. As Rengger noted with his customary paternalism: "There used to be, before, no such thing as a dextrous workman in Paraguay," but El Supremo created many by fiat—by simply ordering (in a very detailed manner, to be sure) that certain things be made. "Thus . . . he created a race of whitesmiths, saddlers and architects."[46] Though perhaps overstating the case, the assessment is essentially correct. Paraguay was reduced to providing virtually all articles on which it depended for daily life and convenience save weaponry.

It was, however, the birth of a relatively thorough state socialism that had more impact on Paraguay and, in fact, permitted much of the above diversification to take place. One of the most salient features of the Caraí's rule was the gradual accretion of economic power and resources to the state. The revolutionary junta inherited not only political power in 1811 but also all imperial resources within Paraguay, which included some forty almost-unused and unproductive royal ranches, spread throughout the nation, plus large chunks of land near the borders. Renamed "estancias de la República" in 1813, the former royal ranches were not parceled out and sold, as was the case in other republics, but were used and expanded to foster national self-sufficiency.[47]

The Dictator saw in the state estancia system a great natural resource. Facing interruption of commerce and hostile neighbors, he used the neglected ranches to meet the nation's food and clothing needs and to provide meat, hides, and remounts for the fast-expanding military. As a foreign observer noted approvingly, Francia rendered "the domains productive, and has, by so doing, created a branch of revenue, which aided by time, and a wise Government, may be found sufficient of itself alone, for all the wants of the State."[48] This judgement was astute.

The estancias provided not only pastoral bounty but also crops such as yerba, tobacco, and wheat. A major share of this production after 1822 was destined to Pilar and Ytapúa, where it represented the government's share in the international trade.[49]

By 1818, the Dictator had built up the estancia network (adding to it the property of foreigners who died in Paraguay) to a total of fifty estancias and twenty-two smaller puestos, in addition to a number of state farms spread from Concepción in the north to Ytapúa in the south and Yhú in the east. Fourteen were located near the capital (where most of the army was), ten near Villa Rica, seventeen in the Tebicuari zone, four near Pilar, and several close by Ytapúa.[50]

The state patrimony was soon augmented. All lands of the 1820 conspirators were confiscated, and many of the nation's finest ranches passed into the state system. Also becoming part of the patrimony were the lands of the seminary and the much larger holdings of the religious orders.[51] The slaves and free Blacks living on these lands all became state property as slaves.

Yearly each Francia-appointed foreman tendered reports and inventories to the government, and these documents reveal a thriving network. An inventory of the Tabapí estancia in 1826 shows not only its large slave labor force but 4,000 head of livestock, 145 local families renting some estancia lands, 700 pesos in cash, and lumber and straw as well as animals collected for sale.[52]

Most estancias rented out portions of land for crops or pasturage, and other state lands not part of the estancia system were also let out to the public, as a visitor noted, "at a very moderate rent, and for an unlimited period, under the single condition, that they shall be properly cultivated."[53] As "moderate" as these rents were, they contributed a great deal to state revenues, averaging perhaps 5 percent of all state ingress in the years 1825-1840.[54]

If the Caraí's state absorbed into its patrimony huge amounts of land, and often the labor and livestock on it, it also monopolized the export of fine woods and established several state stores through which it sold to its own people. These retail stores, situated at Pilar, Ytapúa, and the capital, sold produce from state lands and certain items purchased from foreign merchants. As a Mr. Hope wrote in 1827, "it seems Francia has five or six shops of his own, and by keeping these supplied with goods, he gradually collects a considerable" amount of money.[55] It may be difficult to picture El Supremo as shopkeeper, but his stores showed a regular and notable profit, returning 5,150 pesos alone in the second half of 1826.[56] In one bizarre document, we find a Cecilia Marecos acknowledging receipt of her 25-peso monthly allowance from a state store. She indicates that Francia ordered ex-subdelegado José León Ramírez to deposit the money there regularly "for having seduced, deflowered, and tricked me with promises of marriage, years ago."[57]

In addition to the revenue from land rents, monopolies, and state stores and the money saved or generated by the consumption or trade of the state estancia bounty, the Dictator kept his ship of state afloat through taxes and fines. The chief tax in coin or kind was the alcabala, or sales tax, which fluctuated downwards from 9 to 4 percent. Although the amount collected at Asunción averaged perhaps only 1,000 pesos annually, the trade at Ytapúa generated as much as 24,597 in 1840. That same year another 1,258 pesos were collected in alcabala elsewhere (we have no figures for Pilar), land rents brought in 7,217, a cattle tax 805, confiscation of goods of foreigners who died intestate 14,326, and the sale of state produce an enormous 80,253.[58]

Other taxes, levied mostly in kind, were those on livestock and crops and the diezmo, or tithe on all rural production. In 1832, citing the "laborious diligence of the Government [resulting in] the Treasury finding itself with more than enough to meet the expenses of the State and also having an abundance of cattle on the estancias" of the state, Francia decreed that "the contribution called the cuatropea [livestock tax] will cease," along with the tax on crops save in a few frontier partidos, where it was necessary for the support of garrisons.[59] The diezmo would be the only pastoral and agricultural impost levied in the future. Growing revenue from the Pilar and Ytapúa trade made it possible to cut taxes dramatically, a rare thing in any nation's history.

Other sources of revenue were the sale of stamped paper for official pleas, fines, the property of the intestate, and occasional "forced contributions." The government paper brought in about 2,000 pesos annually, fines often amounted to massive sums, and special "contributions" were levied on the shrinking Spanish community in 1823, 1834, 1835, and 1838.[60] Contributions were assessed in multiples of 515 pesos, with the wealthiest being mulcted 4,120 pesos each. Obviously, the destruction of the Peninsular elite was not accomplished overnight.

Francia's organization and reorganization of his people and their labors, and his exceedingly close attention to finances, resulted in balanced, indeed, generally surplus budgets. In no year for which we have records did the government spend more than it took in, and frequently it spent less than half. Although cash on hand averaged over 350,000 pesos each January, expenses from the Asunción central treasury averaged only a little more than 100,000.[61] Economically, the Franciata was successful in that, by turning inward, it discovered that the nation by and large could meet its own needs, developing its own resources while lessening its dependence on the outside, often hostile world. In the field of culture this was not the case.

The Spark of Intellect Burns but Weakly

One looks for some sign of cultural progress in the Dictator's Paraguay in vain, for there is almost no hint of healthy intellectual activity. In some ways, perhaps the evaluation by Manuel Cibils is correct, that Francia's ascension "signified the triumph of the interior . . . over the city," where almost all cultural trappings in Paraguay had previously been on display.[62] It is certain that the Dictator closed the seminary, and in secularizing and dispersing the monks (in whose hands had been most private education) he seriously further weakened Paraguayan education. Yet Francia had no desire to extinguish the flame of education. To him, literacy was a respectable national virtue. A well-educated, sophisticated elite, however, was a potential danger.

In the capital, José Gabriel Téllez taught a large number of youngsters in his public primary school, as did the Argentine Pedro Escalada in his private "academy."[63] Carlos Antonio López, graduate and former teacher at the seminary, may have been able to hide his light beneath a bushel in the interior, but his son Francisco Solano, born in 1826, had little difficulty obtaining a modest education, which included modern languages. It would be unwise to paint the educational-cultural portrait of the Caraí's Paraguay in solid black. Carlos Centurión exaggerates when he writes that El Supremo "did worse than doing nothing" in the cultural field and that he almost never paid his much-vaunted 140 rural schoolteachers.[64] Documents reveal their payment, often supplemented with beeves from government herds, personally authorized by Francia.[65] Although Francisco Wisner overstates the case when claiming that the Dictator decreed in 1838 the mandatory education of all boys to the age of fourteen, a number of small, private tutorial schools continued to function in various Paraguayan towns.[66]

Paraguay had never been known for its painting, religious or otherwise, and, "during the government of Francia, without doubt there was little opportunity to acquire nor things to enrich the artistic" spirit. Partly this was due to lack of contact with foreign artistic and cultural currents, partly to the eclipse of the elite. Still, some religious painting was done, mostly on sheet metal, "showing that even in those years of spiritual upheaval the desire to create persisted."[67]

The Franciata is not known for the literature it produced (one should also remember that there was no printing press in the nation), but one José Manuel Arias "found space and humor sufficient" to write a drama for the non-existent stage, entitled *El Rosario perseguido,* which he wisely dedicated to the Caraí. It was, however, never performed.[68] Also, in the noisome dungeons, under difficult circumstances, Mariano Antonio Molas wrote the impressive *Descripción histórica de la antigua provincia del Paraguay,* the one outstanding literary piece of the epoch. Written after his arrest in 1828, the work is a marvelous compendium of natural and political data.

It should also be noted that Francia himself, toward the end of his rule, created Paraguay's first public library, sending it scores of books on various occasions. When Bishop Panés died in 1838, the Caraí ordered his personal effects delivered to the treasury, "except the books, which are destined to the public Library" recently opened in Asunción.[69]

When one considers the cultural vista, one is depressed by its general bleakness. It stretches out to the horizon like the hostile Chaco, with only an infrequent tree or shrub breaking the monotony. Aside from the closure of the seminary, the absence of a printing press, and the proscription of importing books and periodicals, what throttled culture in Paraguay was simply the atmosphere of the Franciata itself. It was a pervasive dictatorship, one that evinced suspicion of learned men and new ideas and that executed many of the literati, arrested others, and frightened the remainder into silent exile on the nation's ranches. This climate of fear, of suspicion and distrust, was what killed learning in Paraguay. The very negative anti-intellectualism of the Franciata, so akin to that of the seventeenth-century Spanish Inquisition, represents the darkest side of the regime and its legacy. It is precisely that which determined Carlos Antonio López to seek talent beyond Paraguay's borders when he decided to modernize the nation. There was no choice, for there remained virtually no native talent.

From Supremo to Difunto

El Supremo, no matter his iron will, endless mission, and indispensability, was not immortal, a fact that eventually surprised his people. In fact, as Pedro Somellera remarked in 1840, "he hardly let us see him as a man of flesh, and only his death has been proof that he was."[70]

In 1839, the Caraí, now in his mid-seventies, began to feel the ravages of age, and his health deteriorated alarmingly. He largely confined himself to Government House, attended only by Patiño and Dr. Estigarribia. Closeted in his book-filled study and adjacent spartan living quarters, he emerged only briefly in the cooler months to take the sun among the orange trees in the patio.

Estigarribia was powerless to arrest the inexorable progress of the ultimate infirmity, age, restricting himself to retarding the aches and pains of a slow death. Probably on the physician's orders, chocolate was purchased at Ytapúa and sped to the Dictator's table.[71] The Caraí, tenacious in death's presence as he was in life's, clung to the latter with both hands, month by month refusing to die, even through the damp and penetrating chills of winter.

On September 20, 1840, he suddenly let go, and El Supremo became El Difunto, the Dead One. The Franciata ended, although José Artigas remarked of Francia that "his shadow will long continue to float over Paraguay."[72] Hearing the slow tolling of mourning bells, "the people flocked in crowds from the most remote quarters of the city to Government House, and in a few moments universal mourning proclaimed that the Dictator" had gone the way of all flesh.[73]

The news spread quickly through the small nation, despite official attempts to retard its diffusion. As Gregorio Benítez reminisced: "His death was bewailed by the people, especially by the women. Although very young at the time, I remember that upon receipt of the news of the death of the Dictator in Villa Rica, there was much sobbing."[74] People ran from house to house with the ominous news: "Omanó yeco caraí guazú"—The Caraí is dead.[75]

Francia was buried in the floor of the Church of the Encarnación in the capital three days after his passing. His body, in a rude coffin, was carried to the church on the shoulders of ranking officers and judges, and much of the military marched as honor guard, while singers and musicians intoned a dirge.[76]

The throne was empty perhaps, but the treasury was full, and at least 122,000 pesos in silver and another 87,336 in gold were found in the vaults. Of this sum, more than 36,500 was in Francia's untouched salary, which was soon divided among several recipients, including the defunct seminary.[77] One irate official noted several months later that "the goods and interests of the dead Señor Dictator had been arbitrarily disposed of to private interests."[78]

On October 20, Father Manuel Antonio Pérez delivered a funeral oration from the steps of the Church of the Encarnación, fittingly stressing the positive side of the Caraí's rule. Claiming that Paraguay in 1813 had been "the skeleton of a giant requiring a master hand to clothe it with flesh," Pérez lauded Francia's many good works. Chief among these was El Difunto's efforts to smash the specter of anarchy, the "dangerous assemblies" that threatened discord. Of the 1820 conspiracy and subsequent repression, the priest, who called the plotters harbingers of civil strife, noted that "he conducted himself on this occasion like a wise surgeon, who when a member threatens mortification, either cauterizes or cuts off the infected part."[79]

Of all legacies bequeathed by Dr. Francia, the concept of indispensability, with its silent implication that Paraguayans were politically childlike and incompetent, remains the most somber. Certain it is that his rule reinforced, if it did not create, this very trait.

A later observer, more familiar with the López regime, was struck by the same characteristic, remarking that Francia, especially late in his rule, was "as unapproachable as a divinity" and that on his death "the people shed tears and divided the garments of Francia as precious relics." In sweeping bombast, the observer concluded that "the people of Paraguay do not endure tyranny; they are pleased with it and love it."[80] A later historian wrote, with considerable insight, that "Dr. Francia elevated his thought to the category of duty and his duty to the category of faith."[81]

The Caraí gave his nation twenty-six years of domestic peace, without which its future would have been very doubtful. Also important, and hardly accidental, he created in Paraguay a relatively egalitarian, rural-oriented society—the most "level" society in the hemisphere. He destroyed the traditional elite, economically, socially, politically, and biologically, yet he did not raise up a new elite. His racial decrees, which affected not only marriage but godfathership and were enforced for a full generation, spurred the ongoing process of miscenegation while breaking the bonds of family connection that for so long had reinforced and strengthened the essentially white elite within a mestizo society.

The ramifications of the Caraí's unique racial and leveling policies were significant. Paraguayan nationalism became coterminous with Paraguayan racial identity. The Paraguayan of 1840 was a mestizo, and this helped set him apart further, psychologically as well as genetically and linguistically, from his neighbors.

Francia also provided, in addition to the sociological revolution, an honest and reasonably efficient government—there was little graft and no official opulence, and the Caraí's personal austerity set the tone. As one distant witness wrote with accuracy, "Spartan food and lodging, two cigars and a cup of mate daily . . . he already had this" well before his ascension to power.[82] Similarly, a Buenos Aires daily wrote that "his household consists merely of two Negros and a woman cook."[83] For his lieutenants, the price of peculation could be high: a one-way trip to Tevegó or a border fort, years on public works, or, perhaps, as in the case of Villamayor, a mysterious demise.

In agriculture, as in livestock and manufacturing, the nation diversified and increased production, while foreign commerce, if reduced, continued to meet the major national needs. The Dictator shored up the national borders and halted a process of territorial attrition centuries old. Forts and garrisons decisively halted the southern advance of Brazil at the Río Apa, and Candelaria became at least de facto Paraguayan. Problems from Indians and bandits along the borders, if not eradicated, were greatly lessened through new forts and aggressive patrolling by well-trained troops. Most Paraguayans, for the first time in history, were reasonably safe.

In the words of Cecilio Báez, "he was a severe despot by calculation, not by natural malevolence."[84] He made demands on Paraguay, chief of which were recognition of his indispensability and consequent obedience to his will. Perhaps this was because, of all major figures of his era, he alone created a nation. It was his work, and he was its.

The average Paraguayan, a farmer, knew, in a mixture of insight and observation, that he lived better with his family than had any previous generation of his ancestors, and better, for that matter, than most Argentines, whose chronic civil wars drove them across the rivers into Paraguay. He also knew, with a sense of quiet pride that had been absent in his youth, that he lived in a nation called Paraguay. And, finally, he understood very well, from what he had seen and what he had been told and what he had surmised, that these things, which for him were good, were not of his own doing—they came as gifts from the Caraí.

6. The Old Order Changeth?

"Paraguay . . . has been dead for twenty-five years"

Thomas Carlyle, safe in his oak-paneled study, examined the policies and seeming xenophobia of El Supremo, concluding before the latter's death that, concerning foreigners, "Paraguay had grown to be, like some mousetraps and other contrivances of art and nature, easy to enter, impossible to get out of."[1]

Despite the frequent but never capricious detention of foreigners in Paraguay, such was the lure of opening that republic that other, for the most part British, merchants continued to seek commercial advantages. One such merchant-adventurer was W. R. B. Hughes, a resident of Montevideo, who answered his own call of the wild in mid-1840, enthralled by a vision of a lucrative trade agreement with Francia. Obtaining special, official passports and letters of introduction from various British, Argentine, and Uruguayan authorities, Hughes met with the British minister at Buenos Aires, Mr. R. Mandeville, who carefully explained "distinctly to Mr. Hughes that he goes to Paraguay at his own risk, and that, in the event of his being detained there . . . H.M. G^t will have no power to render him any assistance whatever."[2]

By the time the intrepid Hughes reached Asunción, Francia was El Difunto instead of El Supremo, and the Briton was well received by the curious consuls and permitted to sell the merchandise he had brought with him. Somewhat prematurely, it was announced that the Paraguayan "mousetrap" was open.

As Hughes conducted his business in Asunción, Paraguayan expatriate Juan Andrés Gelly in Buenos Aires, viewing his nation's place in the world, wrote sadly that "Paraguay is in complete darkness from that which occurs in the world: it has been dead for twenty-five years."[3]

Political Uncertainty and the Magic Rise of Carlos Antonio

In the months between Hughes's departure from Montevideo and his eventual arrival in Paraguay, much had changed. Many people, Paraguayan as well as foreign, expected Paraguay to enter a time of upheaval, riot, disorder, and struggles for power—struggles that were sure to be taken advantage of by Buenos Aires. It was known that, whatever his merits, Francia had done nothing to prepare his nation for "self-rule" and had no designated successor or favorite. Yet, after the stunning news of El Supremo's death, no factions, parties, or caudillos arose, no major disorders, no foreign intrigue.

As messengers sped across the nation bearing news of Francia's demise, Patiño, who alone considered himself legitimate heir to Francia, made his move. The key to his success would be his ability to gain the support of the only other source of power in the nation: the officers of the Asunción garrisons. In his bid to corner the militares, however, Patiño was opposed by the ancient Dr. Estigarribia, to whom some of the patina of close association with Francia still clung, and Asunción Alcalde Manuel Antonio Ortíz, leading politician of the capital. Like most Paraguayans, Estigarribia and Ortíz detested Patiño and were less than enthusiastic about a transferral of supreme authority to his decidedly unsupreme shoulders. Within perhaps ten hours of confused but fervent demagoguery and negotiations, complicated by what appeared to be glimmers of unrest on the part of many Asunceños, a decision was made.[4] The barracks chiefs, Agustín Cañete, Pablo Ferreira, Miguel Maldonado, and Gavino Arroyo, announced to Patiño that a junta would be created to safeguard public order and avoid anarchy. Members of the junta would be Alcalde Ortíz (titular leader) and the barracks chiefs. Patiño would be allowed to serve in the minor, nonvoting position of secretary. José Gabriel Benítez, former treasury minister, was also loosely attached to the new governing body.[5]

Within a very short time of Francia's death, a crisis had been averted, a provisional junta was ruling, and Patiño had been sidetracked from the tracks of power. Among its first acts, the junta ordered the arrest of José Artigas and several other influential foreigners.[6] All entrepôts were sealed off, and none of the some 600 political prisoners jailed by Francia were released. The new government, unsure of itself, was taking few chances. Its first official, public act was to preside over the funeral oration for the late master. That oration, spoken as if with El Supremo's own voice, was, in fact, a junta-sponsored warning to the people, lauding, as it did, Francia's smashing of all "factions" and "destructive parties."[7]

Having duly warned the citizenry that it would not tolerate any deviation from the submission that had been shown Francia, the new government then swore oaths to defend the republic and protect its inhabitants.

Avoiding a decision on suggestions that it convoke a congress, the junta officially installed itself on September 25, amidst music and fireworks, and began the serious labor of ridding itself of secretary Patiño, a link to the past most obnoxious to Paraguayans. Sometime before September 30, Patiño was quietly arrested, charged with embezzlement of public funds, and thrown into a dungeon. There, in fearful uncertainty, the disappointed politician solved a nettlesome problem for the junta by hanging himself with his hammock cords.[8] With rejoicing on the part of the public, his corpse was carried from the jail, as if to prove that he was, indeed, dead, but none of Asunción's churches would permit his interment in their consecrated soil. After many vagaries, his remains were buried in the patio of one of his own, private homes.[9]

The junta soon revealed itself as an ineffectual governing instrument, with none of the semi-divine supreme aura of Francia's assured despotism. Its members were unsure, uncertain, and unimpressive, and the officers, barely literate, were rustic in the extreme. Aside from collecting their self-appointed salaries and disposing of some of the Caraí's properties, the junta did little as warm weather approached. In the face of a growing popular disenchantment, "the government took only one progressive step, which was to open . . . the library founded by Dr. Francia."[10]

With discontent and political passions building in the streets, parlors, and barracks, Don Carlos Antonio López returned from his ranch in the interior and reopened his house at Trinidad, where he met frequently with disgruntled officers, counseling them that the only way to save the nation was to call a congress and create a legitimate government. As one of the republic's leading literate men, Don Carlos Antonio no doubt had considered, as had Francia before him, the part he might play in the new drama.

Supposedly considering the idea of a congress, the junta let October and the next two months slip away without making up its collective mind, and by January Asunceños expected nothing save further delay. On January 23, 1841, an infantry unit led by Sergeants Ramón Duré and José Domingo Campos surrounded Government House. Within minutes, Duré was shackling all the junta members and the barracks coup was over—almost. Duré, with the support of most of the garrisons' officers and men, announced to the public the end of the junta and the formation of a temporary triumvirate composed of him and the two city alcaldes—a triumvirate that would soon call a congress.[11]

As a sweltering dawn broke on February 9, and as yet no congress had been called, the barracks again moved. Led by a junior officer, Mariano Roque Alonso, the barracks deposed the Duré clique and actually began preparations for the long-awaited assembly. Alonso, now calling himself General Commander of Arms, labored long with his new secretary, Carlos Antonio López, on the upcoming congress. With barracks approval, they set the date for March 12 and sent detailed instructions throughout the land.

Before congress met, it became clear that there were three leading contenders for power: Roque Alonso, López, and ex-Francia subdelegado Norberto Ortellado. To cut off the latter, and to avoid a bitter campaign that might lead to disturbances, Carlos Antonio propagandized in favor of a two-man consulate composed of himself and Roque Alonso. As the delegates streamed into Asunción, such propaganda was daily increased.[12] On the appointed day, almost 500 delegates, freely elected in the partidos, met at the Church of San Francisco, determined to end the uncertainty and fill the void left by the Caraí.

With a minimum of debate, perhaps because of noisy military maneuvers by the honor guard in the corridors, the congress named Roque Alonso and López consuls for a term of three years, after which a new congress would review the situation and consider the future. To Carlos Antonio was assigned a salary of 3,000 pesos per annum, for it was recognized that by dint of his education the rotund lawyer would carry the real burden of government; to his military counterpart was allotted a salary of only 2,000 pesos. The congress also disposed of what remained of the salary Francia had not bothered to collect. A large part of this went for the reopening of the seminary, some was earmarked for the army, and 400 pesos was donated to the Caraí's sister, Petrona. The port of Ytapúa was reopened, and Pilar, not the capital, was designated as terminus for the downriver trade. The consuls were enjoined to foster education, were authorized to initiate whatever diplomacy was possible under the circumstances, were allowed to regulate commerce, and were exhorted to defend the republic. With astounding naiveté, even given their lack of practice, the congress went no further in defining the duties of its new chiefs, nor did it consider a written constitution. Instead, it dissolved itself, and with fireworks brightening the dusk and the sound of hearty reveling rending the air, its members, with sighs of relief, headed their horses home.[13]

The Corpulent Despot

Carlos Antonio López was fifty-four years of age in 1841, and extremely obese. By the standards of the time he was wealthy, wise, and educated. His father, an Asunción Creole shoemaker of modest means, had married a mestiza of Guaicurú ancestry and was unable to offer much to his eight children. Financed by a friend of his father, young Carlos Antonio, because of an early demonstrated cleverness, attended and graduated from the seminary in Asunción and, like Francia, skeptical about entering the priesthood, set about on his own to learn the law. Since the legal "profession" was one of the few avenues by which a gentleman could make money, whereas teaching theology was not, López soon gave up interest in the latter and opened an office for the former in 1823. As a lawyer, Carlos Antonio gained a good reputation and, more important, a wide circle of influential clients and friends. He married carefully and well, to Juana Paula Carillo, of similar girth but larger family holdings, and received as dowry a ranch near Olivares, southeast of Asunción.[14] For over a hundred years, most writers have hinted that Doña Juana was pregnant by (the account varies) another man and that Carlos Antonio was bribed with a large dowry to take the embarrassment off her parents' shoulders. Whatever the case, which casts interesting speculations as to the father of Francisco Solano, Carlos Antonio got the better of the deal.[15]

López was now a pillar of society, possessing those three attributes most valued in nineteenth-century Latin America: land, the legal profession, and an education. But the roseate peace of the Franciata had been shattered in 1820 with the plot to blow El Supremo to smithereens, and the resultant repression made it appear that Francia was determined to do away with all literate members of society. As a literate man, Carlos Antonio fled in 1823 with his family to the rural Recoleta barrio, where he tried hard to live at a low profile, and he began to spend more and more time at his Olivares ranch, devoting himself to the gigantic countryside meals the area was famous for and raising both cattle and children. He rarely appeared in the city after 1830, and in 1837, after coming briefly to Francia's notice in an obscure court case, he moved permanently to Olivares, where he remained until after the Caraí's death.[16]

López had survived the Franciata, as few other important Creoles had. In a sense, he had moved several rungs up the social ladder, for those naturally above him had been executed, jailed, or bankrupted. Much like Francia before him, Don Carlos Antonio would be spokesman for the ill-educated militares of his nation, and, like Francia, he would emerge their unquestioned leader.

History Relived: The Consulado, 1841-1844

When one studies the consulate, 1841-1844, one studies not the government of two men but that alone of López. Mariano Roque Alonso, bewildered by the business of government, in effect abdicated his position, preferring to hang around the barracks in the company of men like himself. It is, however, to his lasting credit that he did nothing to interfere with a government that he did not understand. Like Fulgencio Yegros before him, Roque Alonso became a shadow, vaguely present on ceremonial occasions.

Carlos Antonio was immediately faced with myriad problems, not the least of which concerned foreign affairs, a subject truly "foreign" to his experience. The entire subcontinent was a shambles. Argentina, torn by gaucho civil war and partially dominated by a dictator, Juan Manuel de Rosas, was on the verge of war with both Britain and France. Conditions in the Porteño-dominated Argentine were such that a British resident wrote in detail that Rosas and his henchmen were responsible for over 20,000 deaths: 4 by poison, 3,765 by throat-cutting, 1,393 by firing squad, 722 by stabbing, 14,920 in battle, and a further 1,600 by "various persecutions."[17] The situation in Brazil was hardly better. The empire, with its infant prince regent, was in the process of being torn asunder by civil wars, most evident in the secessionist movement in the south known as the Guerra dos Farrapos, and its statesmen suspiciously watched Paraguay for signs of intervention. As a Porteño newspaper reported of Brazilian instability, without comment, "An old man named Barata has been sent prisoner from Bahia to Rio de Janeiro; he had been running about the streets among the Republican Party, with a laurel leaf in one hand and a knife in the other, stabbing all the Portuguese he met with: some think him insane."[18] That only "some" think him insane is an interesting comment on the society and the times. Uruguay, meanwhile, waged her own civil war, in part fomented and backed by Argentine factions. In short, in the words of Thomas Carlyle, the nations of the area were "raging and ravening like one huge dog kennel gone rabid."[19]

Carlos Antonio at Work and at Play

López, as he faced these and other problems, was a physically imposing man. Of medium height, he was not stout but alarmingly fat, with a huge head made even larger by immense slabs of fat which hung from both sides of his chin, effectively hiding the collars on his dress uniforms. This obesity, marked from youth, became accentuated with age as the despot used his regal position to indulge in an almost superhuman effort to ingest food of all description. He lived well, eating immense meals (but abstaining from strong drink), and chain-smoking long black cigars rolled for him by his wife.[20] Described by one who knew him as "this great tidal wave of human flesh . . . a veritable mastodon," Carlos Antonio affected a huge, plumed hat, "quite appropriate to him and equally suitable for a museum of curiosities or for the Buenos Aires carnival."[21]

With one leg shorter than the other, López, who despite his bulk had his share of vanity and more, preferred to remain seated when in the presence of others. Besides his slight limp, obesity disfigured his gait, and simply rising from a chair was a major undertaking. He did not often mount a horse.

He was, however, a reasonably pleasant man, with a perpetual smile and a sonorous speaking voice. He had, in the words of one who knew him well, the facial expression of a "man well satisfied with himself," and he frequently conversed in a manner that could be described as patronizing. The abundant black hair and dark complexion were paired with thin lips, fine wrists, and tiny feet.[22]

Carlos Antonio's wife, Juana Carillo, "was an old lady as robust as her children," according to one who observed her, and almost as rotund as her husband.[23] She also shared his love of food and black cigars, and had a complexion that "revealed her the daughter of a European father and an Indian mother." She generally dressed in rather plain clothes and eschewed the use of stockings.[24]

The López rarely visited their estancia at Olivares after 1841, and normally lived in a spacious home near the Cathedral, close by Government House. A large interior patio garden was cluttered with "pedestals that sustained trophies and coats of arms of the Republic."[25] When the heat crackled in from the Chaco, the López were wont to move to their quinta at Trinidad (today's Botanical Garden) on the outskirts of the city. There, on high ground with beautiful lapacho and palo santo trees, the First Family summered instead of simmered. Many visitors came to the sprawling quinta, and López conducted much government business there in the summer.[26]

Except on state occasions, Carlos Antonio was not a formal man, as had been Francia. His clothes were somber and simple, his jackets always open (perhaps because of his girth), and he often went about half-dressed. Typical was the manner in which the Corpulent Despot received Ildefonso Bermejo when the Spaniard arrived on contract in Asunción. Called to enter the president's office, Bermejo was surprised that "the President was seated in white shorts on a hammock," with a pile of official papers and French magazines on a nearby chair. Motioning the Spaniard to be seated, Carlos Antonio explained his informality, telling Bermejo that "we are republicans," and hence do not stand on ceremony. As they were talking, a barefoot barber entered with hot water and shaving gear, and Doña Juana also arrived, handing her husband a batch of cigars that she had just prepared.[27] Such was a typical López audience.

Carlos Antonio arose early, about five in the morning, and after a swift, if large, breakfast, received in his house certain officials, passing across the plaza to Government House a few hours later. About mid-day he would return home, where he would dine and then climb into his huge hammock for siesta. Returning to work, he would deal with paperwork in his own home in the late afternoon, and then, after a massive dinner, he would retire early, except on Thursday, when he hosted an informal get-together at home, attended for the most part by his children and their friends.[28]

It seems that Carlos Antonio spent a good deal of time with his children, especially with his favorite, eldest son Francisco Solano. He arranged "the best possible education" for his sons, beginning with tutoring by Argentine schoolmaster Juan Pedro Escalada and followed by more tutorial work with learned priests, culminating, for Francisco Solano, in a year or so of studies in a private school under Jesuit direction. He was later sent by his father on the 1843 mission of Manuel de la Peña to Buenos Aires so that he might better understand the wider world. Later, of course, he was sent to Europe, as much for his own broadening as for diplomatic purposes.[29]

There were two other sons, Venancio and Benigno, and Dr. Chaves asserts that they were united only in their intense dislike (and perhaps jealousy) of their older brother. Both would pay the ultimate price for their sibling rivalry, dying in agony in the mud. Venancio, who dabbled in the career of arms, became Asunción garrison commander and, for a while, minister of war. He was something of a nonentity, even at the time, and was known only for his almost religious attendance at all dances given in the city. Benigno took after his father in his zest for the good life, eating often and well, and spending most of his evenings at the Club Nacional, which he had helped to found. Reasonably sophisticated, he had studied for two years (on his father's orders) at the Brazilian Naval Academy at Rio de Janeiro, and later accompanied his elder brother on his European junket. It is notable that Benigno, the only Paraguayan of his time to possess even a smattering of naval training, never, even during the war, associated himself with the ill-fated national fleet.[30]

The two daughters are even less well known. Inocencia, the eldest, married an officer, Vicente Barrios, whose career looked up immediately. He became the first real general in the Paraguayan army and later served as minister of war before Francisco Solano put him against a wall in 1868. Rafaela, the youngest López, who was saved from death by Alfred Demersay in a simple but hectic operation, was a spoiled child. Dying in 1845, despite the ministrations of a brace of curanderos and the prayers of her parents, Rafaela was to be operated upon by visitor Demersay, but Doña Juana had her superstitious doubts. "The mother had less confidence," the surgeon remembered, "and in explanations twenty times repeated and always useless, I lost precious hours," and almost the patient.[31] Definitely her father's girl, Rafaela often accompanied him on his travels throughout Paraguay and acted as "first lady," replacing her overweight mother at many official gatherings. She married very young, to Saturnino Bedoya, a public auctioneer who, to nobody's expressed surprise, next became minister of the treasury in time to be executed by the Mariscal in 1868.[32]

By 1850, all the López had their own relatively sumptuous homes, summer places, and ranches, forming in themselves the Paraguayan elite and mingling, as isolated aristocrats must in a rural land, chiefly with sophisticated foreigners and the small diplomatic community. At the Club Nacional, and in their own homes, the López children often hosted dances for the select circle, dragooning military bands to provide the music. This became even more frequent after the arrival of Madame Lynch in 1855. The Irish consort "had, without a doubt, an important part in the introduction of dances and danceable music, all of European origin."[33]

Bermejo, always the observer, described one such ball at Tacumbú in a jury-rigged ballroom composed of boat decks. On a raised dais "was hung a frame with a portrait of the President, so badly painted that it seemed, in truth, a caricature." There were almost a hundred guests and a military brass band, and, sniffed the somewhat arrogant Spaniard, though no woman present wore gloves, "they had not forgotten their rings, which all shone in greater quantity than could be contained on their fingers; the majority were shoeless." That evening, the elite mostly danced the quadrille, and Bermejo was briefly paired with Inocencia López, noting with approval that she was perhaps fat, "but well shod." With the music "more thunderous than harmonious," the revelers were being observed by scores of curious soldiers: "They were transfixed, mouths agape, with arms crossed over their chests, with heads inclined and a semblance of astonishment" on their faces.[34]

Doña Inocencia, enchanted by Señora Bermejo's gown, unabashedly asked the Española to make her one like it: "That is to say, they wanted to know my wife so that she could serve them as seamstress." Taken aback, Bermejo diplomatically lied his way out of the embarrassing problem and passed to the other room, where a group of men were smoking and drinking imported beer, catching a notable glimpse of Doña Juana on the way: "I saw Doña Juana Carillo, the presidenta, resting, with a hand on her belt, leaning on a table, and with a great cigar in her mouth." The party, "a picturesque spectacle," lasted until two in the morning, some men "grabbing handfulls of sweets and filling their girlfriends' skirts with them" before leaving for home.[35]

Such dances were indeed spectacles for those not invited, and unashamedly, by the hundreds, people gathered to watch the elite in their colorful clothes and to hear the music. A British traveler present at one official ball in 1851 wrote that "the people not admitted into the salon adopted a novel method of watching: they stuck their naked legs through the grillwork of the windows, and, holding onto the bars so as not to fall, they let their smiling faces be seen, illuminated with contentment."[36]

Carlos Antonio and his family also had a certain fondness for the theater and frequently attended its performances, especially after Bermejo took it in hand and provided his expert guidance. As an Argentine wrote describing Carlos Antonio's first experience with the theater: "During the evening, I watched López I for a sign of any impression produced upon him, on witnessing a play for the first time in his life. It was like watching a stone in a field."[37]

Although by Paraguayan standards well-educated, Carlos Antonio's knowledge had been largely self-acquired and was of a nature addressable to national problems. Never having traveled abroad, even to Argentina, and, before 1844, having met very few foreigners, his outlook tended to be provincial in the extreme. As Chaves has written, "he knows but little of foreign matters."[38] One of the few foreigners who got to know him well, Alfred Demersay, respected him, but noted: "President López does not lack education, but this education, drunk in through books and not controlled by educated people or by experience in the world, carries him to exaggerated appreciations, too absolute and too unjust."[39] Yet this man would shape and mold a modern Paraguay. Unfortunately, it would not long outlast him.

The More Things Change . . .

As Carlos Antonio was corpulent, so was he a despot. It is easy to lose sight of this, his most salient characteristic, yet it was his strong suit. At the mention of the word "dictator," attention seems to swing automatically toward the cloaked figure of Francia, yet El Supremo's variety of despotism was merely a bit more exotic than that of López.

The elder López controlled his nation as thoroughly as had Francia before him, yet, because it was coming to be a slightly different nation as the years passed, his dictatorship at times appears to be of a new variety. López sought what Francia had sought, and, because of the superb groundwork done by the Caraí, López could begin to achieve the long-term goals. Virtually every government program initiated by Carlos Antonio had but one aim—the defense and preservation of Paraguay. There were few, if any, reforms in the epoch of the Corpulent Despot, merely changes made to effect the overriding goal. There was no more opposition permitted under López than there had been under Francia, and, in fact, an exile community of considerable size grew in Buenos Aires.

Not only did Paraguayans and foreigners require special licenses to move around within Paraguay, but López, as intent on details as had been Dr. Francia, turned down a request from a free Black who asked permission to marry, with the words, "There is no reason for the intended marriage of free with slave."[40]

If López opened schools, he did so because literacy was a basic key to national strength and unity, to say nothing of effective propaganda. When he opened commercial floodgates, it was not to acquaint his rustic people with the blessings of corsets and champagne, but to purchase arms and machinery. As he built a railroad he did not think of Sunday outings or national prestige, but directed the track to military purposes. If he entered the world of diplomacy, he did so to protect his weak nation in other nations' flags and insure its survival. When he constructed ships at Asunción, he built them to guarantee Paraguayan control of the rivers, to preclude future blockade. As British and other foreign technicians poured into the country, they were set to work almost entirely on the creation of a military-industrial complex, and the greatest project of the era was the huge, sprawling fortress of Humaitá, the "Sevastapol of the Americas."

The congresses that met during his rule were less expressions of a confused, rustic popular will than a series of rubber stamps wielded by López. The congress of 1842 was composed of 400 delegates, that of 1844 by 300, and later ones by about 200 delegates.[41] The rudimentary "constitution" of 1844 not only put all powers in his hands, representing the utter abdication of his people, but limited to property-owners the right of election to future assemblies.

If López permitted the release of political prisoners jailed by Francia, he soon had, albeit in lesser numbers, sufficient of his own.[42] In education, which he boasted was largely his creation, he was careful to limit anything that looked like superior studies, for although the nation required literacy, López did not desire a generation of thinkers who might challenge him. Those he sent abroad for technical education were few and very carefully selected. What passed for journalism in Paraguay was a series of state-directed rags, all edited at least partially by López himself and dedicated to fostering an almost rabid nationalism and paranoia among the people. The country had not yet reached the point where "censorship" was a meaningful word.

In 1844, Carlos Antonio accepted from a congress a presidential term of ten years, while that august body itself would reunite only once each five years. When it convened in 1849, about all that could be said of it is what Julio César Chaves has noted: "It approved and sanctioned all acts of Government" during the previous half decade. "Congress dissolved itself without labors or glory, without discussing government acts or raising fundamental questions."[43] In addition to his control over army and police, Carlos Antonio had inaugurated "a practice a bit divorced from the parliamentary ethic: he himself presided over the congresses, over which his influence was visible." So pronounced was the sheeplike resignation of the 1849 deputies that many foreigners in Asunción made fun of the situation, causing the government newspaper, *El Semanario,* to rebut its humorous critics in a decidedly unhumorous manner.[44]

Within this context of iron control and Francia-like sense of purpose, then, Carlos Antonio completed the Paraguayan Revolution begun by the Caraí and took the inevitable but danger-fraught steps into the wider world.

Plate 2. Carlos Antonio López

7. A New Paraguay Is Stirring

Although Carlos Antonio received his sobriquet "the Builder" due to large construction projects carried out in the 1850s, one must look to the previous decade to note the sweeping changes that made the renovation of Paraguay possible. The 1840s have been virtually ignored by historians, who traditionally have preferred to focus on the "flashy" aspects of the Corpulent Despot's rule.

Asunción, Mother of Cities

A traveler arriving at Asunción in the 1840s would not be impressed unless he came from Corrientes. In fact, his ship might sail past the city accidentally, for the low buildings were largely hidden from the river by thousands of trees and lush vegetation. While there are few descriptions of the city in this epoch, a partial picture may be painted.

Asunción's population of about twelve thousand was scattered in a wide arc from the bay far inland, and many of its actual suburbs, such as the Recoleta and Ybiraí, can only be classified as rural. The streets were not paved (work only began on this project in 1874 and is continuing slowly), and deep ditches in the dirt main roads were constantly scraped out by convict chain gangs in a vain attempt to channel torrential rains, sewage, and garbage down the low hills to the bay. Near that body of water a series of low walls had been constructed to keep parts of the city from sliding into the river during cloudbursts, and two decrepit wooden wharves jutted uncertainly about sixty feet from shore.[1]

A foreigner described the city a few years later, expressing his "surprise in seeing that the capital of the Republic did not have paving, and that the stroller was obliged to walk with . . . his feet sinking deep in the sand." The heat also bothered this gentleman, who further noted that "a fresh egg put into the sand of the street and taken out ten minutes later was hard, and, if one were so disposed, one could eat it."[2]

Perhaps the government itself best described the city in an 1842 municipal decree. The first article called on the people to improve, clean up, and wall in their downtown lots, warning those who would not or could not do so that they would be required to sell to more willing people. Another article directed that buildings "threatened with ruin" were to be repaired or torn down, at the owner's cost. The citizens were further enjoined not to gallop in the streets, discharge firearms, or "shoot rockets among people who are passing through the streets." It also "prohibited the throwing of trash, dead animals, or pestilent waters into the streets and plazas," and it was also forbidden to "have sheep or pigs outside the interior of the house." Drinkers in the taverns were not to "proffer obscene, scandalous, or insulting words to the people passing by," on pain of a month on public works, and those found guilty of "committing any dishonest acts on the streets" would face four months' hard labor. Article 21 promised that the government would figure out some way "to moderate the customs of the savage Indians who live in the suburbs of the capital and on the river beach, to avoid their public drunken orgies and other acts that offend public morals." Anyone who got drunk in his home with "a child, runaway Indians, slaves, vagabonds, intruders, or suspicious persons" could end up "in chains on public works" for two years or more. All begging by those who "are not absolutely poor or do not have an impediment" was forbidden, except for "the insolvent prisoners of the jail who with moderation ask for alms," as was traditional. Asunción, continued the decree, was for Asunceños, and visitors to the capital could remain no longer than two days without special license.[3]

Of the four barrios of the capital (Cathedral, Encarnación, Recoleta, and San Roque), the first-named was where the better families (and later many foreigners) dwelt. In the Cathedral barrio in 1843 were sixty-one shops (twelve of which were owned by foreigners) and twelve taverns (three owned by Spaniards). In addition, the barrio boasted fifty-seven licensed peddlers, ten scribes, thirty-three carpenters, forty-nine silver workers, forty-two iron workers, a surprising hundred and six tailors and seamstresses, fifty-one hatmakers, eighteen hairdressers, thirty-six shoemakers, fifteen bricklayers, six playing-card makers, a German watchmaker, five painters, four straw-roofers, two barbers, two liquor distillers, a jeweler, a herbalist, a river guide, four shipwrights, and eighty-two day laborers.[4] The other barrios, in lesser degree, also had their businesses, but none could match the elite Cathedral barrio.

A later report on the silverworking trade, by tradition a large one in a land where both men and women invested in jewelry, silver spurs, scabbards, and yerba mate gourds, shows nine silver shops in the city, six of which were located in the Cathedral barrio, with one each in the other barrios. The largest was owned by Gerónimo Legal in the Cathedral barrio, who provided employment for six masters and eight apprentices. In all the city there were forty-seven master silversmiths and fifty-two apprentices, and it would seem that they were all kept busy.[5] Although there was little cultural life and less foreign influence in the inland city in the 1840s, and it was very rustic, there were Sunday evening serenatas in the streets and wandering guitarists to create a patina of sophistication, and the city was not devoid of charm.[6]

Before the coming of the foreign technicians in large numbers and the creation of a national theater, most social pleasures took place in the home, usually restricted to dinners for visiting friends. In the early 1850s, the omnipresent Ildefonso Bermejo attended such a dinner at the home of an upper class Paraguayan family, and he left us his impressions. A large table, set with silver and a white tablecloth, was presided over by the visitor's friend, Don Vicente. Also on the table were two large pieces of chipa, a coarse bread made from mandioca flour, corn, milk, and cheese. The guests, nibbling the thirst-inducing chipa, cast their eyes about in vain for wine, a very rare treat in Paraguay at the time. Their thirst was soon to be assuaged, however, for a Black servant brought in "a great earthenware bowl in the guise of a soup toureen, filled with broth and rice, which signified to me that here was the soup; but seasoned with cow fat," which gave off "an odor little agreeable to the nose and a taste not at all agreeable to the palate. Much time has to pass before one can accustom oneself to sample this type of food without visible repugnance."

As he was recovering from that dish, a new bowl was set on the table, containing another broth, this one studded with chunks of meat and corn. The main dish, which followed, was a large "piece of veal, barbecued in its skin," followed by sugarcane honey and fresh goat cheese. When the desserts were finished, "a mulata came, who, not only being very ugly and dirty, had a nose so turned upward that it seemed to be fleeing from her mouth." Clearing the table, the mulata "announced that the hammocks were ready." The substantial midday meal could not but terminate, as it does today, with a siesta.[7]

A View of the People

One of the frustrating, and at times amusing, aspects of dealing with Paraguayan history is the utter ignorance of just how many Paraguayans there were at any given time. The demographic side of Paraguayan history, so vital in assessing the importance of a certain army size or annual trade statistics, has remained untouched, especially for the nineteenth century. We have estimates based on the incomplete censuses of the late eighteenth century,[8] these positing just under 100,000 inhabitants, and, on this exceedingly fragile base, later writers have claimed totals as diverse as 200,000 and 1,337,439 for the population on the eve of the Paraguayan War.[9]

In late 1845, Carlos Antonio López ordered a detailed census to be taken by the priests of each of the nation's eighty-six partidos. The completeness of the information varies greatly from area to area, because, with no specific guidelines, the clerics recorded whatever seemed significant to them. The result, however, is clear. With a small margin of error, it can be said that in 1846 there were 238,862 Paraguayans, plus another 20,000 or so migratory, stone-age Indians.[10]

Some general observations can be made from the census data. More than 100,000 people, or about 42 percent of all Paraguayans, lived within a fifty-mile radius of Asunción, a pattern resulting from three centuries of Indian warfare. Other major nuclei, although far less densely concentrated, could be found around Villa Rica and within fifty miles north and south of the Tebicuari River. Almost no one dwelt in far eastern Paraguay, and few along the track of the Alto Paraná. Equally important was the lack of population in the large and strategically vital region between the Ypané and Apa rivers, and it hardly needs mention that the entire Chaco, a "Quebracho Curtain," was home to none save painted M'Bayá and Guaicurú.

There were 17,181 Blacks in Paraguay, some 7.19 percent of the total population (considerably less than had been guessed).[11] Of these, 7,866 were slaves and 519 libertos (or slaves until their majority). Almost 15,000 Paraguayans were classified as agregados, or "people in service to another," a category spanning such diverse groups as debt peons and concubines. The 1,229 Indians listed is an absurd underestimation, resulting from several notable factors. As the census taker at San Joaquín noted, "wild" Indians were simply ignored, as there was no way to gauge their numbers. Also, an "Indian," then as now, was a person who lived like an "Indian." That is to say, that to be a Paraguayan in 1846 was to be settled, Christian, and mestizo: only those who failed those three tests could be "Indians."

One striking thing revealed by the census is that the average Paraguayan household was composed of only 6.97 people, a figure that includes servants, slaves, and distant relatives. This means that the average Paraguayan lived with his nuclear family—a wife and two or three children—even in isolated rural areas. Average household size ranged from 4.48 in the Indian section of Caazapá to 15.85 in Curuguatí-North. Only in the latter and in Piribebuy does the data indicate genuinely large families. Extended families under the same roof were rare, and most widows and widowers remained on their own with only immediate family or servants.

The census takers occasionally reflected on the genetic local color. In Asunción, an English bachelor resident, William Lir (Lear?), had a brood of sixteen children, while for some reason in San José de los Arroyos, families with from ten to twenty-six children were uncommonly common. The national procreation champion, however, appears to have been the widow Simeona López of Villeta, who boasted the survival of twenty-seven offspring, all living under her roof in 1846!

In Asunción's Recoleta barrio, Anastacio Rodríguez and his wife Petrona (aged eighteen and seventeen respectively) joined her father, Pantaleón Cubillas (aged thirty-six), in playing with their five-year-old son: not only the land was fecund in Paraguay. In Curuguatí, the census-taker, more graphic than most, recorded thirteen people as "stupid and dull and retarded in their senses," and one Modesto González, "who crawls like a snake and is absolutely mute."

Aside from indicating the number of Paraguayans in 1846, the census has important implications regarding the Paraguayan War eighteen years in the future. If there were 238,862 people in 1846, given the lack of any significant immigration, the 1864 population can be estimated. Using annual growth rates from 2½% to 5%, we find:

	2½%	3%	3½%	4%	4½%	5%
1864	372,545	406,643	443,239	483,888	527,523	574,851

These figures do not take into account the death toll from various epidemics that swept Paraguay in the late 1840s. Although the difference between the highest and lowest rates of growth amounts to an impressive 200,000 in 1864, even the highest figure is far short of what is normally claimed by writers not utilizing hard data. A 5 percent growth rate for Paraguay during the period under consideration is unthinkable, and the oft-repeated figure of a million or more Paraguayans in 1864 would have required such a libidinous effort as to be unique in the annals of demography. A 3 percent growth rate would be a high, but acceptable, calculation, resulting in about 400,000 Paraguayans when the war began.

Pardos y Pobladores: The Black Community

Despite the fact that Blacks were a vital segment of nineteenth-century Paraguay, very little is known about their role and place in society. Paraguayans, with a long tradition of nationalism firmly rooted in racism, have paid but little attention to the pardo, or Black, minority. In 1785, Azara estimated that Blacks composed perhaps 11 percent of the population.[12] This figure is not surprising, as a much more complete record shows that, in Buenos

Aires during the same epoch, one in three inhabitants was a pardo.[13]

There is not much information on Blacks during the Franciata, but general outlines can be drawn. Hundreds of pardos were sent from Tabapí to the ill-fated colony at Tevego, 1812-1823, and Emboscada and Areguá were pardo communities. We are also aware of sizeable pardo groups in the capital and at Laurelty, Guarambaré, and Cambá Loma.[14]

What is far more important was the growth of state slavery during the Caraí's rule. He, as the government, had inherited several hundred state slaves when sworn in in 1814, offspring of property confiscated from the Jesuits in 1767. Most of these lived and worked on what became estancias de la República, of which there were seventy-two in 1818. When Francia smashed the elite in 1821, he also confiscated the properties of those he executed. Among these were the heads of most of the elite families of Paraguay, whose wealth was based on extensive rural properties. In one stroke, El Supremo added perhaps a thousand slaves to the national patrimony and almost doubled the national land holdings.[15]

If Francia multiplied state lands and slaves while crushing the elite, he perhaps doubled both by strokes of the pen in 1823 and 1824. In the former year he closed the seminary, gaining its substantial lands and slave work force. The following year, he secularized the monasteries and huge tracts of land, and yet hundreds more slaves became government property.[16] Also, although it is not clear how or why, many free Blacks became slaves at about the same time. The Tabapí pardos had almost all been freemen in 1812, yet an 1826 census shows the community composed of 392 slaves and only 23 free pardos.[17] It would seem that El Supremo simply decreed slave any Black living on confiscated lands, thus expanding the number of state slaves not only at the expense of the elite and the Church but also at the cost of the free Black community.

At the congress of 1842, the Law of Free Womb was enacted. This law, contrary to what many have written, did not end slavery, but merely the slave trade. It also stipulated that any children born of slave parents after December 31, 1842, would be classified libertos de la República and would be fully freed on reaching the age of twenty-four for females and twenty-five for males. Before reaching their majority, the libertos would have to serve as if they were slaves.[18]

This law had an interesting effect on slave birth rates. For example, at the large Tabapí estancia, a detailed 1854 census reveals a total of 682 slaves, of whom 310, or 45 percent, were aged ten or under. The number of those aged eleven to twenty, or twenty to thirty, is not at all in proportion to that of the children. What seems clear is that birth rates spiraled upwards as slaves learned that future offspring would not spend the rest of their lives as someone's property.[19]   So fast did the state slave population grow after 1843 by natural means that Carlos Antonio ordered major sales of "excess" slaves and libertos. From Tabapí alone, 143 slaves were sold in 1848, and a further 49 slaves and 82 libertos between 1855 and 1861. Yet the population did not decline.[20]

Certainly, as the 1846 census attests, slavery was far from defunct in López's Paraguay. The same census also tells a good deal about the geographical distribution of the Black minority. Although there were pardos in almost every partido, there were two major concentrations that reveal something about the purposes of Paraguayan slavery. In the capital's barrios there were 1,636 pardos, some 14.87 percent of the city's population (San Roque barrio was 46 percent pardo). If one adds to this the nearby towns of Limpio, Emboscada, and Villeta, one finds 32.48 percent of all pardos but only 10.96 percent of all Paraguayans.

Far more surprising is the large concentration of pardos in the lovely, rolling grasslands just north of the Río Tebicuari, which was then, as now, a region devoted almost entirely to ranching. The seven partidos of Caapucú, Ibicuy, Mbuyapeí, Quiindí, Quiquió, Tabapí, and Ibitimí, with only some 8 percent of the national population, were home to 26 percent of all pardos. Caapucú, in fact, an important ranching center, was almost half pardo, both slave and free. There were no large-scale agricultural endeavors in the region, and almost none of Paraguay's major crops were produced there. Some corn, wheat, and mandioca were grown, but not on farm units large enough to justify slave labor. It may be assumed that most Tebicuari Blacks, slave and free, were involved in ranching, a situation very rare in the annals of New World slavery.

In all Paraguay there were no truly immense ranches or plantations dedicated to the regimented exploitation of cash crops. Nor were there any very large private slaveholdings that could compare with those elsewhere in the hemisphere. In 1846, there were 176 Paraguayans who held 10 or more libertos and slaves. Together, this elite claimed 2,583 slaves and 186 libertos, 32.84 percent of all the former and 35.84 percent of the latter in the republic. Of these, 145 owned from 10 to 19 slaves and libertos, 22 held between 20 and 29, and 6 claimed from 30 to 39. Only 3 people held 40 or more slaves, and Juan Bernardo Dávalos, a rancher at Bobi, owned the greatest number, 43. Some 51 of the large slaveholders lived in the Tebicuari zone, a figure in keeping with the large number of pardos there.

There were also a few pardos who themselves held slaves, including one Nolasco Merino in Caapucú, a free pardo who listed five slaves and four agregados in his household. In addition, the Church was claimant to several hundred slaves in 1846. The Asunción Cathedral owned one, the chapel at Pirayú held eleven, the Virgin of Tobatí claimed thirty-five, and the Christ

Child at Quiquió owned another five. It was very common for a wealthy person of the epoch to include a clause in his or her will leaving one or more slaves to the local church or patron saint.[21]

Perhaps due to the burgeoning birthrate, the price of slaves fell steadily after 1820. The destruction of the economic base of most of the elite diminished a large share of the market and demand, and the state, as not only the largest corporate slaveholder of the nation but also the principal seller, perhaps flooded the market. Whatever the case, a strong, healthy slave who fetched a price of 500 pesos in 1820 would commonly sell a generation later for less than 200 pesos. A survey of sales prices during the López years reveals that the 200 pesos paid in 1859 by Dolores Mongelos for a slave "healthy and with no vices" was perhaps the top price paid at the time. More common was 100-150 pesos.[22]

Earlier, Francia had decided to free his personal body servants, who were also state property, and he paid the treasury 250 pesos for José María and 150 pesos each for two mulatas, "because of their advanced age."[23] Yet when the state itself began selling Tabapí slaves a few years later, the average price was only 50 pesos, while a liberto, with ten or so years of service left, normally brought only 30 to 35 pesos.[24]

Carlos Antonio did not restrict the labor of state slaves to the estancia system, but required them to work on other official projects as well. As the nation slowly modernized, so did the tasks of many government slaves. They worked side by side with mestizos and foreign experts in every major state enterprise from the 1840s through the war. They were numerous at the Ibicuy foundries and at the Asunción arsenal and shipyard. They labored at the treasury, on the wharves, and in the various state workshops throughout the land. Fifty-eight slaves worked at semi-technical tasks in the Asunción barracks, one was master gunsmith at Concepción, and others were employed by the state as tailors, iron workers, and carpenters. Still others were loaned to visiting foreigners, and thirty libertos were sold in 1855 to Francisco Correa Madruga, "with the object of teaching them to work in a cigar factory."[25]

Free blacks, ever since El Supremo's creation of a pardo lancer squadron in 1833 for use as an escort unit, served in the regular units of the army. Parts of the 2nd and 3rd infantry battalions under the López were pardo, as were various cavalry units, although most of their officers were not.[26] In the ranks of the militia, they were represented, as were all Paraguayans, in accordance with their proportion of the population.

Many Paraguayans manumitted their slaves, as had Francia, some through their wills, others before their demise, as a reward for loyal service. In at least one case, a slaveowner, Señora Francisca Ferreyra, had to take out a small loan to pay for the certificate of liberty for her ex-slave Sebastián.[27]

More common was the granting of freedom by testament. A sampling of such documents indicates that at least half of the nation's slaveholders included manumission of at least one of their slaves on their deaths. This would help explain the large and constantly growing free pardo community. As Matías Ramírez of Limpio wrote in his 1843 will: "I have already given the certificate of Liberty" to some of his slaves and "I declare that it is my wish that all of my slaves remain free upon my demise."[28]

Many another slave, especially among those belonging to the state, purchased their own certificates of liberty with money earned in the practice of their skills. For example, the treasury notified Carlos Antonio that "the slave called María de la Cruz Ferreira, 26 years of age, of the state slaves of this Capital, intends to free herself, offering 80 pesos for her liberty." López affixed his approval to the margin of the note, and María de la Cruz paid the treasury and was free.[29] Two state slaves at the estancia of Tacuacorá "propose to free their children" and were permitted to do so upon payment of the agreed-upon, rather small price.[30] In July, 1855, Carlos Antonio assented to the self-purchase of two slaves and their children. All four escaped bondage for a combined price of only 140 pesos.[31] Apparently freedom, like most other things, was cheaper when purchased in quantity.

The nature of Paraguayan slavery was, though certainly not benign, reasonably humane. Most Paraguayan slaves were ranch hands or personal servants rather than field hands on large plantations. The work was neither excessively difficult nor dangerous, and the birth rate of the Black community appears to have been continuously high. Self-purchase, manumission, and freedom through testament were all very frequent, and the Law of Free Womb gave hope for future generations. The skills they were permitted and even encouraged to develop and practice allowed them a place in society, a means of mobility, and a pride in themselves. According to a list of oficios dated 1843, a third of the "professions," from silversmith through hatmaker in the capital, were filled by pardos, free and slave.[32]

Perhaps because they participated so actively in most facets of Paraguayan life, they tended to share the vices as well as the virtues of their lighter-skinned compatriots. In fact, the pardo community was noted for its contribution to Paraguayan criminal statistics. Aside from a small but notable slave insurrection at Ycuamandiyú in 1812, where "the Negroes, armed with knives and garrotes," had to be crushed by the local militia,[33] and frequent runaways, Blacks were industriously participating in their share of mayhem and more. Twenty-three percent of those in the Asunción jails in 1819 were pardos, as were 17 percent of those arrested in 1847 and 39 percent of those incarcerated in 1863.[34] The robbery of El Supremo himself by his "trusted" and newly-freed servant José María was merely the most audacious of pardo crimes.

Slavery existed, but it certainly did not breed docility.

The New Paraguay Stirs

The decade of the 1840s witnessed not only a series of reforms relating to education and the beginning of the outside world's influence on Paraguay but also a number of internal improvements. Among these was a network of roads in the interior, which for the first time put Asunción in contact with the hinterland, commercially and politically. Villa Rica was linked to the capital by a decent road, with primitive but effective bridges crossing the numerous streams, cutting transit time in half. Another road, with six new bridges, connected Villa Rica with the rich yerbales of Caaguazú, previously a very isolated region. A road was made in the Curuguatí zone, opening the vast yerbales there to exploitation, and carts could then proceed where only peasant cargadores with tump lines could go before. Interior San Joaquín was linked to other centers and another highway connected the southern pueblo of Jesús to its ancient stands of very fine caá-miní yerba two hundred kilometers north near Acaraí. Elsewhere there were scores of shorter roads, bridges, canals, and dams, all of which acted to open the vast interior of the nation and break the isolation of the capital from the rest of the republic— no small contribution to a modern Paraguay.[35]

Many families from Candelaria were brought across the Paraná and settled in newly-opened lands in the interior, where they could live and work without the dangers encountered in their chaotic birthplace. These families, most of whom were brought north in 1842, received free lands and other government aid, and an official encharged with making a census of the immigrants expressed surprise that some of the new arrivals "say they do not know which pueblo they came from."[36]

In the late 1840s, the old system of segregating many Indians in pueblos de Indios was ended by fiat, and thousands became Paraguayans in the full sense of the word, although this was far from an unmixed blessing. Also, Carlos Antonio, hoping to further reduce dependence on expensive imports of cloth and clothing, ordered most of the state estancias and farms to grow cotton and produce cloth for the government. Reports from 1850 and 1851 reveal success in this endeavor, as estancias at locations as diverse as Altos, Santiago, and Atirá produced thousands of yards of passable cotton cloth each year.[37]

Important progress was also registered in another vital area as López, directing his energies toward resolving national problems, vastly improved the defense of his people against marauding Indians. As Swedish savant Eberhard Munck wrote in 1845, "still wandering around here are many tribes of Indians . . . who have become very aggressive, and are feared for the accuracy and force with which they launch their arrows."[38] Carlos Antonio minimized this omnipresent danger that had for so long defined the existence of his land, constructing a large number of forts and guard posts, modernizing the equipment and training of the militia, and ordering swift, retaliatory campaigns against intractable tribes. In 1845 he decreed that all southern pueblos maintain a "ready" militia force to pursue raiding Indians, and three new forts were built along the Alto Paraguay to help shield Concepción and Salvador (Tebegó).[39] This combination of offensive and defensive measures, plus gradual expansion of the regular army and purchase of modern arms, acted to restrict the Indian threat except on the Río Apa frontier, where M'Bayá and Guaicurú were being encouraged by the Brazilians. The fact that serious smallpox epidemics hit the Chaco in the 1840s (as they did eastern Paraguay) and laid waste to many a camp of hostiles was providential as far as most Paraguayans were concerned.[40]

To prepare the way for pacification and eventual settlement of the Chaco, a series of military posts and army estancias were created there in the 1840s, presenting a thin cordon that further reduced the opportunities of hostiles to raid across the river. All of these army establishments were located close to the river, if not actually on its banks, but a start had been made. In 1844 and 1845, large outposts called Potrero del Chaco, Pilcomayo, Rinconada, Espinillo, Tuyú, San José, and Puesto Primero were founded, and their garrisons, buttressed in some cases by small cannon and supported by regular canoe patrols of the river fords, made most of the eastern shore of the Río Paraguay safe for the first time.[41]

Also in this epoch, Carlos Antonio created a police force that soon expanded to most population centers. First functioning at Asunción and Pilar, the police were to take over such routine duties as customs inspection, management of the jails, and public works. The Asunción police were organized into a battalion and paid standard army wages. Allotted few modern arms, they were mainly occupied with making nightly rounds of the city, an indication that there must have been something to patrol against. In 1849, the battalion, commanded by Pedro Nolasco Fernández, counted three companies totaling 194 officers and men, plus a huge cavalry detachment of 4 officers and 195 men.[42]

Reflecting his concern for his nation's military strength, Carlos Antonio in 1845 decreed creation of a national guard, a sort of prestige militia on a semi-professional basis. In his decree he stated that it was the duty of all citizens not only to defend their nation but also to assure "public order." For the national guard, which was not to be permitted "to come together and take up arms" without López's explicit orders, almost all healthy men between the ages of 16 and 55 were to be enlisted. In theory divided, as was the regular army, into battalions of infantry and regiments of cavalry, the national guard units would also have standard officer and non-com complements.

The national guard, however, much touted by later writers, never really existed as a fighting force. The only unit actually created was the first battalion, of 407 officers and men drawn from the capital, commanded, as one might suspect, by Francisco Solano, the president's eldest son. Second Lieutenant Venancio López was given command of the unit's second company, and no doubt both brothers were disappointed to learn that their first glorious assignment was to aid the police in guarding the main jail.[43] There is no evidence that any further units were created, save possibly on paper, and national guard battalions do not appear on military musters during the mobilization of 1864 and 1865.

And the Teachers Shall Be Paid

When Carlos Antonio became president, perhaps 90 percent of his people were illiterate, and the educational "system" was almost defunct. El Supremo had purged most of the educated men and had destroyed many educational institutions, rare enough to begin with. The purge of letters and lettered men, in fact, was so effective that it severely retarded Paraguay and dramatically limited López's plans for the modernization of his country. The simple fact that Carlos Antonio himself had to educate his own boys through tutors indicates that the best Paraguay had to offer was none too good.

In 1840 there was but one public school in Asunción, along with a few clerical private schools and a handful of more or less educated tutors. There was no secondary school at all, and in the interior the scene was even more grim, with militia sergeants and other volunteers barely maintaining their own literacy and trying to impart some of the basics to their selected but rustic charges, while they themselves struggled to survive on scant and irregular salaries.

There can be little doubt that López, from the start, saw education as one of the keys to national progress. He early recognized that a modern Paraguay must be a literate Paraguay, and he acted on his convictions. In 1841, a sizeable sum of money was set aside for the reopening of the seminary, though the institution did not actually open its doors for many years.[44] The public Library, founded by the Caraí, was opened on a fixed schedule, and a literary academy began to function as a sort of groundwork institution for future secondary education. The academy, directed by Padre Antonio Maíz, in 1841 offered work in Spanish (important in a land where it was often the *second* language), Latin, fine arts, philosophy, and theology to its first 50 students. In the following year, Maíz could point with a certain pride to the 149 students enrolled, and Argentine Padre José Joaquín Palacios, previously tutor to Francisco Solano López, was awarded the chair of theology.[45]

Throughout the decade, the López regime showed a strong interest in education, and, well before a host of foreigners set up specialized private and semi-private schools in the 1850s, very considerable progress had been made. With no empty rhetoric, López wrote the president of France in 1850 that "time has shown that if on the one hand there exists the need for order and public tranquility, on the other there prevails the urgent necessity for a more rapid intellectual development . . . in this nation, so that it might flower, grow, and prosper."[46]

In 1845, Carlos Antonio set standard salaries for the rural primary school teachers at a hundred pesos annually, plus a bonus of twenty-four beeves. Though not a generous salary, it was sufficient, given living costs in the interior, to remove the job from the ranks of the "hardship posts" and make recruitment of maestros much easier.[47]

Although we lack documentary evidence concerning most educational development in the 1840s, the best proof that López made progress may be found in a report sent him from the Ycuamandiyú area in 1848. An official there wrote López that in his rural district there were currently 15 primary school teachers, busily spreading literacy to some 420 students. The list shows that almost every pueblo in the region now had its own teacher, whose load varied from 13 students to 55.[48] If an almost entirely rural district such as Ycuamandiyú now had its own rudimentary educational infrastructure, things were indeed stirring in Paraguay.

In 1845, the new state printing press ran off the first of its educational pamphlets (although it never unleashed the hoped-for flood of textbooks), and in both Asunción and the interior the government sponsored free schools for the poor and orphans. In Quiindí, the school for orphans enrolled 50 students, and by 1860 almost a score of such schools existed, providing an education partly practical, partly intellectual.[49]

It would be easy to exaggerate the progress made in education in the 1840s and its effect on the Paraguay of the era, and this is too frequently done. Almost all of the education purveyed by 1850 was on the primary level, and most students attended school on a part-time basis for only a few years. Literacy acquired in San Estanislao was of the most rudimentary nature and was often rubbed off like a stain by the irresistible force of further years in the pueblos. But progress was definitely made, for whereas Francia throttled education out of a sense of nationalism and fear of disruptive, alien ideas, Carlos Antonio's nationalism prompted him to spur education as a necessary armament in a hostile world. Inheriting a unified nation, López did not have to concern himself with creating nationalism but could instead educate and train it. The fact that the first Paraguayan "newspaper," *El Paraguayo Independiente,* which he himself edited, was dedicated to a historical defense of Paraguayan independence is not coincidental. Literacy could be and was a vehicle of nationalism and was a prerequisite for the acquisition of the technical skills that would transform Paraguay.

Thieves Were Unknown?

Dictatorships, ancient and modern, are frequently defended against their detractors with the dicta that crime is all but unknown and that the trains (or oxcarts) run on time. Neither was the case in Paraguay, then or now. Virtually everything written about the 1820-1870 period, whether by foreigner or Paraguayan, seems to assert that Paraguay's continual iron dictatorship assured the country almost total freedom from crime. As Ildefonso Bermejo put it in the 1850s, "Any traveler could walk alone in the countryside."[50] What the erudite Spaniard, who himself avoided the interior, failed to mention is that such a traveler had better be armed to the teeth. Far from being a land free of crime, where even minor infractions were punished in Draconian style, Paraguay had its share of people who knew and practiced every known crime, shattering every legal statute from Hammurabi through the Ten Commandments to the Napoleonic Code. The Paraguayan countryside was home to much violent crime, and free-flowing aguardiente often unleashed the machete or dagger without warning.

Let us consider a sample of the mayhem of the epoch. In 1847, an inspection of the main calabozo in Asunción revealed a veritable catalogue of rogues. One Black was serving on public works for having murdered two women, a citizen was doing time for "having cut the ear off a Portuguese," a man called Antonio Ayala had killed two slaves, and a character called "the Throatcutter" had been caught rustling cattle. Further, there was a woman in chains for infanticide, an official Protector of Indians for abusing his charges, two pardos for "various excesses," and a slave "for his immoral life." One man was serving a sentence for "adultery and other excesses," while Manuel Tabayú, an Indian, was under close guard "for the deaths painfully caused to the persons of Don Blas García, his wife, a legitimate daughter, and another child that he had adopted." Finally, a French resident, Santiago Tibot, had been incarcerated for kidnapping.[51]

Two years later, much the same story was evident. Of the more than a hundred prisoners in the central jail, one encounters a man who had severely beaten a government official, many who stole animals of various types, and others jailed for false accusation, calumny, various and at times imaginative woundings of other people, beatings, general theft, stealing silver stirrups, and wife-killing. A young pardo was arrested "for the crime of bestiality," and another was "remitted, along with the documents, with his daughter María Salome, for incest." Although rape was rare, other sexual crimes were very common.[52]

Nor were crimes harshly punished. Bestiality was rewarded with forty lashes, and most theft merited from thirty to seventy lashes. Theft of livestock was punished by a set interval, about six months, on public works, and many other perpetrators of minor infractions were sent to serve in the navy (considered a hellish fate) or to work gangs or state estancias for redemptive labor. The death penalty was reserved almost entirely for those guilty of political offenses and subversion. Other criminals, including most murderers, became, one might say, temporarily part of the state patrimony and contributed their labor to the new nation. Bermejo, soon after his arrival, encountered "a string of prisoners tied two by two with thick and heavy chains and conducted by a foreman. I counted some seventy-two condemned," who were on their way to public works.[53] Throughout the López years, much of the work force at Ibicuy, the arsenal, and the railroad were prisoners, and colonies such as that of Tevegó were settled by cutthroats and cutpurses who made amends to society by holding the frontier.

8. The Economic Pulse Quickens

The coherent society inherited by López was about to open to the wider world, but slowly, like the petals of a new flower, and hesitantly. Carlos Antonio, almost as cautious as Francia had been, was first to complete the socialization of his people, extending his control dramatically over almost every facet of their economic activities.

"A considerable trade, carried on in an idle, irregular way"[1]

There are several fundamental aspects of Paraguayan life in the Carlos Antonio López years that accurately reflect the scope not only of change but also of his drive to make the state the nation and the nation the state. One of these was the new commercial activity that began shortly after El Supremo's death.

Eberhard Munck arrived at Pilar from his native Sweden in 1843, one of the first learned Europeans to enter post-Francia Paraguay. He was immediately struck by the suspicion with which Paraguayans, including the authorities, regarded foreigners, writing a friend that "Paraguay today is not open to other foreigners than merchants."[2] His observation was correct. Rustic, long-isolated Paraguay, desirous of commerce, was nonetheless wary of the new ideas that might accompany it. As a result, most trade with the outside was carefully channeled not through spacious Asunción Bay but into the squalid little port of Pilar. There, the interchange was closely regulated and monitored, and foreign merchants were confined to the limits of the pueblo, where by design there were few accomodations, thereby encouraging them to sleep aboard their vessels.

The old Brazil trade overland from São Borja to Ytapúa (called Encarnación after 1848) continued with no interruption, and privileged Brazilian merchants operated wholesale and retail outlets in the small riverine village. This entrepôt, vulnerable to bandits, Indians, and Correntino troops who plagued the passage of caravans through Candelaria, steadily dwindled in importance vis-à-vis the growing trade at Pilar. In 1841, a Brazilian merchant, Jordan Luis de Trayo, was operating a retail store at Ytapúa whose shelves displayed a surprisingly large and varied inventory of imported goods valued at 22,244 pesos, a major endeavor for the period.[3] Trayo, however, was the exception, and by the late 1840s Paraguay considered the Ytapúa trade important only for weapons acquisitions from Brazil. That specialized trade *was* important, prompting Paraguayan retention of part of Candelaria, with the subsequent risk of renewed hostilities there.

Although a fairly steady trade had been driven by Paraguay during the Franciata, Paraguayan exports had suffered in their traditional markets. This was especially true of yerba, which before 1810 had been exported by the millions of pounds to markets in the Río de la Plata, Chile, Peru, and even Ecuador. There is no doubt that during the rule of the Caraí these markets were largely lost, as only a trade sufficient to finance arms purchases was permitted.

With Paraguay restricting its exports of the tea, Brazil and Corrientes both expanded theirs to satisfy the thirsty millions. One Brazilian historian has pointed out that, due to Paraguay's isolation, "Paraná mate encountered an open door for its implantation and consolidation of markets." Later, when Carlos Antonio opened his nation's commercial arteries more fully, he found his yerba, collected wild, having to compete with plantation-grown tea from Brazil. He responded by "selling its product at a price much lower than" Brazil's. He cut the profit margin drastically on the government yerba commerce because of the need to re-enter the old markets and generate the cash needed for arms purchases.[4]

By 1845 there were enough foreign merchants calling at Pilar, despite the dangers along the river route, for López to publish a decree defining their status. This decree, which allowed the merchants freedom in their own transactions, also stipulated that they were not to move about Paraguay without special license. They were to pay only standard import-export taxes, and, if they did not openly flaunt it, they were free to practice the Protestant version of Christianity.[5]

Complete data on this commerce exists for the year 1846 and provides insight into a changing Paraguay. Despite the very difficult conditions present that year downstream, the trade survived. In the first half of the year, twenty-six vessels put into Pilar for trade. Thirteen of the ships were Paraguayan (of small dimensions), seven were Argentine, four were Correntino, and two were Spanish. Together, the ships registered cargos valued at 97,966 pesos at the Pilar customs house, on which a duty of 21 percent was paid. Paraguayan vessels carried, by value, some 35 percent of the total.[6]   The cargos were varied. Paraguayan ships, for the most part state-owned, carried goods acquired by the government. Foreign vessels generally hauled consumer articles. A frequent part of many cargos was "armaments and other articles of war," and bars of iron and other metals, chains, and gunpowder were also common. One Paraguayan ship carried, among other things, a hundred bayonetted rifles, listed at eleven pesos each. In addition, one could find wool, silk, hardware, wine, cotton cloth, hats, handkerchiefs, thread, paper, and salt.

At Ytapúa there was far less activity. In the same period, a caravan arrived from São Borja or towns in Corrientes about once a month. These well-guarded caravans of high-wheeled, leather-roofed carts, two Brazilian and four Correntino, carried goods whose value totaled 27,701 pesos, mostly cloth and clothing. Three individual Paraguayan carts also made the trip from São Borja, carrying 2,118 pesos' worth of iron, and "a machine for working iron."[7]

The second half of the year witnessed a decrease in activity at Pilar, even though this is normally the season for high water in the river. Fourteen boats— ten Paraguayan, two Brazilian, one Portuguese, and one Spanish—dropped anchor in the shallow port, carrying 46,603 pesos' worth of cargo. National vessels hauled 86 percent of all goods by value. By land, five caravans—three Correntino and two Brazilian—arrived at Ytapúa between July and December, with 5,354 pesos' worth of cloth. In all the year, the Paraguayan government collected some 35,832 pesos of import taxes and an unknown amount in export duties (which averaged only 5 percent of value).[8]

Additional data for 1847 suggest that the above pattern was common until the opening of the rivers in 1852. A slightly higher percentage of foreign vessels reached Pilar in 1847, with a more variegated cargo, mainly of European origin, such as chocolate, Spanish cloth, French "spirituous beverages," and Portuguese silk. Although several Uruguayan vessels made it upstream, most foreign commerce was carried under the Argentine flag. Thus, as during the Franciata, neither hostility nor non-recognition precluded trade.[9]

In these years a foreign merchant community was building at Pilar, and police reports of the era mention Italians, Spaniards, Correntinos, Entrerrianos, Chileans, Germans, Swiss, Uruguayans, and Colombians, as well as a sizeable number of French and British merchant-adventurers.[10] Many of the men who applied for naturalization in this decade were merchants (for the most part Spaniards and Argentines), perhaps seeking to guarantee their commercial position in Paraguay. With citizenship they could, and often did, travel to and reside in Asunción, establishing their import businesses and retail outlets there.[11]   All foreign merchants, however, had to keep in mind that although they could seek diplomatic aid in other exotic ports, in Pilar they could not. In all Paraguay there was no European diplomatic representative until 1853, and only Brazilian interests were maintained on a fairly steady basis.[12]

Carlos Antonio, to achieve even part of his plans for his nation, would have to do better. Lack of foreign recognition, anarchy in the Litoral provinces, and control by Rosas of the rivers, permitted only a trickle of the potential commerce to seep through to Pilar. After 1852, with both recognition and free navigation assured, the Corpulent Despot could at last turn the trickle into a veritable stream and embark on his startlingly rapid modernization of Paraguay.

The State Transcends the Man

As has been noted, El Supremo vastly expanded the scope of the national patrimony through major expropriations of private and Church lands. Carlos Antonio went farther, claiming new lands and properties for the state, creating a lucrative network that probably came to include at least half of all lands in eastern Paraguay as well as the entire Chaco. So much revenue did the state lands provide that López had almost no need for internal taxation to help finance his modernization campaign.[13] The millions of pesos in rents and from the sale of state produce explain how a small, rural, and supposedly poor nation could pay for its own modernization in the markets of Europe without the need for foreign investment capital or loans, all on a cash and carry basis.

By a series of decrees in 1843, López simply laid claim to all abandoned lands, under the fiction that these had always been government lands and that he was merely reclaiming them. If a terrain was not in use by a titled possessor, it was, by definition, state property.[14] At the same time, he asserted state ownership of most lands near "vital" frontiers, and allowed the sale of certain state lands to private individuals, who, if they actively worked them, could pay the government off in twenty years at 5 percent of the value per year.

In 1846, in a controversial move, Carlos Antonio declared that all yerba and lumber of export quality was state property, regardless of the fact that it might be growing on private land. Such products could only be exploited with government license (on a bid system), and commerce in the two items was made a state monopoly. The following year, the government began granting licenses to harvest yerba in specified areas.[15]

To round out this domination of man and land by the state, López issued a decree in 1848 that has usually been interpreted in light of its impressive "liberal" rhetoric. The decree "declares Citizens of the Republic the natural Indians of the twenty-one pueblos of . . . Ypané, Atirá, Guarambaré, Ytá, Yaguarón, Altos, Tobatí, Belén, San Estanislao, Ytapé, San Joaquín, Caazapá, El Carmen, Yutí, Santa María de Fe, Santa Rosa, San Ygnacio, Santiago, San Cosme, Trinidad, and Jesús."[16] A lovely sentiment, followed by more sinister articles. Each pueblo would be divested of its cabildo and its segregated status, and its men would be liable for regular military service. They would also, beginning in 1852, pay all agricultural and pastoral taxes, *and* almost all of the communal pueblo lands, in addition to the considerable properties owned by the cabildos, passed to the state. With little exaggeration, it may be said that the state acquired perhaps 45,000 new sharecroppers and renters, placing under its control the last demographic nuclei that had been somewhat independent.

As social historian Carlos Pastore, one of the few scholars to fully understand the decree, put it: "The volume of the contribution of the pueblos of Indian origin to the patrimony of the state was important. It consisted of extensive areas of pastoral and agricultural lands, huge forests of yerba and construction lumber, and no less than 200,000 head of cattle and horses."[17]

Nor was Carlos Antonio as selfless as had been his predecessor. "The President ordered the transferral to members of his family important properties of the state." Son Francisco Solano received a state estancia at Catiguaá, Venancio that of San Joaquín, and Benigno that of San Ygnacio.[18] The identification of the state with its ruler was now almost complete. None of the López family worried much in the future about pocket change, and, in fact, over the years each accumulated (often with title) huge landed domains, as if aping the great estancieros of the pampas. As Harris Warren has written with only slight exaggeration: "Don Carlos loved Paraguay—so much, in fact, that he owned about one-half of the land."[19] The story of the almost psychotic acquisitions of land by Madame Lynch, which would have made her the world's largest individual landowner, is found in a later chapter. A byproduct of state and López family ownership of the bulk of the Paraguayan tierra, and one not coincidental, was its preclusion of the growth of a landed aristocracy in Paraguay. Such a new elite might well have presented a potential danger to the jealous López family, and they effectively blocked the avenue of landowning. So successful were they that when one refers to the Paraguayan elite in the 1840-1870 era, one refers only to the extended López clan.

The Asunción Archive is filled with documents concerning state land rents, and the overall impression given is that Carlos Antonio was bent on creating a nation of tenant farmers. In 1854, in Luque, there were 290 families renting government lands, paying 540 pesos as well as a share of lumber and farm products.[20] In tiny, isolated Caraguatay, 161 men paid 294 pesos, in San Antonio 145 paid 300 pesos, whereas, in Asunción itself, 51 paid 134 pesos. In Quiquió, the lands "that the Yegros used to own but that reverted to the state" were let out to 26 men for 51 pesos, and in miniscule Jesús 167 family heads paid 663 pesos.[21] Rents were kept low and tied to the amount and quality of land rented. In Jesús, for instance, the widow of Antonio Coronel, who rented lands sufficient to graze her 540 beeves and 75 horses, paid 121 pesos rent in 1864; most other renters paid between 1 and 2 pesos for their few hectares.[22]

A very substantial revenue thus flowed in from land rents. Other major components of the state finance system, beyond its profits from yerba and lumber, included the sale of various products collected in the annual agricultural and pastoral taxes levied in kind. These taxes brought a flood of goods to government coffers that was then diverted to auctions, state retail stores, and the state's foreign commerce, being translated into negotiable cash.

Many rural taxes were farmed out. Even foreigners like Eberhard Munck found it profitable to bid at auction for a government license to collect livestock taxes in a given area. In his case, he annually bought the license to collect along the Tebicuari, and he was able to make a very good living by flashing his license, collecting the animals, chasing down deadbeats, and selling the newly-acquired herds at auction, remarking in a letter to a friend that "Here I have good earnings, without need to work more than I care to."[23] Thus the López government was assured of a steady revenue without having to maintain a large, permanent body of tax collectors on salary. Any hostility generated by harsh collectors was directed not at the government but at individual, often foreign licensees.[24]

Beyond the cascade of livestock was the regular sale of surplus animals from the state estancias, involving tens of thousands of head annually. Normally sold at huge public auctions in Asunción, the animals became a major economic, or hard cash, mainstay of the treasury. One brief example: on May 16, 1854, eighty-one piglets from state lands at Carapeguá were sold in a Recoleta auction for 178 pesos, 4 reales.[25]

In all the hemisphere, this political domination of most of a state's natural and other resources was unique, and the López government profited immensely from it. It may be worth noting in some detail one facet of the patrimony and how it served both the state and López.

Tabapí and Surubí: A Tale of Two Estancias

Two typical state estancias of the epoch were those at Tabapí, a slave-run ranch north of shallow lake Ypoá, and Surubí, somewhat larger, just south of Asunción. A glance at Tabapí reveals a good deal about both the Black race in Paraguay and the state estancia system. When Dr. Francia absorbed the lands of the Dominican order at Tabapí into the national patrimony in 1824, the hundreds of free pardos working on the large estancia there ceased to be freemen and became, like the land itself, property of the state. The extant censuses of 1826 and 1830 show an increase in their numbers from 417 to 486 and indicate that between those dates 109 were born, 37 died, and 3 fled: a surprisingly high rate of increase.[26] This extraordinary birth and survival rate continued.

Records reveal that in the two years 1848 and 1849 there were 112 births and only 34 deaths; in 1853, 24 were born and 3 died.[27] A more detailed census of 1854 provides even more graphic proof of a very high birthrate, showing a total population of 682, of whom 44 percent had been born after the Law of Free Womb in 1843. The Tabapí community in that year was composed of 279 males and 403 females. There were 34 complete families with 215 members, 25 widows and 7 widowers as heads of families, and 45 bachelors. Thirty-one percent of all Tabapí pardos were listed as "sick," "blind," or "useless."[28]

Tabapí's heroic birthrate was such that even large-scale sales of "excess" pardos did not reduce the total number, nor did frequent self-purchases. In 1857, an official noted that state slave "Dolores Samaniego wishes to free herself and her liberto children, called José Concepción, six years old, Tereza de Jesús, four years old, and Marco Antonio, five months old, offering . . . 110 pesos." Carlos Antonio assented. At least fifty slaves purchased their freedom and/or that of family members at Tabapí during the López years.[29]

Tabapí, like every state estancia, was expected to be almost entirely self-sufficient and to produce substantial surpluses of animals and other grown or manufactured staples as well. The foreman sent detailed reports to Asunción, and his effectiveness was constantly monitored. The main functions of an estancia continued to be to produce meat on the hoof for the army, cavalry remounts, oxen, hides, wool, and certain foodstuffs. Also common was donation of cattle to help feed the indigent poor or victims of drought, flood, and other natural disasters.[30]

Insight into the livestock production cycle can be had through the remarkably complete reports covering the years 1843 through 1851; these reports show for each year how many animals were consumed on the estancia, were born and died there, and were delivered to the government. In 1844 and 1845, Tabapí, like all estancias, was visited by an epidemic of some kind that killed large numbers of animals. The data show the birth of 14,577 animals, of which 7,092 were delivered to the state, 2,303 were consumed on the estancia, and 3,519 died of disease, snakebite, or accident. A total of 12,914 animals appears in the debit column, leaving a net increase at the end of the period of 1,663 head. In addition, 599 oxen, then as now very valuable animals in a land that moved at the pace of a high-wheeled cart, were delivered to the government, and 771 died. When one remembers that there were eighty-one other estancias and puestos of the state, the importance of the system and its sheer magnitude become apparent. The words "national patrimony" in Paraguay were anything but empty. It is interesting to note that a high level of efficiency was evidently not a major requirement, for, during the period considered, fully a quarter of all animals appearing on the debit side of the ledger died.[31]

An 1861 report indicated the varied scope of production at Tabapí. In that year an inventory showed 5,185 cattle, 436 oxen, 1,831 horses, 2,453 sheep, 16 mules, 7 burros, 52 arrobas of wool, 11 of wax, 1,940 roofing tiles, and 4 iron pots. That year's consumption and delivery[32] was noted:

	Delivered to the state	Consumed or died
hides	70	153
cattle	820	119
bulls	20	0
oxen	49	54
mules	0	2
horses	21	70
sheep	0	136
pigs	9	0
wool	60 arrobas	28
beans	102 sacks	20
rice	1,082 sacks	50
starch	149 sacks	10
corn	1,228 sacks	80
tiles	0	100

Even by current standards in Paraguay, a ranch boasting almost 10,000 head of livestock is the exception.

Other documents afford an idea of what was done with the cattle delivered by Tabapí to the state. In the decade 1855 to 1865, Tabapí drove some 6,475 beeves into the capital to feed the growing garrisons there. In 1864 and 1865, 300 cattle were sent to the army camp at Cerro León, and in 1863 and 1864 a further 550 were dispatched to help provision workers laboring on the railroad.[33] Incomplete as they are, the records do provide at least a partial picture of usage.

Surubí was one of the state's largest estancias, acquired originally from confiscated Jesuit lands. As early as 1832, that estancia reported to El Supremo the branding of 4,000 calves and 414 colts, most of which were added to its already extensive herds.[34] Surubí, however, despite its reputation as a huge and efficient operation, apparently fell on bad times after Francia's death, for we find Carlos Antonio angrily writing a judge at Villeta in 1844 about "the abandonment and bad management of the horse herds at Surubí," noting that "if something is not done soon, there will be no more production." He ordered the judge to visit the estancia with "two intelligent men, to inspect and observe the state and regimen of the estancia" and make a full report to Asunción.[35]

Conditioned to obedience, the judge and his two "intelligent men" reviewed the Surubí operation and sent a long report to López a week later. Describing his companions as "men instructed in the management of rural enterprises," the official had ordered a round-up of all horses on the estancia and its smaller puestos, finding a pathetic 58. He reported to López, however, that the lack of horses was due less to malfeasance than to a current epidemic, and "the extreme scarcity of pasturage caused by the flood that these fields have experienced" recently. The cattle had also suffered, and hundreds had died due to a lack of fodder. He then reviewed the attached puestos:

Paso Laguna: 103 horses, 700 cattle (in poor condition)
Lobato: 150 horses
Ñanducuá: 52 horses, "a few cows"
Ygarapé: 82 horses, "a lot of very thin cows"

More than 500 cattle had died of the epidemic that was sweeping the area, and the survivors were described as "exceedingly thin."[36] A later note concerning available labor indicated that the estancia was understaffed, with only five foremen and nineteen peons.[37] In August, 1848, after labor drafts had almost tripled the workforce but had failed to halt the decline of the herds, the president again wrote the judge, incredulous at the latest report, which showed only 600 cattle remaining at Surubí. "I cannot understand how fifty peons could be maintained there in service to this so-called estancia."[38] With all of this labor available, the judge responded, the government would still have to requisition cattle and horses from other estancias to rebuild the herds.[39] Carlos Antonio went into a rage at this admission, firing back an order to the judge to remove all the foremen, "with their families," from the estancia immediately. He then himself appointed new foremen and ordered the puesto at Nanducuá abandoned, its lands rented out.[40]

On López' orders, an army sergeant went to Surubí and carried out a detailed inventory. Perhaps not to anyone's surprise, he found 147 oxen, 1,499 cattle, 2,266 horses in decent condition and another 66 "ancianos," 463 sheep, 7 mules, and 2 burros. Obviously, foul play was afoot, for the missing animals were not missing after all. Carlos Antonio, after rediscovering his "missing" herds, remedied the situation by sending a force of fifty light-infantrymen to garrison the estancia and discourage further rustling and account juggling.[41]

Strange to say, with only four foremen and eighteen peons, but with fifty guards, Surubí once more began to prosper.[42] In 1850, the estancia reported 3,527 horses, 478 oxen, and 2,223 cattle, plus "a few" sheep and other animals.[43] A note from the new judge at Villeta in mid-1850 goes far to explain the earlier problem. He wrote concerning the expulsion of Cayetano

Aquino and Miguel Ortíz, both "known thieves." Aquino had been foreman at Paso Laguna and Ñanducuá during the time of the disappearing animals and was "a convicted cattle thief." Ortíz had practically looted the Nanducuá puesto, his booty "hauled away by his family in carts belonging to the state."[44]

Reports from 1851 reveal tranquility and prosperity, the only problem being "the tigers [jaguars] that prey on the state production."[45] In 1845, 1,286 calves and 440 colts were branded, and a state slave, Juan Rodríguez, was named foreman at Paso Laguna.[46] Two years later, another slave, Anacleto Dias, was named foreman at Lobato, and a new puesto was established at Chaparro with an initial 1,050 animals. The estancia was again on its feet.[47] Due to control of thieves, careful management, and extra, "seed" cattle brought in from other ranches, Surubí was rebuilt and between 1856 and 1865 contributed many thousands of head of cattle to the Asunción garrisons. The 1864 survey describes a flourishing estancia, again one of the nation's largest, running 12,000 cattle, 603 oxen, 1,714 horses, and 100 sheep.[48] The peculation at Surubí was a rare occurrence, but it illustrates not only that crime had failed to disappear in Paraguay but also that "white collar crime" existed even in the bosom of the state.

9. The Diplomacy of Frustration

If Carlos Antonio was astonishingly successful in organizing his state internally, he faced frustration, threat, confusion, and disappointment in his dealings with foreign powers. Until 1852, this was due for the most part to the continued enmity of Juan Manuel de Rosas and his control of the Río Paraná. After that date, Paraguay caused its own problems.

The Corrientes Connection

Paraguayans, for geographical, racial, and linguistic reasons, have always felt a certain closeness to the people of Corrientes, a sentiment often reciprocated, for the Guaraní-speaking mestizos of Corrientes were more often in accord with policies emanating from Asunción than those from white Buenos Aires. As a result, the first Paraguayan diplomatic "success" came with their provincial neighbor—a success that was to prove an embarrassment, and a costly one, in a number of ways. That province had openly rebelled against Rosas in 1839, in effect establishing itself as an independent state. Underpopulated, with only some 20,000 inhabitants, Corrientes was beset by almost as many problems as it had people. Harassed by internal factionalism that approached civil war, mauled by institutionalized banditry and invasion by pro-Rosas forces, Corrientes had in vain asked the aging Dr. Francia for aid, and many of its people had escaped northward to save their lives.

Carlos Antonio hoped that the Correntinos would be successful in weakening the power of Rosas, but he was unwilling to take an active role in the struggle. Despite his reticence, he was willing to negotiate with the beleaguered Correntinos, and in mid-1841, to the surprise and disgust of the Porteños, two treaties were signed by representatives of Paraguay and Corrientes. The July 31 treaties, which were speedily ratified, dealt with boundaries and commerce. The river fords of Itatí, Yabebirí, and Ytapúa on the Alto Paraná were declared open for commerce, as was the port of Pilar, and Paso de Patria was designated as the route for all official contact, to be jointly patrolled. Tax schedules would be worked out by a future joint commission. López took advantage of Corrientes's desperate position to stipulate that Candelaria was Paraguayan, but the Paraná island of Apipé was recognized as Correntino. In homage to the racial and linguistic unity of the two parties, it was declared that "the sons of both States will be considered native of one and the other. . . with free use of their Rights." On ratification, some fifty Correntinos languishing in Paraguay jails were released.[1]

It is fair to say that the treaties were viewed by López as temporary measures to restore stability and some commerce along the volatile border.[2] The cost of these treaties, however, was to be inordinately high for Paraguay, for in recognizing Correntino independence López weakened the Paraguayan position in the more crucial negotiations with Rosas. Porteño foreign minister Felipe Araña wrote in 1842 that "if it had not been for the infamous [General Pedro] Ferré," rebel governor of Corrientes, an accord would have been possible between Rosas and López. The Paraguayan leader compounded his problems with Buenos Aires by permitting Ferré, fleeing from the collapse of his government, to pass through Paraguay, when it was well known that Rosas wanted to capture and make an example of the Correntino.[3]

Alarums and Excursions: The Early Diplomacy

How to steer Paraguay through the treacherous shoals of regional anarchy would be López's main concern for many years. His problem was twofold: to obtain recognition of Paraguayan independence from important nations and to negotiate free transit of the Plata River system. Rosas was violently opposed to both goals, and other nations hesitated to accede to either for fear of antagonizing the Porteño leader. Some powers would recognize Paraguay *if* the rivers were open, and others would deal with the free navigation issue only once Rosas had recognized Paraguay. In this conundrum, Carlos Antonio would have to deal first with Rosas. While he was plotting the course of his Argentine policy, news reached him of an "official" British visitor. Mr. George R. Gordon, consular official at the British legation in Rio de Janeiro, had, on Foreign Office orders, traveled the long, overland route to Ytapúa, whence he rode on to Asunción in October, 1842. Ordered "to direct his attention to the political condition of the Country—the disposition of the Gov^t with respect to commercial intercourse . . . and, generally, the commercial resources and capabilities of the Country," Gordon carried no authority to conclude any formal acts or treaties.[4] López, hoping otherwise, received the envoy with as much opulence as the city could provide. Over a period of weeks, between fetes, dinners, and other evidence of hospitality, López slowly learned that Gordon had no powers at all, and when that gentleman talked seriously of Paraguayan trade concessions, the consul made it clear that until the issue of recognition was considered there could be no Paraguayan concessions. Having worn out his welcome, Gordon very unwisely became involved in a pet scheme to inoculate Paraguayans against smallpox. Shocked by the visitor's taking such liberty without government permission, López had him ejected from the country preemptorily. An angry and disillusioned Carlos Antonio would not in the future be so gracious and open to a British representative, and the British foreign minister noted in a report on the Gordon fiasco, "It would not be prudent to make this defeat public."[5]

The three weeks spent by Gordon in Asunción sufficed to impress on López the need to deal directly with Rosas, since it seemed that European powers were not about to dignify his nation's independence with formal recognition as long as the Porteño considered it a mere province rightly ruled from Buenos Aires.

In late 1842, to provide sanction for his diplomatic offensive, López decided to call a congress. When it met, some of its members were not sure just why they were in the capital and proposed López as president, but, when the dust had settled, Carlos Antonio had full consent to conduct negotiations with foreign powers as he saw fit. This congress, for the books, and to avoid confusion abroad, formally stated that "Independence and Emancipation are solemn and incontestable," and went on to state that Paraguay, as an independent nation, was not the property of any one man or family—a statement that would have brought guffaws a decade later. For reasons not at all clear, congress also chose this moment to pass the Law of Free Womb. Before dissolving itself, the assembly also presented Paraguay with the trappings of sovereignty, choosing a new flag and coat of arms and authorizing the coining of money.[6] With this formal affirmation of independence and with his own authority buttressed, Don Carlos began his campaign to open Paraguay.

Having learned a bitter lesson from the Corrientes connection, López on December 28, 1842, sent Rosas an official reportage of the recent congress, duly informing him of Paraguayan independence, now ratified by the "People," and his country's strict policy of "Neutrality in the dissentions which are agitating neighbor States." It was also announced that, as a sovereign state, Paraguay would soon send "an accredited Citizen" for diplomatic talks with Porteño authorities.[7]

This "open" policy failed to impress the caudillo of the south, and the Paraguayan envoy, Government Secretary Andrés Gill, though well treated in Buenos Aires, was completely rebuffed on the question of recognition. In fact, in a classic diplomatic put-down, Rosas wrote López in April, 1843, ignoring the entire question and complimenting Gill's personal qualities, stating that "he has been lodged and received as an employee of Your Excellency."[8] Playing it safe, the Porteño refrained from discussing the major Paraguayan issues, yet took care not to overtly offend the upriver supplicants.

Perhaps because of this blasé tone, López decided to send another special agent to Buenos Aires, Manuel Pedro de la Peña, who brought in his entourage the young Francisco Solano López. Again the Paraguayans met with a run-around, although it seems that this time Rosas was a bit more frank, admitting that the times were not auspicious for talk of Paraguayan independence, because the regional anarchy made such a distinction meaningless and quite possibly dangerous. One thing the mission did accomplish was to introduce the young López to a wider, more sophisticated world, a world to which he would long to return. Rosas wrote the consuls in mid-1844 that he had permitted the envoys to sell the trade goods that had accompanied them, but, as far as more "important" decisions went, "this Government is not obliged to consider anything else, impelled by circumstances of war."[9]

The rivers remained closed because of unrest and rebellion in the Litoral provinces, and, beginning in 1845, an Anglo-French blockade of Buenos Aires. Hoping to assuage Rosas, Carlos Antonio cut off all contact with Corrientes, but, in spite of renewed supplications to the Porteño, no advantages were gained. As the chaos downriver worsened, López ordered Paraguayan warships to convoy national and foreign commercial vessels through dangerous Correntino waters, prompting the governor of that province to demand in 1844 "a satisfactory explanation of this hostile act."[10]

Although he had no success with Buenos Aires or other major powers on the issue of recognition, Carlos Antonio had learned in mid-1843 that the Republic of Bolivia had officially recognized Paraguayan sovereignty, a small crack in the dike, widened within a year by Chile's following suit. But for all this, the central problem remained the attitude of Rosas.

As Carlos Antonio was also busily organizing his own political recognition within Paraguay, much of 1843 and early 1844 was spent in domestic campaigning. It was known that Roque Alonso was almost an inert mass and that López had carried the government alone on his flabby shoulders, so the outcome of the congress scheduled to meet in March, 1844, was never in doubt.

On March 13, some 300 delegates assembled at the Church of San Francisco to hear Assembly Chairman López regale them with nationalistic speeches and tales of his own heroic achievements. Within two days López was chosen president "by acclamation," and an embryonic organic law was promulgated. This proto-constitution, drafted by López himself, was simply entitled "The Law That Establishes the Political Administration of the Republic of Paraguay." It may well have been, as Dr. Chaves assures us, "a step forward toward democracy,"[11] but it is notable, if not unique, among organic laws in not containing anywhere in its text the word "liberty." The 1844 document created an extremely centralized, legitimized dictatorship, allowing all powers to reside with the president. Despite a theoretical tripartite division of government functions, the president was supreme arbiter in all spheres and was permitted to do virtually anything so long as he justified his actions with the phrase "maintain order." Democratic trappings notwithstanding, the "constitution" basically institutionalized and legalized the system created by El Supremo, cloaking it scantily with modern rhetoric.

Before breaking off its meetings, the congress enjoined the president to send six students to Europe for training in law, pharmacy, and art, to serve on their return as teachers. He was also authorized to contract foreign medical experts. Within a decade these first seeds would become mighty oaks. López, who was to rule for a period of ten years, was assigned 8,000 pesos per annum in salary.

The Corrientes Connection: Part Two

In mid-1845, with an Anglo-French squadron blockading Buenos Aires and with Porteño strength tied up in an imperialistic war in Uruguay, López, quick to sense an opportunity, again began serious talks with Corrientes, newly disaffected. After months of these talks, the Corpulent Despot signed a treaty on November 11, 1845, that committed Paraguay and Corrientes to an offensive-defensive alliance against Rosas. Paraguay agreed to send troops to Corrientes to join forces with General José María Paz, "Allied" commander. Corrientes formally recognized Paraguayan independence.[12]

Within weeks, several thousand Paraguayan infantry and cavalry, led by newly-commissioned, eighteen-year-old Brigadier General Francisco Solano López, crossed into Corrientes. The youngster, however, was not entirely left to his own devices, as is commonly thought, for Carlos Antonio did not see him as so precocious as have later historians. A Paraguayan flotilla went along, commanded by Hungarian Cavalry Lt. Col. Francisco Wisner de Morgenstern, who was also chief advisor to the teenage general. Physically closer to López was the eccentric Colombian freebooter Col. Pedro Abad Oro, one of the first foreign military experts contracted by Carlos Antonio. He acted as Francisco Solano's chief of staff.[13] Guided by a set of almost laughably complete instructions from his father, the younger López had with him only a fraction of the troops called for by the recent treaty.[14]

These troops were, in the eyes of their allies, in deplorable condition. Commanding General Paz, recovering from his shock at seeing the Paraguayan force for the first time, commented, "It was an unformed mass, without instruction, without organization, without discipline, and ignorant of the first rudiments of war." He continued, "The Paraguayan Infantry was so rustic that it did not know how to load or fire its weapons," and, of the cavalry, Paz bemoaned their lack of officers, noting that "they were so badly mounted . . . not through not having been given horses, but because they did not care for them and destroyed them in a few days." Of the young general, Paz was more sympathetic: "Perhaps the young General Francisco S. López is adorned with lovely personal qualities, but [he has] no military knowledge and, what is more, not the slightest idea of war and how to wage it."[15]

While Carlos Antonio belatedly mobilized the militia, his son chose to retreat toward the border as enemy forces approached the allied army in March, 1845. Due to his discretion, the ineffectual Paraguayan contingent was not destroyed with the rest of its allies and was able to cross the Paraná without casualties in early April, just before a disenchanted General Paz himself fled into Paraguay. So ended Paraguay's first military diplomacy and Francisco Solano's second trip abroad.

In late April, his forces once again safely in Paraguay, Carlos Antonio dissolved the Correntino alliance, charging his neighbors with failure to cooperate and writing that "the European intervention mysteriously continues." As long as it did, wrote López, any alliance between the two Guaraní-speaking entities "would be premature and dangerous." With this cryptic note, he cut the Correntino connection, although in 1847 he did send Wisner and some warships to Corrientes port to aid some friendly Correntinos.[16]

A Light in the Tunnel

López did not expend all of his diplomatic energies on the Rosas government, but simultaneously attempted to gain recognition from the United States, Brazil, and the European powers, especially Britain. Recognition from several of these would go far to open the river system, regardless of Porteño policy.

As early as 1842, Consul López had initiated a steady correspondence with British diplomats in Buenos Aires, and although he was chagrined that those commerce-minded gentlemen would not agree to "explicit recognition of our Independence," he several times sent them "relevant documents" that sustained the Paraguayan case.[17] These documents were forwarded to the Foreign Office for consideration, and López hoped that growing tension between Rosas and Britain would work in his favor.

Diplomat W. E. Ouseley wrote López from Buenos Aires in 1845, in gratifying, if over-optimistic, terms that the wishes of his government "accord entirely with those of Paraguay in seeking the liberation of that State from the political isolation and commercial dependence enforced by Buenos Aires." Ouseley then asked that special Paraguayan agents be sent to Montevideo under British protection, and informed López that he had recently urged his government to recognize the independence of Paraguay without delay.[18] In a later note, in which he personally recognized that independence, Ouseley waxed enthusiastic concerning future ties between the two nations.[19] This note arrived in Asunción about the same time the last troopers of the Paraguayan adventure in Corrientes were crossing the river into Paraguay.

In July, 1845, the anti-Rosas government of Uruguay recognized Paraguayan independence, and late that year France and Britain, themselves blockading Buenos Aires, determined to free the interior Paraná system by smashing Rosas's Litoral blockade. A convoy of some seventy merchant ships, escorted by the French war steamer *Fulton,* proceeded upriver. An Anglo-French squadron cleared the way, defeating a Porteño blocking flotilla in the short, sharp combat at Obligado in December.

On January 15, 1846, the merchant fleet dropped anchor in Asunción harbor. On board the *Fulton* were the commanders of the British and French fleets blockading Buenos Aires and some diplomatic agents from Montevideo. As trade commenced, so did diplomatic soundings, but despite the flattering attentions of the European envoys, López remained aloof, claiming that there could be no serious commercial agreements without prior and formal recognition of Paraguayan sovereignty.[20]

American diplomat-entrepreneur Edward Augustus Hopkins, in Asunción at the time, noted that the *Fulton* was considered a true wonder in the city, the first steamer to appear in Paraguayan waters. "She, therefore, naturally excited a degree of wonder" of tremendous proportions among the isolated Paraguayans.[21] Despite the novelty, Hopkins made a point of mentioning that not one official Paraguayan accepted an invitation to come on board. The steamer did carry, however, Bernardo Jovellanos and Anastacio González when it cast off, López's agents bound for Montevideo.[22]

When the fleet departed Paraguayan waters, little had changed. The net again dropped over Paraguay, and the Porteño stranglehold on the river resumed. Bearing López's terms for trade concessions and treaties, the European agents were rebuffed by their home governments, which were unwilling to offer recognition to Paraguay until the regional situation stabilized.

Enter Edward Hopkins, Stage Right

The United States also vacillated in its attitude toward Paraguay. Failing

to respond to preliminary feelers from Carlos Antonio, the State Department
became upset with the Anglo-French intervention at Buenos Aires, interpreted
in Washington as a dangerous adventure contrary to the tenets of the vague
Monroe Doctrine. In mid-1845, Secretary of State James Buchanan ordered
Edward A. Hopkins to proceed to Asunción and report on the general situation.
Hopkins's voluminous instructions called for a good return on his six-dollar
daily wage. He was to investigate the "character" of Paraguay and the "intel-
ligence of its inhabitants," and report on the nature of the government, the
nation's military potential, its financial status, its leading citizens, and the
racial makeup of its people. He was also to "take advantage of any favorable
occasion to inform the Paraguayan Government of the danger of forming
embarrassing alliances with other nations or conferring commercial advantages
to one nation at the cost of others."[23]

After a hectic journey, Hopkins arrived at Asunción on November 8, 1845,
and was very cordially received by López, who assumed more of the mission
than he should have. The optimistic president welcomed the American with
uncharacteristic ostentation and warmth. But the warmth soon disappeared
as the president learned in the course of one interview that Hopkins brought
no solid credentials, no notice of diplomatic recognition, and no powers to
propose treaties. Carlos Antonio, affronted by the fact that Hopkins was
merely a well-dressed spy, terminated the audience abruptly.[24]

The American envoy was disappointed but hardly undone. He soon let it
leak out that his mission *would* permit him to act as mediator between Paraguay and Rosas, and once the news reached López, the president gave his
blessing to the idea, indicating also a degree of interest in Hopkins's personal
scheme to link Paraguay with the world beyond through a steam navigation
company. Well did the American realize that if he were successful in the
former, he could count on a Paraguayan government charter and perhaps
financial support for the latter endeavor.[25]

After two months in Asunción, Hopkins parted for Rio de Janeiro to
begin his mediation with the aid of American Minister Henry A. Wise and
Argentine chargé General J. Guido. Buoyed by Wise's enthusiasm and by
Guido's naive and presumptuous belief that his nation would soon recognize
Paraguay, Hopkins traveled to Buenos Aires, hoping to directly negotiate with
Rosas. The Porteño, however, aware of Hopkins's total lack of authority,
refused to meet him, and the issue was handled through the offices of United
States chargé William Brent, Jr. In March, 1846, after discussions with Brent,
Rosas announced his government's recognition of the territorial integrity of
the *Province* of Paraguay and its independence in internal administration.[26]
This announcement, in itself almost a bad joke, deflated Hopkins and he left
Buenos Aires, writing López from Montevideo concerning his failure but

promising to work for United States recognition. The quixotic Hopkins would rise from the ashes.

The Candelaria Dream

The problem with Argentina remained, heightened by an accord signed in 1847 by Buenos Aires and Corrientes reestablishing peace and the subordination of the latter to the former. Paraguay was invited to join in the signing of this agreement, but López refused, and, fearing that Rosas would turn his full attention to Paraguay, he prepared his nation for war.[27]

Toward the end of 1847, new military units were raised, some militia forces were mobilized, and a major military camp was established near the main ford at Paso de Patria. In January, 1848, López announced that Paraguay would "not tolerate, as in the past, that inhabitants of the neighboring Province of Corrientes enter the Río Paraná and establish harvests or lumbering on the banks or islands of said river." He ordered that the Paraguayan commander on the Paraná island of Atajo (who had just expelled all Correntinos from that island and Apipé) vigorously patrol the river and, if necessary, use force to guarantee Paraguayan rights there. The small fleet was sent to aid defenses along the southern border.[28]

In April, López extended permission for people of the district of Santa Rosa to harvest yerba in Candelaria.[29] More and more, Paraguay was staking a claim to the "disputed" borders. Carlos Antonio wrote the Pilar police chief in August, warning him that "the enemy of the Republic, Governor Rosas of Buenos Aires, will be attempting to introduce emissaries and agents into Paraguay who will sow division among" us.[30] At about the same time he ordered an expedition into the Chaco to check for unauthorized foreigners and report on potential invasion routes that an enemy might utilize during wartime.[31]

He also reorganized the frontier militia, decreeing that all pueblos along the Alto Paraná maintain picked units of fifty cavalry each, ready to ride at a moment's notice. He informed a senior officer in the south, Wisner, that he should watch out for spies and arrest every person found on the islands of Apipé and Yaci-retá, since no commerce was now permitted there. Wisner was to exercise emergency powers over the threatened southern partidos.[32]

The following year, as Francia had done a generation earlier, López moved to assure physical control of Candelaria and easy communications with Brazil. In June, he instructed Wisner to take a force of 1,000 infantry, 600 cavalry, and an artillery battery and cross into Candelaria. He was to garrison several points, patrol the area all the way to the Río Uruguay, and, if possible, purchase up to 2,000 muskets from Brazilian authorities.[33] López next informed his people of his precautions, explaining that "the right of the Republic to the territory between the Paraná and the Uruguay is incontestable." Further: "This operation presents the advantage of breaking the isolation of the Republic by land, putting it in correspondence with the Empire of Brazil in order to allow the purchase and introduction of armaments, munitions, and all types of warlike instruments."[34]

Apparently the less than brilliant leadership displayed by Francisco Solano in Corrientes led the senior López to utilize a true professional to conduct this important campaign. Wisner handled himself and his troops well, and Candelaria was once more effectively Paraguayan. Building large military complexes at Tranquera de Loreto and San Miguel, he requested and received reinforcements in 1849. A report shows that late that year an artillery squadron, a cavalry regiment, and an infantry battalion were concentrated at San Miguel, and that at the Tranquera there were another artillery squadron, several war vessels, three infantry battalions, parts of two cavalry regiments, and assorted smaller units. The combined strength in these places was a well-armed elite force of 117 officers and 2,656 men. An interesting note was appended to the report: two officers were carried as "executed."[35] These had displayed more fright than fight in the face of the enemy.

To more fully animate the defensive and preemptive operations, Carlos Antonio left Asunción to tour the potentially threatened border areas and inspire local garrisons. Leaving treasury minister Mariano González behind as temporary vice-president and his son Venancio as military commander of Asunción, the Corpulent Despot traveled south to Villa Oliva, Villa Franca, Pilar, Curupaití, and Paso de Patria, at which point he tarried two months encouraging his soldiers to stand fast. At Paso de Patria, he issued a stirring paean of praise to his recruits, who "are invincible, struggling for their homes, their families, and National Independence." In fact, they were really only struggling with boredom and dysentery, but he reminded his troops: "Soldiers, I repeat and assure you, we do not arm ourselves except to command respect for our territory and maintain neutrality."[36]

Even though there were certain problems to be faced with Brazil, López knew that the land bridge across Candelaria offered the only possible route out of isolation as long as Rosas kept the rivers closed. For this reason he risked war. Paraguayan forces were divided into several divisions, and, after the campaign had begun, Francisco Solano took command of one himself, moving deep into Corrientes, where he collided with units from that province and from Entre Ríos, engaging in short battles in July, August, and September, 1849. Bested by troops almost as rustic as his own, López was forced to retreat, ceasing operations in Corrientes proper.[37] In late 1849, a Paraguayan expedition crossed the Paraná to briefly hold the small but venerated religious center of Itatí, aiding the escape of refugees from Rosas's forces. As they recrossed the river, the troops brought along the famous image of the Virgin of Itatí.[38] In 1850 and 1851, Paraguayan forces again moved into Correntino territory on limited maneuvers, and cavalry "made circuits through the terrain of Santo Thomé." War was averted largely by luck and the fact that Entre Ríos caudillo Justo José Urquiza turned against Rosas about the same time that Brazil and Paraguay signed an alliance.[39]

In control of an expanded Candelaria and a secure southern border, Carlos Antonio once more turned to Rosas in 1849, urging a long-overdue rapprochement. This detente, as it were, should be based on a treaty of friendship, commerce, and free navigation, leaving questions of recognition and limits to be discussed later through formal diplomatic channels.[40] Rosas, however, angered by what he considered a Paraguayan invasion of Candelaria and Corrientes, hardened his position. In November, 1849, the Buenos Aires Provincial Assembly authorized Rosas "to dispose, without any limits, the reincorporation of the Province of Paraguay into the Argentine Confederation."[41] This authorization, coming as it did with the end of the European intervention, worried López, who now suspected that the Porteño would turn his full energies to settling the "Paraguayan Problem."

The Opening of Paraguay and the Return of Edward Hopkins

It was at this juncture that Edward A. Hopkins returned to Paraguay, in a purely unofficial capacity. Having lost all faith in the idea of negotiating with Rosas, the young American had other plans. He blithely proposed to López that he be appointed an admiral in the Paraguayan navy, and offered to build a ship of his own special design. This ship, captained by "Admiral" Hopkins and manned mostly by North Americans, would sail to Buenos Aires, where its commander would simply kidnap Rosas, thereby solving the thorny diplomatic questions with gaudy yanqui flair. All he needed from López, said Hopkins, was about 100,000 pesos to help finance the venture. Carlos Antonio, perhaps not knowing whether to laugh or cry, demurred.[42]

Partly owing to the deterioration of the situation in the south, López turned to Brazil and in December, 1850, signed an alliance with the empire. Clearly directed against Buenos Aires, the treaty called for offensive and defensive military cooperation in the event of hostilities and guaranteed free transit of internal waterways.

In May, 1852, caudillo Urquiza raised an anti-Rosas army in his province of Entre Ríos, and less than four weeks later his agents in Montevideo signed a treaty committing Entre Ríos, Corrientes, Uruguay, and Brazil to go to war in order to depose Rosas. One article mentioned that "the Government of

Paraguay is invited to enter in the alliance," but López showed himself cautious. When the allies overthrew the Porteño levies later in the year, there were no Paraguayan units in their army and Paraguay had lost the opportunity to influence the diplomatic future of the region.[43]

At last and at least, however, the rivers were about to open. Victorious Urquiza sent Dr. Santiago Derqui to Asunción to negotiate the recognition question, and on July 17, 1852, the Argentine Confederation officially recognized the independence of Paraguay and its rights to free navigation.[44] A slight snag developed the same year, however, when Argentine troops entered Candelaria, which was eventually to be turned over to the Confederation, and López wrote a sharp note to Buenos Aires, warning those authorities not to expect "the delivery of the Territory of Misiones before definitive ratification" of the 1852 treaty by both signatories. He did, however, offer Urquiza up to 20,000 Paraguayan troops in case of a Porteño revolt.[45]

Within a year, Britain, France, Sardinia, and the United States followed the Argentine example, dominoes in the wake of Rosas's fall. In each case, recognition was followed with treaties of friendship, commerce, and navigation.

The Empire: Friends as Enemies

Closely related to Carlos Antonio's jousting with Rosas was his policy toward his other giant neighbor. As with relations with Argentina, this became an unreal kaleidoscope of abrazos and military clashes. There seems little doubt that the Brazilians, aware as they were of the balance of power problem in the region, tended to favor the interests of buffer state Paraguay so long as it was threatened by Rosas. Certainly they did not want to see in Paraguay a replay of Rosista intervention in Uruguay. As the larger of the regional behemoths, Brazil wished to further its own short- and long-term interests by restricting Argentine territorial expansion and protecting both buffer states: however, it was hoped that this could be done without causing a war. The only complication in the parqueted halls of Cateté and Itamaratí was an almost reflexive Brazilian compulsion to nibble away at Paraguay's borders.

Brazilian commercial and, in fact, semi-official diplomatic contact with Paraguay had never halted, but in the first years after Francia's demise the regency council in Rio, awaiting the coming of age of the new emperor, split factionally within itself and, trying to hold Brazil together in the face of endemic revolution, made no move to incur the wrath of Rosas. By late 1843, however, the regency considered it more dangerous to placate than annoy him, and official policy swung 180 degrees. The decision was made to recognize Paraguayan independence.

Claiming that Brazil had recognized Paraguay in 1824 by posting Correa da Câmara to Asunción and hence was not embarking on a new policy but merely formalizing an old one, the Brazilian government sent special diplomatic agent José Antônio Pimenta Bueno to Paraguay in mid-1844. His ride from Ytapúa to the capital became, in one writer's words, "a veritable triumphal march." Great things were expected from him.[46] On September 14, dressed in the garish diplomatic costume of the epoch, he presented his official credentials, together with letters from the young emperor, to Carlos Antonio, in what to Paraguayans was an emotional ceremony. Among the documents presented was a formal recognition of Paraguayan sovereignty by the empire. Pimenta Bueno was authorized to remain in Asunción as Brazilian minister resident, with full powers to negotiate treaties. Brazil had done what it could, by this maneuver, to strengthen Paraguay's position vis-à-vis Rosas.[47]

The Brazilian immediately proposed a treaty with Paraguay, a proposition quickly accepted by López. The accord was signed on October 7, 1844, an agreement on alliance, commerce, extradition, free navigation, and limits. Because it saw war with Rosas as inevitable in 1844 after witnessing his intervention in Uruguay, Brazil was desirous of guaranteeing its flanks and gaining an ally at the same time, and both signatories agreed to come to one another's aid in case of attack by a third party. In this epoch, Rosas was becoming "third party" to many a treaty. A commission was to be appointed to "establish and recognize the limits indicated by the Treaty of San Ildefonso of October 1, 1777," and the 1844 accord itself would be considered for renewal in 1852.[48]

Carlos Antonio was a happy man on October 7, for it seemed that he had gained more than a protective alliance with an erstwhile enemy. If indeed the borders stipulated in 1777 were restored to Paraguay, the republic would gain some 30,000 square miles of territory currently held by Brazil. Quickly the Corpulent Despot dispatched a team of military engineers north to draw maps of the contested territory.

Unfortunately for López, the treaty was too good to be true. In Rio de Janeiro, Emperor Pedro II and his advisors were horrified when they read the section on limits, which constituted, in effect, Pimenta Bueno's promise to return to Paraguay a large chunk of what had been for a century Brazil. For a long year, silence was the only message from Cateté and, late in 1845 only, came a short note explaining that the treaty would not be ratified in Rio because of the question of limits.[49]

This news depressed López, coming as it did when his eldest son was leading forces into Corrientes, an expedition that might well prompt Rosas to retaliate, which threat in turn made the Brazilian treaty all the more valuable to Asunción. Carlos Antonio would not have plunged into Corrientes if he had previously known of the death of his major insurance policy, the accord of 1844. Despite the contretemps, little had been lost: Paraguay was still recognized, a Brazilian diplomat was posted in Asunción, commerce between the two nations was growing, and relations were at least stable and courteous.

López, out on a limb, responded to the Brazilian negative in several ways. Early in 1846 he appointed urbane Juan Andrés Gelly to be "Temporary and Special Agent" to the imperial court. Gelly, a Paraguayan more than thirty years absent from his homeland, had but months before returned, and had impressed López by his patriotism and cosmopolitan nature, the one trait so common and the other so rare in Paraguay. He would be sent to Rio not only to represent Paraguay but also to obtain Brazilian accession to another treaty of alliance, even at the cost of Paraguay's surrendering some of its territorial claims. The growing pressure from Buenos Aires and the collapse of the Corrientes rebellion made such a sacrifice tolerable in Asunción. An added duty of Gelly's was to open relations with diplomats of important nations in Rio, to convince them of the commercial potential of Paraguay and hence, through their good offices, gain their nations' recognition. He was to focus his efforts especially on the United States, Britain, and France.[50]

As Gelly left Asunción in September, 1846, Paraguayan troops were frantically constructing a whole new line of forts along the Río Apa to guarantee that Brazilian territorial appetites would not get out of hand. To the old fort at San Carlos were added those of Bella Vista, Rinconada, Ytaquí, Observación, Quién Vive, Arrecife, and Confluencia, as well as scores of pickets. A number of army estancias were also established from ten to twenty miles south of the river for logistical support.[51] The fortification of the north and the Corrientes, Candelaria, and Paraná islands maneuvers were all part of Carlos Antonio's bid to define, occupy, and strengthen his most easily defended national borders, a consolidation fatalistically based on an acceptance of the probability of war.

In Rio, Gelly was unsuccessful in his major mission. Brazil was afraid that a strong treaty of alliance with Paraguay would lead to an open break with Rosas. So much had imperial policy vacillated to the rhythm of Porteño strength and weakness that the emperor even refused a commercial treaty at this time for fear of angering Buenos Aires.[52] The Porteño envoy at Rio, General Guido, was active in playing on the young emperor's fears and almost succeeded in having Gelly's credentials annulled. Although Carlos Antonio in frustration bestowed on Gelly in 1847 the power not only to propose but also to *conclude* any sensible treaty, the Brazilians remained unimpressed. As one author noted concerning the proposed alliance, "No one doubted that Paraguay could mobilize from 20,000 to 30,000 men," but it was also known that "it has no materiel of war," military experience, or leadership.[53] Pedro II and his cabinet were not impressed by teenage generals, and the recent "show of force" in Corrientes was hardly reassuring to a potential ally.

Gelly was, none the less, busy in Rio. He loved the city, its beauty, relative culture, and sophisticated diplomatic community. While there, he took time to write his *El Paraguay. Lo que fué, lo que es y lo que será,* basically an explanation of Paraguayan rights and potential. Published simultaneously in Portuguese, Spanish, and French, it was a consummate piece of literary diplomacy, although there is no indication that it affected events in the slightest.[54] He also found time to contact and contract a number of foreign specialists among the large, floating population of foreigners in Rio, men whose skills were so much needed in Paraguay: technicians like Henry Godwin and physicians such as Jorge Frederick Meister.[55]

With these minor feathers in his cap, Gelly returned to Asunción to find not only new forts along the Apa but renewed hostilities as well. Perhaps due to the new Paraguayan military activity in the area, Indian attacks on the Apa line, often fueled by Brazilian aguardiente and accompanied by Brazilian soldiers, escalated in 1847 and 1848. In the latter year, the situation had gotten so out of hand that Carlos Antonio irately posted a new decree denouncing "the vileness and cowardice" of workers in the northern yerbales. These "flee at the least movement" of the Indians, "leaving them all of the tools and other things . . . even the firearms" given to them by the government, which López caustically called merely "a hindrance in their accelerated flight." The Indians, with Brazilian aid, then "collect those arms and tools and . . . burn the ranchos." This was not the worst of it, wrote López, but, "above all, the discredit that this incurs abroad." As a result: "From today on, deserters from the yerba stations will be dealt the capital punishment imposed on deserters in combat."[56]

Even with added reinforcements rushed north and a spate of stern decrees, the situation deteriorated, and spies reported new Brazilian army posts almost overlooking the Río Apa. At times, Brazilians even crossed the river for commercial reasons or to rustle cattle.[57]

In 1849, the Brazilian court once again swung pendulum-like toward Paraguay and appointed Pedro Alcántara de Bellegarde, a very influential soldier-statesman, to be new resident minister in Asunción. Arriving in that city, Bellegarde at once impressed López by his openly pro-Paraguayan attitude, and he indicated that Brazil would remain benignly neutral should Paraguay actually invade Corrientes.[58]

Although on the official level Bellegarde was making many friends in Asunción, those same friends were growing increasingly upset with the empire because of new encroachments in the north. This was especially true after the foundation of Pão de Açucar, very close to the Río Apa, was learned of by López. The president, unable to force Brazilian withdrawal from Pão de Açucar through diplomatic channels, did what the empire's experts least expected: he attacked. A large force was sent across the Río Apa in mid-1850, driving Brazilian pickets and settlers before them After a brief siege and an even shorter action, the Brazilian garrison slipped out the conveniently unblocked back door of the fort and disappeared into the jungle.[59]

Carlos Antonio, who understood the balance of power concept far better than would his son, did not overreach himself. After razing the fort and setting pickets out nearby, he had the Paraguayan troops recross the Apa: he had proved his point. Bellegarde, who had departed Asunción for São Borja on learning of the Paraguayan attack, was in that pueblo when he received orders from Rio to return to Asunción and begin negotiations for a new alliance.

Brazil's leaders had at last decided that Rosas must be confronted. This decision had been facilitated by a series of painful border incidents and by the caudillo's recall of General Guido from Rio in 1850, signaling a break in relations and probable war. In this situation, Paraguay again became a valuable pawn in the Brazilian game, and the imperial court was willing to excuse the recent border hostilities and even assure Paraguay that it would not move again into the area between the ríos Blanco and Apa.[60]

After a month of talks in Asunción, Benito Varela, government secretary, and Bellegarde signed a treaty of alliance on Christmas Day, 1850. Various clauses in the treaty assured Paraguay that Brazil would aid her in obtaining recognition abroad, that both nations would come to each other's side in the event of an attack by Rosas, that both would work for the free navigation of the rivers, that the Candelaria highway would be jointly defended, and that both would act to insure the independence of Uruguay. The accord would be in force an initial six years, and it was ratified and exchanged on April 26, 1851.[61]

López must have heaved a hefty sigh of relief on the ratification, for the treaty had been a priority goal of his for a full decade. It represented as much security as was possible at the time and signaled the end of an epoch and a guarantee of the existence of the republic.

All in all, the 1840s had been disappointing diplomatically for López, despite the Brazilian accord of 1851. Although now under a sort of Brazilian umbrella, Paraguay still faced the enmity of Rosas and most Argentines and had not yet been recognized by any major power save Brazil. The rivers were not yet free for Paraguayans, and the border issues, after more violent deaths, were no closer to settlement. Paraguay in 1850 or 1851 still considered itself, and with some reason, as a state under siege.

If the following decade would bring recognition from the United States, Britain, France, and other great powers, the fall of Rosas and freedom of navigation as well as a dramatic modernization within Paraguay, it would also, ironically, bring massive threats from Brazil, the United States, and Britain and bitter wrangles with France. In 1860, Paraguay would be stronger, more unified, and more technologically advanced than could be foreseen in 1850, but would also be infinitely closer to the major war that would destroy her.

10. Threat and Counter-Threat: The 1850s

It may have seemed, after the defeat of Rosas, that Paraguay was about to enter at last into an epoch of international acceptance and tranquility. Between 1850 and 1853 it gained an alliance with Brazil, recognition and free navigation from the Argentine Confederation, and commercial accords with the United States and many European nations. Yet the 1850s were fraught with diplomatic crises, border clashes, and threats of foreign military intervention, and the foundation was laid for a future war. The "opening" of Paraguay, so necessary for its development, exposed the nation to a new host of dangers.

The questions that arose were largely unexpected and involved Paraguay in embarrassing military confrontations with the United States, Britain, and Brazil. From these and other crises, Carlos Antonio and his elder son learned but one lesson—to strengthen Paraguay to the point where further humiliation could not occur. Thus reinforced in their defensive nationalism, the López channeled their modernization of Paraguay into basically military avenues.

Brazil at the Borders

Despite the 1850 alliance with the empire and its implied commitment on the part of the latter to keep its citizens out of the area between the Blanco and the Apa, trouble was brewing in the jungles within months. As one scholar has pointed out, the Paraguayan fixation with the Río Blanco stems from their recognition that the Apa was by no means "a genuine barrier" to Brazilian expansion, being dried to a trickle half the year. The land between the rivers, intrinsically worthless, was seen as a necessary buffer.[1] Just as Paraguay had never doubted its legal claim to the region, never had Brazil doubted its physical possession: Brazilians continued to enter the area.

Operating from their bases at Miranda, they began to enter the "neutral" land, trading with the Indians, establishing ranches, mapping the area, and building forts, all of which was soon known to Carlos Antonio. When the Brazilian government, through its chargé, Felipe José Pereira Leal, insisted that Paraguay sign a treaty allowing Brazil absolutely free passage of the Alto Paraguay (as per the 1850 accord), López saw the move as dangerous. Overland routes to the Mato Grosso were so tortuous as to be almost unusable, and Carlos Antonio, acting as had Rosas before him, decided that if Paraguay controlled river access to Brazil's interior province, it could prevent its military buildup and expansion.[2]

To counter what he saw as a renewed Brazilian push in the north, he responded by stipulating that he would not agree to free navigation until Brazil signed a definitive treaty of limits. To make his point, he ordered the expulsion of Pereira Leal in August, 1853, and suspended relations with Brazil.[3]

The Brazilian reaction was stronger than López had anticipated, and the empire's minister of foreign relations warned bluntly that "only war could cut through the difficulties with Paraguay."[4] A compromise was reached within the Brazilian government, and in 1854 a large fleet was pulled together from all over Brazil. Late that year some twenty ships mounting 120 cannon were ready to sail, and Brazilian border forces were beefed up and incursions made across the Río Blanco.

In January, 1855, thoroughly worried, López ordered a partial mobilization and informed his officers of the gravity of the situation. He condemned "the assaults made by the Savages of Miranda mixed with Brazilians" on several Paraguayan forts and the continual theft of Paraguayan livestock. In retaliation, a small Brazilian post at Salinas, north of the Apa, was overrun by Paraguayan troops.[5]

In February, the Brazilian fleet, whose admiral, Pedro Ferreira de Oliveira, was invested with diplomatic powers, set sail. Oliveira's orders were to allow Paraguay eight days to consider granting free navigation, after which he was, if necessary, to proceed upstream and land troops to physically occupy the contested zone.[6]

Unfortunately, just at this time, Paraguay's problems multiplied in an unexpected manner. The previous year, Capt. Thomas J. Page of the USS *Water Witch* had received permission from López to chart the waters of the Río Paraguay and its tributaries. His work finished, he returned with his ship and expelled United States Consul Hopkins (see below) to his base at Corrientes. In February, 1855, the *Water Witch* was involved in a shoot-out with a Paraguayan shore battery, and this incident was to have grave consequences, as it afforded the young North American nation a chance to show its muscle.[7]

As the Brazilian fleet sailed north, the mauled *Water Witch* headed south, both boding ill for Paraguay. As López wrote an official after the *Water*

Witch incident, the Yankees "have received punishment and an example," but "the *Water Witch* heads downriver, surely to seek reinforcements and unite with the Brazilians."[8] Though correct in the first assumption, he was mistaken in the second. The United States would rely on no third party to settle its diplomatic complaints.

A truly depressing prospect faced Paraguay, and there was little that López could do. Flying in the face of reality, in February he reiterated a prior decree that "foreign warships are prohibited entry into waters of the Republic without previous permission."[9] At the same time, he instructed commanders on the northern frontier to abandon the Río Apa line if faced with "a superior force of Brazilians and Savages" and wage mobile, guerrilla warfare as they fell back to the more realistic and more defensible Río Ypané. Admonishing the people of the north not to fight for their homes but to retreat with their posessions if necessary, Carlos Antonio appointed a Capt. Toribio Martínez commander and chief of the north, with his base at Bella Vista. He was given temporary emergency powers.[10]

In late February, nature and luck came to Paraguay's aid. It seems that no one in the Brazilian navy had researched the route of the punitive expedition, and when the fleet reached Corrientes its keels were already scraping the mud: even the lowliest grummet realized that with the river so low, the fleet would be unable to proceed for months. Thus, instead of floating an imposing array of cannon past Government House, Admiral Ferreira, rather humiliated, went upstream in a small auxiliary vessel in mid-April.[11]

After two weeks of negotiations, López signed a treaty of free navigation, but, taking advantage of the empire's temporary impotence, he stipulated that ratification would be postponed at least a year, to be simultaneous with ratification of a treaty of limits.[12]

The imperial government, angry at its equally irate admiral for accepting the advantage-less treaty, prepared for war, hoping to frighten Paraguay. The policy succeeded brilliantly, and López, with major diplomatic crises with the United States and France, sent Foreign Minister José Berges to Rio, where in April, 1856, Paraguay capitulated to Brazilian demands. The new treaty conceded free navigation without mention of the question of limits, which was to be shelved for several years. Until such discussions, both sides would consider possession to be law but would refrain from making any major changes in their parts of the contested territory.[13]

The crisis averted for the present, López began to hedge his grant of free navigation with a series of restrictions, including illegal duties levied on goods in transit. The Brazilians preferred the real to the image and were not accustomed to dealing with the Paraguayan despot. In retaliation, agents of the court initiated contact with the growing Paraguayan exile community at

Buenos Aires, perhaps hoping "to repeat the success achieved" in Uruguay through the same tactics.[14]

In order to stave off yet another crisis, yet desirous of obtaining truly free navigation, the Brazilian government decided to send in its diplomatic first team: Imperial Chancellor José Maria da Silva Paranhos. That august figure reached Asunción in January, 1858, and, after negotiating with Francisco Solano López, signed a convention on February 12 ending restrictions on Brazilian transit of the Alto Paraguay. Paranhos had made it clear that Brazil was exasperated and dead serious: it would go to war, if necessary, to enforce its rights.[15] One remaining limit was agreed to by both parties: that no more than three ships of either nation would at one time ascend the river. Also signed was a protocol dealing with limits. In this document, Bahia Negra (at the confluence of the Negro and the Paraguay), some seventy miles north of the Blanco, was recognized as the limit between the nations.[16]

With the convention and protocol (which bear Paranhos's name), it seemed that diplomatic issues between the signatories were at last resolved. López realized that he could not enforce a Rosas-like blockade of his neighbor. He also knew that, despite claims, reality would interfere with Paraguayan control in the Mato Grosso. He merely settled for what, on paper, was the best bargain he could strike, knowing that the protocol was but a piece of paper. In effect, that document only ended the issue by giving a green light to Brazil, and, as if physically propelled, Brazilians by the hundreds began settling in what had been Paraguay's claim.

Francisco Solano Goes to Europe

On June 12, 1853, as relations were worsening with Brazil, Francisco Solano López, named minister plenipotentiary by his father at the still tender age of 26, sailed from Asunción on the ancient Paraguayan war vessel *Independencia* on his way to Europe. Having mastered the mechanics of war, the young López set out to dominate those of diplomacy. His trip was the high point of his life and his nation's diplomacy. What he gathered in Europe— treaties, recognition, accolades, a new ship, contracts for experts and colonists, and a red-haired Irish mistress—exceeded even his own expectations.

Aboard with him traveled his retinue, composed of his brother Benigno, secretary Juan Andrés Gelly, brother-in-law Comandante Vicente Barrios, and three lesser officers. He also brought considerable spending money so that he would not have to "do" Europe on five pesos a day, and some bales of yerba to be distributed as gifts. On September 14, the Paraguayan ship docked at Southampton "with its brilliant embassy aboard," and Francisco Solano went to work.[17]

In Britain, he made a three-month tour, visiting Liverpool, Manchester, and other squalid birthplaces of the Industrial Revolution, reserving an afternoon for a visit to Madame Tussaud's famous wax museum. Having exchanged treaties of recognition, friendship, and commerce, López was treated very well, and the British went out of their way to impress him with the commercial and other advantages to be had from fair Albion.

Especially interesting and fruitful was López's business deal with the firm of J. & A. Blyth of Limehouse. With those gentlemen he placed an order for a modern steam warship, the *Tacuarí*, at a cost of some £50,000. He also authorized Blyth and Co. to act as general agents for the Paraguayan government in contracting expert technicians, the purchase of industrial and military hardware, and the sale of Paraguayan products. This bond lasted for more than a decade, and it could be said that Blyth and Co. supervised the exceptionally rapid modernization of Paraguay (although, incidentally, it lost some money uncollectible after 1864 when war destroyed its client).

From Britain, López passed to France, where he spent several months basking in the attention of Napoleon III, whose very name thrilled him. Not all of his acts in Paris were official, for as one commentator who knew him well put it, "On arriving at Paris, young López left the details of all business to his secretary, gave loose rein to his naturally licentious propensities, and plunged into the vices of that gay capital."[18] Under the care of Napoleon III, Francisco Solano "studied" the military sciences and was even permitted to review and drill the imperial guard. With the treaties exchanged in Paris, the minister plenipotentiary then traveled to Sardinia, where he remained two months as royal guest, also exchanging treaties signed at Asunción.

In April, 1854, the López mission arrived in Rome, where López hoped to convince the pope in private audience to recognize uncle Basilio López as auxiliary bishop of Paraguay. He got as far as the Vatican secretary of state, Cardinal Antonelli, who received his petitions but effectively blocked his path to the Holy Father, who apparently did not wish to honor his nepotistic request. The López family was still awaiting Basilio's confirmation when that cleric died in 1859. His successor, Father Urbieta, was immediately confirmed by the pope.[19]

Disappointed in Rome, Francisco Solano then moved on to Spain, where he hoped to attract peasant immigration to Paraguay as well as to obtain various treaties from Queen Isabella II. He was informed, however, that Spanish and Paraguayan views on citizenship, recognition, and a host of other points precluded any accords. After three months of unfruitful negotiations, López returned to Paris, where he continued to hold talks with the Spanish government through its ambassador to the City of Lights. In frustration, the young man finally gave in, accepting the basic Spanish conditions, but by the time Madrid finally drafted a treaty to its liking, López was stepping aboard a boat at Bordeaux, and it was too late.[20]

While in France, López concreted with officials at Bordeaux a pact for the immigration of at least five hundred settlers from that area, promising on the part of his father's government to subsidize transportation and settling-in expenses.[21]

Much more romantic was the premier acquisition of the entire trip, Elisa Alicia Lynch, whom he encountered for the second time on his return to Paris. "A woman of abandoned Character," as United States Minister to Asunción Washburn later described her, "she belonged to that class of public women so numerous in Paris, always on the watch for strangers with long purses and vicious habits."[22] Elisa, or, as she became known in Paraguay, "La Lynch," was to remain with Francisco Solano for the remainder of his short life.

The mission terminated, if not entirely accomplished, López prepared to leave Europe. The newly-constructed *Tacuarí,* commanded by Capt. George Francis Morice (on leave from the British navy) and served by a British crew recruited by Blyth, steamed into Bordeaux harbor flying the Paraguayan tricolor. On November 11, 1854, the *Tacuarí* took aboard the Paraguayan delegation and its many souvenirs and departed, colliding with a large buoy. The damage repaired in movement, Morice then steamed into a tempest, and the somewhat nauseated passengers, landlubbers all, were relieved to see Lisbon appear through the fog. To compound an already inauspicious voyage, a quarantine was slapped on the Paraguayan ship for four days, as Bordeaux was reputed to be choleric, and Portuguese authorities balked at accepting another *mal français.*[23] The quarantine ended, López and his retinue piled ashore for four days of tourism, sailing for home on November 24, directly through the path of a frightening storm.

Having by now proven that the ship was well made, Morice touched at Madeira and the Cape Verdes, and in late December dropped anchor at Rio de Janeiro, where the Paraguayan flag was given thrilling, if standard, salutes by Brazilian naval units present. Gelly was proud to note during his stay in Rio that the ship made a good impression with its modern design and "the great swivel cannon on the poop."[24] Touching briefly at Montevideo and Buenos Aires, the *Tacuarí* dropped anchor in Asunción harbor January 21, 1855, cheered by a crowd of hundreds as government functionaries filed on board to welcome and congratulate General López, returning hero.

Yanqui Quixote: Edward A. Hopkins Returns

If to some degree the diplomatic problems with Brazil were to be expected, those with the distant United States were not. Two problems coalesced to strain relations to and beyond the breaking point. One was the peripatetic Hopkins. That gentleman, still transfixed by the vision of a steamboat monopoly and interested in other commercial activities, was again in Asunción in 1851. It was not easy for him to deal directly with Carlos Antonio, for the president had grown weary of Hopkins's pretensions, schemes, avarice, and lack of diplomatic status, yet the young American, who seems to have predated the dictum of Phineas T. Barnum, succeeded. Such a fine flim-flam man was Hopkins that even before United States's recognition of Paraguay, López consented to name him special minister of Paraguay to the United States, hinting broadly that personal commercial advantages might follow if he could obtain his country's diplomatic recognition.[25]

Hopkins left Asunción in late 1851, apparently assured that if he returned as United States consul in a suitable steamship, the monopoly he had so long sought would be his. Once home in the United States, he was pleased to learn that he had, indeed, been named consul to Paraguay (he was, after all, the only applicant for that previously non-existent post), and divided his time equally between giving speeches about Paraguay and its untapped resources and organizing a company to tap them.

In 1852, the United States and Paraguay Navigation Company was incorporated in the state of Rhode Island with an initial capital of $100,000, raised from some of the most experienced businessmen in the land. The old Hopkins charm had struck again. It should be noted that, as general manager of the company, his own salary was an immodest $2,000 per annum plus 5 percent of all future profits. With the company formed, Hopkins expanded his plans to include the lumber industry and the export of cigars, sugar, bricks, alcohol, and cotton. With this in mind, and hoping to become virtual export czar of Paraguay, the consul purchased a large steamer that, after repairs, cost the company $70,000. Two smaller vessels and a huge load of machinery and trade goods used up the rest of his capital, but in early 1853 he was at last ready to return to Paraguay.[26]

Laden with a score or so of company technicians and a huge cargo, the steamer, the *Paraguay,* ran a gauntlet of storms, the last of which resulted in its wreckage on the coast of Brazil. Having insured the ship, Hopkins shrugged off the loss and, with his brother Clement and the technicians, traveled to Asunción via Montevideo. On his way up the Paraná, he met and talked with Francisco Solano, at the time on his way to Europe. He produced a very bad impression on the future Mariscal.[27]

On October 11, 1853, he arrived at Asunción, where he was received warmly despite loss of the *Paraguay* and its expensive machines. He soon presented his credentials, explained to a stunned López his grandiose industrial plans, and set to work building his new empire. Showered at first with favors from the Dictator, who allowed him free importation of technical goods, government housing for his team, and the purchase of both land and slaves, Hopkins opened a cigar factory in Asunción and a brick factory at San Antonio. Within months, however, he was forced to turn to Carlos Antonio for a 11,500-peso loan, which was given at 6 percent interest. López even arranged a fixed labor supply (mostly state prisoners), which performed at very low wages.

The calm was soon to be shattered by several events. One was Hopkins's overbearing arrogance, which constantly offended López and most other Paraguayans. Soon after his 1853 arrival, he had proposed to Carlos Antonio the creation of an agricultural school funded by the government but directed by that jack-of-all-trades, the American consul. Long a fond dream of López's, the proposal elicited his interest and enthusiasm, but his ardor cooled when he read the fine print on Hopkins's plans, which called for the American to be the school's "Supreme Authority" and did not permit López any say at all. If this shocked the president, he was truly horrified by the consul's request that he turn over to brother Clement Paraguay's official (and only) newspaper, *El Semanario,* in return for American establishment of a ministry of agriculture and immigration. Almost in a catatonic state, López demurred, much to the surprise of Hopkins.[28]

Complicating matters was Hopkins's unusual relation with the Guillemot family, with which he was residing. His host was the French consul, and his attractive wife Jeanne, it was said, was a distant relation of the American. To put it kindly, the relation did not remain distant, and rumors of a scandal circulated, doing the American no good in the rather puritanical atmosphere of Asunción. As one writer notes, "they began to exhibit in public a recip-rocal inclination too warm to be attributed only to" being distant relatives. The scandal eventually reached even the French consul himself, and he complained to the López government that the American should be jailed.[29]

While the scandal, Hopkins's inherent arrogance, and perhaps financial mismanagement as well were taking their toll of López's patience, a crisis occurred as Hopkins, his brother, and his "relative" were on a country ride. The fiery lady, confronted with a herd of cattle belonging to the government blocking her way, ranted, raved, and shook her fist at the soldier herding them and then stampeded the beeves, scattering them in all directions. The poor, bewildered soldier, who probably did not speak Spanish, did understand certain gestures and imprecations, and proceeded to whack Mme. Guillemot about the midsection with the flat of his sabre. On their return to the city, with Hopkins "wounded in his self-love and dignity and the lady in her ribs," the American demanded that López have the uniformed lout shot. An angry

Carlos Antonio ordered the soldier confined to quarters for a few days and informed Hopkins that since a foreigner could not legally own land in Paraguay, his claim to the cigar factory was voided. This was, of course, a legal fiction, for the president could and always did give or sell anything he wanted to. Knowing this, Hopkins demanded in August, 1854, that López reverse his decision, writing his own, distant government for support. The following day, he was given his passports and told to leave the country immediately. One authority has written that the consul had "insulted López and Paraguay so intolerably that one wonders if he was not deliberately attempting to invite expulsion to conceal" the imminent collapse of his financial ventures.[30]

If López believed that he could iron out his problems with the United States easily, it was because no one could foresee the next inept moves of United States and Paraguayan diplomacy. In October, 1853, the *Water Witch* had first arrived at Asunción, sent by the Navy Department to chart the region's many rivers. Its commander, Lt. Thomas Jefferson Page, was well received by López and made an excellent impression on him, especially after presenting a new 12-pounder howitzer as a gift from his government to Paraguay. With López's permission, he then began exploring and taking soundings, but he also passed all the way north to Corumbá, angering López, who had not authorized such a route and who was afraid that Brazil itself would see Page's passage as a precedent, demanding the same right for its own vessels. On his return downstream, the lieutenant puzzled over his cool treatment at several Paraguayan ports at which he had been well received on the way north. Later, apprised of his gaff, he ruefully noted that "it is astonishing with what rapidity the commands and wishes of the government are here transmitted to every part of the Republic."[31]

López at first refused to meet again with Lt. Page, although he later relented and expressed great interest in the naval officer's scientific observations. Once more in good graces, Page explored Paraguay on horseback before taking his ship south to Corrientes in July, 1854. While at that port, he received an urgent letter from Hopkins demanding his return to Asunción, where the consul intended to use him as an implied threat in his bargaining with López. Page, however, who knew Hopkins well by this point, wrote that "if Mr. Hopkins expects to complicate myself and the *Water Witch* in the opprobrious business between the government of Paraguay and himself, he is fooling himself."[32]

When he reached Asunción, Page at first declined to take the consul's side and merely requested that López provide transportation for Hopkins and his retinue downstream. López refused until the consul would hand over the land titles that the government had abrogated. Faced with the humiliation of the American diplomatic representative, Page grew sympathetic to Hopkins and sent a series of notes to Government House. Unfortunately, since some of these were written in English, they were unacceptable to Paraguayan authorities, who chose this moment to stand on ceremony. Page, in the tradition of his service, saw red, writing his government that if López did not permit Hopkins to exit as a gentleman, he would be proud to capture the Paraguayan fleet and tow it to Corrientes. As sailors on the *Water Witch* gleefully polished their armaments, López decided that the game was not worth the risk, and on September 30, 1854, Hopkins was allowed to board the *Water Witch* for the voyage south.[33]

While the naval vessel was in Corrientes, the Paraguayan government decreed that the *Water Witch* would be singularly unwelcome again in Paraguayan waters,[34] and López readied his small river fleet and coastal defenses to resist any return of that vessel. Unfortunately, Page was at that time intending to sail the proscribed vessel to Asunción to test López, carrying, as a pretext, United States official correspondence. He was, however, denied permission to do this by Washington, and was sent instead on other, local missions.[35] Early in 1855, the lieutenant ordered his second-in-command, Lt. William Jeffers, to take the *Water Witch* into the Alto Paraná as far as the island of Apipé, to chart some rapids there. Although Page described his decision as a rational one since the Alto Paraná, as a border between two nations, was an international waterway, there seems little doubt that the move was a calculated insult to López.[36]

On February 1, 1855, Jeffers took his ship into the Alto Paraná, nervously noting much activity at the numerous Paraguayan shore batteries. Declining a written warning message because it was written in Spanish (which he could not understand), Jeffers continued until he approached the elevated, six-gun battery at Itapirú. There, ignoring several blank warning shots, he later professed surprise when a cannon ball "carried away the wheel, broke the rudder cables, and mortally wounded the rudderman." With his crew of twenty-eight Jeffers beat a retreat, firing as he went, a retreat speeded up by the appearance of the brand-new *Tacuarí* with its six modern, rifled cannon.[37]

López was worried when informed of the Itapirú skirmish, and all the more so as the very powerful Brazilian squadron was approaching. He wrote one of his officials that "the Pirates went to bury their dead at Corrientes," but that he expected the United States to retaliate.[38]

Lt. Page was, of course, enraged, and he wrote Commodore Salter of the Brazil station, intending to use all available United States naval power to "knock Itapirú into rubble," but that officer was distinctly unenthusiastic.[39] Failing to interest Salter, Page next tried to borrow several large cannon from another United States war vessel at Buenos Aires, intending to use them to "destroy" the Paraguayan navy. Luckily, he was dissuaded, for this could only have led to the sinking of his own ship and quite probably a war between the two nations.[40]

In the United States, the treatment and expulsion of Hopkins came together as one issue with the confiscation of American-owned properties and the *Water Witch* incident in the minds of politicians and public, and President James Buchanan requested and received from Congress the authority and appropriations to defend national honor.

Only in October, 1858, forty-four months after the Itapirú incident, did a United States fleet set sail. Commanded by Commodore William B. Shubrick, the fleet was composed of eleven steamships and nine sailing vessels of the regular navy, manned by almost 2,500 men and mounting over 200 cannon.[41] This was, by standards of the day, an imposing armada, especially for such an exotic voyage. The ships, however, were more a diplomatic than a military tool, and it was hoped that the real threat it posed would be conducive to "flexible" negotiations with Paraguay. If not, the sailors could amuse themselves by blowing apart the entire chain of river defenses erected by Paraguay and perhaps even lob a few shells into Asunción as well.

In late 1858, most of the fleet reached Corrientes, and, giving previous notice to the López government, Commissioner James B. Bowlin proceeded upriver aboard a single vessel to negotiate. Bowlin was probably unaware that 12,000 Paraguayan troops and most of the national artillery park were then massed at Humaitá to contest passage of the river if necessary. Already in Asunción was Argentine President Urquiza, who had been accepted as mediator by both sides. He was not at all happy with the idea of a massive intervention in his region of the world, an intervention that might seriously weaken Paraguay and upset the precarious balance of power. Bowlin, treated with distant formality, entered negotiations on January 25, 1859, and agreement was soon reached, the crisis averted.

By this agreement, López assented to pay $10,000 compensation to the family of the dead *Water Witch* seaman and to ratify the old commercial treaty of 1853. Although he laughed off claims of the United States and the Paraguay Navigation Company for a million dollars in damages, he did agree to submit the issue to a special arbitral committee. Bowlin left Asunción amidst the noise of a reciprocal twenty-one-gun salute.[42]

The arbitral commission, which included Paraguayan José Berges, met in Washington in 1860 and, after hearing the company's lawyers and their exaggerated claims, declared that Paraguay owed not a cent to the Hopkins group.[43]

The Corpulent Despot had reason to be pleased. He had mastered the second threat of massive naval coercion by a superior power at minimal cost to his pride or reputation. In a sort of footnote to the affair, J. Blyth wrote Francisco Solano from London of European newspaper coverage of the Paraguayan crisis, remarking that "not withstanding the very questionable taste of" the style employed by some editorialists, "their general tone is not unsatisfactory and it is evident that they are pleased with the pacific arrangement that has been made."[44] So was everyone save Hopkins. That an incident so grotesque and potentially dangerous could be permitted to grow from a series of minor misunderstandings reflected no credit on either contestant. López, father and son, however, were alike in their determination to make Paraguay so strong that further intervention was impossible.

The Displeasure of Her Britannic Majesty

As had El Supremo, Carlos Antonio had an almost childlike faith in the magic of British industrial and commercial power. Although he had not been able to obtain early recognition from the Foreign Office as he had hoped, López was pleased by Britain's treatment and its use of its own warships to escort commercial convoys through Argentine waters. It is ironic that Paraguayan treatment of a British subject would occasion the greatest humiliation Paraguay was to experience in this epoch.

In December, 1852, free now to deal openly with Paraguay because of Argentine acquiescence, Charles Hotham, special British minister plenipotentiary, landed at Asunción, together with representatives from France and Sardinia. He and his colleagues recognized Paraguayan sovereignty in the name of their governments on January 4, 1853, signing treaties the following March.[45]

Soon, British merchants were operating in large scale at Pilar and Asunción, represented on the spot by Consul Charles A. Henderson, an imperious diplomat of the old school. In London, Benjamin Green became Paraguayan consul, a post he held for many years. After Francisco Solano's European sojourn, relations with Britain became rather close, not only through expanding commercial contact but also due to the hundreds of British technicians on contract who were supervising the transformation of Paraguay. Things were going well, and Henderson was a sort of social lion and father figure for the small, isolated diplomatic community.

This pleasant situation, however, was not to last. In 1858, a special British envoy, W. D. Christie, was sent to Asunción on what seemed a routine matter—to renew the 1853 commercial accord—but he was so long delayed by López's turgid bureaucracy that he left in high dudgeon and the treaty expired. A few months later, a dozen or so men were arrested for supposedly plotting to kill Carlos Antonio while he dozed at the National Theater. The significance of the affair is that one of the men arrested, Santiago (or James) Canstatt, a well-know merchant of confused origin, faced with charges of attempted regicide, screamed for the British consul. Canstatt, who seems to have had a British father and a Uruguayan mother, did indeed have two sets of passports and papers, one for each parent's native land. The López government claimed that not only was he Uruguayan but in any case was guilty of a heinous crime—and, incidentally, that he was an agent of the Paraguayan exile community in Buenos Aires as well.[46]

Consul Henderson took up the cudgels, but, denied an audience with López on the matter, he fumed and began an intemperate exchange of notes with various government figures. He also wrote London for instructions, informing his government that Canstatt and four others had already been sentenced to death. The Foreign Office gave its typically Victorian response: Canstatt must be released, a cash indemnity paid, and a complete act of apology made by the López regime for "its lack of respect." If these terms were not met within three days, Henderson was to leave Asunción, and the Foreign Office would reflect on sterner measures.[47] Carlos Antonio was less impressed than angry when he received the ultimatum, and Henderson left Paraguay in September, 1859.

Meanwhile, in Buenos Aires, another act of this zarzuela was about to be played. Francisco Solano, ever the diplomat, had been in that port for most of 1859, mediating a dispute between President Urquiza and the province of Buenos Aires. With him were his staff and the *Tacuarí,* which had almost become his family's yacht. After doing a creditable job of mediation, he boarded the Paraguayan steamer in late November for his return home. He did not make it. Slipping out into the port channel, the *Tacuarí,* still commanded by Capt. Morice and manned mostly by Britons, was confronted in a distinctly hostile manner by a British corvette, aptly named the *Buzzard,* and a companion gunboat, equally properly called the *Grappler.* Gunports agape, these vessels blocked the *Tacuarí* and put a warning shot across her bows, and López, nervously pondering the probable reaction of his own British crew, did not force the issue. Instead, he sent the *Tacuarí* back to its berth, humiliated as never before in his life. Again moored, he was informed by a British rating that his vessel would not be allowed to leave until the Canstatt affair was suitably settled.[48]

In a biblical rage and feeling his humiliation more deeply with each passing hour, López wrote to Urquiza and port authorities, requesting that they do something about Britain's flagrant abuse of international law. Those, however, admitted their impotence, for Britannia did, after all, rule the waves, even the small ones of the Río de la Plata.

Covering his shame with a cloak, López left the pride of his navy and rode north to Santa Fe, whence he took ship for Asunción, where he and his father pondered how to escape their new problem without loss of the *Tacuarí*. It was a touchy time for the many British citizens in Paraguay, especially as they had little faith in the French consul delegated to represent them.[49]

Early in 1860, Canstatt was given a full pardon, and only two of the accused plotters went to the wall. It was carefully pointed out by Paraguayan authorities that the pardon bore a date anterior to the British threats, but all knew that this was mere face-saving. To handle the indemnity question, López named Argentine jurist Carlos Calvo (then in London) to negotiate with the Foreign Office. This was no easy task, for the Victorians were still upset, and it was almost impossible for the sophisticated envoy to gain appointments with any but the lowliest officials. These made it clear that Britain would not at all be flexible in such matters of honor, although they did release the *Tacuarí* prior to agreement on other points. Only in 1862 did Canstatt receive his indemnity and the British their apology, when an accord was signed renewing the 1853 treaty. Perhaps in pique, Her Britannic Majesty did not deign to assign a full-time diplomat to Asunción after that, but instead had its minister at Buenos Aires make infrequent trips upstream.[50]

The Paraguayan Pulse Accelerates

If the 1850s represented a difficult epoch for Paraguay in the intricate field of diplomacy, it was also a period viewed by later generations as a golden age. Never before or after were Paraguayans so unified, internally pacific, and externally self-assured. The Indian menace had greatly abated, the Argentine danger had all but disappeared, and although problems with Brazil still lingered, the modernization and militarization of Paraguay served to offset that ancient anxiety.

If a significant number of disaffected Paraguayans were slipping across the borders bound for Buenos Aires, that was all the better for Carlos Antonio, who saw no need for dissidence *within* Paraguay. If this exile community found time and bile to publish virulently anti-López newspapers such as *El Grito Paraguayo* (1858-1859) and *El Clamor de los Libres* (1859) in the Port City, the Corpulent Despot worried not at all, for within Paraguay only his personally-edited sheets, *El Eco del Paraguay* (1855-1857), *La Epoca* (1857-1859), *La Aurora* (1860-1862), and the irregular *El Semanario* circulated and shaped what little public opinion existed.[51]

Carlos Antonio, who had what he wanted, was not molested by the occasional whining of exile mosquitos. The foreign technicians were successfully molding a new Paraguay, and to a lesser extent a new Paraguayan, from the soft red clay of his nation. Public works were physically transforming the country, and genuine prosperity—for the privileged sectors—had appeared in Paraguay for the first time in its history. In the positivist world view, Francia had given "order" and Carlos Antonio was achieving "progress." Unhappily, his son would achieve "ruin."

The 1853 treaties had assured a limited goldrush to Pilar and Asunción, and a few years later, identical treaties were signed with Portugal, Austria, Sweden, Prussia, and Belgium.[52] With these guarantees on paper and with Paraguay's voracious demands for certain European goods, trade volume rose meteorically, and Asunción, with its new wharves and port facilities, became a bustling port. In 1852, only 90, relatively small vessels put into Asunción in trade, but by 1855 the annual traffic had risen to over 300 larger boats. The value of Paraguay's foreign commerce increased in even greater proportion, from an estimated 572,000 pesos in 1851 to about 4,000,000 in 1859.[53] The value of most Paraguayan exports also increased in value. Between 1851 and 1860, the sale price of tobacco in Asunción jumped by 90 percent per arroba, and in the last of those years over 3,000,000 pounds of the leaf, plus 6,000,000 cigars, were exported. Yerba earnings tripled in the course of the decade. In 1860, some 4,500,000 pounds of yerba were exported from Paraguay, mostly to Argentina, and foreign merchants were fighting one another in Asunción to purchase yerba licenses. There were healthy balance of trade surpluses throughout the decade, despite large foreign arms and machinery purchases—more than sufficient to build sumptuous homes for the López clan, pay the foreign experts, and maintain the growing but rather low-cost military.[54] The overly precise figures that appear in the various records may be somewhat at variance with reality, but the general trend was clearly one of sizeable annual surpluses of foreign exchange, aided by an upward adjustment of the import tax scale to the point where it averaged 20 percent of value.[55]

Typical of the commerce of the epoch were the 1855 dealings of two foreigners. David Bruce, arriving on the Porteño vessel *Buenos Aires* in July, brought with him 500 large boxes of "general merchandise," 8 kegs of wine, 20 kilos of iron, 22 large flasks of olive oil, 3 huge rolls of paper, 10 copper bars, and 10 cases of champagne.[56] Perhaps Paraguay was not the commercial Eden some expected, but there was enough trade to interest many a European merchant. Pascual Savie, a Spaniard, was in his turn an exporter, and when he sailed for Buenos Aires early in 1855 he carried a very large load of Paraguay's most common products: 1,105 cow hides, 75,000 pounds of tobacco, 25,000 pounds of salt pork, 6 large "pipes" of aguardiente, and 40,000 cigars. It is probable that much of Savie's cargo originated on state lands.[57]

Even the various diplomatic and military contretemps of the epoch did not keep merchants from flocking to Pilar and Asunción. They would continue to do so until the sound of guns wafted across the muddy waters.

Paraguayans Were So Nubile

Perhaps in part due to luck and in part to better medical knowledge available from the foreign medicoes and to large-scale inoculation against smallpox, the 1850s were not pocked by the massive epidemics of "fevers" that had decimated the pueblos in the previous decade. With little to check the natural increase of the population and a general abundance to stimulate it, Paraguayans were being born at an increasing rate and surviving longer than before. One European traveler who toured much of the nation in this period noted that "the Paraguayans are so fecund; they are nubile at the age of eleven or twelve."[58] This peculiar fecundity, however, occasionally bothered the somewhat prudish Carlos Antonio, and in 1855 he issued a decree, indicating that if smallpox was no longer a worry, the social pox was: "A growing number of Women coming in from the Partidos, most of them without license [are] resulting in the demoralization of the Troops and the consequent loss of many Soldiers infected by corrupted Women." López ordered that none but "the least suspicious" of women would be permitted to enter the city, and those only after having registered with the police.[59] Paraguay was indeed catching up with the rest of the world.

So placid and halcyon were the 1850s that in 1858, when congress met at the appointed time to re-elect him, Carlos Antonio could smugly and safely demur. Ildefonso Bermejo, the only eyewitness to the farce who took the time to record it, wrote that López, as if on a stage, was suitably dressed "with the trappings of a French Marshal." Smug he may well have been, but Carlos Antonio took care to announce that "I prohibit all manner of heated discourse, vivas, and other analogous noises," after which he pointed out that the cavalry escort that ostentatiously guarded the doors "has not come to intimidate." Thus having defined the congress's limits, López presented his message, which had to be translated into Guaraní for the rustic deputies: "A recompilation of all the administrative acts of the executive power for ten years." His audience suitably impressed, if not actually asleep, Carlos Antonio announced that he did not desire re-election: "Do not put your eyes on me; leave me to rest. Your persistence in re-electing me has broken my health in an irreparable manner. Search the Republic for a meritorious Citizen with whom to replace me."

As expected, the assembly declined the generous offer, as they were pleased with López's rule, deeply afraid of uncertainty, and desirous of avoiding more time and effort than a mere acclamation would take. Amid "vivas" and huzzahs, a pleased López, having acted his part well, told the congress, "I resign myself in submission to the new sacrifice," but for a shorter term of five years. It was a Paraguayan tragedy that he did not outlive his new mandate.[60]

The Woman on Horseback: Elisa Alicia Lynch

As with so many other visitors, Francisco Solano had fallen in love with Paris. The Paraguayan, with his beautiful dress uniforms and glittering medals, there met the loveliest woman in the world. In truth, Elisa Lynch was a strikingly handsome woman, a fact mentioned by nearly everyone who met her. She was almost the exact opposite of Francisco Solano. She was tall, quite slender, calcium white in complexion, red-haired, green-eyed, and sophisticated. Perhaps no figure in Paraguayan history has been so little understood and so wildly slandered. Elisa was born in Ireland in 1835 to a middle class family. In 1850, at age fifteen, she married Jean Luis Armand de Quatrefages, a French military surgeon, the unhappy marriage dissolving three years later, when Jean Luis decamped without warning. Long after she moved to Paraguay, her marriage may have been annulled: it is clear that her husband remarried in 1857.[61]

Whatever the case, she was living in Paris with her mother, and perhaps a Russian nobleman as well, when she met López in 1853. It was love at first sight. Francisco Solano was overwhelmed by her beauty, grace, charm, wit, and fluency in French and the apparent prestige value she would represent at home. Elisa, for her part, "loved" López because of the security he offered with his position as heir to the throne, his large landholdings, and his Paris expense account.

Soon after knowing one another in the Biblical manner, López knew that he must take her back to Paraguay, but, as she was instantly pregnant, not on the same ship. Despite arguments with brother Benigno, who did not want the affair carried across the ocean, the elder brother left Elisa with a kiss, a large purse, and instructions on how to get to Paraguay. He then departed.[62]

The strong-willed Lynch arrived at Buenos Aires in October, 1855, with 800 ounces of gold and incipient labor pains; she barely got to the hotel before giving birth to Juan Francisco, who was baptized in a private ceremony as Juan Francisco López after her arrival in Asunción in December.[63]

Apparently it took her some time to get over her depression on encountering Paraguay and its people, but she persevered, taking advantage of the few available niceties. She soon discovered that anything she desired, from champagne through furniture to clothing from Paris, could and would be ordered direct from Europe by her consort, who never counted his change.

She also soon learned that she could dominate what passed for society in Asunción despite her "unofficial" position and the López family's clear dislike of her. Francisco Solano's position and her own social graces assured

a good turnout when she decided on a party. In fact, by 1858 she was the
social leader of the community, even though she was almost always pregnant
and known to be "living in sin."

La Lynch was something of a snob and delighted in displaying her new ways
to the more rustic Paraguayans, refusing to ride sidesaddle and serving elegant
French cuisine to guests more at home with half a barbecued beef. No matter
that she offended some, she became a lady to emulate if not like, and her
social example almost places her in the ranks of the British contract technicians,
for she too did her part to modernize Paraguay, since that nation "wanted to
become modish, and not only in its ships and cannon."[64]

Early in her stay in Asunción, she began hosting formal dinner parties
and afternoon teas in her spacious downtown house, inviting government
officials and foreign technicians and diplomats. Her home was very ornate
and very European; her salon was described as "set with excellent taste, which
constituted a delightful sight." Under her watchful eye, the salon of her lover's
house also became a showplace: "The furniture of the room would be perfect
in Paris," according to one visitor.[65]

La Lynch also set the syle with her clothing, leading to a deluge of orders
on the few French seamstresses in town as Paraguayan matrons "substituted
the *aho poi* [native embroidery] for printed fabrics."[66] The same may be
said for cuisine, tokay, champagne, cosmetics, sewing machines, certain music,
formal dances, and lithographs and other objets d'art. An amusing view of one
aspect of change is that in 1853, Carlos Antonio had hosted a 600-guest banquet
commemorating the anniversary of Argentine recognition. The food was traditional—barbecued beef and Paraguayan sweets—and cost the government about
one peso per guest. "A few years later, Elisa Lynch was spending 500 pesos
monthly on food brought in from the Club Nacional."[67]

Perhaps it was her taste for sauce Béarnaise or coq au vin that accounts for
Elisa's growing stoutness: a few photographs taken around 1860 show her to
have "filled out" considerably, less now a young lady and more a matron. No
doubt a contributing factor in her expanding girth was her successful effort to
guarantee heirs for herself and Francisco Solano. In all, between 1855 and
1861, she gave birth to five sons—Juan Francisco, Carlos Honorio, Federico
Lloyd, Enrique Venancio, and Leopoldo—all of whom openly carried the
López name.

She clearly rose high in the world in a material sense, recipient of gift
after gift from her admiring general. Aside from a veritable deluge of jewelry
and an open account with many shops in London and Paris, she became the
world's largest female landowner. It is known that by 1865 she owned several
large ranches and at least twenty-six urban properties. During the war, perhaps
to place in her name huge properties in order to protect some wealth in case

he lost the conflict or had to abdicate, "Marshall López ordered the sale to Elisa Lynch of 437,000 hectares of lands and forests of the state" located in the Chaco. In addition to these lands, she acquired a further 12,000,000 acres in eastern Paraguay and another 9,000,000 acres of yerbales and forests in the contested area north of the Río Apa.[68] If these lands (state property) were truly "sold," it must have been for the proverbial token shilling, for La Lynch, no matter her many charms, did not have any wealth of her own. Further, when the war was clearly going against Paraguay, Francisco Solano made out a will leaving all of his many properties to the consort, depositing that document with United States Minister General Martin McMahon. Although the provisional government in 1869 decreed all properties of the López family and Lynch confiscated, postwar litigation continued for many years as Elisa attempted to salvage something of what she considered was her legitimate wealth. She failed.

Plate 3.   Elisa Alicia Lynch

11. Foreigners and the Modernization of Paraguay

During the Francia years, official policy greatly reduced the impact of foreigners on Paraguay by restricting access to that nation to a small number of merchants (mostly Brazilian) at the segregated entrepôts of Pilar and Ytapúa. The few foreigners who by accident or ill luck penetrated into the interior were normally forced to remain there for years.

With the death of the Caraí, the situation radically changed, and Paraguay's new leaders began to look outward, seeking recognition of sovereignty and commercial advantage. Both of these goals were partially frustrated until after 1852 by the very hostile attitude of Juan Manuel de Rosas, who saw Paraguay as an errant appendage of the Argentine state. The crux of the issue continued to be Buenos Aires's control of the rivers.

"How on earth came you to Paraguay?"[1]

Although Sir Robert Peel of the Foreign Office had written sadly in 1842 that "it does not appear that the right of Bs Ayres to close the Parana can be disputed,"[2] the voracious British merchant community in Buenos Aires was not to be put off. Impelled by a vision of Paraguay as a vast potential market, a vision based in part on a gross exaggeration of that nation's population and in part on the fact that Paraguay alone in South America was known to be free of civil strife, the British commercial factors at Buenos Aires almost salivated at the thought of prying open that huge tropical storehouse.[3]

If Britain and her merchants sought a lucrative trade with Paraguay, a commerce enhanced due to growing discontent with the Rosas regime, the leader of Paraguay sought not only trade but, more important, development for the nation. Basing his vision on the legacy of El Supremo—a unified, disciplined, and prosperous country—Carlos Antonio realized that it would be necessary to seek in the modern world for the hardware and skills needed to produce a new and stronger Paraguay. This turn outward was not the product of any liberalism or rejection of defensive dictatorship, but a course rationally plotted toward the goal of a strong and modern Paraguay. The nation must be strong enough to survive in what was presumed would be a hostile world. To achieve this goal, it would be necessary to open the rivers, and this, as we have seen, was a long-term project.

Carlos Antonio, aware in 1845 of heightening tension between Britain and Argentina, wrote the British minister at Buenos Aires, offering "to contribute to the pacification of the Río de la Plata," even if this would involve sending Paraguayan troops to help oust Rosas.[4] Minister Ouseley, flattering as always in his missives, responded by intimating that Britain would soon recognize Paraguay, writing that Paraguay, "her population and resources equal to those of all the Provinces over which the Gov^t of Buenos Ayres has exercised jurisdiction," was a natural South American partner for London.[5] It would be years before Britain would recognize the absurdity of that assumption, but its mere consideration underlines the fact that Britain's actions were less humanitarian than financial in origin.

It seemed on the surface that López would achieve his premier goal, and he must have basked in the light produced by the truly glowing missives from the British minister. All that had really been done, however, was to partially open the door to foreign merchants, and the first such traders and technicians began to slip in to work their share of the new Paraguayan revolution: the commercial and technological.

The First of the Foreigners

Despite lack of official recognition of Paraguay by major nations, an increasing number of outsiders entered Paraguay, for the most part to make their fortunes by getting an early start in what they assumed was a vast, American China. López promulgated a decree in 1845 defining their status and limiting their physical presence to Ytapúa and Pilar, where they "will enjoy the most complete Liberty in their traffic and in the exercise of their Industry and Art." They were, with great vision, also guaranteed protection in the event of a break in relations between their own governments and that of Paraguay.[6]

Even before the decree was written, foreigners were assuming an important role in Paraguayan commerce and business. As Swedish savant Eberhard Munck wrote in 1843, "foreigners are still looked upon by the Government with certain suspicion," yet this in no way checked their growing numbers or financial transactions.[7] The same year, of the sixty-one retail stores in the capital, twelve were owned by foreigners. Others owned taverns or silver shops or earned their livelihoods as merchants, scribes, carpenters, or ironmongers.[8] Some were even becoming Paraguayan citizens: in 1845 alone at least fifteen immigrants completed the red tape required to be Paraguayan. Most of these were Spaniards or Argentines. More were naturalized each year thereafter.[9]

If foreigners were entering Paraguay in fairly large numbers in the 1840s, it should also be said that they dominated much of Paraguay's fluvial commerce as well. The vast majority of ship captains and owners (often the same), many of whom were legal alien residents of Asunción, were Italians, and, despite the anarchy along the river, scores of Italian vessels were involved in the trade before 1852.[10] A Pilar report from 1849 reveals a sizeable, largely resident foreign commercial community in the unprepossessing port. There were four British and three French merchants, and others from Switzerland, Colombia, Spain, Uruguay, Portugal, and various Argentine provinces, based at Pilar,[11] and many others were constantly passing through.

Also appearing in this epoch were the first foreign experts to work on contract for the modernization of Paraguay—the first wave in a tide that would radically transform the nation. In 1845 came Lt. Col. Francisco Wisner, a cavalryman and engineer of great capacity, whose services were eagerly purchased by López in order to train and modernize the army. Not only was Wisner used as drillmaster, cartographer, and advisor, but at least twice he was given command of Paraguayan units in the field.[12] He remained in Paraguay for thirty years, exercising an astounding variety of important positions in both military and civil spheres. At times, however, he fell from grace. In 1854, Lt. Page of the *Water Witch* encountered him living in apparent retirement on a small ranch in the interior with his Paraguayan wife. Page was impressed with the soldier, but noted in an aside that "his labors were poorly requited" by the López regime.[13] Well before war clouds were plainly visible on the southern horizon, however, he was back in Asunción plying his trade. Wisner's influence on the transformation of the Paraguayan army was great, and many of the later military contractees served under his supervision. He was personal military advisor to both López, designed the huge fortress-complex at Humaitá, and wrote the "official" biography of Dr. Francia.

Other technicians, especially medical men, arrived in the 1840s, mostly on their own initiative, either to offer their services to the government or to pursue their own scientific studies. In both activities they were elements in the sweeping changes affecting Paraguay. One of the earliest physicians to accept a legal contract to serve the government was Germán Federico (Johann Frederick) Meister, who signed up in Rio de Janeiro at the urging of Juan Andrés Gelly. Meister's contract stipulated that he would be "Chief Surgeon to the Army" for two years, receiving 70 silver pesos monthly in addition to travel expenses and special food "corresponding to your class and rank—fresh meat, rice, flour, etc." Passage and lodging for his family would also be under-written by the government should they wish to come to Paraguay, and Meister would be permitted such private practice of medicine as his free time would allow.[14] He served well for four years before returning to his native land.

Eberhard Munck, who arrived in 1843, did not formally serve the govern-ment until after 1864, but he was given permission in 1845 to practice medi-cine outside the capital, even though he was not a medical doctor.[15] In medicine, as in most other technical fields, the shortage, or utter absence, of trained natives impelled the government to use what talent it could find at hand. Even aged José Artigas was offered (but refused) a post as instructor to the army in 1845.[16]

The only index of the size and complexion of the foreign community in this period is a report on foreigners living in the capital's Cathedral barrio in 1850. This, merely one of four barrios, contained 166, including 35 Spaniards, 45 Italians, 19 French, 24 Brazilians, and lesser numbers of Argentines, Swiss, Germans, Portuguese, Bolivians, and British. Only 61 of these are listed as merchants. There were also 9 carpenters, 7 sailors, 6 shopowners, 5 tinworkers, and others with such "arts" as physician, shoemaker, baker, tailor, pharmacist, silverworker, and even miller.[17]

Despite the steady trickle of foreigners, it was not until after 1852 and the liberation of the rivers that the Paraguayan government could embark on its program of enticing foreign experts to collaborate and direct, in a coherent and large-scale manner, the development of the nation. While Gelly in Rio had contracted what experts he encountered on the spot, such as British engineer Henry Godwin and Germans Henry Graf and John George Bechman, to work on the birth of the Paraguayan iron industry, it was not until Francisco Solano was sent to Europe in 1853 that the major steps could be taken.[18]

Whytehead and the Blyth Connection

Blyth and Co. not only built the *Tacuarí,* it also agreed to act (for a fee, of course) as general agent for the Paraguayan government in the recruitment of European technicians and the purchase of needed hardware. Until the outbreak of the war in 1864, Blyth would have an enormous input into Para-guayan development. The British firm, one of the largest and most techno-logically advanced in the world, hired many hundreds of experts, bought equipment and arms, and provided sophisticated apprentice training for dozens of Paraguayan youths selected by the Paraguayan government to become the first native technicians.

To open its recruitment drive, Blyth permitted the contracting of its own chief consulting engineer, William K. Whytehead, one of the finest civil engineers of his age. In spite of his youth, Whytehead awed the López government with his reputation as a technical genius, and Carlos Antonio awarded him the title of "Chief Engineer of the State" on his arrival in Asunción in 1855 (a title never given again). His salary was a rather princely £600 per annum, plus an amazing variety of fringe benefits and travel allowances. He was to be master-builder of the new Paraguay, coordinating all major technical projects, including the iron foundry and factory at Ibicuy, a new and modern arsenal and weapons factory at Asunción, a major shipyard there as well, a railroad, and the telegraph system. The young engineer would be engaged in all of these projects and more, paying especial attention to Carlos Antonio's pet scheme, the arsenal. With him, also contracted by Blyth, came at least eighteen other Britons, for the most part machinists. Within the next four years, at least seventy would follow from Britain alone, and many more would appear unbidden in this skill-hungry land by then known for its generally high contract wages.[19] Those contracted as general technicians or machinists were paid according to experience. First class (men of long experience) were salaried at 80 pesos monthly, and second class specialists drew 60 pesos, or £200 and £144 per annum respectively. Those wages were about double the going rate in London, and were rounded out with fringe benefits and bonuses. A man near the top of his field, such as Whytehead, could earn a truly unusual salary, and as the war approached and finally broke out, the salary scale zoomed upwards. This is the reason that so many technicians chose to remain in Paraguay and take their chances with the nation they helped to arm.[20]

Whytehead immediately went to work on the problem-plagued iron foundry at isolated Ibicuy, which Henry Godwin had failed to get established years before. He ordered the channeling of the Arroyo Mbuyapeí to provide water power, began the mining of iron at Caapucú and San Miguel, and sent long lists of needed equipment to Asunción for transmittal to Blyth. Even given the carte blanche of the López government, his band of British colleagues and plentiful (if unskilled), often convict labor, Whytehead was forced to begin his projects from scratch, building the basic machines *in situ:* a brass furnace, a heavy crane, metal water wheels, a crucible-making machine, ad infinitum.

Other problems encountered at Ibicuy, aside from those linguistic, included poor relations with the Paraguayan officers who oversaw the "captive" work force and the security guard. One, a sergeant Melgarejo, was especially detested by the technicians for his harsh treatment of the workers. Called the "Barbarian-in-Chief" by Whytehead and William Richardson, the Paraguayan appears in many of their letters. In one written by the latter to the former, Richardson decried the heavy-handedness of Melgarejo, "who not only ordered my boys in the foundry to be flogged, but who horse-whipped one himself." Richardson, evidently not devoid of a sense of humor, went on to gossip that

> I found that Sergeant Melgarejo had been visited by a flash of lightning the night before . . . striking the door which opens into the shop. The door was open, his wife was seated in the shop close to the door, it struck her in the breast and melted a portion of a gold necklace that she had on, it scorched her breast, but I think not dangerously . . . it flashed out the front door and killed a dog.[21]

Conquering such difficulties as learning to live with the Barbarian-in-Chief, Whytehead wrote in 1856 that, "thus equipped, the Establishment . . . has answered to all the appeals made to it either for the army or the navy." He sent iron samples from Caapucú to his homeland for analysis and reported to Carlos Antonio with pride the "favorable opinions expressed by Scientific men in England" as to its properties. He fairly bubbled that "there is reason to hope that when the mines of Paraguay are explored and worked on a suitable scale, she will be able to supply La Plata with the best quality of iron at a cheaper rate than is now paid for an inferior quality of iron imported from Europe." Urging that Paraguay use its resources to create a major shipbuilding industry, the engineer informed López that "a Country which can transport cheaply is master both of the producer and consumer and shares the profits of both." In fact, he wrote again with evident pride, the first steamship built in Paraguay (under British direction), the *Yporá,* was already in service, and "her performance leaves nothing to be desired." Two other steamers of advanced design were in the final stages of construction, and Whytehead closed his euphoric report by praising "the aptitude displayed by the young men who are being trained in the different mechanical arts."[22]

Within a surprisingly short time, Whytehead and an increasing number of his colleagues made notable progress. The Asunción shipyards, under the guidance of a dozen or so British experts using recently purchased or constructed machinery, began to hum. The British-built *Tacuarí* and the newly-purchased *Río Blanco* were joined in 1856 by the *Yporá* and *Salto de Guairá,* in 1857 by *El Correo,* in 1858 by the *Río Apa,* and in 1859 by the *Río Jejuí,* all sizeable, modern river steamers designed for both commercial and military service.[23] Not only were these vessels built at Asunción, in a shipyard that became progressively more modern, but extensive repair work and maintenance was also carried out on ships locally built or purchased abroad. On all Paraguayan steamers, foreign (mostly British) machinists served. Many, in fact, worked in the engine rooms of the Paraguayan flotilla for ten years or more, well into the war itself.

A British civil engineer, Thomas Norton Smith, with the rank of "Ship

Constructor to the State," managed the shipyard under Whytehead's supervision from 1855 to 1860, at a salary of £275 annually. Among other works, he constructed a massive, modern wharf and drydock designed by his chief. Many young Paraguayans, selected by the government, toiled there, learning their new trades, as well as hundreds of common laborers.[24]

Under the unswerving gaze of the chief engineer, an arsenal was created in Asunción in 1856 to provide not only heavy caliber weaponry but also massive metal naval gear such as boilers. Whytehead appointed Frederick Garton its first director, and then his good friend Alex Grant, who worked with a team of British and Paraguayans and master caster engineer William Richardson, who was later replaced by colleague and compatriot William Newton. Mechanical drafting at the arsenal was entrusted to William Marshall, who arrived in 1857, and architect Alonzo Taylor was put in charge of designing more modern facilities. A foundry was built for the arsenal, and moulding shops, drafting rooms, and metal-cutting circular saws were installed. By 1858, the arsenal was producing cannon, shot, machine tools, propellors and assorted naval equipment.[25]

The projected railroad, which was to link Villa Rica with the capital (by way of the central military camp at Cerro León), was another major concern of the government and its hired experts (perhaps the most expensive of all). Blyth sent the locomotives, some of which had chugged through the Crimean War, and some of the rails, as well as a team of technicians led by North American civil engineer George Paddison, who began his work in 1858. Soon joined by three well-known British contract engineers, George Thompson, Henry Valpy, and Percy Burrell, Paddison made outstanding progress in the difficult undertaking.[26] Thompson, who demonstrated unusual skill in designing fortifications, worked with and for the army during the war, and, as a colonel, was given active command over a Paraguayan defense line in 1868.[27]

Health care, especially for the growing army, was yet another priority of the regime, and to this end López recruited a number of medical men to replace Dr. Meister, who left Paraguay in 1852. Blyth handled most arrangements, and in 1856 sent Dr. John H. Johnston and pharmacist James Prickett, at excellent salaries. The doctor died shortly after his arrival (one of the first of many to expire in Paraguay before their contracts) but was quickly replaced by the team of Drs. John Fox, George Barton, and William Stewart. Prickett stayed on until 1861. Barton, who was made chief of the military medical service, received £500 annually for his skills, plus horse, house, servants, and living allowance. This is, no doubt, why he renewed his contract two years later. The other doctors were remunerated at only slightly lesser rates. All salaries moved upward by 1863 as international tensions mounted, and Stewart, only in his mid-thirties, earned £800 annually by the end of that year. The medical men, a smoothly functioning team, established several military clinics, treated the sick and wounded, and formally trained a large corps of Paraguayan paramedics who served brilliantly during the war.[28]

One Could Find a Few Feet of Clay

Other foreigners were contracted to work with the military, for the most part as advisors, as had Col. Wisner earlier. In addition to those serving in the navy, other experts acted as technical advisors to both naval and terrestrial artillery units, teaching skills acquired in less peaceful lands. The Paraguayan military benefited greatly from their guidance, and the placement and handling of artillery throughout the war was superb. As with other areas of contract service, however, not all worked out well with foreign military advisors. Witness the case of one Claudius B. Piers.

That gentleman, sent out by Blyth, was appalled by Paraguay, by Paraguayans, and by his treatment at the hands of both. After one year of service, we find him complaining to the government about alleged indignities he had suffered. A minor official, José M. Téllez, was detailed to respond, and he minced no words, accusing Piers of inflating his own military credentials. Instead of having served as Captain of British Horse Artillery and Lt. Col. of Osmani (Turkish) Cavalry on detached duty, as Piers claimed, Téllez wrote that an investigation revealed no Turkish service at all and only very junior rank in the British Army. The official also sarcastically informed the officer that he could not expect the title of "Chief of Engineers," as that was reserved for those who actually *were* engineers, which Piers most decidedly was not. Reminding the foreigner that he was both "without any rank" whatsoever and subject to Paraguayan military law, Téllez then insisted that Piers's salary was £600 annually and not the £700 claimed. Finally, he would receive no special food unless he chose to pay for it himself, and Téllez chided the officer for being but one of a number of foreigners who harbored absurd and arrogant pretensions.[29]

A deeply-stung Piers retorted, claiming that inaccuracies in his service record were due to poor translation by an English clerk. He also asserted that, contrary to official Paraguayan views, he was not *in* the Paraguayan Army, "for I have neither contracted nor do I intend to enter it—the fact of my duty being Military and not Civil Engineering in no way warranting such a conclusion." "I acknowledge no laws," wrote Piers, "but those to which a British Subject residing in this country, apply to me, and I do not hold myself accountable to the ordinances of the Army." Explaining in a condescending manner that "it is the duty of every English Gentleman to vindicate his honor," he noted that he had requested Blyth to send a full and clear explanation "of what they consider I am entitled to under said contract."

According to the officer, this included higher pay, a full expense account, two servants, and two horses, and he reiterated his demand "that Your Excellency will either give directions that I be supplied with fit and proper rations or an allowance in lieu of the same."[30]

When the government suggested that Piers might be better off canceling his contract, it was stunned by his exorbitant response. Seizing an opportunity to gouge the López regime and escape the rustic country at once, Piers demanded £300 in travel and transportation expenses, £900 in compensation for early termination of contract, and a further £100 in miscellaneous allowances.[31] The López government, never long on patience, irately responded that "if there has been a breaking of the Contract, it has been on your part," and so, no compensation was due. Piers was bluntly informed that *if* he abandoned Paraguay on the first available ship, López would authorize payment of his "simple passage" and half salary until his arrival in England. His pride severely ravaged, Piers *did* immediately depart.[32]

Paraguayan authorities found a host of other headaches with their contract intellects, some of whom served inexpertly, if at all. In 1859, J. Blyth wrote Francisco Solano, admitting that "we hear with surprise of the disappearance of Assistant Surgeon Mr. Henry Wells, and we shall not of course make any payments to his order" until he turns up and resumes work. He never did so.[33] It was also necessary to arrest experts from time to time for brawling and other visibly poor conduct. At root in most of these cases was the pronounced predilection of many foreign contractees for the extremely potent Paraguayan aguardiente. As George Masterman wrote in 1870, after his "seven eventful years" as a contract pharmacist, the liquor was dangerous, and "the English Mechanics in Asunción, with the usual recklessness and improvidence of their class, consumed it in enormous quantities, and the death of nearly half their number could be traced directly or indirectly to its abuse."[34]

Also a problem, accentuated by cultural shock, ennui, and firewater, was laziness and absenteeism. Probably the British Empire record-holder was machinist John Twiddell, who "has lost 239 days in a period of twenty-six months, for no reason." Twiddell was fired on the spot, along with his friend and fellow-malingerer Andrew Bryson.[35] Anger over sloth often resulted in the arrest of the expert, as in the case of foundry technicians Smith and Boothby, jailed in 1865 "for not wanting to work."[36] Rare was it, however, for an expert to languish. Conditions in the jails were so medievally harsh that even the most slothful became charged with a desire to honor his contract.

Telegraphs and Foreign Intellects

In general, despite the contretemps, foreign experts worked and worked out surprisingly well. The shipyard was finished and functioning smoothly in 1860, the arsenal and Ibicuy foundry poured forth a stream of cannon and shell, the railroad, despite some spectacular early accidents, connected the capital with Pirayú and the military camp at Cerro León and was pushing eastward, and many another work was underway.

In addition to these major undertakings staffed and directed mainly by English-speaking experts, one should note the telegraph, directed by Whytehead but effected by a German team led by Robert von Fischer Treuenfelt. That engineer, contracted especially to create a telegraphic network that would link Humaitá with Asunción and other military nerve centers, arrived in Paraguay only in mid-1864, just before the war. Within three months, Villa Rica was connected to the capital by wire, and in the following year the line, part of which passed under the turbulent Río Tebicuari, reached strategic Humaitá. As the war progressed, Treuenfelt extended the line all the way to Curupaití. The German engineer also trained Paraguayan telegraphers and, during the war, created a national paper industry at Luque. He was repaid in 1868 by being beaten to death by orders of the Mariscal, one of the many victims of the San Fernando "purge."[37]

Besides these proofs of modernity, foreigners also had much to do with the renaissance of Paraguayan culture and education. In addition to the several dozen Paraguayans sent to England for education in the "mechanical pursuits," many in the factories of Blyth and Co., individual foreigners were salaried to expand modern education at home, to correct the anti-intellectual legacy of El Supremo.

One of the most fruitful of the educational experts was Ildefonso Bermejo, a Spaniard who arrived at Asunción in 1855. He had contracted to act as a sort of literary agent and consultant to López, and he began his work with some trepidation after seeing a young German photographer, his fellow passenger on the trip upstream, thrown in jail because he could not adequately explain his "infernal machine" to customs officials.[38]

Among his early assignments was to edit one of the first newspapers published in Paraguay, *El Eco del Paraguay,* after which he edited, with Carlos Antonio, *El Semanario* from 1857 to 1863, also training a few Paraguayan youth to take his place when he left the country. He also founded the first Paraguayan normal school in 1855, an ill-fated venture that was closed for lack of interest and support the following year. He then created the Aula de Filosofía, where advanced students faced a modern curriculum, and this school lasted until his departure. In 1857, Bermejo earned about £600 annually, an excellent salary, even for a top-flight medical or engineering expert. He magnified his cultural impact by giving lectures, organizing social events such as costume parties, and in 1859 enticing a Spanish light opera company, then in Buenos Aires, to voyage upriver and present to Asunción's elite a piece of his own authorship.[39]

Bermejo, despite his almost frantic commitment, was never content in Paraguay (few experts were), uncomfortable in such a rustic society, noting that "Paraguayans are naturally docile and susceptible to all forms of teaching," but also "fearful and servile, . . . fake and suspicious." In 1860, with some misgivings, he returned a government slave who had been put at his disposition, writing with disappointment that although he had taught the slave reading, writing, and carpentry, he had become "an incorrigible drunk." The government, showing more faith in Bermejo's teaching than in the slave's drinking, employed him henceforth in the military carpentry shop.[40] In 1863, with the Corpulent Despot dead and international crises multiplying, Bermejo finally returned to his native land.

Another leading educator was Pedro Dupuis, who appeared in Asunción in 1854 and opened a school of mathematics to prepare students chosen by the government for careers in the mechanical arts. Many of the fifty-one students who appear in his first official report, such as Natalicio Talavera, Cándido Bareiro, and Juan Crisóstomo Centurión, would become important cultural and political forces in the future. Much of the work was basic—in fact, remedial—in nature, but Dupuis was generally pleased with the activity and eagerness shown by his charges. An exception, he noted, was one José Dolores Valiente, who displayed "an irregular conduct, not wishing to work— on the contrary, trying to distract his neighbors." Carlos Antonio, in his inimitable way, soon notified Dupuis that "the denounced José Dolores Valiente will be sent to the Navy" for corrective labor.[41]

Dupuis, who left Paraguay shortly before the war, returned soon after its conclusion to become director of the new Colegio Nacional, in 1875. His wife Ana taught piano at her private music school in the capital during both stays. Other foreigners, in the main French, were involved in Paraguayan education, for the most part in the private sphere. Among these were Dorotea Duprat, who opened a private girls' school on the eve of the war, a Mons. DeCluny, who taught his native tongue in the 1860s, and Francisco Sauvegeod de Dupuis, who founded and directed a music school from 1853 until his death in 1861. The latter also contracted to teach six military bands to play martial music and also to direct a military band "anytime that there are comedies at the National Theater."[42] Shortly before the war, in 1864, a German, Gustavo Mackenson, arrived, after having taught for years in Uruguay. In Asunción he set up a commercial and linguistic school, dedicated to the teaching of five modern languages and basic financial skills. Like many other foreign teachers, he supplemented his income by doing considerable in-home tutoring.[43] A European lithographer, Carlos Riviere, taught engraving and other sophisticated specialties in Paraguay at the government's request, and was contracted in 1856 to print paper money for Carlos Antonio. He was to teach at least ten Paraguayans his trade, and his pay was to be a percentage of the bills he produced: a substantial sum of local money.[44]

Yet another area in which foreign experts worked with great success was that of architecture. Aside from numerous sumptuous private homes (most of which were owned by the López clan) planned and directed by foreign architects, a number of larger projects were undertaken, mostly by Alejandro Ravizza or Alonzo Taylor. The former, a professional Italian architect, came to Paraguay with his brother in 1854 to begin a series of impressive private structures for the elite. While his brother engaged in commerce, Ravizza accepted the post of "State Architect," and over the next decade designed and supervised construction of the Oratory (today's Pantheon of Heroes), the National Theater (which he never finished, owing to difficulties with the roof), the Club Nacional, and several city churches. He was still constructing while the Allies were destructing during the war.[45] Alonzo Taylor, a British engineer and draftsman who worked on the new arsenal and elsewhere, left his mark on Paraguayan architecture by designing and building the harmonious Government Palace, which has been used by every chief executive since Francisco Solano. It is perhaps the one outstanding building to be seen today in Paraguay. Taylor was also responsible for most of the excellent railroad stations near the capital (that at Areguá is a minor classic), and his work was enhanced by the skill of two contracted sculptors, John Owen Moynihan and Andrés Antonini, whose delicate work and artistic balance softened many a harsh line in the angular Paraguayan sun.[46]

The Informal Technicians of Caaguazú and Beyond

The individual and highly skilled contract experts represent only the tip of the foreign iceberg that entered Paraguayan waters under the López. Engaged in less spectacular but ubiquitous endeavors were literally hundreds of foreigners, most of them resident aliens, who constituted much of the middle class of the host country. In 1863, foreigners were granted over half of all business licenses given in the capital. Outsiders dominated the wholesale trade, owned ten taverns, shoe shops, three pharmacies, billiard parlors, paint stores, and silver shops, and engaged in many occupations tied into domestic and external commerce. In all the republic, foreigners were granted 44 percent of all licenses awarded that year, a striking phenomenon.[47]

During the same period, partial passport lists (February, 1857, through June, 1861), show that 516, or 62 percent, of the 836 passports issued at Asunción went to foreigners. Of these, 112 were issued to Italians, 78 to

Spaniards, 77 to Portuguese, 57 to French, and 29 to British citizens. In all, 308 were made out to Europeans. Virtually all nations of the hemisphere were also included, as was every Argentine province.[48]

In Asunción, in a short period of months, Italians Santiago Caniza, Gerónimo Falcón, and José Vagliani opened a tavern, a billiard parlor, and an "Optical Cabinet which contains the best European views, for public recreation," all in the Encarnación barrio, where a growing number of foreigners lived.[49] Also in the capital were a German watchmaker, a North American cigar maker, and an English printer, as well as scores of other resident specialists. Much of what was available in Asunción—much of what made it a city—was owed to the presence of diverse foreign elements.[50]

Another perusal of the scene shows Luis Mysznowski purchasing licenses to collect taxes in Limpio, Henrique Cramon, a French resident of the capital, asking permission to construct a sawmill in the Chaco, and Italian Lázaro Costa buying tobacco harvests at Villa Rica. A surprising number of foreigners could be found in the interior, although few actually lived there. Swedish naturalist Munck supported his studies by buying and selling livestock taxes along the Tebicuari, Italian Miguel Queirolo ran a yerba station at Caaguazú, Agustín Piallo regularly purchased tobacco at Caraguatay, and Madame Lynch's brother, John Pablo Lynch, did the same at Villa Rica.[51]

The War and the Technicians—End of a Dream

The foreign impact on Paraguay through limited industrialization, training, education, and general economic activity helped strengthen the nation in a formal sense. The hundreds of heavy-caliber guns at Humaitá and elsewhere, the navy, railroad, telegraph, and munitions manufactures all helped bring about the horrendous War of the Triple Alliance. The war, in turn, all but destroyed that which had been essential to Paraguay's strength. The hardware that enabled Francisco Solano to become "Mariscal" and self-appointed arbiter of the Río de la Plata did not long outlast him. The dizzying speed with which his nation was modernized tempted López to flex his new muscle and seek an activist role in international affairs. Even as war approached and tensions mounted, foreigners continued to sign up, and Blyth and Co. was kept busy purchasing materiel for its best customer. So good, indeed, was the government of Paraguay that at one point Blyth allowed Francisco Solano to carry an impressive £50,612 on the cuff.[52]

When Mariscal López declared war on Brazil in 1864, he immediately turned to his technicians, ordering Whytehead to prepare newly-confiscated or purchased ships for war. For months, the chief engineer ran his shipyard workers ragged, converting a half-dozen vessels to warships.[53] Only a few technicians opted to leave despite the war, and López was so confident as to actually refuse to renew contracts for men he thought to be slackers. He did, however, raise salaries across the board.[54]

Conditions soon deteriorated for all in Paraguay, foreign workers included. López's blunders cost the cream of his army and an Allied blockade was soon felt. Absence of contact with their loved ones and friends in other nations, increased hours of labor, and, occasionally, combat duty all tended, as Josefina Pla has noted, to accentuate (especially among the British) an already noted fondness for strong spirits as well as acute depression, listlessness, illness, and suicide.

In the only major naval engagement of the war, the battle of Riachuelo, in June, 1865, the Paraguayan fleet was crushed, despite the heroic efforts of a score of British machinists aboard, at least two of whom died of their wounds. Two others, Cuthbert Westgarth (who later died of cholera) and John Watts (later executed by López), were decorated in a formal ceremony by the Mariscal himself, for exceptional bravery.[55]

After Riachuelo, it became clear to all foreigners who cared to think about it that the war would be long and probably disastrous to Paraguay. What this resulted in psychologically cannot be known, but the work, at an increasingly frantic pace, continued. In July, for a combination of reasons unknown, Chief Engineer Whytehead killed himself by an injection of concentrated nicotine. He had been ill and depressed and was neither the first nor the last to take his own life. An inventory of his effects revealed a telescope, a portable pump, 258 books, a magnesium lamp, two horses, and 324 pesos in paper money: a poor estate for a man who orchestrated the development of Paraguay for almost a decade.[56] Although many technicians continued their labors, some deserted to the Allies and others sought refuge in foreign legations or in the winding sheets of death.

In 1868, when Allied forces overran Ibicuy, some twenty British specialists were evacuated at the last minute by orders of López and rushed to "safety." No doubt, at that point, their definition of safety differed markedly from that of the Mariscal. Most of these were set to similar work at the Asunción arsenal, which increased its output remarkably as they were joined by machinists from the abandoned remnants of the Paraguayan fleet. When the capital itself was threatened, the technicians and many loads of machinery were transported to Caacupé, where the arsenal was reestablished. Despite the fact that many of the technicians knew little of casting and rifling cannon, they showed themselves very adept at doing just that. Until the last days of the war they produced scores of very high quality cannon and mortars, although the pace and strain of events killed at least fifteen of them.[57] When Brazilian troops finally captured the make-shift arsenal in mid-1869, they were surprised to find there twenty-two recently-produced cannon and some nine hundred thousand projectiles. Twenty-three British technicians and a few others of different nationalities were captured there as well.[58]

The foreign medical men, as well as scores of other foreigners, were notable for sticking to their posts to the very end, several dying in the last week of the war, along with López. During the Mariscal's paranoid reaction to the supposed 1868, or San Fernando, conspiracy, Drs. Rhynd and Fox and pharmacist Masterman, as well as hundreds of other foreigners, were arrested. All were treated abominably, tortured, starved, and beaten, and few lived to tell the tale of their sufferings. John Watts, the decorated machinist of Riachuelo, Eberhard Munck, a British merchant named Stark, German engineer Neuman, United States citizen James Manlove, and as many as five hundred other foreigners were either beaten to death, shot, or lanced. So also died the majority of the small corps of diplomats stuck in Paraguay by the war.[59]

Those who survived told tales of horror, of sadistic mistreatment, interminable interrogations, and snap decisions of life or death by drum-head military tribunals. As haggard survivor Masterman wrote shortly after his release, "the blind obedience of the rest to the orders of López, an obedience almost as unreasoning as that of an ox to his master, but which has been mistaken for devotion and patriotism," was the true tragedy of Paraguay. A tragedy written in blood.[60]

When the war terminated, there was precious little evidence of the titanic work that had been done. Gone were the experts and the hundreds of Paraguayans trained by them. Those foreigners who came to Paraguay after 1870 would in many cases be parasites, buying the natural resources and alienating the public domain of the shattered nation.

The Paraguayan experience with rapid modernization was a unique one. The government of Carlos Antonio alone of South American regimes achieved a large measure of industrialization without inviting massive amounts of foreign investment capital that was waiting impatiently in the wings, and hence Paraguay in the 1840-1870 epoch did not mortgage her financial future, escaping the pressures that were brought to bear on neighboring nations by European investors. Paraguay paid cash for what it needed and only purchased what it could pay for. Paraguay relied not on imported capital but on imported skills. Paying as it went, Paraguay not only made use of selected foreign experts who represented fortunes spent in other lands on research and education, to construct a new Paraguay, but also to build, through training, a new, technologically-oriented Paraguayan to manage the future nation. Had it not been for the war, it might have worked out. There is no doubt that in 1864, Francisco Solano ruled a nation unified, debt-free, and technologically advanced in relation to other nations of the continent.

It should be noted that virtually all of the modernization and "industrialization" carried out in this epoch was military, or defensive in nature. It would not be an understatement to say that Paraguay's leap into the mid-nineteenth century was on one foot only, an unbalanced development at best that left the average Paraguayan scratching in the soil with the same ideas and instruments used two centuries earlier. One cannot say that the progress noted above "caused" the war, but there is no doubt that it made the war possible. Even El Mariscal would not have dared do more than defend his borders had not his military materiel encouraged him to redefine those borders and play the more dangerous role of fulcrum in the regional balance of power.

The Bordeaux-Asunción Axis

Apart from the importation of technicians, but conceptually allied with that phenomenon, was the strange case of Nueva Bordeaux. Francisco Solano's trip to Europe witnessed agreements to found a sizeable French farming colony in Paraguay, to be merely the first of many. This effort reflected the elder López's ardent desire to aid the modernization of his land through fostering the immigration of sturdy, hard-working European farmers, and also to fulfill the ancient Paraguayan dream of settling the still wild Chaco.

Between 1537 and 1855, a combination of hostile Indians, horrible heat, drought, flood, dangerous flora and fauna, and frightening insect life had frustrated Paraguayan attempts to settle and utilize the Chaco. In the 1840s, a few forts and army estancias had been established across the river from Asunción, and some Blacks settled near the river, but these endeavors barely managed to survive, and were a constant drain on the treasury.

Responding to Francisco Solano's overtures while in France, the French government agreed to permit the sending out of a pilot agricultural colony of some four hundred people as soon as it could be organized, *if* the settlers were given guarantees of land and good treatment. In May, 1855, as the immigrants were arriving in Paraguay, the López government issued a decree, almost in contract form, specifying in thirty-two articles the rights, duties, and privileges of the colonists. According to this sanguine document, each able-bodied man would receive a portion of his own land (with title), a house, food for a year, seeds, and livestock. The government would also provide tools and tax exemptions. The colonists, for their part, were to work hard, and after the third year they would be required to deliver to Paraguayan officials one quarter of all their harvests of "cotton, honey, anil, cochinilla, and tobacco" to repay the cost of their passage. No greater proof of López's naive faith in Europeans can be imagined than this pipedream concerning the production of "strategic" crops in the poor soil of the eastern Chaco! [61]

Within months of their arrival, the colonists were beginning to melt away. Most of them were not farmers by trade and were totally unprepared for the grim reality of the Chaco, and the López regime was less than lavish with its support. Most dwellings were not complete, there were immediate shortages of food and other basic goods, and the French settlers showed themselves singularly reluctant to become pioneers. From the outset, many simply fled, usually to Asunción, where, being conspicuous, they were arrested for violation of a contract that few had seen and none had signed. Indeed, some of the fleet-footed French were put on public works in chains.[62]

Within six months after its initial foundation, Nueva Burdeos was spewing its dismayed settlers throughout Paraguay, and local authorities were picking them up as far into the interior as San Ysidro Labrador, where one, Jean Roulac, was arrested as "one of the French colonists involved in the plot to leave the colony of Nueva Burdeos and turn themselves over to the Chaco Indians."[63] Things must have been absurdly difficult indeed for such an alternative to be considered, and, in any case, San Ysidro is in the wrong direction for those seeking the Chaco nomads. As Lt. Page put it after surveying the scene, many immigrants preferred "to run the gauntlet of Indians, jaguars and starvation to living under such oppression."[64]

In the last days of 1855, responding to an almost unanimous petition of the colonists who wanted to leave the colony, López agreed to its dissolution. At this time there were 339 colonists at Nueva Burdeos: 41 bachelors, 7 unmarried women, and the rest in 72 families. As Carlos Antonio wrote in a postscript to the affair, the French immigrants would be allowed a term of fifty days "to pay their debts to the National Treasury," an unrealistic demand in the face of their impecunious condition.[65]

As López attempted to collect from the Chaco-shocked colonists, he sent soldiers to the settlement to guard buildings and what few crops had been sown. One French family requested to remain, and they were allowed to, helping the soldiers with the meager January harvest.[66]

The Paraguayan government was never repaid for its expenses of passage, and most of the colonists, disillusioned, headed for France, their way paid by the charity of compatriots in Asunción. Those few who chose to remain in Paraguay did not take part in the recriminations that burdened diplomatic correspondence between Paraguay and France for years concerning the misguided venture. The López government eventually assented to pay a small cash indemnity to cover the "inconveniences" experienced by the French settlers.

Plate 4. Francisco Solano López

12. "Francisco Solano's Error: The War"

"I consider López to be a monster without parallel"[1]

Carlos Antonio López, the Corpulent Despot, died a lingering death on September 10, 1862, despite the ministrations of a brace of British medicoes. As he left this world, he called in his son Francisco Solano, appointed him vice-president, and counseled him, according to one account, to avoid bellicose gestures in foreign affairs, especially in the case of Brazil.[2] It is a pity the young man did not heed his father.

As the old man's rotund frame was being prepared for burial, his son sent out a call for a congress that would decide on the future of the Paraguayan government. On September 16, a nervous, thirty-six-year-old Francisco Solano, in his shaky position as vice-president, opened the first session of the two-hundred-delegate assembly, perhaps the first Paraguayan congress that really had something to decide. Several prominent Asunceños were notably absent from the assembly, for López, rightly fearing an opposition party, and desirous of nipping dissidence in the bud, had discretely ordered a score or more arrests in the previous few days.[3]

Even with those precautions and with a stronger than normal honor guard highly visible, not all was serene for the young López. In the very brief initial debate, at least one delegate doubted the legality and propriety of Francisco Solano's assuming his father's mantle. After all, had not Carlos Antonio, in his quasi-constitution of 1844, declared that the presidency would not be the property of any one family? Another daring Paraguayan suggested that perhaps it was time to draft a genuine constitution, but he was shouted down by the pro-López faction, which was clearly in a majority, Within a few hours, despite the efforts of a small "liberal" group of delegates, Francisco Solano was named president by acclamation, for a term of ten years, and Asunción that evening was treated to a series of political arrests as well as a Te Deum and fireworks. A wealthy gentleman named Florencio Varela, known to believe that López was ineligible for election, was thrown into a dungeon, his properties confiscated by the state. A high-ranking magistrate, Pedro Lescano, was also jailed, as was Father Fidel Maíz, a supposed leader in the "liberal" party. Maíz, a boyhood friend and classmate of the new president, was kept in chains for almost four years, brutally beaten, threatened with death, and barely kept alive on a minimal diet. He was released only in 1866 by a López made ecstatic by his victory at Curupaití. As a grateful Maíz later wrote of his surprise salvation: "Curupayty! Place of my second birth."[4] His experience was fairly typical of those arrested—capricious release or death, all without benefit of accusation, trial, or any other basic rights. Dozens of important Paraguayan families, such as the Saguiers and the Decouds, as well as a number of resident foreigners, left Paraguay to join swelling exile ranks at Buenos Aires.[5]

Francisco Solano López inaugurated his rule, then, with a short, sharp repression, and no matter congratulatory form letters from the rulers of many nations, the climate of fear in Asunción was so palpable in the next few months that British Minister Edward Thornton, visiting that city from Buenos Aires, warned British citizens to leave what he considered an unstable dictatorship.[6] To help explain his purge, López told various diplomats that Fidel Maíz and his own brother Benigno López had been conspiring to place the latter in the presidency, a maneuver, said Francisco Solano, that boded ill for Paraguay.[7]

That López had enemies before the congress cannot be doubted, and, equally clear, he created some new ones through his harsh reaction of September, 1862. Aware that he faced a certain "popular discontent,"[8] it is quite possible that the new president felt it important to win the respect, if not the love, of his people as well as those abroad by assuming an international role commensurate with his nation's growing power.

Francisco Solano was, in his own way, an impressive man. Short of stature and full-bearded, the younger López was quite slim in his youth, "though in later life he developed a decidedly Napoleonic paunch as well as bandy legs from early riding."[9] Unlike his informal father, there was nothing slovenly about Francisco Solano, who affected an imperious manner, rarely being seen in less than formal dress uniform.

There is little doubt that he had been spoiled in his early years. In the words of one author, he "lived the life of a Crown Prince: from an early age, his every whim was indulged and he was encouraged to expect instant obedience from all about him."[10] Yet he was a conscientious student in both school and life, and showed a certain aptitude for languages, eventually speaking, if not with perfect fluency, French, German, English, and Portuguese in addition to his native Spanish and Guaraní.

López learned fast, if not always by choice. His father, lacking trust and confidence in most of his compatriots, early entrusted major military, administrative, and diplomatic tasks to his favorite son, beginning in 1844 with Francisco Solano's titular command of the expedition to Corrientes. From that time on, the young man, and not his brothers, was chosen to direct every important undertaking not handled directly by the Corpulent Despot himself. The elder López was grooming his son for power. As a result, Francisco Solano, able and hardworking, was well prepared to assume the presidency in 1862. Or so it seemed at the time.

Francisco Solano, Statesman

López's perception of his nation's neighbors was basically faulty—in fact, it lagged several decades behind a swiftly advancing reality. He well knew that Paraguay's survival as a nation owed much to the fragmentation of Brazil and Argentina in the 1830-1850 era. Both nations, suffering from great centripetal forces, had almost been torn apart by regional differences that exploded time and again into major civil wars. In the 1860s, however, the situation had drastically changed. The old scars and perhaps some bitterness remained, yet the old caudillos were dead, discredited, or withdrawn from the scene. Argentina, despite its pronounced regionalism, was a constitutional republic, no longer a snarling congeries of provinces. Brazil, a constitutional empire, faced serious social, economic, and political problems, but by 1860 was united by bonds of nationalism tied personally by Pedro II.

In any serious contest, Brazil and/or Argentina would react as a nation reacts and would not revert to "ravening" caudillo-ridden regionalism. Failure to appreciate the maturity of his neighbors and overconfidence in his own nation and its increasingly modern military led Francisco Solano to redefine Paraguay's borders outwards, to figuratively include Uruguay, and to play the part of arbiter of the Río de la Plata: the Provincia Gigante reborn. Playing on his people's conditioned nationalism, a species of chauvinism largely racial in complexion, López felt he could gain both international stature and tranquility within Paraguay. A tragic misapprehension.

The Uruguayan Enigma Unfolds

A history of Uruguay in the nineteenth century is really a history of the intrigues of Brazil, Argentina, and to a lesser extent Paraguay, and of their respective parties within the small country. Its complexity rivals that of

Schleswig-Holstein, yet there was no Metternich to unravel the skein.

What had transpired in Uruguay since 1810 had always been of interest and perhaps, in a limited way, of consequence to Paraguay. Potentially the other buffer state of the subcontinent, Uruguay was, from the beginning of the century, subjected to great pressures from both Argentina and Brazil. The latter, desiring to round out its centuries of expansion with a southern boundary on the Río de la Plata estuary, hoped to dominate that broad fresh and saline waterway and hence exercise influence over Argentina. The former, aware of this possibility, was historically opposed to such a future.

When one considers the matter, it made little difference to Paraguay who controlled Uruguay. The various civil wars in the Banda Oriental, 1810-1830, barely affected the Guaraní Republic, and open Brazilian annexation of what they called their Cisplatine Province brought Paraguay neither boon nor ill. Even the major Cisplatine War (1825-1828) between Argentina and Brazil went almost unnoticed in reclusive Paraguay, as did the official creation of the Republic of Uruguay through British mediation in 1828.[11]   After El Supremo's death in 1840, Paraguayans continued to live their lives blissfully ignorant of civil wars, Rosas's intervention, gaucho raids, and Garibaldi's exploits in Uruguay. They remained unaware of the mass rape of Uruguay because it had no significant repercussion in Paraguay.

Neither Francia nor Carlos Antonio cared much what happened in Uruguay: certainly they never dreamed of intervening there in favor of one cause or another. This lassitude was an intelligent one owing to a clear appreciation that Uruguay was unimportant to Paraguay, whereas the dual policies of neutrality and non-intervention were essential to national survival. Only Francisco Solano, once in power, saw a connection between the two buffer states that better minds had previously (and have since) failed to discern. This connection was a creation of the young López, and he acted as if he had discovered what the *philosophes* had spent their lives searching for: the motive force of nature. In his decision to tie the future of Paraguay to that of distant and different Uruguay, López made a disastrous error. When he claimed that the "perfect and absolute independence" of Uruguay was a precondition of the maintenance of the regional balance of power, Francisco Solano spit in the face of reality, for such had never been the case.[12]

López's discovery of the balance of power principle in 1863 was for rhetorical rather than material purposes. What he really discovered after one brief year in office was that Paraguay was, in the regional context, a major nation, a force to be reckoned with. What upset the dictator was the fact that his nation and he were *not being reckoned with*. Events in Uruguay, prompted in large part by Brazil and Argentina, were taking place without regard for Paraguay's new stature. Hence his decision to enter the chaotic international power plays taking place in Uruguay. It can be cogently argued that Francisco Solano, far from maintaining the fragile balance of regional power, shattered it when he moved into the Uruguayan arena. He acted out of a wish to win the recognition that he knew his country and he personally were due. After all, he had personally mediated at Buenos Aires in 1859 between the forces of Urquiza and Mitre and had won the kudos of all involved, bringing Paraguay for the first time to center stage of the regional theater. As one observer noted astutely: "The diplomatic attention shown to Paraguay caused him to overestimate her influence; at the same time, he attributed the attitude of his neighbors to fear."[13]

If, then, López sought recognition, he had to stir his nation from its traditional, passive (and peaceful) role of spectator, and lead the country into the boiling cauldron. It should also be noted that Paraguay was still not being treated as an equal by either Brazil or Argentina in the vexatious and interminable boundary disputes. Despite her growing strength, Paraguay was no closer to a settlement of its claims in the north or in Candelaria than it had been in 1840. In fact, the reverse was true, for Brazil had bullied López into the 1858 accord, which allowed virtually free access to the Mato Grosso without settlement of the border issue. Similarly, the Argentines, while possessing increasingly more of disputed Candelaria in the physical sense, had continued to postpone serious talks and decisions on the issue.

Further indicative of a certain disdain for Paraguay was Brazil's neglect to post a diplomatic representative of any rank in Asunción between late 1858 and late 1863, preferring to handle affairs through the good offices of the Portuguese resident consul there.[14] The Argentines had similarly entrusted their diplomatic business, not to a regular envoy, but to infrequent missions by ministers plenipotentiary.

Slighted, overawed by his own importance and that of his nation, and confused by Brazil's and Argentina's lack of the same appreciation, López opened the Uruguayan version of Pandora's box. What came out confused him as much as it had the Argentines and Brazilians, and it was this confusion that brought about the war that devoured Paraguay.

Inside Uruguay

The chaotic Uruguayan scene cannot be plumbed in a few brief pages, but its general outline may perhaps be delineated.[15] The basic instability of Uruguayan political life was caused by its two parties, the Blancos and the Colorados, each of which was itself fragmented into extremist and moderate wings. The salient characteristic of these parties (beyond their inability to acquiesce to each other's rule) was that the Blancos generally represented rural, pastoral, and traditional segments of society, whereas the Colorados drew most of their support from commercial, urban, "liberal" interests. Aside from this very general portrait, each party derived considerable, although fluctuating, support from neighboring states. For years, Brazil had tended to back the Blancos, but, by 1863, displeasure with Blanco policies led to a shift in support to the Colorados, who often had received moral and physical aid from Buenos Aires. Argentine and Brazilian intrigues by 1863 were for once not directed at opposite goals but at bringing down the ruling Blanco party.[16]

To add to the confusion, Argentine and Brazilian domestic situations were complex. In Argentina, many of the Litoral caudillos, including ex-President Urquiza, were very sympathetic to the Blancos and proffered them aid. Urquiza, cattle baron of Entre Ríos, was a kindred spirit to the pastoral Blancos and often came to their support.[17] Brazil was no less split. The emperor, who sought influence in Uruguay, not war, was often embarrassed by caudilhos of Rio Grande do Sul who raided across the border into Uruguay. By 1860, perhaps fifty thousand Brazilians dwelt within Uruguay, and border clashes were dishearteningly routine.[18]

Under pressure from his influential southern caudilhos, Pedro II agreed to a stiffer policy toward the Blanco government, which by 1863 was again fighting a major guerrilla war against Colorado dissidents armed by Buenos Aires. The Argentine attitude was also hardening, in part because in 1861 Buenos Aires had triumphed over the Confederation. Within a year, the nation called Argentina was in full existence, the epoch of the caudillos was all but a bad dream, and central rule from Buenos Aires was a reality. Provincial leaders such as Urquiza began to cut off their support to the Blancos while Mitre, now president of the entire nation, permitted clandestine aid to the Colorados.

At this juncture, the increasingly isolated Blanco government looked "north to Paraguay, distant, armed and silent . . . far-off Paraguay is the only hope."[19] The Blancos began a diplomatic offensive in Asunción in 1863, just as a Colorado invasion led by José Flores came ashore with Porteño backing. Chief Blanco diplomat Luis Alberto de Herrera was sent to Paraguay to convince López that it was in his interest to help his beleaguered government. It is probable that it was from Herrera that López learned of the balance of power and the supposed mutual interests of the two nations.

In July, 1863, José Lapido arrived in Asunción with the draft of a treaty between the two buffer states. The Uruguayans were not without their plausible arguments, and pointed to the Flores invasion as proof of Porteño duplicity, telling Francisco Solano that if only Paraguay would take decisive action, Urquiza's Litoral provinces would also enter the fray. This would maintain an independent Uruguay, seriously weaken Argentina, give pause to Brazilian interference, and permit Paraguay to take her place in the sun as arbiter.[20]

Although he refused to sign a treaty, López was impressed by these arguments. He was still wary of a formal commitment to a very unstable and distinctly unimpressive Blanco regime, declaring that Asunción "could not trust the Uruguayan government sufficiently to ally itself with so shifty a neighbor." López preferred to maintain freedom of action at this point, but made it clear that he would not accept domination or dismemberment of Uruguay by its neighbors.[21]

In late 1863, with the Flores revolution in full flower and the Blancos on the verge of declaring war on Argentina, Pedro II announced his willingness to arbitrate, the Blancos responding that they were in agreement *if* President López were the emperor's co-arbiter. This request was laughed off in Brazil and angrily rejected in Argentina—further evidence to López of his neighbors' lack of respect.[22]

It was at this point that Francisco Solano made his open commitment by delivering to the Asunción diplomatic corps a circular declaring that he considered the sovereignty of Uruguay crucial to the balance of power and that Paraguay would not idly sit by and watch that nation disappear.[23]

Early in 1864, ignoring the bombast from Asunción, Pedro II acceded to the demands of his southern warhawks, sending an insulting list of demands to the Blanco government that constituted blatant intervention in Uruguay's internal affairs.[24] New Blanco President Atanasio Aguirre was not the man to give in, drafting a counter-list of forty-eight claims based on alleged mistreatment of Uruguayan citizens and property. He also sent a note to López concerning the Brazilian demands, and noting that a Brazilian army was concentrating on the frontier. Then, refusing to accept the Brazilian demands, he did agree to begin talks designed to end the domestic civil war. After bitter negotiations, an accord was shaped in June, 1864, that, it was hoped, would reunite the two political parties in the face of foreign intervention. Unfortunately, in keeping with Uruguayan tradition, the agreement decomposed within days.

On August 4, Brazil presented the Blancos with an ultimatum, demanding that Aguirre agree to a series of demands similar to those earlier presented, under threat of Brazilian military "reprisals," which, according to the Brazilian envoy, would not be considered "an act of war" under international law.[25] Aguirre, counting too heavily on Paraguayan support, refused.

Before Brazil went so far as to present its May demands or August ultimatum, its diplomats had worked cannily to assure Argentine acceptance of their tactics and goals. In fact, they were so successful as to almost convince Mitre to agree to a joint military intervention and pacification. Ultimately, however, they had to settle for his approval of their gun-boat diplomacy.[26]

On September 14, units of the Brazilian army in Rio Grande do Sul crossed the border into Uruguay. The dice had passed to Francisco Solano.

López Picks Up the Gauntlet

While Uruguay was going through its agonies, all of which were swiftly communicated to López by Blanco diplomats, the Paraguayan president was fully aware of the gravity of the Uruguayan situation but showed astonishing ignorance of the gravity of the regional problem. In late August he was asked by the Uruguayan minister to intervene and forestall the impending Brazilian invasion, and on August 30 he tendered his own counter-ultimatum, informing Brazil's resident minister that Paraguay would not permit any manner of Brazilian military operations within Uruguay, hinting broadly that war would result from such a course of action.[27]

López, unsure of what to do next, emphasized his point by calling up the army reserves, but avoided the Blanco minister's entreaties for a last-minute military alliance. Ironically, such an alliance was the only gambit open to López that might have checked the Brazilian invasion of Uruguay. In the first days of November, Francisco Solano learned how ineffectual had been his vague warnings to Brazil, for in mid-October an imperial army had openly invaded Uruguay.

On November 11, the Brazilian steamer *Marquez de Olinda* dropped anchor at Asunción to take on coal and debark mail before resuming its voyage to Corumbá. López, who was at Cerro León drilling his soldiers, learned that aboard the steamer was a considerable trove of arms bound for the Mato Grosso garrisons, a chest of hard currency, and Col. Federico Carneiro de Campos, new president-designate of the state. He also learned of the Brazilian aggression in Uruguay.[28]

López, about to become El Mariscal, sent an urgent message back to Asunción, and on November 13 the *Tacuarí* caught up with the slower Brazilian steamer, captured it, and guided it back to Asunción, where its imperial flag was lowered, to be soon made into a rug for the presidential office.[29] The war had begun, and López, embarrassingly naive and totally ignorant of the Brazilian/Argentine rapprochement, prepared to invade Brazil.

The Absurdity of It All

In the first two weeks of March, 1864, as international tensions produced a distinct sense of strain in Asunción, fourteen people purchased round-trip tickets for the train from that city to Areguá; four traveled first class, seven second class, and three, legs hanging over the edge of an open platform, rode third class.[30]

While some rode the rails, others amused themselves at the theater, which, though a harmonious building, still lacked a functional roof. Architect Ravizza, who began work on the building in 1858, could find no apt technique or material for roofing the complex mixture of vaultings, buttresses, and columns he had designed. Despite occasional discomfort from tropical downpours, patriotic plays produced by the young Natalicio Talavera were performed to packed houses, which often included many of the López family.[31]

In the capital and the interior, it was said that 435 public schools were busily imparting knowledge to precisely 24,524 students, an observation made all the more interesting when one calculates that this would result in a farcical average of some 570 students per school![32]

To celebrate his July 24 birthday, Francisco Solano hosted "a great ball" for the elite, both foreign and native. There, in public, he for the first time "inaugurated the new throne . . . given by the citizens of Asunción . . . more grandiose than anything ever seen before in Paraguay."[33] So pleased was López on his thirty-eighth birthday that he graciously permitted vast celebrations, featuring horse races, bullfights, and dances, to continue for an entire month throughout the republic. It was a last party before the lights went out. One would scarcely realize that the dogs of war had been loosed and that Paraguay was about to begin a frantic, rabid dance of death.

A Militarized Paraguay?

When Francisco Solano López ordered the seizure of the *Marquez de Olinda,* he signed his nation's death warrant, for Paraguay was by no means prepared for a major war. The total population of Paraguay was smaller than the number of those enrolled in the Brazilian National Guard in 1864.[34]

The Paraguayan Army, so carefully nurtured by Carlos Antonio and his vainglorious son, was neither so powerful as its leaders believed nor so large as its enemies feared. Following the tradition and political caution of El Supremo, the López had curtailed the growth of the officer corps. A few colonels, with good connections but no field or classroom experience, represented the top level of this overestimated force, except for Francisco Solano himself, general and later Marshal. Despite the growing regional tensions, the officer corps in 1864 was totally inadequate. The army counted one general, five colonels, two lieutenant colonels, ten sergeant majors, fifty-one captains, and twenty-two first lieutenants. Several hundred junior officers and the equally skeletal non-commissioned officer ranks rounded out the picture of an army drastically short on key personnel even for routine peacetime duties. There was no military manual available, and six youths sent to the French military academy had barely finished their first semester when the war began.[35] Military salaries were low, with colonels earning a meager forty pesos per month, junior lieutenants seventeen, sergeants twelve, corporals ten, and common soldiers a pauperish eight.[36]

A few individual units were large, and, thanks to foreign arms purchases, many regular battalions were fairly well equipped. The infantry was organized into battalions, which at full strength would each count about a thousand men. The organization of the elite First Infantry Battalion of Asunción was the ideal. Its 977 officers and men were divided into four rifle companies, a reserve, a grenadier and a light infantry company, and two small bands. What was untypical was the simple fact that this unit, alone of all battalions, was at or near full strength on the eve of the war. Most units were very undermanned. The Second Infantry Battalion showed 483 officers and men in mid-1864, and this seems to have been the norm for regular units. It is very doubtful that the oft-mentioned figure of fifty battalions existed in 1864, save on paper, and before the major mobilization during the first months of the war, the regular infantry did not exceed fourteen thousand men of all ranks.[37]

Each cavalry regiment was normally composed of three squadrons of two or three small companies each, but several unattached squadrons also served, especially on the frontier, without regimental affiliation. The famous First Cavalry Regiment was made up of two squadrons of three companies each, and a large staff, totalling 355 officers and men. Most cavalry regiments numbered between 200 and 300 effectives in 1864. Some units were armed with modern carbines in addition to sabers, and each had its own, rudimentary medical service.[38] There were several detached squadrons of lancers, artillery units of various sizes, government escort units, medical companies, and the Asunción Police Battalion, which counted 567 men on its rolls.[39]

Asunción, in the muggy month of December, 1864, was heavily garrisoned, being home to the heart of the regular army: infantry battalions 1, 2, 6, and 7, the police battalion, a company of Villa Rica police, the First Cavalry Regiment, a squadron of Concepción cavalry, a lancer squadron, a composite regiment of dragoons, light infantry, and riflemen, three artillery companies, the Acá Carajá escort regiment, several military bands, a forty-eight-man medical "corps," and Francisco Solano's personal staff—in all, some six thousand regulars.[40]

There were sizeable forces elsewhere, however, especially along the borders at Concepción, Pilar, and Encarnación. In the latter, an artillery unit, infantry battalion 28, cavalry regiment 24, and a lancer squadron kept vigil over the muddy Paraná. Battalions of infantry were stationed at Ypacaraí and Villa del Rosario, and three more, some marines, and a regiment each of artillery and cavalry were based at strategic Humaitá. The infantry carried European-made muskets throwing 54-caliber balls and mounting bayonets, and many officers carried revolvers. Cavalrymen had short carbines and sabers, except for the picturesque but deplorably armed lancers.[41]

Aside from scattered, smaller garrisons sweltering in the year's-end heat in their isolated frontier posts, the only other body of regulars (in large part composed of recent conscripts being turned into regulars) was found at the large military camp and training grounds at Cerro León.

In some ways more crucial to Paraguayan survival in a protracted struggle than its army was its navy, which would have to keep the rivers open, transport men and supplies, and maintain contact with the outside world. Paraguayan river defense did not rest alone on the batteries of Humaitá. By the outbreak of the war, the López navy was not inconsequential by the standards of the day and was considered a respectable force for fluvial combat. The flagship of the Paraguayan flotilla was the aging *Tacuarí*, the only López vessel to have been constructed especially as a warship; it mounted six large guns. Other steamers in the Paraguayan navy were the *Yporá, Salto de Guairá, El Correo, Río Apa, Río Jejuí*, and *Río Ygureí*, all built at Asunción between 1855 and 1858 as government merchant vessels. To these were added the *Olimpo, Río Negro*, and *Paraná*, second-hand steamers purchased by Carlos Antonio, and the larger, well-built commercial steamer *Paraguarí*, best of Paraguay's ships, bought almost new in London in 1862. As the war began, Francisco Solano purchased the strife-stranded foreign steamers *Ranger, Salto*, and *Cavour* and confiscated the *Marquez de Olinda, 25 de Mayo*, and *Gualeguay*, encountered at Asunción or Corrientes. With the exception of the *Tacuarí*, all of these vessels had to be hastily converted to military use, with the addition of a brace of cannon and much hardwood planking. Foreign technicians labored almost around the clock to ready this hybrid Paraguayan fleet for action, and many British machinists were recruited to serve aboard on active duty. Orders for the construction of two modern, iron-clad warships designed for river use were given by López in mid-1864 to Blyth, but these were never constructed.[42] Most of the ships present in 1865 were small, averaging about two hundred tons, and only the *Paraguarí* and the *Tacuarí* exceeded four hundred.

The fluvial fleet was rounded out with the antique *Río Blanco*, the sailing vessel that had brought the French colonists upriver in 1855, and other, smaller sail- and oar-propelled craft: the bark *Bermejo* and the diminutive *Yndependencia, Oliva*, and *Giacovina*, each mounting a single cannon. Also one-gunners were the seven chalanas, or barges, long in service. Normally stationed at Humaitá, these small, clumsy craft mounted a single heavy-caliber weapon, and its gun crew sheltered behind thick hardwood gunnels.

Although most vessels carried marines or sharpshooters after the war began, crews were small. The largest crew seems to have been that of the *Río Ygureí*, which had a captain (Flotilla Commander Pedro Ygnacio Meza), two junior lieutenants, a sergeant, a fifer and drummer, six corporals, two helmsmen, and fifty-one other effectives. Most steamers carried less than fifty crewmen; the sailing vessels averaged about fifteen and the barges only seven. As reassuring as the seventeen steamers and handful of other ships must have appeared to the Paraguayans who saw them chug south to the Humaitá station, they were to prove no match for Brazilian ironclads.[43]

Auto-Destruction and the End of a Dream: 1865

By the time the Paraguayan congress got around to declaring war on Brazil in March, 1865, the nation was already at war with two other nations as well and a good deal had changed. Francisco Solano, realizing that time was of the essence, had decided to strike immediately at Brazil and bring the empire to its knees at the same time he rescued Uruguay.

Almost immediately on the capture of the *Marquez de Olinda,* López dispatched some thirty-five hundred men by river and a further twenty-five hundred by land to conquer the Mato Grosso, so long a bone of contention. These troops, including most of the army's pardo regulars, were exhorted by their president: "Honor, national dignity, and the preservation of the most dear of Rights provoke us to war. You are the first to give testimony to the force of our Arms, gathering the first Laurel. . . . March serenely to the field of honor, gathering glory for the Fatherland. . . . Show the world the worth of the Paraguayan Soldier!"[44]

The combined northern expedition was successful almost from the minute it crossed the border, and its exploits constituted almost the only laurels gained by Paraguayan arms in the entire war. Capturing the main centers of the Mato Grosso within weeks, the expedition was soon sending back downriver large military stocks encountered in the jungled region, stocks that would soon be of inestimable value to the defense effort. Encouraged by results from his first offensive, Francisco Solano launched the second, which would be his biggest disaster.[45]

Expanding his levies daily and hurredly training new recruits, creating new units and mobilizing the militia, López determined to strike against Brazil in Uruguay and Rio Grande do Sul, destroying the empire's main field army. Preferring to use the swiftest, most direct route, which would entail transit of a part of Corrientes, López formally asked permission of President Mitre to do so, and, when Mitre refused, Francisco Solano had his congress declare war on that state as well on March 18. He erroneously believed that provincial separatism would prevent Argentina from participating in the war until after he had annihilated his Brazilian enemy.[46] That separatism, largely based on the mistaken notion that Urquiza would oppose the war, did make itself felt, but at best it retarded rather than crippled the Argentine war effort.

On April 13, Paraguayan forces landed at Corrientes city, and within a few

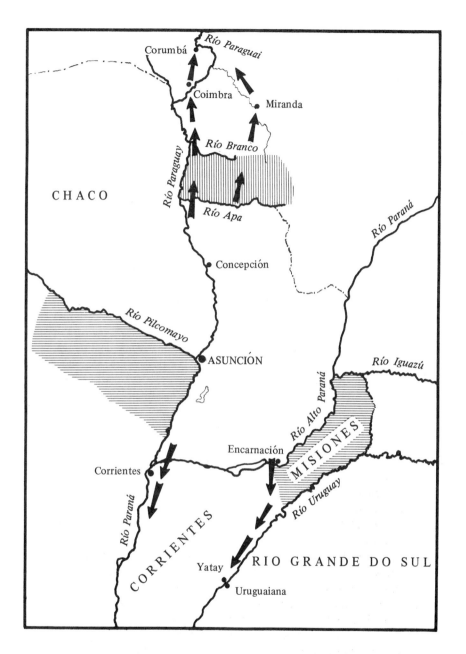

MAP 3. PARAGUAYAN OFFENSIVES, 1864-1865

Areas claimed by
Argentina and Paraguay

Area claimed by
Brazil and Paraguay

days the main force of the army, some thirty thousand troops, entered Corrientes in several columns, intending to strike south along the Paraná at Argentine ports and down the Uruguay to come to grips with the Brazilian army. The enemy, however, was swifter to mobilize its political and military potential than López had foreseen.

On May 1, representatives of the empire, the Flores government in Uruguay, and Argentina signed the Treaty of the Triple Alliance in Buenos Aires. The treaty, whose text was soon leaked, declared that the Allies would prosecute the war against the "tyrant," but not against the Paraguayan people, until his government was destroyed. Although the independence of Paraguay would be guaranteed by the signatories, the Allies would, as a matter of course, redefine their borders with Paraguay and would expect that nation to bear the cost of the war. President Mitre was named Allied commander-in-chief. As one historian has noted, "Argentina and Brazil were generous in agreeing to territorial claims: each was to receive its maximum demands."[47]

The Allies were equally rapid in the mobilization and concentration of their military resources. A Brazilian squadron of ironclads headed north on the Paraná as Brazilian, Uruguayan, and Argentine troops converged on López's green striking force in Corrientes. Perhaps here the chronic civil strife of the region came to the aid of the Allies, for their troops were, for the most part, veterans of many campaigns, and their arms were vastly superior to those of their enemy. The Paraguayan Legion, a unit of disaffected Paraguayan exiles, was raised and equipped in Buenos Aires, and its several hundred men were soon at the front, albeit of chiefly political value.[48]

On June 11, to safeguard his forces operating in Corrientes, López ordered the best of his fleet to sally south and destroy the Brazilian squadron anchored near the city of Corrientes. In a confused dawn action, the Paraguayan flotilla was repulsed with very heavy losses at the battle of Riachuelo, the only genuine naval engagement of the war. Brazilian vessels, propelled by screws instead of paddlewheels, proved more maneuverable. Their iron plating and modern, rifled Whitworth cannon assured a victory for Dom Pedro despite the almost suicidal bravery of Paraguayan boarding parties, who tried to achieve with the machete what their outgunned vessels could not.[49] Remaining units of the Paraguayan navy were largely inactive for the rest of the war, and Paraguay underwent an almost airtight blockade. Had it not been for the overrated Humaitá batteries, the Brazilian fleet would have bombarded Asunción into rubble, landed troops, and probably ended the war in 1865.

The army fared no better in the south. In addition to high casualties suffered throughout the province of Corrientes in actions large and small, a wing of López's invading army was annihilated at Yataí in July with a loss of seventeen hundred dead and fifteen hundred prisoners. Much worse, however, for Paraguayan hopes was the fate of a larger force, commanded by a Col. Estigarribia. After a brief siege, the colonel surrendered his force of more than six thousand regulars at Uruguaiana to a mixed Allied army.

This was a shattering blow. In the four months of operations in the south the fleet had been emasculated and as many as eighteen thousand troops, largely regular units, had been lost; half their number surrendered. With them was lost much of Paraguay's best small arms and fieldpieces, a loss that much more than offset the acquisition of arms in the Mato Grosso. In a state of angry shock, López ordered the remainder of his southern invasion force, now under command of General Isidoro Resquín, to retreat across the Paraná. Resquín did extricate his forces, no easy task in itself, and also brought back a hundred thousand head of rustled cattle.

The López offensive was over. From this point on, Paraguay would be forced to fight a defensive war, against Allies whose strength increased daily, and would have to fight without benefit of foreign trade in weapons, food, or medicines. The stage for tragedy was set within six months of the outbreak of war. The core of the Paraguayan army was gone, along with its irreplaceable equipment. Recruiters scoured the pueblos in preparation for an invasion of the homeland.[50]

13. The Immolation of Paraguay

While the Allies regrouped, argued about strategy, and awaited the arrival of new regiments in Corrientes, Francisco Solano was busy creating a new army with which to guard the southern frontier. Absorbing almost all active militia units into the regular army, he was able to expand the size, if not better the quality, of his forces. New battalions and regiments, after the most cursory training, and with few arms, were rushed off to Humaitá, Curupaití, Encarnación, and other border bastions. News of the Treaty of the Triple Alliance and its contents had the effect of increasing Paraguayan patriotism, and if the levies were short of small arms, they were long on dedication, and the foreign technicians kept them well supplied with shot and shell.

One reason for the general exaggeration of the size of the Paraguayan army in 1864 is the later rapid expansion and creation of new units in 1865 and 1866. A list of eighteen infantry battalions and twenty-six cavalry regiments stationed at Paso de Patria early in 1866 to repel the expected invasion reveals that most of the units had been recently created. Very few appear in the quite complete pre-war military lists.[1] After the debacle in the south, López was forced to scramble to put together a respectable army in the face of a serious threat. The fruits of a gradual military buildup, 1850-1864, had been squandered, and piecemeal recruitment had to fill the gaps. Typical was the experience of the pueblos along the Tebicuari. By fiat, their militia units were combined, remolded, and labeled battalions 31-33 and 41-43, and regiments 26, 28, 35-39, and 46. With a few instructors and little modern weaponry, these, units only in name, were sped to the threatened frontier.[2]

The Crucible: 1866

After a year of cautious preparations, an Allied army of more than 35,000, led by General Mitre, crossed the Paraná near Itapirú in April, 1866. Its basic goal was to march north toward Asunción, capturing the fortress of Humaitá on the way. Francisco Solano, perhaps hoping to shatter the invading force before it became even stronger, left his prepared positions and foolishly threw his army at the superior foe in a series of battles between May and September. These bloody encounters, taken together, awed and slowed the Allies, but they also destroyed the bulk of the Paraguayan army. López, whose concept of tactics was to pit the acknowledged, almost fanatical bravery of his men against Allied cannon, was horrendously wasteful of his human resources. The result was not only a litany of lost battles but casualty rates often double those of his enemies.

At Estero Bellaco, on May 12, the first major battle on Paraguayan soil, the Mariscal lost twenty-five hundred men to his opponents' fifteen hundred. Stung by this reverse, López's response was to throw most of the rest of his forces in a vast banzai charge at the massed enemy twelve days later. When the smoke cleared from the battlefield of Tuyutí, it revealed the death of the Paraguayan army. The carnage was impressive, for on that day the Paraguayan cause lost some fourteen thousand of its most ardent supporters, while only about four thousand Allies fell. Smaller combats, such as those at Yatayty Corá (July 10-11), Boquerón (July 16, 18), and Curuzú (September 3) merely resulted in Paraguayans' continuing to die at a rate far greater than their enemies. Only at Curupaití, on September 22, could López claim a victory (he himself was not present on the field). There, the Allies, convinced that they now faced an exhausted, decimated enemy, attacked fixed Paraguayan positions well protected by artillery. This imitation of López's tactics left over four thousand Allies littering the slopes while merely a handful of Paraguayans were struck down.

After Curupaití, both antagonists needed and sought rest and recuperation. Although Allied forces could probably have completed the destruction of the remnants of the Paraguayan army, they instead idled, awaiting reinforcements and preparing for the big push on Humaitá, which would open the river and, they hoped, end the war. Despite the fact that the 1866 campaign was far less costly in lives to the Allies than it was for Paraguay, battles such as Tuyutí and Curupaití had a sobering effect on their leaders. They were now convinced that the war would be a long and bloody one. Shocked by the ferocity of the fighting and overestimating the strength both of the opposing army and of Humaitá, Allied strategists allowed López almost a year to rebuild his forces. Only when the Allied army could count more than fifty thousand effectives, mostly drawn from Brazil, would it move warily against the refilled Paraguayan ranks. In the meantime, at their bases at Curuzú and Corrientes, cholera hit the Allied Forces with a vengeance, killing more than bullets had.[3]

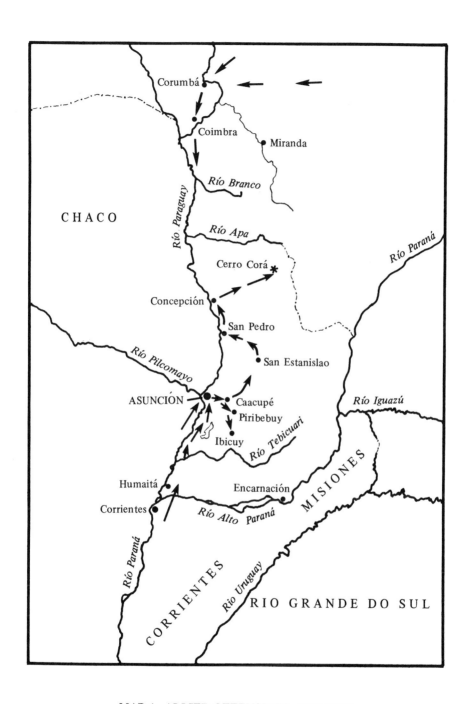

MAP 4. ALLIED OFFENSIVES, 1866-1870

The Demographic Catastrophe

Refilling those depleted ranks was a more difficult task than Allied leaders would have believed or historians have since written. By 1867, before the chronological midpoint of the war, the López government had reached the bottom of the demographic barrel—Paraguay was running out of people. Too many of her young men had surrendered at Uruguaiana, too many had been sacrificed at Tuyutí and a dozen less-remembered battles, and many thousands more had died of a host of diseases in the army camps and hospitals of 1865 and 1866.[4] Battalions, more numerous now, often numbered fewer than two hundred effectives. Battalion 6 "was armed with machetes that had been captured in Corrientes,"[5] notes one historian, and a contemporary observer reported that the shrunken cavalry units were "mostly on foot" for lack of horses.[6] Paraguay simply lacked the manpower and the material resources for a war against her giant neighbors.

From a population base of perhaps four hundred thousand in 1864, at least sixty thousand young men were dead, captured, or hopelessly mutilated within two years, and another sixty thousand had been called to the colors. As an Uruguayan officer wrote in 1866, the toll exacted in the first eighteen months of the war had crippled Paraguay: "The veterans had been exterminated."[7]

That the manpower shortage had become critical was admitted by the government on September 6, 1866, when it ordered local authorities to enroll as many slaves and libertos as was practical. Slave owners who voluntarily released their property were to be reimbursed by the treasury. Thus in September through November, we find Villa Rica "volunteering" 34 slaves and 31 libertos for army service, tiny Yacaguazú sending 8 of each category, and Ibicuy dispatching 59 young libertos and 33 slaves. Partial data show twenty-one partidos contributing 279 slaves and 296 libertos to the war effort. The probable total was about seventeen hundred for the nation. Many of these were rushed directly to Humaitá, then desperate for soldier-laborers.[8]

Even earlier in 1866, militia surveys revealed that most able-bodied men had already been stripped from their villages by the recruiters. Typical was a militia report of March 14, which showed that populous Carapeguá had only 304 men left in its local militia. Close examination, however, shows that 11 of these were "of great age" and 219 were sick or convalescing from serious wounds. Of the 304, only 74 were listed as "ready."[9]

Within months of López's decision to recruit available slaves, many patriotic Paraguayans were "donating" their human property to the state. One of the many to do so was Concepción rancher Pascual López, who wrote that

I give full liberty from the slavery in which he finds himself my servant

Juan José, 36 years of age, whom I obtained through inheritance, and whom I present to the Commander of the Villa so that he be enrolled as a free man and sent to the service of Arms in the present war against the enemies of Liberty and National Independence, without demanding any price.[10]

That in 1866 López would have to recruit slaves, both private and public, is indicative of the human crisis, as was his clean sweep of 1867, when he ordered the foremen of the state estancias to immediately forward all slaves and libertos "from the age of twelve years to sixty" to help slake the army's endless thirst for recruits. Tabapí sent its last twelve slaves and twenty-three more libertos, while at Gasorí only thirteen youngsters were to be found. Women would tend the state estancias, as well as the private farms, for the rest of the war.[11]

To the toll of new battles was added in 1866 and 1867 the horror of epidemics, as smallpox swept through the camps, followed by massive outbreaks of a new, Asiatic cholera, which littered the trenches and hospitals of both armies with dead. By late 1866, at the army hospital at Cerro León, thirty-three wounded died each week of "diarrhea" and others of smallpox, and conditions in other hospitals appeared like scenes from the brush of Hieronymus Bosch. In January, 1867, the death toll from disease reached sixteen daily at Cerro León, merely a prelude to still grimmer tolls. In April and May, cholera hit the Paraguayan army in full force, aided by the rudimentary sanitation conditions. Spread through Brazilian prisoners, the disease killed thousands of Paraguayans within a few months and undermined the health of many more. The epidemic, which was combatted with massive doses of coffee and aguardiente, did not last long in the Paraguayan camp, but spread inland, arriving at Asunción with terrible results later in the year.[12]

To offset these steep losses, which were aggravated by an increasing incidence of desertion, El Mariscal dug deeper into his scant remaining human resources.[13] On December 12, 1866, the *Yporá* moored off Humaitá with a cargo of fifty youngsters from Villa Rica, aged ten to fourteen. These had volunteered "to form a military unit, the first entirely of children, which would be incorporated into the army on campaign."[14] The war newspaper, *El Centinela*, took time off from its reportage of fictitious victories and praise of López to report late in 1867 that "the daughters of Ybitimí have just placed one more jewel in the Fatherland's splendid crown, offering to take arms in defense of independence." They were seconded by the girls of Lambaré, while yet others shouted, according to the editors, "A rifle! A rifle! is the shout of the women . . . such a commendable thought."[15] Few women actually served with military units, but they, aside from donating their jewels and gold, played active roles in supporting positions behind the lines.

Also in 1867, El Mariscal ordered that "arms be distributed among the wounded and sick of the hospitals," and this was done "little by little, to not alarm the people." He also instructed that prisoners from the Asunción and Villeta jails be sent to labor in the foundries of Ibicuy.[16] A recruiting bulletin was published in April that called up children of twelve to fifteen years of age, granting no exceptions, and, as cholera continued to kill at least fifty soldiers daily in the Paraguayan camp despite the efforts of Doctors Stewart and Skinner, López decreed that crippled and mutilated veterans should be mobilized and sent to man all telegraph offices, railroad facilities, and other vital endeavors, freeing healthier men for active service. At the same time, all pueblos were drained of "soldiers convalescing from their wounds or illnesses."[17] The borders were denuded of their already understrength garrisons, and even strategically important frontier Villa del Salvador was left protected after May, 1867, only by its small "banda de músicos."[18] Yet still the new drafts continued as the military situation worsened. In June, 1867, faced with a major Brazilian offensive in the Mato Grosso, López ordered north the only reserves he had on hand—eighty Asunción policemen. It was disease more than Paraguayan strength that turned back this threat.[19]

The condition of those actually serving in the military was in a perpetual state of decline from the war's beginning, oscillating between the appalling and the comic. Prussian military observer Max von Versen described Paraguayan soldiers in 1867: "They were semi-nude, without shoes or boots, covered with shoddy ponchos . . . even colonels go about barefoot."[20] Colonel Palleja, concluding that López's "plan is to exterminate all the young men capable of bearing arms," noted that "this afternoon a deserter arrived from the enemy, a dirty youth, almost naked, with a hunger that radiated" from him like a halo. He further observed after a battle that "the wounded are dying of hunger; they are on the point of death and ask for food. The dead are thin and only skin and bones." The Uruguayan officer, who respected the Paraguayan soldier and considered him a "soldier of the first order," lamented the destruction of "this pure and virile race, not effeminated by vices and comforts, but strengthened by misery, nudity, and sufferings. . . . I look with pain upon the extermination which the Paraguayan people are suffering."[21]

The Paraguayan army also suffered a severe and growing shortage of arms, having littered a dozen battlefields with its best ordnance. Although the arsenal and Ibicuy produced sufficient heavy-caliber weapons until the last stages of the war, including such monstrous cannon as "The Christian," cast from melted church bells and throwing an awe-inspiring 200-lb. ball, infantry weapons were scarce. Much of the close-in fighting in 1867 and succeeding years was waged by Paraguayans wielding machetes, pikes, spears, lances, knives, and sabers, which helps explain the high incidence of ghastly, mutilating wounds suffered by both sides. Shortly before the war, Francisco Solano had purchased twenty thousand muskets from Brazil to round out his much smaller but higher-quality European acquisitions. With the capture of the arms-bearing *Marquez de Olinda* and military storehouses in the Mato Grosso, thousands more light weapons were encountered, but not enough to compensate for catastrophic losses in Corrientes in early 1865.

In February, 1865, the last arms-carrying ship arrived at Pilar, unloading large stocks of cartridges, balls, assorted equipment, and a battery of Congreve rockets.[22] Paraguay would now have to manufacture or capture its light arms, and this was to prove impossible. As the manpower pool spat up increasingly young or defective recruits, so did the ordnance department come up with increasingly variegated and shoddy arms.[23]

And yet an official newspaper could still thrill its readers with reports of well-armed, happy recruits, eager to kill the Black Brazilian invaders: "Kill the Niggers! This is the enthusiastic voice that is heard from our robust recruits who daily travel to the General Barracks. They all go full of happiness, as if marching to a great fiesta . . . "[24] Paraguayan nationalism, always built on the dual props of race and language, increasingly leaned on the former and used the latter as a vehicle. Sarcastic, often Guaraní-language insults were printed in the official war press, presenting the enemy, represented usually by the Brazilians, simply as "niggers" or Black monkeys. Many of the empire's troops who faced them were indeed Black, serving for the duration in exchange for their freedom, but many cartoons even painted the emperor Black as well. This racial aspect of the war, the identification of the nation's enemies with enemies of the race, was an important factor in stimulating Paraguayan resistance to the Allies. After all, what might happen if the Black monkeys overran the country?

The Home Front

Within weeks of the declaration of war, Paraguay was a mobilized nation. Tens of thousands of men flocked to the colors, government industries went on extended shifts to produce everything from cannon balls to underwear for the troops, and women were pressed into farm and ranch work. With the Allies in control of the rivers by mid-1865, it became clear to all that Paraguay must become self-sufficient to survive. The labor was herculean, the goal almost attained.

Production of the staple, yerba mate, which in 1863 had totaled 1,681,000 pounds, began to decline almost immediately, in part due to the proximity of many of the best yerbales to threatened border areas.[25] Concepción, one of the richest yerba partidos, was especially hard hit, its men called to arms to fight both Brazilians and a new round of Guaicurú raids. The eight yerba licensees in the partido, who together had produced some 480,575 pounds of the green tea in 1862, yielded only 17,500 pounds in 1865 and virtually none thereafter.[26] By February, 1867, the government announced in a state of shock that "the General Treasury informs us that there is no current, active harvesting of yerba, all having been allowed to stop due to enlistment of personnel." The announcement further noted that the only yerba then available in the entire nation was in 9,096 bales held in government warehouses, a few weeks supply for a nation of addicts.[27] That Paraguay was forced to fight the rest of its greatest war without its beloved yerba was in itself a war crime.

Production of crops, however, was maintained at rather high levels. Early in 1866, a government survey was carried out, examining plantings in each partido. Tiny, ephemeral Villa Occidental, with its 284 "casas," reported sizeable plantings of tobacco, cotton, corn, mandioca, sugarcane, beans, peanuts, peas, onions, and potatoes, as well as lesser amounts of wheat, rice, squash, watermelons, and fruit trees—all of this in the harsh soil of the Chaco. Estimating plantings in liños (1.85 acres), the report reveals mandioca, corn, and beans to have been, in that order, the nation's most important crops. Almost no yerba was listed in the national survey, and very little wheat, but cotton production was booming.[28]

On the eve of the war, the government had begun to increase cotton production, hoping to lessen the nation's dependence on outside suppliers of good-quality cloth. In 1863, two types of North American long-fiber seeds had been distributed gratis to farmers throughout the nation, together with a handy guide, the *Agricultural Catechism.*[29] From that date, cotton production spurted, and during the war it appears that Paraguay was self-sufficient in cotton, if not in available labor to turn it into finished clothing. Minimum needs were met from domestic production, partly from crops planted by fiat on most state lands, and the government maintained a corps of female seamstresses to make uniforms for the army.[30] In 1867, López announced a series of 310 cash prizes for those presenting the government with the most cotton. First prize was a hefty 8,000 pesos, the rewards ranging downwards to 50 pesos, but there is no record of the prizes ever being awarded.[31] Cash prizes were also offered for other patriotic endeavors, such as the production of handkerchiefs and barrels.

Vice-President Domingo Sánchez, elevated to that new post early in the war, was put in charge of fomenting agriculture in 1866, and devoted a substantial proportion of his time to that important task. By use of threat, reward, and the general coercive power of the state, Sánchez could proudly report that in the first three months of 1866, some 6,805,695 liños of foodstuffs and cotton had been planted in the republic as well as 215,000 fruit trees. A year later, however, suffering the ravages of increasing recruitment, disease, and loss of a portion of the nation's land to the enemy, the first quarter saw the planting of only 4,192,520 liños and 135,757 fruit trees.[32]

Despite this substantial decrease in cultivated land, Paraguayan food production was sufficient to keep the nation on its feet for the rest of the war. That the army was often ill-fed should be ascribed to logistical problems and atrocious roads rather than to a lack of production. When one considers that by 1866 agriculture was almost entirely in the hands of old men, women, and young boys, the level of production appears more impressive.

So was the yield of the huge state estancia system, which continued to supply enormous amounts of meat on the hoof and cavalry mounts during the war despite an agonizing lack of manpower. Food poured in from private ranches as well, some of it donated, some through a quota system introduced in 1867. Under this system, the government requisitioned cattle from each partido to feed the troops, demanding thousands of beeves each month. In general, the quota worked well, but it was from the state's own lands that the major bounty came. In a sense, the state socialism constructed and nurtured by three despots justified itself during the war.[33]

Donations of all sorts flowed in to the treasury, from every corner of the nation. Baskets of gold jewelry were sent by women whose husbands had gone off to war. Some of these baubles were perhaps kept by Madame Lynch, but others went to finance the limited trade with Bolivian merchants in the occupied Mato Grosso. Money, clothing, and food continued to flow in to the government until, perhaps by late 1867, there was little left to give, and that was being prudently buried in cornfields to finance personal post-war reconstruction. In July, 1867, the people of Villa Rica sent 500 shirts and 515 pairs of shorts to the army, those of Quiquió gave 231 ponchos, and those of Ytauguá donated 530 eggs, 14,890 cigars, candles, flour, cheese, and 794 pieces of chipa.[34]

Public spirit, reinforced by government action, was also the mother of invention during the war years. In 1867, to slake a national thirst, it was reported that "in various parts of the interior has begun the fabrication of orange wine . . . with the best properties of European wine."[35] The finest of this improvised beverage was said to be made at Curuguatí, and although the report exaggerated the quality of the liquid, it shows that few doors were left unopened by Paraguayans in need. Orange wine and the continued distillation of aguardiente ensured the Paraguayan of at least one way to escape the reality of war.

During the war a saltpeter factory was opened at San Juan Nepomuceno by Pedro Jara, and a new paper factory was opened near the capital to produce newsprint for the war newspapers, making the editors "as happy as if Gutenberg was in one of their workshops firing with his invention at the Negroes of the Empire," in the words of one editor. Shortly thereafter, a new gunpowder plant went into production in Asunción, and a coco-fiber weaving establishment also opened its doors.[36] In late 1866, copper mining got underway near Ytapúa, as did extraction of saltpeter at Ypané and some manganese ore in the north, and, as the February heat felled cattle and soldiers in the Chaco, an ice factory was opened in Asunción, five boxes of ice being sent daily to El Mariscal.[37]

In April, 1867, the first issue of *El Centinela* was printed in the capital, announcing itself as "born amidst the thunders of war and baptized by the great Priest of the Fatherland on the Mount of Martyrdom."[38] It thus displayed a standard for rhetoric that it would maintain throughout its short life, a standard cheerfully imitated by other war papers. Joining the older *Semanario,* which was still in publication, *El Centinela* devoted itself to denouncing the enemy as "hordes of cowards and abject mercenaries who come in search of pillage and crime," purveying almost nonsensical war news and sarcastic cartoons and lampoons of Black Brazilians, often replete with tails. Occasionally it would present patriotic poetry:

Long live Democracy!
Long live free Paraguay!
Long live the Champion of the Century, the hard-working Marshal López!
Liberty or death!
Down with slavery! [39]

That piece was among the more literary of those thrown at the public during the war.

In May, a bilingual military weekly, *Cabichuí,* began publication at the army headquarters at Paso Pucú, its bitter, anti-Brazilian diatribes and rather brilliant artwork directed by Natalicio Talavera and Juan Crisóstomo Centurión. In this hemorrhage of patriotic literature two more journals were born. *Cacique Lambaré,* published almost entirely in Guaraní, began its life at Paso Pucú in July, 1867, and *La Estrella,* tolling the last bells of suicidal nationalism, was briefly printed at Piribebuy in 1869.[40]

To those periodical publications must be added works written for and staged by the National Theater, which continued its shows virtually until Brazilian soldiers overran the capital. Included in its repertoire were the popular "Enjoyable History of the Triple Alliance," a satire written by North American Cornelius Porter Bliss, and "The Protest," from the pen of Bolivian Tristán Roca. The former was later arrested and tortured, the latter bayoneted to death by order of López. The plays were well attended by the elite and the foreign community, and by El Mariscal and his faithful consort when they were in town.[41]

It is hard to reconcile the ghastly toll of the war and the growing sacrifices of the Paraguayan people with a decision to collect money for an equestrian statue of the Mariscal, or with the massive collections in all parts of the republic of thousands of pesos to prepare a golden sword for presentation to López on his 1867 birthday.[42]

There is a totally unreal quality to Francisco Solano's actions during the war: actions of a man who in his journey through life has left reality far behind him. This great leader spending the lives of his people as if they were small copper coins; a man who could arrest two British doctors because they could not morally leave the mangled youngsters at Paso Pucú immediately and fly to Asunción to treat his ill mother;[43] a man who would order the execution of a prominent European scientist, Dr. Munck, "for having declined to obey an order of the Marshal to combat the enemy with witchcraft";[44] a man who could appoint a commission to regularize Guaraní orthology while not providing medicines to the military hospital at Cerro León;[45] a man who could enjoy a satire at the theater while battalions of young boys died to defend him. Something unknown seems to have insulated the Mariscal as his nation died around him.

It is impossible to gauge the extent of the human tragedy on the home front, for there are few records. Certainly there was hunger, omnipresent cholera, and chronic shortages of almost everything. One of the few measures of rural reality extant is the fragmented annual census of libertos carried on from 1844 until 1868. It is a grim record. Dealing only with libertos, it does not reflect the mortality of slaves, or of older people in general, but it is a harrowing glimpse of another aspect of the demographic tragedy. Not only, given the absence of most men, were fewer libertos born, but a much smaller proportion of those born survived. In the four partidos for which we have good records,[46] we find:

		1850	1853	1856	1868
Caapucú:	born	20	11	19	8
	died	9	6	11	37
Tabapí:	born		24	35	4
	died		3	10	13
Quiindí:	born	112	47		4
	died	34	15		36
Quiquió:	born	11	14	14	2
	died	4	2	5	8

Somewhat similar statistics might be expected from other groups within the population due to disease and dietary imbalance.

The War Grinds Slowly, yet Exceeding Small

The war year of 1867 passed with only one major battle, the second combat at Tuyutí, a slightly less sanguinary rerun of the first, applauded in the Paraguayan press as a great victory.[47] There were other, lesser clashes, and Allied warships ran the gauntlet of Humaitá to frighten inhabitants upriver, but much of the year was wasted by the invading army, now perhaps 80 percent Brazilian in content and commanded by the Duke of Caxias, who had gained fame in his youth in crushing a series of revolts throughout Brazil. Caxias fell prey to a masterly bluff prepared by El Mariscal. To flesh out his weak army, López had removed most of the garrison from Humaitá, and many of its guns as well. He left behind a small force instructed to act like a large one. The Allies, falling for the ruse, cautiously began major siege operations, tying down their army for many months in 1867 and 1868 while López, from a safe distance, was granted yet more time to reshuffle what was left of his army.

What he saw was what he had, for the full horror of the war must have finally penetrated as he read the results of his final militia mobilization order of November 24, 1867. In human terms, the report is almost unique. On that date, he ordered local authorities to call together all their remaining militiamen and send complete reports to him. The results were shocking. The partido of Yutí counted 371 men, of whom 94 were "youngsters of twelve years, more or less," and 35 were in their 70s or 80s. A further 120 were aged from 60 to 69, and the litany of ills afflicting the last third ran from venereal disease, gout, lung sickness, and smallpox through "wounded in the leg."

More pathetic was the report prepared by Commander Ramón Marecos of heavily-populated Villa Rica. He listed 563 men. These were composed of 238 boys aged 12 to 14, 7 more boys in a church band, 5 slaves, 8 libertos, 29 wounded soldiers, 260 militiamen aged 50 and above, and a scattering of defectives. Among the latter were 6 labeled "insane," 4 "totally blind," and 3 "deaf and dumb," and one, Ygnacio Benítez, 90 years old, was reported as having "problems all over his body." In short, Villa Rica had no manpower at all.

The same could be said of most partidos that answered the government circular. Atirá was reduced to one officer and 90 men, about equally divided between wounded, children, and the elderly. Caazapá carried on its rolls the blind, the deaf, and several lepers, and Concepción claimed that three of its remaining men were over 100 years old. Quite typical was the militia company remaining at San Joaquín: it listed 7 men (70-90 years old), 12 (60-69), 8 (50-59), 4 (40-49), 2 (30-39), none (20-29), and 7 (12-19).[48]

By January, 1868, Paraguay was, in terms of human resources, shattered.

That many Paraguayans decided to struggle on for two more years is an astonishing phenomenon that bears witness to the strange racial, cultural, and linguistic bases of the war. General Martin McMahon, United States minister in Paraguay at the time, graphically described what was left of the Paraguayan army after a skirmish in 1868: "There were children of tender years who crawled back, dragging shattered limbs, or with ghastly bullet-wounds in their little, half-naked bodies. They neither wept nor groaned nor asked for surgeons or attendance."[49]

In August, 1868, when Humaitá at last surrendered, the Allies were embarrassed to find only some thirteen hundred prisoners. From this point on, the war became truly disastrous to Paraguay as a nation. El Mariscal, continually in retreat, forced much of the civilian population to follow him, and where the caravans traveled so too did cholera and a host of other diseases in their wake, an unseen albatross on the shoulders of the republic. He declared Luque his new capital after the fall of Humaitá removed all obstacles from the path of Allied occupation of Asunción, and then had to shift to Piribebuy. Losing battle after battle, López was pushed deeper and deeper into the interior, trailing thousands of emaciated and mangled soldiers and civilians along the bumpy via dolorosa.

Combats in 1868 and 1869 such as Ytororó, Avaí, Itá-Ybaté, and Pikysyry were less battles than ritual sacrifices, and thousands more Paraguayans died in indefensible positions for a cause long lost. Legends to the contrary, Paraguayans, appalled by the slaughter, began deserting in droves in this epoch rather than continue the suicidal struggle. For the first time since Corrientes, prisoners were more numerous than other casualties.[50]

San Fernando and Beyond: The Beast Is Loose

In 1868, El Mariscal, beset with defeat, perhaps hearing rumors of dissatisfaction, and himself in poor health, gave in to a carnival of paranoia, envisioning a vast, silent plot to depose and kill him. As far as can be ascertained, these laudable goals were never considered in a concrete conspiracy, but López was sure that they were. Arresting a thousand or more unfortunates, he turned them over to drumhead military tribunals, and, after brutal tortures, overworked firing squads did away with many hundreds, including Francisco Solano's two brothers, his two brothers-in-law, dozens of ranking government and military personnel, the bishop, and at least five hundred foreigners, including many a diplomat.[51]

The trail of misery that began at Villeta with the execution of Bishop Palacios and eleven others and rose to a crescendo at San Fernando cannot be painted in dark enough hues. Nor did it end there; mass executions continued at Itá-Ybaté, Pikysyry, San Estanislao, Igatimí, and Panadero, adding new cadavers to those marked by cholera, smallpox, and simple exhaustion that lay rotting in the cart tracks of defeat.

Brother Venancio López, suspected by the Mariscal of coveting the crumbling presidency of a devastated nation, was arrested and subjected to a regimen only Goya could have depicted. He was flogged daily, given almost no food, and followed the army on its retreat, led down the dusty dirt roads of the via crucis barefoot "by a cord attached to his belt." Finally, near San Estanislao, "there died Venancio like a beast."[52]

The victims were dumped in mass graves, especially at San Fernando, and in late 1868 the half-decomposed corpses were encountered by the Duke of Caxias when his vanguard approached the village. These "vestiges of the tragedy" were examined, and many a prominent body was identified and shown the horrified Duke.[53] In the last months of the war, even more brutal massacres were carried out under López's orders, especially around Horqueta and Concepción, where hundreds from the area's leading families were rounded up and lanced like animals for supposedly waiting for instead of fleeing the arrival of a Brazilian flotilla.[54]

Having massacred those he felt implicated in the non-existent plot, López and his family, together with Vice-President Sánchez and his family, continued the retreat, surrounded by a daily diminishing nucleus of dedicated, scarred troops. Finally, at Cerro Corá, seventy-five miles northeast of Concepción, López's personal drama reached its operatic climax. With him were fewer than four hundred men and boys, "reduced to the saddest prostration, without clothes or food." Acting on the tip of a deserter, Brazilian cavalry surprised his last, makeshift camp, and, in a brief action, El Mariscal, firing his pistol to the last, was wounded by a lance thrust and killed by a carbine bullet. His eldest son, Juan Francisco, and Vice-President Sánchez also died in the jungle clearing. Barely beyond the eyes of her Brazilian captors, La Lynch buried her lover and their son with her own hands in the red clay, and the war was over.[55]

Asunción, 1869

Unfortunately, the suffering did not die with López, but merely the sound of the guns. Hunger and disease stalked Paraguay for years. The Duke of Caxias, entering Asunción in 1869, was moved by its ruined state, its lack of sewers, drains, and lighting, and remarked that the inhabitants were, "in the most part, families in complete misery."[56]

People in rags were seen by the thousands on the roads leading to the city, mainly women, children, and grotesquely wounded veterans. The provisional government, composed of "loyal" Paraguayans who had opposed López, wrote in 1869 of "the Paraguayan people, escaping from their martyrdom . . . destroyed, dispersed, naked and hungry, prey to epidemics and annihilated by sufferings." Describing the growing exodus from the countryside to the capital, the authorities deplored "these same streets covered with the cadavers of the unhappy" people who sought escape from the tyrant López.[57]

The new government, with little help from the Allies, who were bitterly arguing over the potential boundary changes and indemnities soon to be demanded, attempted to save what they could of their nation, passing a spate of decrees abolishing slavery, setting food prices, and reallocating vacant lands.[58] The pathetic announcements in the *Registro Oficial* tell a grim tale. The many families in Asunción with neither food nor lodging were sent to work camps at Trinidad to plant the crops so necessary for their own survival. Able-bodied men were sent to Luque for special public works. A commission was created to oversee relief for the thousands of hungry orphans, the properties of the López clan were declared confiscated, as was that of "the woman Elisa Lynch, concubine, accomplice of the criminal Traitor Solano López," the siesta was abolished because "it is prejudicial to the activity that is demanded in these times" (a decree that was obviously ignored), and the teaching or use of the Guaraní language was banned from the schools (because it was correctly considered a primary vehicle of nationalism).[59]

Conditions were so deplorable that on December 1, 1869, the government admitted "the difficulty in conducting corpses to the public cemeteries . . . because of the lack of conveyance . . . and also a lack of men." The militia, newly created of men not closely identified with the López war effort, was ordered to aid "the weak and hungry" women in the task of burying the dead, "who shall continue to be buried anywhere," thus saving trips to the often distant burial grounds.[60]

Paraguay was prostrate, groaning under the burden of a large Brazilian army of occupation, forced to accept a dictated constitution in 1870 and the loss of territory. As many as a hundred thousand Paraguayan men were dead or otherwise lost forever to the nation, and many returned to their homes after the war as shambling, partial people. Many thousands more, of both sexes, from infancy through senility, had been carried away by disease. Great areas of land lay abandoned, many pueblos were empty, the huge herds had long since been turned into food, and the provisional government reported 529 adult men in Asunción capable of bearing arms.[61]

The Costs of Unity

Geographically, Paraguay is an aberration, an artificial entity, being a continuation of the rolling plains that begin south of Buenos Aires. As a nation, it has from the first based its existence, its national awareness, on its distinct racial and linguistic characteristics, characteristics reinforced by centuries of hostilities with Brazil and the Chaco nomads and capped by the growing pretensions of Buenos Aires. When Dr. Francia midwifed his nation into existence, he had to reinforce the racial and linguistic unity of his people and create from it an identification with the nation. Quietly for the most part, and under constant threat from outside his borders, he did just that. Carlos Antonio López inherited a homogeneous people enjoying rural prosperity and sure of their place as Paraguayans. Whereas Francia had to devote himself to essentially creating a nation, the Corpulent Despot could develop it, turning it gradually outward in time and space. The modernization of one facet of Paraguay and Paraguayan life was astoundingly rapid, perhaps too rapid, for it never had a chance to broaden, and there was no time for a new generation of Paraguayans to be its masters.

Francisco Solano López in 1862 took over a nation that had great potential for its own people. Forged, however, in a world of enemies both real and imagined, it was sufficiently strong to guarantee its own borders and more. Facing the same traditionally arrogant and often hostile enemies, as well as a few new ones, Francisco Solano, a great egotist if nothing else, redefined his nation's borders outward. He did so not only to gain recognition of regional big-power status but also as a further guarantee of national survival, as a defensive measure. Sure of his nation's military potential, he widened Paraguay's sphere in the region. Perhaps a pre-emptive measure to restrict the influence of Brazil and Argentina and hence make them less of a potential threat to Paraguay, the tactic failed utterly. Impressed by the unity and strength of his own country, López did not notice the growing cohesion of his neighbors, which were fast becoming nations. Armed with a certain degree of modern militarization (that lacked basic infrastructure), Francisco Solano was fooled by memories of a fragmented Argentina (he had, after all, as recently as 1859 mediated between two warring regional caudillos) and a disunited Brazil (whose people had in the past fled *into* Paraguay for peace). He felt that Paraguay could weaken and perhaps cause the collapse of one or both neighbors and create a new balance of power. Brazilian and Argentine machinations in Uruguay were but a symbol, albeit a powerful one, of the ancient Paraguayan fears. They justified Paraguayan paranoia and Paraguayan racial nationalism.

Unfortunately, so did the war, and the Treaty of the Triple Alliance, and the Black Brazilian regiments, and the sacking of Asunción, and the destruction of Paraguay, and the death of El Mariscal itself. Once started, the war was seen (and is often seen today) as proof that the regional behemoths were indeed enemies. Paraguayans suffered once again, economically, territorially, and in human terms, at the hands of traditional foes. Francisco Solano, dying heroically in the red Paraguayan mud at the hands of a Brazilian invader, did nothing to diminish either the legend of "the leader" or Paraguayan conviction of the implacable hostility of its neighboring states. Paraguayan racial nationalism is alive and well today, as is the cult of the indispensable man.

Notes

Key to Archival Citations
 The following information, in its abbreviated form, is sufficient to locate any document cited in the notes of this book. The numbers in the right-hand column are random examples of the citation form for each archive.

Archivo Nacional, Asunción	ANA
Sección Historia	SH
Sección Nueva Encuadernación	SNE
Libros de Caxa	SLC
Sección Propiedades y Testamentos	SPT
Sección Judicial y Civil	SJyC
Volume, folio, page (where applicable)	199-3-7
Archivo General de la Provincia de Corrientes	AGPC
Correspondencia Oficial	CO
Expedientes Administrativos	EA
Legajo	12
Archivo General de la Nación, Buenos Aires	AGN, BA
Room, cabinet, shelf, legajo	X-1-9-12
Museo Mitre, Buenos Aires	MM
Cabinet, box, no. of pieces, order no.	B-2-1-39
Biblioteca Nacional, Rio de Janeiro	BNRJ
Coleção Rio Branco	CRB
Coleção de Angelis	CA
Room, cabinet, drawer, legajo	1-30,22,17
British Museum, London (Manuscripts Section)	BM
Additional Manuscripts Series	Add. Mss.
Series no., vol. no.	40,245

Public Record Office, London	PRO
Foreign Office Series	FO 207
Volume, page	vol. 7, p. 19

Archivo Histórico Nacional, Madrid	AHN-M
Sección de Estado	SE
Sección de Consejos	SC
Legajo	19

| Real Academia de la Historia, Madrid | RAH-M |
| Room, cabinet, shelf, vol., page | 9-12-5, 2, p. 7 |

Chapter 1: The "Provincia Gigante" in the Eighteenth Century

1. Bernardo de Velasco to Señor Buenaventura, July 12, 1807, in BM, Add. Mss. 32,607, pp. 129-130.

2. J. P. and W. P. Robertson, *Letters on Paraguay*, II, 178.

3. Thomas Carlyle, *Critical and Miscellaneous Essays*, p. 32.

4. Vicente Pazos Kanki, *A Narrative of Facts Connected with the Change Effected in the Political Conditions and Relations of Paraguay*, pp. 9-10.

5. Martín Dobrizhoffer, S. J., *Historia de los Abipones*, I, 148, 221, and Ludwig Kersten, *Las tribus indígenas del Gran Chaco hasta fines del siglo XVIII*, pp. 48-66.

6. Carlos Zubizarreta, *Historia de mi ciudad*, p. 112.

7. Francisco Pérez de Saraiva from Buenos Aires to Pedro de Cevallos, March 14, 1759, in BM, Add. Mss. 32,604, pp. 117-125. Also, Branislava Susnik, *El indio colonial del Paraguay*, III, 165-169. See also Interim Governor Gutiérrez to Comandante Fodevila at Corrientes, April 28, 1808, in ANA, SH, 207-3-1.

8. Dobrizhoffer, *Historia*, I, 215. Juan Francisco de Aguirre, in his "Diario del Capitán de Fragata," in RAH-M, 9-21-5, vol. 2, p. 357, estimated that there were 31,700 hostile Indians in the Chaco.

9. Guillermo Furlong, S. J., *Misiones y sus pueblos de Guaraníes, 1610-1813*, pp. 102-132.

10. Ibid., pp. 383-388; Viceroy Manuel Amat y Junieu, "Estado del Perú—1776," in BM, Add. Mss. 19,572, pp. 84-119, 132-134, on the Portuguese threat.

11. See "Varios documentos sobre los proyectos de los Portugueses de fundar poblaciones en los Dominios de S. M.," 1748-1749, in MM, B-18-1-12, especially Bernardo Nusdorfer to governor of Paraguay, May 29, 1749; Interim Governor Gutiérrez to the viceroy, March 19, 1809, in ANA, SH, 208-13-7.

12. Efraím Cardozo, *El Paraguay colonial*, pp. 93-103.

13. Furlong, *Misiones*, pp. 357-364.

14. Ernesto J. A. Maeder and A. S. Bolsi, "La población de las Misiones guaraníes entre 1702 y 1767," *Estudios paraguayos* 2, no. 1 (June 1974): 111-138. See unpaginated population chart.

15. Cardozo, *Paraguay colonial*, pp. 91-108.

16. Furlong, *Misiones*, passim.

17. For the War of the Seven Missions, see AHN-M, SE, Legajo 2499. Nothing serious has yet been written on this conflict.

18. See "Buenos Ayres. Expulsion of the Jesuits, 1767-1770," in BM, Add. Mss. 32,605, p. 1049.

19. Viceroy Marqués de Aviles report of 1801, in BM, Add. Mss., 19,576, pp. 57-68.

20. Magnus Mörner, *Political and Economic Activities of the Jesuits in the Plata Region—Habsburg Era*. For the most comprehensive account of the Jesuits in Paraguay, see the illustrated and impressively documented *Misiones*, by Guillermo Furlong.

21. José María Ramos Mejía, *Rosas y el Dr. Francia (Estudios psiquiátricos)*, pp. 245, 248.

22. Bishop Nicolás de Videla to Interim Governor Gutiérrez, Aug. 20, 1807, in ANA, SH, 207-7-19.

23. Bishop Manuel Antonio de la Torre report, Dec. 17, 1765, in AHN-M, SE, Legajo 2581.

24. Viceroy Arredondo to governor of Paraguay, March 16, 1790, in MM, B-25-108-21, No. 3.

25. Andrés Millé, *Crónica de la orden Franciscana en la conquista del Perú, Paraguay y el Tucumán*, pp. 291, 299, and Rafael Eladio Velázquez, *El Paraguay en 1811*, p. 95.

26. Robert Southey, *A Tale of Paraguay*, p. 110.

27. Velázquez, *El Paraguay*, pp. 69-72, 73, 77.

28. Juan Francisco de Aguirre, "Diario del Capitan de Fragata," in RAH-M, 9-21-5, vol. 2, pp. 210-211 (1782).

29. Anon., "Breve noticia histórica de la vida y singular gobierno del Dr. D. José de Francia en la Provincia del Paraguay," in RAH-M, 27-6-183, p. 268.

30. Cosme Bueno, "Descripción del Obispado de la Asunción del Paraguay, 1772," in RAH-M, 27-3-92, pp. 23-36.

31. Charles IV to viceroy at Buenos Aires, May 17, 1803, in ANA, SH, 215-7-1.

32. See Pablo Hernández, S. J., *Organización social de las doctrinas guaraníes de la Compañía de Jesús*, I, 544-555; Nicolás González inventory of Santa María de Fe, Aug. 23, 1790, in ANA, SNE 3374.

33. Juan Pablo Thompson inventory of San Cosme, April 30, 1797, in ANA, SH, 160-4-1/6.

34. Viceroy Arredondo to Governor Joaquín Alós y Brú, Dec. 18, 1789, and same to same, March 22, 1790, in MM, B-25-108.

35. Report of Viceroy Amat y Junieu, Lima, 1776, in BM, Add. Mss.

19,572.

36. Félix de Azara, *Geografía física y esférica de las provincias del Paraguay y Misiones guaraníes,* p. 442.

37. Silbestre Collar from Madrid to viceroy at Buenos Aires, April 3, 1797, in MM, B-27-1.

38. Zubizarreta, *Historia,* p. 215.

39. Report of Asunción síndico procurador, Jan. 3, 1806, in ANA, SH, 211-3-1; report of Interim Governor Gutiérrez, Jan. 19, 1808, in ANA, SH, 207-8-3.

40. Velázquez, *El Paraguay,* pp. 71-84.

41. Olinda Massare de Kostianovsky, *La instrucción pública en la época colonial,* pp. 188-189, 190, 204.

42. Carlos R. Centurión, *Historia de la cultura paraguaya,* I, 161-163.

43. "Padrón de Españoles netos sin mescla de casta," 1790, in ANA, SNE 3374.

44. Governor Joaquín Alós y Brú to the viceroy at Buenos Aires, in ANA, SH, 155-5-1/7.

45. "Notas oficiales de los corregidores de las Misiones sobre atestamiento de sus milicias," 1761, in MM, B-18-27-32.

46. "Reglamento para las milicias disciplinadas de infantería y caballería del Virreinato de Buenos Aires," Madrid, Jan. 14, 1801, in MM, B-27-1-39.

47. "Expedición a Coimbra . . . 1801," in ANA, SH, 184-2-1/40. See also Col. José de Espínola to Governor Lázaro de Ribera, Feb. 19, 1802, in BNRJ, CRB, 1-30, 26, 7.

48. See, for example, Governor Ribera to Viceroy, Jan. 28, 1803, in ANA, SH, 209-1-4/6; Tomás Fernández to Lt. Col. Gregorio de la Cerda, Jan. 30, 1808, in ANA, SH, 208-1-11/12; Gregorio de la Cerda to Governor Velasco, Feb. 24, 1808, in ANA, SH, 208-1-34/35.

49. Governor Velasco to Señor Buenaventura, July 12, 1807, in BM, Add. Mss. 32,607, p. 127.

50. See Gregorio de la Cerda to Governor Velasco, Jan. 12, 1807, in ANA, SH, 204-4-10/14; Juan F. Pérez Acosta, "Repercusión de las invasiones inglesas de 1806 y 1807," *Universidad Nacional. Boletín del Instituto de Investigaciones Históricas* 20 (1942): 150-190. See also Jesús Blanco Sánchez, *El Capitán Don Antonio Tomás Yegros,* pp. 7, 9.

Chapter 2: José Gaspar de Francia and the Paraguayan Revolution

1. Fulgencio Moreno, "Origen del Dr. Francia," *Historia paraguaya. Anuario* (1958), pp. 15-19. See also Julio César Chaves, *El Supremo Dictador,* pp. 26-28; Governor Pinedo letter lauding Francia, Jan. 3, 1778, in ANA, SH, 438-7-10.

2. Chaves, *El Supremo,* pp. 28-29.

3. Viceroy Arredondo to Governor Alós, March 22, 1790, in MM, B-25-108-21, about the Yaguarón malfeasance.

4. Chaves, *El Supremo,* pp. 33-34.

5. Prudencio de la C. Mendoza, *El Dr. Francia en el Virreynato del Plata*, pp. 41-42.

6. Chaves, *El Supremo*, pp. 36-37.

7. José María Ramos Mejía, *Rosas y el Dr. Francia (Estudios psiquiátricos)*, pp. 245, 248.

8. Mendoza, *El Dr. Francia*, pp. 44-45.

9. Kostianovsky, *La instrucción pública*, p. 182.

10. Cecilio Báez, *Ensayo sobre el Dr. Francia y la dictadura en Sudamerica*, p. vi.

11. José Antonio Vázquez, *El Dr. Francia visto y oído por sus contemporáneos*, p. 116; Chaves, *El Supremo*, p. 45.

12. Mendoza, *El Dr. Francia*, p. 48.

13. Centurión, *Historia de la cultura*, I, 161-163; Chaves, *El Supremo*, p. 46.

14. Chaves, *El Supremo*, p. 53.

15. Centurión, *Historia de la cultura*, I, 163; certificate of the examiner of the bishopric of Asunción, Feb. 1, 1789, in ANA, SH, 439-8-3.

16. Chaves, *El Supremo*, pp. 54-55.

17. Ibid., pp. 58-60.

18. Governor Alós appointment of Francia to the teaching post, March 27, 1789, in ANA, SH, 439-1-4/5.

19. Mendoza, *El Dr. Francia*, p. 52.

20. Ibid., p. 53; Ramos Mejía, *Rosas*, p. 267; Chaves, *El Supremo*, p. 62.

21. Chaves, *El Supremo*, pp. 65-67.

22. Ibid., pp. 68-69.

23. Mendoza, *El Dr. Francia*, p. 57.

24. Chaves, *El Supremo*, p. 72.

25. Mendoza, *El Dr. Francia*, pp. 57, 60-61, erroneously notes 1803 as the year Francia entered politics.

26. Viceroy Cisneros to Asunción cabildo, Sept. 17, 1809, in ANA, SH, 328-10-7.

27. See list of French citizens arrested on Velasco's orders, Dec. 16, 1809, in ANA, SH, 208-13-75; Velasco to comandante at Concepción, Feb. 12, 1810, ibid., p. 84; Asunción cabildo to Velasco, March 1, 1810, in ANA, SH, 212-6-6.

28. Chaves, *El Supremo*, pp. 91-92.

29. Buenos Aires junta to provincial authorities, May 26, 1810, in ANA, SH, 211-2-2.

30. Mariano Antonio Molas, *Descripción histórica de la antigua provincia del Paraguay*, p. 97; Chaves, *El Supremo*, p. 92.

31. Rafael Zavala Rodríguez Peña to Velasco, July 4, 1810, in ANA, SH, 211-25-6/9; Molas, *Descripción*, p. 97. See also Velasco bando, July 2, 1810, in ANA, SH, 211-8-1.

32. Julio César Chaves, *Historia de las relaciones entre Buenos Aires y el*

Paraguay, 1810-1813, p. 31.

33. Gregorio Benítez, *La revolución de Mayo,* pp. 23-25; partial resolutions of the open meeting, July 24, 1810, in ANA, SH, 211-13-1/2. See also Chaves, *Relaciones,* p. 41; Blas Garay, *Historia del Paraguay,* p. 155.

34. Velasco bando, Aug. 1, 1810, in ANA, SH, 212-6-22.

35. Julio César Chaves, *La revolución del 14 y 15 de Mayo,* p. 13; Efraím Cardozo, *Afinidades entre el Paraguay y la Banda Oriental en 1811,* p. 6. See also Buenos Aires junta to Governor Elías Galván at Corrientes, Oct. 3, 1810, in AGPC, CO, EA, Legajo 1.

36. Fulgencio Moreno, *Estudio sobre la independencia del Paraguay,* p. 108; Chaves, *La revolución,* p. 15; Cornelio Saavedra to Governor Galván at Corrientes, Oct. 4, 1810, and Saavedra to Corrientes cabildo, Oct. 3, 1810, both in AGPC, CO, EA, Legajo 1.

37. Molas, *Descripción,* p. 106; Belgrano to Governor Galván at Corrientes, Oct. 2, 1810, in AGPC, CO, EA, Legajo 1.

38. Bartolomé Mitre, *Historia de Belgrano y la independencia argentina,* I, 332; Molas, *Descripción,* p. 108.

39. Blas Garay, *Independencia del Paraguay,* p. 64; Belgrano to the people of Paraguay, n.d., in ANA, SH, 211-21-1; Velasco bando, Dec. 18, 1810, in ANA, SH, 211-20-2; Zubizarreta, *Historia,* pp. 251-252. See also Chaves, *Relaciones,* p. 78; Molas address to congress, June 11, 1811, in ANA, SH, 213-1-48/52.

40. Belgrano from Tacuarí to Col. Cavañas, Feb. 20, 1811, in AGN, BA, X-2-3-4; Atilio García Mellid, *Proceso a los falsificadores de la historia del Paraguay,* I, 139.

41. Moreno, *Estudio,* pp. 143-144; Mitre, *Belgrano,* I, 362-364; Col. Cavañas from Tacuarí to Belgrano, March 14, 1811, in AGN, BA, X-3-2-4.

42. Belgrano to Governor Galván at Corrientes, March 18, 1811, in AGPC, CO, EA, Legajo 1; Cecilio Báez, *Historia diplomática del Paraguay,* I, 129.

43. Velasco bando, July 2, 1810, in ANA, SH, 211-8-1; Chaves, *El Supremo,* p. 96; Col. Pedro Gracia to Lt. Pedro Juan Caballero, Sept. 3, 1810, in ANA, SH, 212-6-75, enjoining him to stamp out sedition in his area.

44. John Hoyt Williams, "Governor Velasco, the Portuguese and the Paraguayan Revolution of 1811," *The Americas* 28, no. 4 (April 1972): 443-446.

45. Velasco from Yaguarón to Lt. José T. Fernández, Jan. 7, 1811, in ANA, SH, 215-16-1; Col. Juan Manuel Gamarra to Velasco and Velasco to Gamarra, both Jan. 13, 1811, in ANA, SH, 182-2-178, 179.

46. Velasco bando, April 18, 1811, in ANA, SH, 214-1-8.

47. Chaves, *Relaciones,* p. 58; Mitre, *Belgrano,* II, 9-10.

48. Gregorio Benítez, *La revolución,* p. 28; Chaves, *La revolución,* p. 33.

49. Col. Cavañas to Col. Francisco das Chagas Santos, Feb. 3, 1811, in ANA, SH, 432-1-26.

50. Captain General Souza from São Borja to Velasco, Feb. 25, 1811, and March 22, 1811, in ANA, SH, 432-1-24, 40.

51. Acuerdo of Asunción cabildo, May 13, 1811, in BNRJ, CRB, 1-29, 22, 9.

52. Ibid.; Williams, "Governor Velasco," pp. 441-443.

53. Velasco to Captain General Souza, May 13, 1811, in ANA, SH, 184-2-181. See also Williams, "Governor Velasco," pp. 446-447.

54. Pedro Juan Caballero to Velasco, May 15, 1811, in ANA, SH, 213-1-1.

55. Oath of office signed by Francia, Zevallos, and barracks officers, May 16, 1811, in ANA, SH, 213-1-8.

56. Barracks bando, June 9, 1811, in ANA, SH, 214-1-51/53.

57. Molas, *Descripción*, pp. 135-140; Francia's speech to congress, June 17, 1811, in ANA, SH, 213-1-45/48. See also Molas's resolution to congress, June 18, 1811, in ANA, SH, 213-1-48/52.

58. Paraguayan junta to Buenos Aires junta, July 20, 1811, in ANA, SH, 214-1-90/93.

59. Captain Antonio Tomás Yegros from barracks to Francia at Ybiraí, Aug. 9, 1811; Fray Fernando Caballero to Francia, same date, in ANA, SH, 214-1-115, 116.

60. Paraguayan junta (minus Bogarín) to Francia at Ybiraí, Aug. 6, 1811, in ANA, SH, 214-1-114.

61. Francia to junta from Ybiraí, Aug. 7, 1811, in ANA, SH, 214-1-118.

62. Francisco Wisner, *El Dictador del Paraguay: José Gaspar Francia*, pp. 41-42; Antonio Tomás Yegros, in the name of the barracks, to Asunción cabildo, Sept. 2, 1811, in ANA, SH, 214-1-121.

63. Francia to Asunción cabildo, Sept. 3, 1811, in ANA, SH, 214-1-125/126.

64. Buenos Aires junta to Paraguayan junta, Aug. 28, 1811, in ANA, SH, 214-1-81/83.

65. Instructions of Belgrano and Echevarría, Aug. 1, 1811, in ANA, SH, 213-1-213/214. Mitre, *Belgrano*, II, 15, notes the choice of envoys "was well calculated to treat with an innocent and suspicious people."

66. Efraím Cardozo, "El Plan federal del Dr. Francia," *Revista de Derecho y Ciencias Sociales* 5, no. 17 (July 1931): 20-22.

67. See the author's Ph.D. dissertation, "Dr. Francia and the Creation of the Republic of Paraguay, 1810-1814," University of Florida, 1969; Chaves, *El Supremo*, pp. 125-126; Charles Ames Washburn, *History of Paraguay*, I, 181. See also R. Antonio Ramos, "Juan Andrés Gelly en la revolución de Mayo de 1810," *Historia paraguaya. Anuario* (1956), p. 8.

68. October 12, 1811 treaty, with signatures, in ANA, SH, 214-1-155.

69. Francia from Ybiraí to Asunción cabildo, Dec. 15, 1811, in ANA, SH, 214-1-169/170.

70. Junta to Francia at Ybiraí, Dec. 16, 1811, in ANA, SH, 214-1-174.

71. Vázquez, *Francia*, p. 195.

72. Artigas instructions to Capt. Juan Francisco Arias, Dec. 7, 1811, in ANA, SH, 215-1-9/11; Gregorio Benítez, *La revolución*, p. 47; Paraguayan

junta to Buenos Aires junta, Jan. 29 and Feb. 12, 1812, in ANA, SH, 217-4-46, 58/59.

73. Chaves, *Las relaciones,* pp. 173-179; Paraguayan junta to Governor Galván at Corrientes, Jan. 29, 1812, in AGPC, CO, EA, Legajo 2.

74. Paraguayan junta to Buenos Aires junta, May 19, 1812, and same to subdelegado at Santiago, May 9, 1812, in ANA, SH, 218-1-44/45, 53.

75. R. Antonio Ramos, *La política del Brasil en el Paraguay bajo la dictadura del Dr. Francia,* p. 21; Hipólito Sánchez Quell, *La diplomacia paraguaya de Mayo a Cerro Corá,* pp. 26-27.

76. Gregorio Benítez, *La revolución,* p. 62.

77. Báez, *Historia diplomática,* I, 200.

78. Paraguayan junta bando, Nov. 11, 1812, in ANA, SH, 220-4-11/12.

79. Paraguayan education code, Feb. 15, 1812, in ANA, SH, 216-1-39/52.

80. Luis G. Benítez, *La junta superior gubernativa,* p. 9; Paraguayan junta to Dr. Luis de Zavala, Jan. 9, 1812, in ANA, SH, 219-3-1; acuerdo of Curuguatí cabildo, Aug. 24, 1812, in ANA, SH, 222-7-6. See also junta to comandante at Concepción, Oct. 6, 1812, in BNRJ, CRB, 1-29, 23, 11.

81. Luis G. Benítez, *La junta,* pp. 11-12; Carlos R. Centurión, "La obra de la primera junta gubernativa," *Historia paraguaya. Anuario* (1962), pp. 37-51. See also junta order to investigate the encomienda, Jan. 18, 1812, in ANA, SH, 215-7-28.

82. John Hoyt Williams, "Tevegó on the Paraguayan Frontier: A Chapter in the Black History of the Americas," *Journal of Negro History* 56, no. 4 (October 1971): 272-276.

83. Antonio Tomás Yegros to Francia at Ybiraí, May 15, 1812, in ANA, SH, 218-2-4; junta to Asunción cabildo, May 14, 1812, ibid., p. 40; Archivo Artigas, Comisión Nacional, *Archivo Artigas,* VIII, 139. Also, Chaves, *El Supremo,* p. 147.

84. Chaves, *El Supremo,* pp. 144-146.

85. Washburn, *History,* I, 169, 202; John P. and William P. Robertson, *Letters on Paraguay,* II, 306, 308. The quotation is from Robertson, p. 306.

86. Junta to Francia at Ybiraí, Nov. 12, 1812, in BNRJ, CRB, 1-30, 2, 80.

87. Agreement signed by Francia, Yegros, and Caballero, Nov. 16, 1812, in ANA, SH, 218-6-1/2; junta to Asunción cabildo, Nov. 17, 1812, in ANA, SH, 218-1-162.

88. Nicolás de Herrera instructions, March 4, 1813, in AGN, BA, X-1-9-12.

89. Efraím Cardozo, "La proclamación de la República del Paraguay en 1813," *Boletín de la Academia Nacional de la Historia* 34 (1964): 774-775.

90. Ibid., p. 777.

91. Báez, *Historia diplomática,* I, 233-235; Artigas to junta, July 3, 1813, in ANA, SH, 222-6-1/2.

92. Herrera to Buenos Aires government, July 13, 1813, in AGN, BA, X-1-9-12.

93. Same to same, twice on Aug. 19, 1813, ibid.

94. Acuerdo of Villa Rica cabildo, Sept. 4, 1813, in ANA, SH, 383(2)-1-530.

95. Garay, *Historia*, p. 175; Wisner, *El Dictador*, pp. 57-58; testimony of Francia, Yegros, and Caballero, Sept. 18, 1813, in BNRJ, CRB, 1-30,2,30. See also junta bando, Sept. 24, 1813, in BNRJ, CRB, 1-30,2,30.

96. Herrera, "Reflexiones políticas," n.d., in AGN, BA, X-1-9-12.

97. Cardozo, "La proclamación," pp. 779-780.

98. Johann R. Rengger and Marcel Longchamps, *The Reign of Dr. Joseph Gaspard Roderick de Francia in Paraguay*, p. 16.

99. Gregorio Benítez, *La revolución*, p. 79; Cardozo, "La proclamación," p. 780.

100. Consuls bando, Oct. 20, 1813, in ANA, SH, 222-3-14/17.

101. Herrera to Buenos Aires government, Nov. 7, 1813, in AGN, BA, X-1-9-12.

102. Same to same, Oct. 13, 1813, ibid.

103. *Gaceta Ministerial del Gobierno de Buenos Ayres* no. 83 (December 15, 1813): 495; Andrés Riquelme, *Apuntes para la historia política y diplomática del Paraguay*, I, 33-34; consuls bando, Jan. 5, 1814, in ANA, SH, 223-4-3.

104. Justo Pastor Benítez, *La vida solitaria del Dr. José Gaspar de Francia, Dictador del Paraguay*, p. 79; Rengger and Longchamps, *The Reign*, p. 17.

105. Chaves, *El Supremo*, p. 167.

106. Robertson, *Letters on Paraguay*, II, 18, 37-38.

107. Ibid., pp. 19, 29.

108. John Hoyt Williams, "La guerra no-declarada entre el Paraguay y Corrientes," *Estudios paraguayos* 1, no. 1 (November 1973): 37-39.

109. Guillermo Cabanellas, *El Dictador del Paraguay, Dr. Francia*, p. 182.

110. Chaves, *El Supremo*, p. 179.

111. Jacinto Ruiz to comandante at Concepción, Sept. 26, 1814, in ANA, SNE 815.

112. Jacinto Ruiz summary of 1814 congress, Oct. 10, 1814, in ANA, SH, 223-4-3/8. This document is the only valid source for the congress and its decisions.

113. Ibid.; Wisner, *El Dictador*, pp. 75-77.

114. Ruiz summary of 1814 congress, in ANA, SH, 223-4-3/8.

115. Ibid.

116. Francia circular letter, Oct. 6, 1814, ibid., p. 27.

117. Rengger and Longchamps, *The Reign*, pp. 20-21; Washburn, *History*, I, 216; Justo Pastor Benítez, *Páginas libres*, p. 11.

Chapter 3: Perpetual Means Forever: Francia and the Remodeling of Paraguayan Society

1. Rengger and Longchamps, *The Reign*, pp. 7-8, 39.

2. José Miguel Ibáñez from Concepción to Francia, May 28, 1815, in ANA, SH, 382-4-47.

3. Same to same, Sept. 19, 1815, in ANA, SH, 367-1-565/566.

4. Same to same, Nov. 25, 1815, ibid., p. 594.

5. Francia to Ibáñez, Sept. 20, 1815, in ANA, SH, 224-5-54. By 1819, the main stream of immigrants would be from anarchic, famine-ridden Corrientes.

6. Williams, "Tevegó," passim.

7. Buenos Aires government to Francia, March 15, 1815, and May 19, 1815, in AGN, BA, X-1-9-13. See also José Torre Revelo, "El fracaso de la expedición española preparada contra el Río de la Plata," *Boletín de la Academia Nacional de la Historia* 33 (1962): 421-438.

8. Francia to José Joaquín López at Pilar, July 5, 1815, in BNRJ, CRB, 1-30,24,19.

9. López to Francia, July 30, 1815, in BNRJ, CRB, 1-29,23,1.

10. Juan Antonio Montiel from Santiago to Francia, Aug. 26, 1815, in BNRJ, CRB, 1-29,23,20, and Sept. 16, 1815, ibid.

11. Francia to López at Pilar, Oct. 20, 1815, in ANA, SH, 224-5-58.

12. Same to same, Oct. 24, 1815, ibid., p. 63; Diogo Arouche de Moraes Lima, "Memoria da campanha de 1816," *Revista do Instituto Histórico e Geográfico Brasileiro* nos. 26-27 (July-October 1845): 125-170, 373-378.

13. Francia to López at Pilar, July 15, 1815, in BNRJ, CRB, 1-30,24,19.

14. Chaves, *El Supremo*, pp. 192-193.

15. Ibid., p. 192.

16. Ibid., p. 194.

17. Acts of the 1816 congress, in ANA, SH, 226-1-2.

18. Francia decree, June 16, 1816, ibid., p. 11.

19. Denunciation of del Valle, Oct. 14, 1816, in ANA, SNE 750, with other relevant documents concerning the proceso, dated to Sept. 25, 1817.

20. See item 256, Aug. 31, 1816, in ANA, SLC 15 (1816); Francia decree, Sept. 8, 1816, in ANA, SH, 226-1-15.

21. Capt. Vicente Iturbe to Francia, n.d. (1817), in ANA, SH, 226-18-3/5.

22. Francia appointment of Asunción cabildo, Dec. 10, 1817, in ANA, SH, 226-15-34.

23. "Visita a los presos," Asunción, Dec. 10, 1817, in ANA, SH, 239-5-1/16.

24. Ramón Gil Navarro, *Veinte años en un calabozo; o sea la desgraciada historia de veinte y tantos argentinos muertos o envejecidos en los calabozos del Paraguay*, p. 77.

25. Wisner, *El Dictador*, p. 96; Washburn, *History*, I, 324-325.

26. Molas, *Descripción*, pp. 52-53; Chaves, *El Supremo*, pp. 270-271; "Visita a los presos," Asunción, Dec. 14, 1819, in ANA, SH, 229-13-1/5.

27. "Visita a los presos," Asunción, Dec. 14, 1819, in ANA, SH, 229-13-1/5.

28. Wisner, *El Dictador*, p. 97.

29. Ibid., pp. 98-99; Chaves, *El Supremo*, p. 273.

30. *El Argos de Buenos Aires* no. 30 (November 3, 1821): 204.

31. Funeral oration, in *British Packet and Argentine News* no. 813 (March 19, 1842): 2.

32. Chaves, *El Supremo*, p. 275; Wisner, *El Dictador*, p. 100.

33. Saturnino Blanco Nardo to Francisco Ramírez, Sept. 10, 1820, in ANA, SH, 414-5-1.

34. For letters of Ramírez to Francia, July-Nov., 1820, see ANA, SH, 431-2-76, 118, 119, 79, and 81, in that order. See also Wisner, *El Dictador*, p. 105.

35. Pedro Nolasco Torres from Pilar to Francia, Nov. 10, 1820, in ANA, SH, 232-6-1.

36. Francia bando, June 9, 1821, in BNRJ, CRB, 1-30,24,64.

37. Gil Navarro, *Veinte años*, pp. 14-15; Wisner, *El Dictador*, p. 108.

38. Robertson, *Letters on Paraguay*, III, 312; Chaves, *El Supremo*, p. 283.

39. Census of Quiquió, Jan. 6, 1846, in ANA, SNE 2846.

40. Norberto Ortellado from Ytapúa to Francia, May 28, 1822, in ANA, SH, 382(2)-3-96; Rengger and Longchamps, *The Reign*, pp. 115-116.

41. John Hoyt Williams, "The Conspiracy of 1820 and the Destruction of the Paraguayan Aristocracy," *Revista de historia de América* 75-76 (January-December 1973): 149-151.

42. Navarro, *Veinte años*, pp. 17, 20-21.

43. Sánchez Quell, *La diplomacia*, p. 72.

44. Molas, *Descripción*, p. 53; Julio César Chaves, *El Presidente López*, p. 11. Also, inventory of Cavañas's properties, Aug. 12, 1833, in ANA, SPT, 542-1-89/90.

45. "Extract of a letter from Mr. Hope to Mr. Parish . . . Corrientes," March 17, 1827, in PRO, FO 354, vol. 7, p. 238.

46. José Tomás Gill from Pilar to Francia, July 3, 1825, in ANA, SNE 3107.

47. Same to same, same date, in Vázquez, *Francia*, pp. 575-576.

48. Francia to Gill, May 22, 1826, in ANA, SH, 238-4-3; Gill to Francia, May 28, 1826, ibid., p. 4.

49. Gill to Francia, Sept. 10, 1826, in ANA, SH, 393-1-331.

50. Testimony of Juan Manuel Barrios, Nov. 15, 1826, in ANA, SJyC, 1514-12-1/3.

51. Cavañas's inventory of property, Aug. 12, 1833, in ANA, SPT, 542-1-89/90.

52. Francia to ?, Sept. 1, 1827, in ANA, SH, 239-1-2.

53. Centurión, *Historia*, I, 195.

54. See ANA, SLC 27 (1827), items 142-144, 236, 241-243, and Francia to subdelegado at Pilar, Dec. 13, 1826, in ANA, SH, 442-1-49.

55. Francia to subdelegado at Concepción, Jan. 20, 1827, in BNRJ, CRB, 1-30,24,45.

56. Francia to subdelegado at Pilar, May 26, 1826, in ANA, SH, 238-5-1; Wisner, *El Dictador*, p. 158.

57. Bishop Panés to Francia, March 9, 1815, in ANA, SH, 224-6-1; Francia to Panés, July 2, 1815, in ANA, SH, 224-5-35.

58. Alberto Nogues, *La Iglesia en la época del Dr. Francia,* pp. 17-18.

59. Francia appointment of Céspedes, Dec., 1815, in ANA, SH, 224-4-6.

60. Washburn, *History,* II, 287; Nogues, *La Iglesia,* pp. 5-8, 21-22.

61. Washburn, *History,* II, 292.

62. See ANA, SLC 15 (1816), items 31, 83-84, 105, 116-121, 234, 264, and 128, 148, 240, 400.

63. Padre Juan Josef de Roo from Buenos Aires to Francia, May 5, 1817, in ANA, SH, 430-1-237.

64. See Francia decree, Jan. 29, 1819, in ANA, SH, 228-6-7, and Francia to Villa Rica alcalde, announcing an end to the taxes, Sept. 20, 1819, in ANA, SH, 228-4-15.

65. Padre Juan Antonio Rivarola from Villeta to Francia, n.d. (1822), in ANA, SH, 412-2-39.

66. Francia to Father Mariano Agustín Goyburú, March 23, 1823, in ANA, SH, 441-20-3; Chaves, *El Supremo,* p. 325.

67. Francia decree, Sept. 20, 1824, in ANA, SNE 3107; Rengger and Longchamps, *The Reign,* p. 109.

68. San José Convent inventory, Oct. 8, 1824, in ANA, SNE 3107; Nogues, *La Iglesia,* pp. 24-25.

69. Francia decree, Aug. 23, 1828, in ANA, SH, 239-10-8.

70. Francia to Asunción cabildo, Dec. 30, 1824, in ANA, SH, 237-7-8/9. It might be noted that among the 1820 conspirators were several cabildantes.

71. The ANA is filled with cabildo records of other pueblos, 1824-1840.

72. Robertson, *Letters on Paraguay,* III, 293, and I, 37.

73. Rengger and Longchamps, *The Reign,* p. 159.

74. Petition of Ybitimí urbanos to Supreme Government, March 1, 1814, in ANA, SH, 383(1)-1-9/11.

75. Francia decree, March 13, 1819, in ANA, SH, 299-9-4/6.

76. See military expense lists in ANA, SLC 21 (1822), passim.

77. John Hoyt Williams, "From the Barrel of a Gun: Some Notes on Dr. Francia and Paraguayan Militarism," *Proceedings of the American Philosophical Society* 119, no. 1 (February 1975): 86, 84-85.

Chapter 4: The Diplomacy of Isolation, 1820-1840

1. John Hoyt Williams, "Paraguayan Isolation Under Dr. Francia—A Reevaluation," *Hispanic American Historical Review* 52, no. 1 (February 1972): 110.

2. Juan A. Domíngez, *Aimé Bonpland. Su vida en la América del Sur,* pp. 503, 508; Adolphe Brunel, *Biographie d' Aimé Bonpland,* p. 83.

3. Bolívar from Lima to Francia, Oct. 23, 1823, as quoted in Juan F. Pérez Acosta, *Francia y Bonpland,* pp. 34-35.

4. Subdelegado Ortellado from Ytapúa to Francia, Aug. 18, 1824, in BNRJ, CRB, 1-30,6,91; Pérez Acosta, *Francia,* pp. 25-26, 31-32.

5. Woodbine Parish to George Canning, April 8, 1825, in PRO, FO 6, vol. 8, p. 191.

6. General Santander from Bogotá to Bolívar, Jan. 21, 1826, as quoted in Vázquez, *Francia,* pp. 593-594.

7. Pérez Acosta, *Francia,* p. 38; Francia to subdelegado at Ytapúa, May 20, 1829, in ANA, SH, 240-2-42.

8. Pérez Acosta, *Francia,* pp. 44-45.

9. Rengger and Longchamp, *The Reign,* passim.

10. Francia to ?, July 19, 1830, in ANA, SH, 240-11-171.

11. John Hoyt Williams, "Woodbine Parish and the 'Opening' of Paraguay," *Proceedings of the American Philosophical Society* 116, no. 4 (August 1972): 343; "Report of the British Committee on the Trade of the River Plata" (1924), in PRO, FO 354, vol. 8, pp. 2-39.

12. See Parish to Francia, July 17, 1824, in BNRJ, CRB, 1-30,7,38.

13. Parish to George Canning, Aug. 22, 1824, in PRO, FO 354, vol. 3, p. 103.

14. Same to same, Feb. 19, 1825, ibid., p. 151.

15. Bernardino Villamayor to Parish, Jan. 26, 1825, in BNRJ, CRB, 1-30, 7,38.

16. Parish to Francia, June 15, 1825, in ibid.

17. Williams, "Woodbine Parish," pp. 348-349.

18. Subdelegado Gill from Pilar to Francia, Aug. 23, 1826, in BNRJ, CRB, 1-29,23,27; Descalzi Documents, in AGN, BA, 7-17-6-1: Doc. 80, pp. 1-3.

19. Descalzi Documents, in AGN, BA, 7-17-6-1, Doc. 80, pp. 11, 22-24.

20. Ibid., Doc. 76, pp. 1-6; Comandante at Concepción to Francia, July 5, 1831, in ANA, SH, 394-1-810.

21. For inventories of several smugglers captured at Ytapúa in May, 1819, see ANA, SPT, 931-5-1/16.

22. Alejandro Audibert, *Los límites de la antigua provincia del Paraguay,* p. 158.

23. Wisner, *El Dictador,* pp. 118-119.

24. Ramos, *La política,* p. 50.

25. Parish to George Canning, Oct. 19, 1824, in PRO, FO 354, vol. 3, p. 182.

26. Ramos, *La política,* pp. 190-193.

27. Ibid., pp. 93-94, 119.

28. R. Antonio Ramos, "Correa da Cámara en Asunción," *Universidad Nacional. Instituto de Investigaciones Históricas* 20 (1952): 62-64.

29. Ramos, *La política,* pp. 129-130.

30. Ibid., pp. 133-134.

31. Ibid.; Ramos, "Correa da Cámara," p. 61.

32. Francia to subdelegado at Ytapúa, April 10, 1830, in ANA, SH, 242-

7-15.

33. Same to same, Dec. 22, 1831, in ANA, SH, 241-7-59/60.

34. Same to same, n.d. (1832), in ANA, SH 241-12-36; Williams, "La guerra," pp. 41-43.

35. Francia to subdelegado at Ytapúa, Sept. 13, 1832, in ANA, SH, 241-12-45.

36. Same to same, Dec. 10, 1833, in ANA, SH, 242-7-49; Williams, "La guerra," passim.

37. Francia to subdelegado at Ytapúa, Aug. 5, 1829, in ANA, SH, 240-2-62.

38. Same to same, June 18, 1831, in ANA, SH, 241-7-22/23.

39. Same to same, Feb. 26, 1831, ibid., p. 8.

40. Same to same, Aug. 7, 1834, in ANA, SH, 242-11-147.

41. Same to same, Nov. 28, 1831, in ANA, SH, 241-7-53; commercial notebook of Manuel Flota, Aug. 20, 1825, in ANA, SH, 229-7-1/10. See also trade licenses for July, 1825, in ANA, SH, 238-11-11/17; Sánchez Quell, *La diplomacia*, p. 63.

42. Subdelegado Casimiro Roxas from Ytapúa to Francia, July 12, 1840, in ANA, SH, 378-1-338/339.

43. Alcabala receipts, Asunción, in ANA, SLC 43 (1840), passim, and export tax scale, July 15, 1829, in ANA, SH, 240-1-3.

44. E.g., proceso against Saturnino Xara, June 19, 1838, in ANA, SH, 243-15-1/3.

45. Vázquez, *Francia*, pp. 742-743.

46. Francia to subdelegado at Ytapúa, Nov. 2, 1831, in ANA, SH, 241-7-42.

47. "Guías de Aduana . . . 1817-1818," in AGN, BA, X-37-1-16.

48. "Guías de Aduana . . . 1819," in AGN, BA, X-37-1-18. See page 369.

49. Héctor José Tanzi, "Estudio sobre la población del Virreinato del Río de la Plata en 1790," *Revista de Indias* 27, nos. 107/108 (1967): 151.

50. Governor Martín Rodríguez from Buenos Aires to Francia, July 4, 1821, in *Documentos para la historia argentina* XIII, 103-107; Bernardino Rivadavia to Francia, July 23, 1823, ibid., 261-264.

51. See ANA, SLC 18 (1821), items for Jan. 1.

52. Governor Juan José Blanco from Corrientes to Francia, Jan. 1, 1822, in ANA, SH, 431-2-83/84.

53. Subdelegado Pedro Nolasco Torres from Pilar to Francia, Jan. 30, 1822, in ANA, SH, 383(2)-1-574/575.

54. Subdelegado at Pilar to Francia, Sept. 4, 1825, in ANA, SH, 393-1-275/276, for a good discussion of the mechanics of the trade, and same to same, Feb. 1, 1827, in ANA, SNE 2568.

55. "Extract of a letter from Mr. Hope to Mr. Parish," Corrientes, March 17, 1827, in PRO, FO 354, vol. 7, p. 240.

56. Ibid., passim.

57. Subdelegado Miguel Castro at Pilar to Francia, Sept. 6, 1831, in ANA,

SH, 394-1-827.

58. Francia to subdelegado Torres at Pilar, Feb. 16, 1822, in ANA, SNE 3106; Torres to Francia, March 17, 1822, in ANA, SH, 383(2)-1-581/582.

59. See Ysasí invoices, 1825, in ANA, SH, 442-1-38/40; subdelegado Gill to Francia from Pilar, July 16, 1826, in ANA, SH, 393-1-322/323.

60. See documents concerning the Pilar smugglers, 1826, in ANA, SH, 442-1-45/89, and Francia to Gill at Pilar, May 26, 1826, in ANA, SH, 238-5-1/2.

61. Parish to George Canning, April 8, 1825, in PRO, FO 354, vol. 3, p. 256.

62. Gill from Pilar to Francia, Feb. 20, 1827, in ANA, SH, 394-1-669/670.

63. Same to same, Aug. 8, 1827, in ANA, SH, 394-1-693, and Aug. 28, 1825, in ANA, SH, 393-1-274. See Williams, "Paraguayan Isolation," pp. 108-109.

64. Tax schedules, 1827, in ANA, SLC 27 (1827), items 307-310, 142-144. See also Gill from Pilar to Francia, July 21, 1827, in ANA, SH, 394-1-688.

65. Francia to subdelegado at Ytapúa, Dec. 5, 1834, in ANA, SH, 242-11-172.

66. Williams, "Race, Threat and Geography," pp. 186-187.

67. Francia to subdelegado at Concepción, May 1, 1820, in ANA, SH, 232-3-7.

68. See Efraím Cardozo, *Artigas en el Paraguay*, pp. 43-44; Wisner, *El Dictador*, pp. 92-93.

69. Parish to the Earl of Aberdeen, Sept. 25, 1828, in PRO, FO 354, vol. 4, pp. 135-136.

70. As quoted in Agustín Beraza, *Rivera y la independencia de las Misiones*, p. 64.

71. Ibid., p. 73; Eduardo Salteraín, *Artigas en el Paraguay*, p. 32.

72. Subdelegado Miguel Castro from Ytapúa to Francia, June 9, 1829, in ANA, SH, 394-1-725/727.

73. Francia to Castro at Ytapúa, Feb. 5, 1831, in ANA, SH, 241-7-4.

74. Castro from Ytapúa to Francia, Feb. 11, 1832, in ANA, SH, 394-1-841.

75. Williams, "La guerra," p. 43; Francia to subdelegado at Ytapúa, Sept. 8, 1832, in ANA, SH, 241-12-43/44.

76. Francia to subdelegado at Ytapúa, Oct. 2, 1832, in ANA, SH, 241-12-52.

77. *British Packet and Argentine News* no. 320 (October 6, 1832): 1. See also *Registro Oficial del Gobierno de Corrientes* no. 9 (1832): 21; *El Telégrafo de Comercio* no. 144 (October 6, 1832).

78. Francia to subdelegado at Concepción, Aug. 18, 1832, in ANA, SNE 3412.

79. General Birón de Estrada to governor of Corrientes, May 19, 1833, in

AGCP, CO, EA, Legajo 44.
  80. As quoted in Robertson, *Letters on Paraguay*, II, 279-280.
  81. Williams, "La guerra," pp. 43-44.
  82. Salteraín, *Artigas*, p. 31.
  83. Francia to subdelegado at Ytapúa, Sept. 21, 1837, in ANA, SH, 377-1-179.
  84. Subdelegado at Ytapúa to Francia, Dec. 16, 1837, ibid., p. 189.
  85. Same to same, April 23, 1839, in ANA, SH, 378-1-286.

Chapter 5: The Supreme Dictatorship, 1820-1840
  1. José F. Bazán, *El Dictador Francia y otras composiciones en verso y prosa*, p. 55.
  2. See funeral oration by Father Manuel Antonio Pérez, Oct. 20, 1840, in BNRJ, CRB, 1-30,25,20, and, for a printed translation, see *British Packet and Argentine News* no. 813 (March 19, 1842): 2-4.
  3. Francia to Ytapúa subdelegado, Aug. 22, 1830, in BNRJ, CRB, 1-30,2,6.
  4. Pedro Somellera, "Notas del Doctor Don Pedro Somellera a la introducción que ha puesto el Dr. Rengger . . . ," *Museo Mitre. Documentos del Archivo de Belgrano*, III, 336.
  5. *British Packet and Argentine News* no. 118 (November 8, 1828): 1.
  6. Nicolás Descalzi diary, in AGN, BA, 7-17-6-1, p. 14.
  7. Vázquez, *Francia*, pp. 29-33, 465-466; *British Packet and Argentine News* no. 813 (March 19, 1842): 1; Rengger and Longchamp, *The Reign*, p. 104.
  8. Rengger and Longchamp, *The Reign*, pp. 99-105.
  9. Robertson, *Letters on Paraguay*, III, 324; Vázquez, *Francia*, p. 829.
  10. Rengger and Longchamp, *The Reign*, p. 202.
  11. Ibid., p. 200; Robertson, *Letters on Paraguay*, III, 323. See also Wisner, *El Dictador*, pp. 148-149.
  12. Vázquez, *Francia*, p. 825.
  13. Cabanellas, *El Dictador*, p. 216; Ramos Mejía, *Rosas*, p. 315.
  14. Testimony of Francia, July 18, 1835, in ANA, SNE 3122.
  15. Rengger and Longchamp, *The Reign*, pp. 40-42, 203; Pilar subdelegado to Francia, July 21, 1827, in ANA, SH, 394-1-832.
  16. Francia to Señora Juana Isabel Francisca de Torres, Nov. 28, 1824, in Asunción Cathedral Historical Museum.
  17. Justo Pastor Benítez, *La vida*, pp. 228, 236; Ramos Mejía, *Rosas*, p. 300.
  18. For a description of his library, see Guillermina Nuñez de Báez, *Dr. José Gaspar Rodríguez de Francia*, pp. 11-14, and Vázquez, *Francia*, pp. 827-829.
  19. Francia to ?, as printed in *El Lucero* (Buenos Aires) no. 273 (August 21, 1830): 2-3.
  20. See ANA, SLC 41 (1838), especially item 44.

21. Rengger and Longchamp, *The Reign*, p. 107.

22. Antonio Zinny, *Historia de los gobernantes del Paraguay*, p. 322.

23. See ANA, SPT, 317-9-29/31, 32/34; vol. 363-3-1/33; vol. 72-8-26/33; vol. 266-2-6, 8; vol. 193-9-15/21, 22; and vol. 410-1-7/9. For Céspedes, see his testament, Dec. 23, 1835, in ANA, SPT, 541-12-1/12.

24. See testimony, March 16 to Nov. 9, 1835, in ANA, SJyC, 1514-11-1/72.

25. Francia to ?, Sept. 1, 1827, in ANA, SH, 239-1-2, concerning Ysasi, and economic records, July 10 to Aug. 24, 1827, in ANA, SLC 27 (1827).

26. Romualdo Agüero from San Estanislao to Francia, July 14, 1825, in ANA, SH, 374-2-25.

27. Plea of Asunción soldier to Francia, April 12, 1817, in ANA, SH, 226-24-7; Báez, *Ensayo*, p. 91.

28. Francia to juez comisionado at Quiquió, Sept. 2, 1818, in ANA, SH, 228-1-2/4.

29. Francia decree, Aug. 16, 1820, in ANA, SH, 232-1-2/3.

30. Instructions for jueces de recursos, Sept., 1820, ibid., pp. 6-7.

31. Francia decree, Aug. 27, 1827, in ANA, SNE 3111.

32. Juez comisionado at Capiatá to Francia, July 11, 1828, in ANA, SJyC, 1514-12-1/2, and Francia's reply, scrawled on the reverse.

33. Bartolomé José Galiano from Atirá to Francia, July 21, 1823, in ANA, SH, 359-2-15.

34. Parish to George Canning, April 8, 1825, in PRO, FO 354, vol. 3, pp. 254-255, and July 28, 1824, ibid., pp. 110-111.

35. Nicolás Descalzi diary, in AGN, BA, 7-17-6-1, pp. 16, 23; Cecilio Báez, *La tiranía en el Paraguay*, p. 16.

36. See jail visitas, 1819 and 1833, in ANA, SH, 229-13-1/5, and 242-8-1/8.

37. Visita of 1827, in ANA, SH, 239-5-1/16. See page 7.

38. Gil Navarro, *Veinte años*, passim; Washburn, *History*, I, 271.

39. Gil Navarro, *Veinte años*, passim.

40. Juez ? to Francia, Oct. 22, 1825, in ANA, SJyC, 1514-11-1.

41. Caesar A. Rodney and John Graham, *Reports*, p. 123.

42. Rengger and Longchamp, *The Reign*, pp. 46-47.

43. Ibid., p. 48.

44. Ibid., p. 49; Rodney and Graham, *Reports*, p. 237.

45. Báez, *Ensayo*, p. 83, and Rengger and Longchamp, *The Reign*, p. 49.

46. Rengger and Longchamp, *The Reign*, pp. 49-50.

47. Manuel Peña Villamil, "Breve historia de la ganadería paraguaya," *Historia paraguaya. Anuario* (1969-1970), p. 89.

48. Rengger and Longchamp, *The Reign*, pp. 174-175.

49. John Hoyt Williams, "Paraguay's Nineteenth Century Estancias de la República," *Agricultural History* 47, no. 3 (July 1973): 208-209.

50. List of state estancias, 1818, in ANA, SH, 229-12-1/2.

51. Williams, "Paraguay's Nineteenth Century Estancias," pp. 209-210; and John Hoyt Williams, "Dictatorship and the Church: Doctor Francia in

246 Notes to Pages 93–98

Paraguay," *Journal of Church and State* 15, no. 3 (Fall 1973): 430-431.

52. Capataz of Tabapí to Francia, April 16, 1826, in ANA, SNE 3110.

53. Rengger and Longchamp, *The Reign*, p. 175.

54. See ANA, SLC 30 (1828), passim, and 34 (1831), 35 (1832), 41 (1838).

55. Cabanellas, *El Dictador*, p. 249; "Extract of a letter from Mr. Hope to Mr. Parish," Corrientes, March 17, 1827, in PRO, FO 354, vol. 4, p. 241.

56. See ANA, SLC 24 (1826), item 233.

57. As quoted in Vázquez, *Francia*, p. 765.

58. See Báez, *Ensayo*, p. 93; ANA, SLC 43 (1840), passim.

59. Francia decree, April 26, 1832, in ANA, SH, 241-11-3; Báez, *Ensayo*, p. 83.

60. See ANA, SLC 35 (1832), passim; also item 431 in ANA, SLC 34 (1831); Juan Natalicio González, *El Paraguayo y la lucha por su expresión*, p. 25. See also ANA, SLC 37 (1834), items 327-329, 168, 338, 427-428, 500, 505, 523.

61. See ANA, SLC 17 through 43, passim.

62. Cibils, *Anarquía*, p. 43.

63. Centurión, *Historia*, I, 187.

64. Ibid., p. 188.

65. Francia to subdelegado at Concepción, June 5, 1831, in ANA, SNE 3412. The eight local teachers were paid and fed "so that they can dedicate themselves with more energy to the teaching of First Letters."

66. Wisner, *El Dictador*, p. 137; Báez, *Ensayo*, p. 83.

67. Josefina Pla, *Los artes plásticos en el Paraguay*, p. 10.

68. Josefina Pla, *El teatro en el Paraguay*, p. 33.

69. Francia to ?, Nov. 22, 1838, in ANA, SPT, 934-2-1.

70. Somellera, "Notas," p. 336.

71. Ytapúa subdelegado to Francia, Jan. 27, 1840, in ANA, SH, 378-1-323.

72. As quoted in Arturo Bray, *Hombres y épocas del Paraguay*, I, 15.

73. *British Packet and Argentine News* no. 813 (March 19, 1842): 2.

74. Gregorio Benítez, *La revolución*, p. 94.

75. Vázquez, *Francia*, p. 789.

76. Ministerio de Interior, *Los restos mortales del Dr. José Gaspar de Francia*, pp. 13-14.

77. See treasury inventory, Jan., 1841, in ANA, SH, 247-3-1; Vázquez, *Francia*, pp. 824-825.

78. Report of comandante general de armas, Feb. 11, 1841, in ANA, SH, 247-2-1.

79. *British Packet and Argentine News* no. 813 (March 19, 1842): 1-2.

80. Ch. Quentin, *An Account of Paraguay*, p. 7.

81. Justo Pastor Benítez, *La vida*, p. 72.

82. Carlyle, *Critical and Miscellaneous Essays*, p. 49.

83. *British Packet and Argentine News* no. 252 (June 18, 1831): 3.

84. Báez, *Ensayo*, p. 122.

Chapter 6: The Old Order Changeth?
1. Carlyle, *Critical and Miscellaneous*, p. 20.
2. Robert Peel to ?, Feb., 1843, in BM, Add. Mss. 40,525, pp. 85-87.
3. R. Antonio Ramos, *Juan Andrés Gelly*, p. 221.
4. Chaves, *El Presidente*, p. 3.
5. Juan Andrés Gelly, *El Paraguay. Lo que fué, lo que es y lo que será*, p. 61.
6. ? to comandante at Curuguatí, n.d. (1840), with orders to confine Artigas under heavy guard, in ANA, SH, 244-10-1; Chaves, *El Presidente*, p. 3.
7. Funeral oration, *British Packet and Argentine News* no. 813 (March 19, 1842): 2.
8. Gil Navarro, *Veinte años*, p. 120; Chaves, *El Presidente*, pp. 5-6.
9. Chaves, *El Presidente*, p. 6.
10. Ibid., p. 7.
11. Ibid., pp. 14-15.
12. Gil Navarro, *Veinte años*, pp. 120-121; Chaves, *El Presidente*, p. 15.
13. Gelly, *El Paraguay*, pp. 66-69; Chaves, *El Presidente*, pp. 17-18.
14. Chaves, *El Presidente*, p. 11; Gelly, *El Paraguay*, pp. 68-70.
15. Phelps, *Tragedy of Paraguay*, p. 34.
16. Justo Pastor Benítez, *Carlos Antonio López*, p. 19.
17. A British Gentlemen, *Rosas and the River Plate*, p. 40.
18. *The British Packet and Argentine News* no. 254 (July 2, 1831): 95.
19. Carlyle, *Critical and Miscellaneous*, p. 44.
20. Ildefonso Bermejo, *Vida paraguaya en tiempos del viejo López*, p. 44.
21. Héctor Varela, as ascribed by Phelps, *Tragedy*, pp. 57-58.
22. Attributed to Alfred Demersay in Francisco Pérez-Maricevich (ed.), *Paraguay. Imágen romántica, 1811-1853*, p. 152.
23. Attributed to Charles Mansfield, ibid., p. 203.
24. Bermejo, *Vida paraguaya*, p. 44.
25. Chaves, *El Presidente*, p. 215.
26. Ibid.
27. Bermejo, *Vida paraguaya*, pp. 41, 44.
28. Chaves, *El Presidente*, pp. 214-215.
29. Ibid., pp. 216-217.
30. Phelps, *Tragedy*, pp. 47-48; Chaves, *El Presidente*, pp. 216-218.
31. Attributed to Demersay in Pérez-Maricevich, *Paraguay*, p. 204.
32. Chaves, *El Presidente*, p. 217.
33. Boettner, "La música," p. 39.
34. Bermejo, *Vida paraguaya*, pp. 152-156.
35. Ibid.
36. Attributed to Charles Mansfield, in Pérez-Maricevich, *Paraguay*, p. 204.

37. Attributed to Héctor Varela, in Phelps, *Tragedy*, p. 58.
38. Chaves, *El Presidente*, p. 213.
39. Attributed to Demersay, in Pérez-Maricevich, *Paraguay*, p. 152.
40. Petition of Manuel Ayala, Nov. 11, 1844, and margin note of López, Nov. 25, 1844, in ANA, SNE 1375.
41. Justo Pastor Benítez, *Carlos Antonio López*, p. 186.
42. Gil Navarro, *Veinte años*, pp. 186-189.
43. Chaves, *El Presidente*, p. 138.
44. Ibid., pp. 138-139.

Chapter 7: A New Paraguay is Stirring

1. Departamento de Cultura y Arte, *Historia edilicia de la ciudad de Asunción*, p. 87.
2. Bermejo, *Vida paraguaya*, pp. 34, 107.
3. As quoted in Departamento de Cultura y Arte, *Historia edilicia*, pp. 89-91.
4. List of oficios, Cathedral barrio, Dec. 17, 1843, in ANA, SH, 259-10-1/13.
5. Report on Asunción silversmiths, various dates (1854), in ANA, SH, 308-9-1/36. For an idea of the magnificent items produced by these shops, see Guillermo Furlong, S.J., *Historia social y cultural del Río de la Plata, 1536-1810*, III, 577-610.
6. Boettner, "La música," pp. 39, 41.
7. Bermejo, *Vida paraguaya*, pp. 88-89.
8. Azara, *Geografía física*, p. 442; Olinda Massare de Kostianovsky, "Historia y evolución de la población en el Paraguay," in Domingo M. Rivarola and G. Heisecke (eds.), *Población, urbanización y recursos humanos en el Paraguay*, p. 227.
9. Kostianovsky, "Historia," p. 222.
10. This author, calculator in hand, tabulated each of the more than 20,000 pages of documents composing the 1846 census during his two-year stay in Asunción, 1973 and 1974. The census data is in ANA, SNE 3288-3319.
11. Josefina Pla, *Hermano negro. La esclavitud en el Paraguay*, passim, and John Hoyt Williams, "Observations on the Paraguayan Census of 1846," *Hispanic American Historical Review* 56, no. 3 (August 1976): 424-437.
12. See Azara, *Geografía física*, p. 442.
13. "Informes de Bucareli y Cevallos, Buenos Ayres, 1770-1778," in BM, Add. Mss. 19,574, p. 127.
14. Pla, *Hermano negro*, pp. 123-127.
15. See my "Conspiracy of 1820," passim, and inventory of properties of Manuel Atanacio Cavañas (1828), in ANA, SPT, 542-1-1/40.
16. Francia decree, Sept. 20, 1824, in ANA, SNE 3107.
17. List of renters at Tabapí, April 16, 1826, in ANA, SH, 239-11-1/4.

18. Pla, *Hermano negro,* pp. 125-126. The decree is printed in full.
19. Slave census, Tabapí, 1854, in ANA, SH, 313-7-1/11.
20. For the 1848 sale, see Pla, *Hermano negro,* p. 109; for later sales, see ANA, SH, 314(B)-1-1/61, and 314(B)-2-1/45.
21. For scores of such testaments, see ANA, SNE 1372, passim.
22. Dolores Mongelos of Caapucú to Juan de Mata Denis, Dec. 17, 1859, in ANA, SH, 328-10-1; Pla, *Hermano negro,* p. 108.
23. Francia to Treasurer Alvarez, Aug. 9, 1834, in ANA, SH, 242-9-3.
24. López to justice of the peace, Ajos, July 24, 1855, in ANA, SH, 314(B)-1-38; Pla, *Hermano negro,* p. 109.
25. See my "Esclavos y pobladores: Observaciones sobre la historia parda del Paraguay en el siglo XIX," *Revista Paraguaya de la Sociología* no. 31 (September-December 1974): 12-16.
26. "Cuenta del caudal del ramo de guerra," Oct.-Dec., 1847, in ANA, SH, 281-6-1/18.
27. Matías Ramírez of Limpio, testament, July 20, 1843, in ANA, SNE 1372. This volume is filled with such documents.
28. Fermín Bazaras to Justice of the Peace Manuel Ygnacio Fernández, Feb. 24, 1853, in ANA, SH, 334-13-13.
29. Collector General to López, June 28, 1854, in ANA, SNE 2733.
30. Mariano González to López, July 23, 1855, in ANA, SH, 314(B)-1-37.
31. López to justice of the peace, Ajos, July 24, 1855, ibid., p. 38.
32. List of oficios, Asunción, Nov. 18, 1843, in ANA, SH, 259-9-1/11.
33. Vicente Iturbe from Ycuamandiyú to consuls, May 27, 1812, in ANA, SH, 220-12-1.
34. "Visita a los presos," 1819, in ANA, SH, 229-13-1/5; "Causas criminales," 1847, in ANA, SH, 281-18-1/47; "Juzgado de primera instancia," 1863, in ANA, SH, 327-8-1/31.
35. Sánchez Quell, *La diplomacia,* pp. 189-190.
36. See Luis Bernardo Benítez report, Aug. 9, 1842, in ANA, SNE 1918.
37. See Manuel Uriarte report, Altos, Nov. 10, 1851, in ANA, SNE 2698.
38. Magnus Mörner (ed.), *Algunas cartas del naturalista sueco Don Eberhard Munck af Rosenschold escritas durante su estadía en el Paraguay, 1843-1868,* pp. 16-17.
39. See militia lists, May and June, 1845, in ANA, SNE 1953, and lists of northern garrisons in ANA, SNE 1990.
40. Susnik, *El indio colonial,* III, 95-99.
41. Bernardino Denis, list of Chaco guardias, June 7, 1845, in ANA, SH, 273-3-67.
42. See reports of police chief Pedro Nolasco Fernández, Jan. 1, 1849, and Oct. 30, 1849, in ANA, SNE 1990 and 1436.
43. López decree creating national guard, Aug. 26, 1845, in ANA, SH, 272-13-1/6, and López decree, Oct. 2, 1845, in ANA, SH, 272-14-1/10.
44. Chaves, *El Presidente,* p. 17.

45. Sánchez Quell, *La diplomacia,* p. 195.

46. López to president of the French Republic, Dec. 25, 1850, in ANA, SNE 2017.

47. López to Antonio Tomás Cabral at Santa Rosa, March 12, 1845, in ANA, SH, 272-4-1.

48. Blas Ygnacio Bazán on Ycuamandiyú schools, June 8, 1848, in ANA, SH, 284-14-1.

49. Sánchez Quell, *La diplomacia,* pp. 196, 199; receipt of teacher Asencio Gómez at Quiindí, March 16, 1861, in ANA, SNE 3246.

50. Bermejo, *Vida paraguaya,* p. 197.

51. See legajo of criminal "causas," 1847, in ANA, SH, 281-18-1/47.

52. "Juzgado del crimen de primera instancia," 1849, in ANA, SH, 323-10-17; López decree, May 16, 1848, in ANA, SH, 282-12-1.

53. Bermejo, *Vida paraguaya,* p. 40.

Chapter 8: The Economic Pulse Quickens

1. George Masterman, *Seven Eventful Years in Paraguay,* p. 32.

2. Mörner (ed.), *Algunas cartas,* p. 11.

3. Jordan Luis de Trayo, Inventory, Ytapúa, April 4, 1841, in ANA, SNE 1918.

4. Themosticles Linhares, *História econômica do mate,* pp. 119, 129.

5. López decree, n.d. (1845), in ANA, SH, 272-9-1/3.

6. "Mapa de importación," first semester, 1846, in ANA, SNE 1410. Though the tax was supposedly 21%, anything between 19% and 22% was collected.

7. Ibid.

8. Ibid., second semester.

9. "Mapa de importación," second semester, 1847, in ANA, SH, 282-2-1/5.

10. Félix Barboza list of foreign merchants at Pilar, Aug. 7 and Nov. 17, 1849, in ANA, SH, 278-5-3/4. About forty were present at any given time.

11. See naturalizations, 1845-1854, in ANA, SH, 273-2-1/101.

12. Schmidt, "Relaciones diplomáticas," p. 69.

13. George Thompson, *The War in Paraguay,* p. 14. Thompson expressed wonder at the almost total lack of taxation or national debt.

14. Carlos Pastore, *La lucha por la tierra en el Paraguay,* p. 121.

15. López decree, Jan. 2, 1846, quoted in ibid., pp. 122-123.

16. López decree, Oct. 7, 1848, in ANA, SH, 282-24-1/3.

17. Pastore, *La lucha,* pp. 128-131.

18. Ibid., p. 132.

19. Harris G. Warren, *Paraguay. An Informal History,* p. 183.

20. List of renters, Luque, April 9, 1854, in ANA, SNE 2733.

21. Lists of renters from many partidos, ibid., and ANA, SNE 2307.

22. List of renters, Jesús, Feb. 24, 1864, in ANA, SNE 2307.

23. Mörner (ed.), *Algunas cartas,* pp. 19-25.

24. See cuatropea lists, 1851, in ANA, SNE 2698.

25. Juan de la Cruz Cañete to ?, May 16, 1854, in ANA, SNE 2733.

26. See censuses of 1826 and 1830, with relevant vital statistics for the intervening years, in ANA, SNE 1858.

27. See vital statistics for Tabapí, 1853-1868, in ANA, SNE 974, passim.

28. "Nómina de esclavos del Estado," Tabapí, n.d. (1854), in ANA, SH, 313-7-1/11.

29. Mariano González to López, May 22, 1857, in ANA, SNE 2753.

30. Williams, "Paraguay's 19th Century Estancias," passim. The 1972 *Area Handbook for Paraguay,* p. 277, notes that "the armed forces produce much of their own food."

31. Tabapí reports, 1843-1851, in ANA, SNE 2049.

32. Diego Félix de Ayala report, Dec. 31, 1861, in ANA, SNE 3246.

33. See reports of various estancias in ANA, SH, 313-7-1/11, and ANA, SNE 2116.

34. Capataz of Surubí to Francia, Aug. 12, 1832, in ANA, SH, 412-2-48.

35. López to judge at Villeta, Aug. 28, 1844, in ANA, SNE 2695.

36. Judge José Vicente Gill at Villeta to López, Sept. 5, 1844, ibid.

37. Same to same, March 3, 1845, ibid.

38. López to Judge Gill, Aug. 14, 1848, ibid.

39. Judge Gill to López, Aug. 29, 1848, ibid.

40. López to Judge Gill, Sept. 3, 1848, ibid.

41. Sergeant Campusano to López, Sept. 18, 1848, ibid., and López to Judge Gill, Oct. 10, 1848, ibid.

42. Sergeant Campusano to López, Sept. 18, 1848, ibid.

43. "Ynforme de Surubí," March 26, 1850, ibid.

44. Manuel Gómez to López, June 12, 1850, ibid.

45. Same to same, Aug. 11, 1851, ibid.

46. Same to same, Oct. 7, 1852, ibid.

47. Same to same, Feb. 16, May 24, and Sept. 19, 1854, ibid.

48. "Detalle de las existencias de las Estancias del Estado," Jan. 30, 1864, signed by Mariano González, in ANA, SH, 339-28-1/2.

Chapter 9: The Diplomacy of Frustration

1. For the full text of the treaties, see *El Nacional Correntino* 18 (August 23, 1841).

2. See Williams, "La guerra," pp. 35-43, for the antecedents.

3. See Enrique Araña, *Rosas en la evolución política argentina,* p. 661; Sánchez Quell, *La diplomacia,* pp. 83-84.

4. Robert Peel to ?, Feb., 1843, in BM, Add. Mss. 40,525, p. 87; Carlos Antonio López, *La emancipación paraguaya,* pp. 288-290.

5. Robert Peel, "Memorandum on Mr. Gordon's Mission to Paraguay,"

Feb. 3, 1843, in BM, Add. Mss. 40,525, pp. 89-90; Chaves, *El Presidente*, p. 32.

6. See *El Paraguayo Independiente* 8 (June 14, 1845): 1-2; Jesús Blanco Sánchez, "Don Carlos Antonio López, figura cimera de la nacionalidad," *Historia paraguaya*. Anuario (1966), p. 26; Rudolfo Puiggros, *Historia económica del Río de la Plata*, p. 226.

7. Báez, *Historia diplomática*, II, 5. The letter appears in full.

8. Ibid., pp. 6-7.

9. Chaves, *El Presidente*, p. 40; Araña, *Rosas*, pp. 664-665.

10. Governor Joaquín de Madariaga of Corrientes to López, Sept. 27, 1844, in ANA, SH, 262-1-7/10.

11. Chaves, *El Presidente*, pp. 45, 44, 46.

12. Clifton B. Kroeber, *La navegación de los ríos en la historia argentina*, pp. 198-199; Sánchez Quell, *La diplomacia*, p. 86.

13. Governor Madariaga from Corrientes to López, July 24, 1827, in ANA, SH, 262-1-22, mentioning the official position of Wisner. See also Ramos, *Juan Andrés Gelly*, pp. 292-294.

14. Instructions of Carlos Antonio López to Brigadier General Francisco Solano López, Dec. 9, 1845, in ANA, SH, 272-22-1/5, in 22 articles.

15. Quoted in Mantilla, *Crónica*, II, 140-144.

16. Quoted in ibid., pp. 187-188, and Araña, *Rosas*, pp. 672-673. See also López to Governor Madariaga at Corrientes, July 24, 1847, in ANA, SH, 262-1-23.

17. López to British minister plenipotentiary at Buenos Aires, Aug. 30, 1843, in ANA, SH, 255-1-4/7.

18. W. E. Ouseley from Buenos Aires to López, Sept. 23, 1845, ibid., p. 14.

19. Same to same, March 7, 1846, ibid., pp. 50-51.

20. Edward A. Hopkins, "The Republic of Paraguay since the Death of the Dictator Francia," *The American Review* (September 1847) pp. 255-256.

21. Ibid.

22. Schmitt, "Las relaciones," p. 68; Mörner (ed.), *Algunas cartas*, p. 17.

23. See Hopkins's instructions and letter of appointment, signed by Buchanan, Aug. 1, 1845, in ANA, SH, 268-2-6. How this "reserved" document ever got into the Paraguayan Archives is a mystery.

24. On the background, see Hopkins, "The Republic of Paraguay," pp. 245-260. See also Hopkins to Buchanan, Nov. 31, 1845, from Asunción, in William R. Manning (ed.), *Correspondencia diplomática de los Estados Unidos concerniente a la independencia de las naciones latinoamericanas*, X, 61-63.

25. Chaves, *El Presidente*, pp. 83, 85-88.

26. Ibid., pp. 103-105.

27. Luis G. Benítez, *Historia diplomática del Paraguay*, pp. 109-110.

28. López decree, Jan. 28, 1848, in ANA, SH, 282-7-1, and report on naval strength, unsigned, Jan. 4, 1848, in ANA, SNE 1990.

29. López decree, April 27, 1848, in ANA, SH, 282-10-1/3.

30. López to Pilar police chief, Aug. 13, 1848, in ANA, SH, 282-16-2.

31. López instructions for Chaco expedition, n.d. (1848), in ANA, SH, 282-33-1/9.

32. López to "General in Chief, Army of the Frontier," Aug. 15, 1848, in ANA, SH, 282-17-1/3.

33. López instructions to Wisner, June 23, 1849, in ANA, SH, 286-14-1/11.

34. López decree, June 10, 1849, in ANA, SH, 286,11-1/4.

35. Wisner report on troop dispositions, Nov. 25, 1849, in ANA, SNE 1436.

36. El Paraguayo Independiente 72 (February 12, 1848). Address of November 17, 1847.

37. Mantilla, Crónica, II, 216.

38. Ibid., p. 217.

39. Ibid.

40. Chaves, El Presidente, p. 148; Báez, Historia diplomática, II, 61-64.

41. Chaves, El Presidente, p. 152, and his "Después de Caseros," Historia paraguaya. Anuario (1956), pp. 103-105.

42. Chaves, El Presidente, p. 154.

43. Ibid., pp. 172-174; Ramos, Juan Andrés Gelly, p. 414.

44. Ramos, Juan Andrés Gelly, p. 417; Chaves, "Después de Caseros," p. 107.

45. López to Luis José de la Peña, Argentine Confederation foreign minister, Oct. 20, 1852, in ANA, SH, 262-1-73/74.

46. Chaves, El Presidente, p. 50.

47. Luis G. Benítez, Historia diplomática, p. 125.

48. Ibid., pp. 126-127.

49. Ibid., p. 127.

50. Ramos, Juan Andrés Gelly, pp. 274-280, 282-283.

51. See list and description of Apa forts, 1854, in ANA, SH, 311-4-3/4.

52. Ramos, Juan Andrés Gelly, p. 289.

53. Ibid., pp. 321, 334.

54. The 1847 edition is very rare, but the book was also published in Spanish at Paris in 1926.

55. See Luis G. Benítez, Historia diplomática, p. 128.

56. López decree, Sept. 16, 1848, in ANA, SH, 282-18-1/11, and Ricardo Franco de Almeida Serra, "Sobre o aldeamento dos Indios Uaicurús e Guanas, com a descripção dos seus usos, religião, estabilidade e costumes," Revista do Instituto Histórico e Geográphico Brasileiro 7, no. 26 (July 1845): 204-207.

57. Chaves, El Presidente, p. 158.

58. Ibid., pp. 141-142.

59. Efraím Cardozo, El Imperio del Brasil y el Río de la Plata, p. 45; Luis G. Benítez, Historia diplomática, p. 129.

60. Chaves, El Presidente, p. 160; Luis G. Benítez, Historia diplomática, pp. 128-131.

61. Chaves, "Después de Caseros," p. 104.

Chapter 10: Threat and Counter-Threat: The 1850s
1. Cardozo, *El Imperio*, p. 49.
2. Pelham H. Box, *Origins of the Paraguayan War*, p. 43.
3. Luis G. Benítez, *Historia diplomática*, p. 133.
4. Cardozo, *El Imperio*, pp. 50-51. See also Virgilio Corrêa Filho, "Portugueses em Mato Grosso," *Revista do Instituto Histórico e Geográphico Brasileiro* 245 (October-December 1957): 204-234.
5. López circular, Jan. 17, 1855, in ANA, SH, 314(B)-1-4; Box, *Origins*, p. 33.
6. Cardozo, *El Imperio*, p. 51.
7. Chaves, *El Presidente*, pp. 236-237.
8. López to comandante at Villa Rica, Feb. 5, 1855, in ANA, SH, 314(B)-1-8.
9. In a letter of José Falcón to British foreign minister, March 22, 1855, in ANA, SH, 255-1-57.
10. López to officers on the Río Apa, Feb. 19, 1855, in ANA, SH, 314(A)-11-1/2.
11. Cardozo, *El Imperio*, p. 52.
12. Luis G. Benítez, *Historia diplomática*, pp. 134-135.
13. Cardozo, *El Imperio*, p. 53.
14. Thomas J. Page, *La Plata, the Argentine Confederation and Paraguay*, p. 285; Box, *Origins*, p. 45.
15. Cardozo, *El Imperio*, p. 54.
16. Luis G. Benítez, *Historia diplomática*, pp. 142-144.
17. Luis Vittone, "El Mariscal Francisco Solano López," *Revista de las FF AA de la Nación* 179 (August 1961): 164.
18. Washburn, *History*, I, 406.
19. Alberto Nogues, "El General López en Roma," *Historia paraguaya. Anuario* (1969-1970), pp. 48-63.
20. See Ramos, *Juan Andrés Gelly*, pp. 419-423; Schmitt, "Las relaciones," pp. 71-72; Vittone, "El Mariscal," pp. 164-168.
21. Ramos, *Juan Andrés Gelly*, p. 428; Luis G. Benítez, *Historia diplomática*, p. 159.
22. Washburn, *History*, I, 407-408.
23. In Ramos, *Juan Andrés Gelly*, pp. 430, 432-434.
24. Ibid., p. 435.
25. Pablo Max Ynsfrán, *La expedición norteamericana contra el Paraguay*, I, 123.
26. Ibid., I, 125-130; Harris G. Warren, "The Hopkins Claim against Paraguay and the 'Case of the Missing Jewels,'" *Inter-American Economic Affairs* 22, no. 1 (1968): 26.
27. Ynsfrán, *La expedición*, I, 137; draft of a letter by Guillemot's translator, n.d., in ANA, SH, 308-1-2.
28. Ynsfrán, *La expedición*, I, 132-135.

29. Ibid., I, pp. 134-138; Warren, "The Hopkins Claim," p. 26.
30. Bermejo, *La vida,* p. 49; Warren, "The Hopkins Claim," p. 27.
31. Page, *La Plata,* p. 126. See also p. 197.
32. Ynsfrán, *La expedición,* pp. 190-193.
33. Page, *La Plata,* p. 279; Ynsfrán, *La expedición,* I, 194-200.
34. Page, *La Plata,* p. 281.
35. Ynsfrán, *La expedición,* I, 211.
36. Ibid., I, 214-216; Page, *La Plata,* p. 307.
37. Page, *La Plata,* p. 308.
38. López to comandante at Villa Rica, Feb. 5, 1855, in ANA, SH, 314(B)-1-8.
39. Warren, *Paraguay,* pp. 194-195.
40. Page, *La Plata,* pp. 308-311.
41. Ynsfrán, *La expedición,* II, 36-37.
42. Chaves, *El Presidente,* pp. 296-299.
43. Warren, "The Hopkins Claim," p. 28. It is probable that by the time of his expulsion Hopkins owed López money! See Edward A. Hopkins, *Historico-Political Memorial upon the Regions of the Río de la Plata,* p. 57.
44. Blyth to Francisco Solano, May 7, 1859, in ANA, SH, 255-1-110, and, on the Canstatt affair, see PRO, FO 527, vol. 11, passim.
45. Schmitt, "Las relaciones," p. 70.
46. Josefina Pla, "Los británicos en el Paraguay," *Revista de historia de América* 70 (July-December 1970): 370-371; Sánchez Quell, *La diplomacia,* p. 179.
47. Sánchez Quell, *La diplomacia,* pp. 179-180.
48. Pla, "Los británicos," p. 371.
49. Ibid., pp. 372-373.
50. Schmitt, "Las relaciones," p. 75; Sánchez Quell, *La diplomacia,* pp. 179-185.
51. Sánchez Quell, *La diplomácia,* pp. 200, 201.
52. Alfredo DuGraty, *La Republique du Paraguay,* pp. 88-91; Schmitt, "Las relaciones," pp. 78-81.
53. Moreno, *La ciudad,* pp. 262-263, 268.
54. DuGraty, *La Republique,* pp. 363-402.
55. Charles A. Henderson Commercial Report, January 7, 1857, in PRO, FO 59, vol. 17, pp. 20-30. Import duties averaged over 20%.
56. David Bruce, cargo manifest, July 18, 1855, in ANA, SNE 2739.
57. Pascual Savie, petition to export, Feb. 12, 1855, ibid.
58. DuGraty, *La Republique,* p. 265.
59. López decree, Jan. 7, 1855, in ANA, SH, 314(A)-1-1/4.
60. Bermejo, *La vida,* pp. 173-174, 179, 180.
61. Bray, *Hombres y épocas,* II, 105-106.
62. Ibid., II, 102-103; Warren, *Paraguay,* p. 204.
63. Bray, *Hombres y épocas,* II, 102-103.

64. Josefina Pla, "Los británicos en el Paraguay," *Revista de historia de América* 71 (January-June 1971): 54.

65. Attributed to Héctor Varela in ibid.

66. Ibid., p. 55.

67. Ibid., p. 56.

68. Pastore, *La lucha,* pp. 148-150.

Chapter 11: Foreigners and the Modernization of Paraguay

1. Anon. (Alex Grant?) to Whytehead, Dec. 12, 1855, in ANA, SNE 707. "How on earth came you to Paraguay? I considered that you were still in France inventing projectiles for the annihilation of the Russians."

2. Sir Robert Peel report on the abortive Hughes mission, Feb., 1843, in BM, Add. Mss. 40,525, pp. 85-86.

3. Brazil was being pulled apart by the decade-long Guerra dos Farrapos, and Argentina was also torn by separatist movements.

4. López to British minister plenipotentiary at Buenos Aires, June 1, 1845, in ANA, SH, 255-1-13.

5. W. E. Ouseley from Buenos Aires to López, Sept. 23, 1845, and March 7, 1846, in ibid., pp. 14, 50-51.

6. López decree, 1845, in ANA, SH, 272-9-1/3.

7. Mörner (ed.), *Algunas cartas,* p. 13.

8. List of oficios, Cathedral barrio, Nov. 17, 1843, in ANA, SH, 259-10-1/13.

9. See naturalizations in ANA, SH, 273-2-1/101. One old Spaniard took the plunge after moving to Paraguay in 1799!

10. Pérez Acosta, *Carlos Antonio López,* pp. 367-393.

11. Félix Barboza list of foreign merchants at Pilar, Aug. 7, 1849, and list of passports given there by same official, Nov. 17, 1849, in ANA, SH, 278-5-4/5, 6.

12. See López instructions to Wisner, n.d. (1846), in ANA, SH, 286-14-1/11.

13. Page, *La Plata,* p. 221.

14. Contract signed by Juan Andrés Gelly and Johann Frederick Meister, Rio de Janeiro, Sept. 15, 1848, in ANA, SH, 284-3-1/2.

15. Eberhard Munck to López, Jan. 27, 1845, in ANA, SH, 272-30-8.

16. López to comandante at San Ysidro, March 21, 1845, ibid., p. 16.

17. List of foreigners resident in the Cathedral barrio, 1850, in ANA, SH, 291-11-1/4. My thanks to Professor Miguel Angel González Erico of the Centro Paraguayo de Estudios Sociológicos for his help in locating this material.

18. Pla, "Los británicos," pp. 345-346, and her *The British in Paraguay, 1850-1870,* pp. 7-10.

19. Pla, "Los británicos," pp. 351-353.

20. Ibid., p. 353.

21. Ibid., p. 353; Richardson from Ibicuy to Whytehead, March 1, 1857, in ANA, SNE 2152.

22. Whytehead report, n.d. (1856), in ANA, SH, 312-2-1/14.

23. Pérez Acosta, *Carlos Antonio López*, pp. 315-317.

24. Pla, "Los británicos," p. 359.

25. Ibid., pp. 361-362.

26. Ibid., pp. 363-364.

27. Thompson, *The War*, passim.

28. Pla, "Los británicos," pp. 365-366, and her *The British*, p. 201.

29. José María Téllez to Claudius B. Piers, July 4, 1857, in ANA, SH, 255-1-91/95.

30. Piers to Francisco Solano López, July 23, 1857, ibid., pp. 96-99.

31. Piers to ?, Jan. 30, 1858, ibid., p. 102.

32. Pablo González to Piers, Feb. 23, 1858, ibid., pp. 103-107.

33. J. Blyth to Francisco Solano López, May 7, 1859, ibid., pp. 112-116.

34. Masterman, *Seven Eventful Years*, p. 71.

35. Venancio López to Whytehead, May 30, 1863, in ANA, SH, 334-13-36.

36. Same to same, April 6, 1865, in ANA, SNE 707.

37. Pérez Acosta, *Carlos Antonio López*, pp. 290-293.

38. Bermejo, *La vida*, pp. 31-32, 43.

39. Ibid., pp. 11-13; Bermejo contract, June 1, 1857, in ANA, SNE 2753.

40. Bermejo, *La vida*, pp. 197, 199; Bermejo to Mariano González, Dec. 12, 1860, in ANA, SH, 329-16-1/2.

41. Pedro Dupuis school report, March 1, 1854, in ANA, SH, 311-8-9.

42. Pérez Acosta, *Carlos Antonio López*, p. 529; Dupuis contract, Sept. 1, 1856, in ANA, SNE 2748.

43. Pérez Acosta, *Carlos Antonio López*, pp. 530-531.

44. Carlos Riviere contract, n.d. (1856), in ANA, SNE 2748.

45. Pérez Acosta, *Carlos Antonio López*, pp. 51-53, 501.

46. Ibid.; Pla, "Los británicos," p. 387.

47. List of licenses given at Asunción, Jan.-June, 1863, dated Sept. 1, 1863, in ANA, SH, 334-28-2; Mariano González report on licenses, April 13, 1859, in ANA, SNE 1579.

48. Passport data from ANA, SH, 323-8-1/15, 326-6-1/30, and 328-11-1/19.

49. López approvals of solicitudes, Feb.-Oct., 1853, in ANA, SNE 1506.

50. Bermejo, *La vida*, pp. 44, 58, 150.

51. Mysznowski solicitude, Nov. 3, 1858, in ANA, SNE 1567; Cramon solicitude, July 1, 1854, in ANA, SH, 312-4-1; Costa solicitude, Jan. 15, 1855, ibid., p. 5. See also Mörner (ed.), *Algunas cartas*, p. 22, and solicitudes in ANA, SH, 314(B)-1-41, 54, 23, 68.

52. J. Blyth to Francisco Solano López, April 8, 1862, in ANA, SH, 255-1-174.

53. Venancio López to Whytehead, Dec. 15, 1864, in ANA, SNE 707.

54. Same to same, April 18, 1865, ibid.
55. Pla, "Los británicos," pp. 24-25.
56. Ibid.; Whytehead inventory, n.d. (1865), in ANA, SH, 255-1-188/194.
57. Pla, "Los británicos," pp. 36-37, and her *The British,* pp. 153-159.
58. Pla, "Los británicos," p. 39.
59. Ibid., pp. 47-60; Mörner (ed.) *Algunas cartas,* p. 5.
60. Masterman, *Seven Eventful Years,* pp. x, 137, 149, 198-203.
61. "Sobre el establecimiento de la Colonia francesa en la Nueva Burdeos," May 4, 1855, in ANA, SH, 314(A)-17-1/3.
62. Luis G. Benítez, *Historia diplomática,* p. 159.
63. Ciriaco Paláez to comandante at San Ysidro, Dec. 12, 1855, in ANA, SH, 314(B)-1-62.
64. Page, *La Plata,* p. 284.
65. "Visita al Juez de Paz de Nueva Burdeos," initialed by López, Dec. 29, 1855, in ANA, SH, 308-1-38.
66. Luis Cominos to López, Jan. 5, 1856, in ANA, SH, 314(B)-2-5.

Chapter 12: "Francisco Solano's Error: The War"
1. Thompson, *The War,* v.
2. Efraím Cardozo, *Breve historia del Paraguay,* p. 86.
3. Washburn, *History,* I, 486.
4. Fidel Maíz, *Etapas de mi vida,* pp. 13-16.
5. Box, *Origins,* p. 183.
6. Schmitt, "Las relaciones," p. 80; Washburn, *History,* I, 544.
7. Washburn, *History,* I, 489.
8. Cardozo, *Breve historia,* p. 87.
9. Phelps, *Tragedy,* p. 48.
10. Ibid., p. 47.
11. Juan Zorrilla de San Martín, *La epopeya de Artigas,* V, 129-225.
12. Box, *Origins,* p. 168.
13. Ibid., p. 186.
14. Schmitt, "Las relaciones," pp. 80-83.
15. For more detail, see Box, *Origins,* passim.
16. Ibid., pp. 157-160.
17. Ramón J. Cárcano, *Guerra del Paraguay,* I, 283.
18. Phelps, *Tragedy,* pp. 79-81.
19. Cárcano, *Guerra,* I, 288.
20. Box, *Origins,* pp. 157-164, 166.
21. Ibid., p. 214; M. Blanca Paris de Oddone, *Cronología comparada de la historia del Uruguay, 1830-1945,* p. 25.
22. Phelps, *Tragedy,* pp. 80-81; Box, *Origins,* p. 169.
23. Box, *Origins,* pp. 167-168.
24. Phelps, *Tragedy,* p. 81.

25. Box, *Origins,* p. 149.

26. Phelps, *Tragedy,* p. 81.

27. Box, *Origins,* p. 212.

28. Ibid., pp. 213-219.

29. Phelps, *Tragedy,* pp. 86-87.

30. José Berges report on train service, March 14, 1864, in ANA, SNE 2307.

31. Pla, *El teatro,* pp. 35-36, 64-69.

32. Sánchez Quell, *La diplomacia,* p. 199.

33. Zinny, *Historia de los gobernantes,* p. 444.

34. Juan Beverina, *La Guerra del Paraguay (1865-1870). Resumen histórico,* p. 104.

35. Cardozo, *El Imperio,* pp. 519-520, 521, provides a lucid counterargument for those who insist that Paraguay was ready for war.

36. Pay list, First Infantry Battalion, Sept. 18, 1863, in ANA, SNE 955.

37. Ibid., and troop list, Second Infantry Battalion, Aug. 31, 1864, ibid. See Charles Kolinski, *Independence or Death! The Story of the Paraguayan War,* pp. 40-41. Col. Luis Vittone, in his *Las FF AA paraguayas en sus distintas épocas,* p. 157, asserts that there were only about 7,000 infantry regulars in mid-1864.

38. Troop list, First Cavalry Regiment, Feb. 28, 1863, in ANA, SNE 959.

39. Troop list, Police Battalion, n.d. (1864), in ANA, SNE 955.

40. Asunción garrison report, Dec. 29, 1864, in ANA, SH, 339-18-6.

41. Encarnación garrison report, Dec. 31, 1864, in ANA, SNE 3278; Vittone, *Las FF AA,* p. 157.

42. Data on naval units was drawn from widely scattered sources. Chief among these were Dec. 31, 1864, reports by individual ship captains, in ANA, SNE 955; naval pay lists of Feb. 28, 1863, in ANA, SNE 959; Pérez Acosta, *Carlos Antonio López,* pp. 314-340; Cardozo, *El Imperio,* p. 536.

43. Ibid.; Capt. Meza report, Dec. 31, 1864, in ANA, SNE 955.

44. López proclamation, Dec. 15, 1864, in ANA, SH, 339-32-1; Thompson, *The War,* p. 32. See also Victor Ayala Queirolo, "Campaña de Mato Grosso," *Historia paraguaya. Anuario* (1966), p. 136.

45. Queirolo, "Campaña," pp. 134-135; Beverina, *La Guerra,* p. 79.

46. Beverina, *La Guerra,* p. 88.

47. Kolinski, *Independence,* pp. 91-93; Beverina, *La Guerra,* pp. 85-89; Harris G. Warren, "Brazil's Paraguayan Policy, 1869-1876," *The Americas* 28, no. 4 (April 1972): 388.

48. Juan B. Gill Aguínaga, *La Asociación paraguaya en la Guerra de la Triple Alianza,* p. 163.

49. For an excellent description of the Brazilian fleet, see Thompson, *The War,* pp. 70-79.

50. Beverina, *La Guerra,* pp. 118-126, 176, 181, 185. Data for other military actions were drawn from Agusto Tasso Fragoso, *História da Guerra*

entre a Tríplice Aliança e o Paraguai, and L. Schneider, *A Guerra da Tríplice Aliança,* passim.

Chapter 13: The Immolation of Paraguay

1. See "Lista de Sres Jefes y Oficiales de la División del Ejército del Sud," Jan. 19, 1866, in ANA, SNE 3278.
2. Vittone, *Las FF AA,* p. 162.
3. Tasso Fragoso, *História,* III, 201-205.
4. Masterman, *Seven Eventful Years,* p. 125. He estimates 50,000 for losses due to disease. This figure appears too high.
5. Vittone, *Las FF AA,* p. 160.
6. León de Palleja, *Diario de la campaña de las fuerzas aliadas contra el Paraguay,* II, 371.
7. One of the most valuable compendia of data on the war, Schneider's *A Guerra,* III, 401, estimates that by September 22, 1866, Paraguay had already lost 38,153 men, a third of whom died on the field. See also Palleja, *Diario,* II, 359.
8. See responses to the Sept. 6, 1866 order in ANA, SNE 2392.
9. Carapeguá militia list, March 14, 1866, in ANA, SNE 3278.
10. Pascual López letter of manumission, Dec. 21, 1866, in ANA, SNE 2399.
11. Pedro Regalado Montiel from Tabapí to ?, May 6, 1867, and José Molina from Gasorí to ?, May 10, 1867, both in ANA, SNE 2463.
12. Efraím Cardozo, *Hace cien años,* V, 155, 71, 238.
13. Palleja and other Allied diarists continually note deserters in their works.
14. Cardozo, *Hace cien años,* V, 159.
15. *El Centinela* 31 (November 21, 1867), p. 4, and 35 (December 19), p. 3.
16. Cardozo, *Hace cien años,* V, 257, 268.
17. Ibid., VI, 91, 117, 129-130, 139.
18. Ibid., VI, 141, 191.
19. Ibid., VI, 272.
20. Ibid., VI, 335-336.
21. Palleja, *Diario,* II, 275-277, 286.
22. Inventory of *Yndependencia,* Pilar, Feb. 9, 1865, in ANA, SNE 2373.
23. Vittone, *Las FF AA,* pp. 161-162.
24. *El Centinela* 17 (August 15, 1867), p. 4.
25. Mariano González report, Dec. 10, 1863, in ANA, SH, 334-32-3.
26. Concepción yerba reports, 1862-1865, in ANA, SNE 2244.
27. Cardozo, *Hace cien años,* VI, 255.
28. Report of 1st-quarter sowings, 1866, in ANA, SNE 3278.
29. Francisco Sánchez to justice of the peace, Ytauguá, Oct. 23, 1863, in ANA, SH, 334-13-62.

30. Rudecindo Areposo of Tobatí to Mariano González, Jan. 28, 1866, in ANA, SNE 2399.

31. Cardozo, *Hace cien años*, V, 287.

32. Ibid., V, 140, and VI, 132; Olinda Massare de Kostianovsky, *El Vice Presidente Domingo Francisco Sánchez*, pp. 89-96.

33. Cardozo, *Hace cien años*, VI, 260.

34. Ibid., VI, 99-100, 329.

35. Ibid., VI, 289.

36. Ibid., VI, 183.

37. Ibid., V, 225, 226, 307, and VI, 150, 183.

38. *El Centinela* 1 (April 25, 1867), p. 1.

39. Ibid., p. 3, and 16 (August 8, 1867), p. 3.

40. See Centurión, *Historia*, I, 301-302.

41. Ibid., I, 293; Pla, *El teatro*, pp. 69-82.

42. Cardozo, *Hace cien años*, VI, 238-239, and V, 18.

43. Ibid., V, 19-20, 24-26.

44. Mörner (ed.), *Algunas cartas*, p. 5.

45. Masterman, *Seven Eventful Years*, p. 117; Cardozo, *Hace cien años*, VI, 188.

46. Censo de libertos, 1850, 1853, 1856, 1868, in ANA, SNE 963, 965, 968.

47. *El Centinela* 31 (November 21, 1867), p. 2.

48. See reports from various partidos, Dec. through Feb., 1868, in ANA, SNE 1012.

49. Martin McMahon, "The War in Paraguay," *Harper's* 220, no. 19 (April 1870): 637.

50. See casualty lists in Tasso Fragoso, *Historia*, V, passim, and Dionisio Cerqueira, *Reminiscencias da campaña do Paraguai*, p. 427.

51. Thompson, *The War*, pp. 323-324.

52. Maíz, *Etapas*, p. 40; Bray, *Hombres*, I, 75-77.

53. Tasso Fragoso, *Historia*, IV, 26-27.

54. Héctor Francisco Decoud, *Guerra del Paraguay: La Masacre de Concepción*, pp. 275-296.

55. Maíz, *Etapas*, pp. 64-65; Silvestre Aveiro, *Memorias militares, 1864-1870*, pp. 61-109, for the best description. Aveiro, then a colonel, was a participant.

56. Tasso Fragoso, *Historia*, IV, 195.

57. *Registro Oficial*, August 15, 1869, pp. 3-4.

58. Herrera, *La diplomacia oriental*, pp. 322-328, 317.

59. *Registro Oficial*, August-December 1869, passim.

60. Ibid., December 1, 1869 decree (unpaginated).

61. Ibid., June 28, 1870.

Bibliography

ARCHIVAL MATERIALS

Archivo Nacional, Asunción
  Sección Historia
  Sección Nueva Encuadernación
  Libros de Caxa
  Sección Propiedades y Testamentos
  Sección Judicial y Civil
Archivo General de la Provincia de Corrientes, Corrientes
  Correspondencia Oficial
  Expedientes Administrativos
Archivo General de la Nación, Buenos Aires
Museo Mitre, Buenos Aires
Biblioteca Nacional, Rio de Janeiro
  Coleção Rio Branco
  Coleção de Angelis
British Museum, London (Manuscripts Section)
  Additional Manuscripts Series
Public Record Office, London
  Foreign Office Series
Archivo Histórico Nacional, Madrid
  Sección de Estado
  Sección de Consejos
Real Academia de la Historia, Madrid

CONTEMPORARY PRINTED SOURCES

A. Books and Articles
It is unfortunate that one finds virtually no Paraguayan collection of printed
documents. There are documents spread throughout many books (all too
often in incomplete form), and a few very valuable memoirs, but the historian

must go directly to the archives if he seeks documents.

Aveiro, Silvestre (Col.). *Memorias militares (1864-1870).* Asunción, 1970.

Azara, Félix de. *Geografía física y esférica de las Provincias del Paraguay y Misiones guaraníes.* Montevideo, 1904.

Bermejo, Ildefonso. *Vida paraguaya en tiempos del viejo López.* Buenos Aires, 1972 (first published, 1868).

Cerqueira, Dionisio (Gen.). *Reminiscencias da campanha do Paraguai, 1865-1870.* 5th ed. Rio de Janeiro, 1974 (1910).

Dobrizhoffer, Martín, S. J. *Historia de los Abipones.* 3 vols. Resistencia, Chaco, 1967-1970 (1747).

Documentos para la historia argentina. 15 vols. Buenos Aires, 1913-1929.

Gelly, Juan Andrés. *El Paraguay. Lo que fué, lo que es y lo que será.* Paris, 1926 (1847).

Gil Navarro, Ramón. *Veinte años en un calabozo, o sea la desgraciada historia de veinte y tantos argentinos muertos o envejecidos en los calabozos del Paraguay.* Rosario, 1903.

Hopkins, Edward A. *Historico-Political Memorial upon the Region of the Río de la Plata and Coterminous Countries.* New York, 1858.

————. "The Republic of Paraguay Since the Death of the Dictator Francia." *American Review* (September 1847), pp. 255-256.

King, Alexander. *Twenty-Four Years in the Argentine Republic.* London, 1840.

López, Carlos Antonio. *La emancipación paraguaya.* Asunción, 1942 (1845).

Maíz, Fidel (Father). *Etapas de mi vida.* Asunción, 1919.

Manning, R. William. *Correspondencia diplomática de los Estados Unidos concerniente a la independencia de las naciones latinoamericanas.* 12 vols. Buenos Aires, 1930-1936.

Masterman, George F. *Seven Eventful Years in Paraguay.* London, 1870.

Molas, Mariano Antonio. *Descripción histórica de la antigua provincia del Paraguay.* Buenos Aires, 1957.

Moraes Lima, Diogo Arouche de. "Memoria da campanha de 1816." *Revista do Instituto Histórico e Geográphico Brasileiro* (July-October 1845), pp. 125-170, 373-378.

Mörner, Magnus (ed.). *Algunas cartas del naturalista sueco Eberhard Munck af Rosenschold escritas durante su estadía en el Paraguay, 1843-1868.* Stockholm, 1956.

Page, Thomas Jefferson. *La Plata, the Argentine Confederation and Paraguay.* New York, 1859.

Palleja, León de (Col.). *Diario de la campaña de las fuerzas aliadas contra el Paraguay.* 2 vols. Montevideo, 1960.

Parish, Woodbine. *Buenos Aires y las Provincias del Río de la Plata.* Buenos Aires, 1958 (1858).

Rengger, Johann R., and Marcel Longchamp. *The Reign of Dr. Joseph*

Gaspard Roderick de Francia in Paraguay. London, 1827.
Robertson, John Parish, and William Parish Robertson. *Letters on Paraguay.*
    3 vols. London, 1838-1839.
Rodney, Caesar A., and John Graham. *Reports.* London, 1819.
Rosas and the River Plate (by "A British Gentleman"). Montevideo, 1844.
Thompson, George. *The War in Paraguay.* 2nd. ed. London, 1869.
Vázquez, José Antonio. *El Dr. Francia visto y oído por sus contemporáneos.*
    Asunción, 1961.
Washburn, Charles A. *History of Paraguay.* 2 vols. Boston, 1871.

B. Periodicals
El Argos de Buenos Aires, 1821-1825.
La Aurora (Asunción), 1860-1862.
British Packet and Argentine News (Buenos Aires), 1828-1848.
Cabichuí (Paso Pucú), 1867-1868.
Cacique Lambaré (Paso Pucú), 1868.
El Centinela (Asunción), 1867-1868.
El Eco del Paraguay (Asunción), 1855-1857.
La Epoca (Asunción), 1857-1859.
La Estrella (Piribebuy), 1869.
El Lucero (Buenos Aires), 1829-1833.
El Nacional Correntino (Corrientes), 1841-1842.
El Paraguayo Independiente (Asunción), 1845-1852.
Registro Oficial (Asunción), 1869 ff.
Registro Oficial del Gobierno de Corrientes, 1826-1839.
El Semanario de Avisos y Conocimientos Utiles (Asunción), 1853-1868.
El Telégrafo del Comercio (Buenos Aires), 1832.

OTHER SOURCES

A. Books
Abadie, Reyes. *La Banda Oriental. Pradera. Frontera. Puerto.* Montevideo,
    1965.
Araña, Enrique. *Rosas en la revolución política argentina.* Buenos Aires,
    1953.
Area Handbook for Paraguay. Washington, D.C., 1972.
Audibert, Alejandro. *Los límites de la antigua provincia del Paraguay.* Monte-
    video, 1892.
Báez, Cecilio. *Ensayo sobre el Dr. Francia y la dictadura en Sudamerica.* Asun-
    ción, 1910.
————. *Historia diplomática del Paraguay.* 2 vols. Asunción, 1930-1931.
————. *La tiranía en el Paraguay.* Asunción, 1903.
Bazán, José F. *El Dictador Francia y otras composiciones en verso y prosa.*
    Madrid, 1887.
Benítez, Gregorio. *La revolución de Mayo.* Asunción, 1910.

Benítez, Justo Pastor. *Carlos Antonio López.* Buenos Aires, 1949.

————. *La vida solitaria del Dr. José Gaspar de Francia, Dictador del Paraguay.* Buenos Aires, 1937.

Benítez, Luis G. *Historia diplomática del Paraguay.* Asunción, 1972.

————. *La junta superior gubernativa.* Asunción, 1964.

Beraza, Agustín. *Rivera y la independencia de las Misiones.* Montevideo, 1968.

Beverina, Juan. *La Guerra del Paraguay (1865-1870). Resumen histórico.* Buenos Aires, 1973.

Blanco Sánchez, Jesús. *El Capitán don Antonio Tomás Yegros.* Asunción, 1961.

Box, Pelham H. *Origins of the Paraguayan War.* Urbana, Illinois, 1927.

Bray, Arturo. *Hombres y épocas del Paraguay.* 2 vols. Buenos Aires, 1955-1957.

Brunel, Adolphe. *Biographie d' Aimé Bonpland.* 3rd. ed. Paris, 1871.

Cabanellas, Guillermo. *El Dictador del Paraguay, Dr. Francia.* Buenos Aires, 1946.

Cárcano, Ramón J. *Guerra del Paraguay.* 3 vols. Buenos Aires, 1939-1941.

Cardozo, Efraím. *Afinidades entre el Paraguay y la Banda Oriental en 1811.* Montevideo, 1963.

————. *Artigas en el Paraguay.* Montevideo, 1952.

————. *Breve historia del Paraguay.* Buenos Aires, 1966.

————. *Hace cien años.* 7 vols. Asunción, 1966-1972.

————. *El Imperio del Brasil y el Río de la Plata.* Buenos Aires, 1961.

————. *El Paraguay colonial.* Buenos Aires, 1959.

Carlyle, Thomas. *Critical and Miscellaneous Essays.* New York, n.d.

Centurión, Carlos R. *Historia de la cultura paraguaya.* 2 vols. Asunción, 1961.

Chaves, Julio César. *Historia de las relaciones entre Buenos Aires y el Paraguay, 1810-1813.* 2nd ed. Asunción, 1959.

————. *El Presidente López.* 2nd ed. Buenos Aires, 1965.

————. *La revolución del 14 y 15 de Mayo.* Asunción, 1957.

————. *El Supremo Dictador.* 4th ed., rev. Madrid, 1964.

Cibils, Manuel J. *Anarquía y revolución en el Paraguay.* Asunción, 1947.

Decoud, Héctor Francisco. *Guerra del Paraguay: La Masacre de Concepción.* Buenos Aires, 1926.

Departamento de Cultura y Arte. *Historia edilicia de la Ciudad de Asunción.* Asunción, 1967.

Domínguez, Juan A. *Aimé Bonpland. Su vida en la América del Sur.* Buenos Aires, 1929.

DuGraty, Alfredo. *La Republique du Paraguay.* Brussels, 1865.

Furlong, Guillermo, S. J. *Historia social y cultural del Río de la Plata, 1536-1810.* 3 vols. Buenos Aires, 1969.

————. *Misiones y sus pueblos de Guaraníes, 1610-1813.* Buenos Aires,

1962.

Garay, Blas. *Historia del Paraguay.* Madrid, 1897.

——. *Independencia del Paraguay.* Madrid, 1897.

García Mellid, Atilio. *Proceso a los falsificadores de la historia del Paraguay.* 2 vols. Buenos Aires, 1963.

Gill Aguínaga, Juan B. *La Asociación paraguaya en la Guerra de la Triple Alianza.* Asunción, 1959.

González, Juan Natalicio. *El paraguayo y la lucha por su expresión.* Asunción, 1945.

Hernández, Pablo, S. J. *Organización social de las doctrinas guaraníes de la Compañía de Jesús.* 2 vols. Barcelona, 1911.

Kersten, Ludwig. *Las tribus indígenas del Gran Chaco hasta fines del siglo XVIII.* Resistencia, Chaco, 1968.

Kolinski, Charles. *Independence or Death! The Story of the Paraguayan War.* Gainesville, Florida, 1965.

Kostianovsky, Olinda Massare de. *La instrucción pública en la época colonial.* Asunción, 1968.

——. *El Vice-Presidente Domingo Francisco Sánchez.* Asunción, 1972.

Kroeber, Clifton B. *La navegación de los ríos en la historia argentina.* Buenos Aires, 1967.

Linhares, Themistocles. *História econômica do mate.* Rio de Janeiro, 1969.

Mansilla, Lucio. *Crónica histórica de la provincia de Corrientes.* 2 vols. Buenos Aires, 1972.

Mendoza, Prudencio de la C. *El Dr. Francia en el Virreynato del Plata.* Buenos Aires, 1887.

Millé, Andrés. *Crónica de la orden franciscana en la conquista del Perú, Paraguay y el Tucumán.* Buenos Aires, 1961.

Ministerio de Interior. *Los restos mortales del Dr. José Gaspar de Francia.* Asunción, n.d.

Mitre, Bartolomé. *Historia de Belgrano y la independencia argentina.* 4 vols. Buenos Aires, 1967.

Moreno, Fulgencio. *Estudio sobre la independencia del Paraguay.* Asunción, 1911.

Mörner, Magnus (ed.). *The Expulsion of the Jesuits from Latin America.* New York, 1965.

——. *Political and Economic Activities of the Jesuits in the Plata Region— Habsburg Era.* Stockholm, 1953.

Nogues, Alberto. *La Iglesia en la época del Dr. Francia.* Asunción, 1959.

Nuñez de Báez, Guillermina. *Dr. José Gaspar Rodríguez de Francia.* Asunción, 1972.

O'Connor D'Arlach, Thomas. *Rozas, Francia y Melgarejo.* Buenos Aires, 1895.

Oddone, Rafael. *Esquema político del Paraguay.* Buenos Aires, 1948.

Paris de Oddone, M. Blanca. *Cronología comparada de la historia del Uruguay, 1830-1945.* Montevideo, 1966.

Pazos Kanki, Vicente. *A Narrative of Facts Connected with the Change Effected in the Political Conditions and Relations of Paraguay.* London, 1826.

Pérez Acosta, Juan F. *Carlos Antonio López: Obrero Máximo.* Buenos Aires, 1948.

————. *Francia y Bonpland.* Buenos Aires, 1942.

Pérez-Maricevich, Francisco (ed.). *Paraguay—Imagen romántica, 1811-1853.* Asunción, 1969.

Phelps, Gilbert. *Tragedy of Paraguay.* New York, 1975.

Pla, Josefina. *Los artes plásticos en el Paraguay.* Buenos Aires, 1967.

————. *The British in Paraguay, 1850-1870.* London, 1976.

————. *Hermano negro. La esclavitud en el Paraguay.* Madrid, 1972.

————. *El teatro en el Paraguay.* Asunción, 1967.

Puiggros, Rudolfo. *Historia económica del Río de la Plata.* Buenos Aires, 1966.

Quentin, Ch. *An Account of Paraguay.* London, 1865.

Ramos, R. Antonio. *Juan Andrés Gelly.* Buenos Aires, 1972.

————. *La política del Brasil en el Paraguay durante la dictadura del Dr. Francia.* Asunción, 1959.

Ramos Mejía, José M. *Rosas y el Dr. Francia (Estudios psiquiátricos).* Madrid, n.d.

Riquelme, Andrés. *Apuntes para la historia política y diplomática del Paraguay.* 2 vols. Asunción, 1960.

Salteraín, Eduardo. *Artigas en el Paraguay.* Asunción, 1950.

Sánchez Quell, Hipólito. *La diplomacia paraguaya de Mayo a Cerro Corá.* Buenos Aires, 1964.

Schneider, L. *A Guerra da Tríplice Aliança.* 4 vols. Rio de Janeiro, 1924.

Southey, Robert. *A Tale of Paraguay.* London, 1825.

Susnik, Branislava. *El indio colonial del Paraguay.* 3 vols. Asunción, 1965-1971.

Tasso Fragoso, Agusto. *História da Guerra entre a Tríplice Aliança e o Paraguai.* 5 vols. Rio de Janeiro, 1956-1960.

Velázquez, Rafael Eladio. *El Paraguay en 1811.* Asunción, 1966.

Vittone, Luis. *Las FF AA paraguayas en sus distintas épocas.* Asunción, 1970.

Warren, Harris G. *Paraguay. An Informal History.* Norman, Oklahoma, 1949.

Williams, John Hoyt. *El Dr. Francia y la creación de la república del Paraguay.* Asunción, 1977.

Wisner, Francisco. *El Dictador del Paraguay José Gaspar Francia.* Buenos Aires, 1957.

Ynsfrán, Pablo Max. *La expedición norteamericana contra el Paraguay, 1858-1859.* 2 vols. Buenos Aires, 1954-1958.

Zinny, Antonio. *Historia de los gobernantes del Paraguay.* Buenos Aires, 1894.

Zorrilla de San Martín, Juan. *La epopeya de Artigas.* 5 vols. Montevideo,

1963.
Zubizarreta, Carlos. *Historia de mi ciudad*. Asunción, 1964.

B. *Articles*

Almeida Serra, Ricardo Franco de. "Sobre o aldeamento dos Indios Uaicurús e Guanas, com a descripção dos seus usos, religião, estabilidade e costumes." *Revista do Instituto Histórico e Geográphico Brasileiro* no. 26 (July 1845): 204-208.

Blanco Sánchez, Jesús. "Don Carlos Antonio López, figura cimera de la nacionalidad." *Historia paraguaya. Anuario* (1966), pp. 21-30.

Boettner, Juan Max. "La música en tiempo de los López." *Historia paraguaya. Anuario* (1956), pp. 31-43.

Cardozo, Efraím. "El Plan federal del Dr. Francia." *Revista de Derecho y Ciencias Sociales* (Asunción) 5., no. 17 (July 1931): 59-90.

―――. "La proclamación de la República del Paraguay en 1813." *Boletín de la Academia Nacional de la Historia* (Buenos Aires) 34 (1964): 771-783.

Centurión, Carlos R. "La obra de la primera junta gubernativa." *Historia paraguaya. Anuario* (1962), pp. 37-51.

Corrêa Filho, Virgilio. "Portugueses em Mato Grosso." *Revista do Instituto Histórico e Geográphico Brasileiro* no. 245 (October-December 1957): 204-234.

Kostianovsky, Olinda Massare de. "Historia e evolución de la población en el Paraguay." In Domingo M. Rivarola and G. Heisecke (eds.), *Población, urbanización y recursos humanos en el Paraguay*. 2nd ed., rev. Asunción, 1970.

Maeder, Ernesto J. A., and A. S. Bolsi. "La población de las Misiones guaraníes entre 1702 y 1767." *Estudios paraguayos* 2, no. 1 (June 1974): 111-138.

McMahon, Martin. "The War in Paraguay." *Harper's* 139 (April 1870): 633-647.

Moreno, Fulgencio. "Origen del Dr. Francia." *Historia paraguaya. Anuario* (1958), pp. 15-19.

Nogues, Alberto. "El General López en Roma." *Historia paraguaya. Anuario* (1969-1970), pp. 48-63.

Pérez Acosta, Juan F. "Repercusión de las invasiones inglesas de 1806 y 1807." *Boletín del Instituto de Investigaciones históricas* (Buenos Aires) 20 (1942): 150-190.

Queirolo, Victor Ayala. "Campaña de Mato Grosso." *Historia paraguaya. Anuario* (1966), pp. 113-146.

Pla, Josefina. "Los británicos en el Paraguay." *Revista de Historia de América* no. 70 (July-December 1970): 336-397; no. 71 (January-June 1971): 23-65.

Ramos, R. Antonio. "Correa da Cámara en Asunción." *Boletín del Instituto de Investigaciones Históricas* (Buenos Aires) 30 (1952): 60-71.

Schmitt, Peter. "Las relaciones diplomáticas entre el Paraguay y las potencias europeas." *Historia paraguaya. Anuario* (1958), pp. 65-87.

Somellera, Pedro. "Notas del Dr. Don Pedro Somellera a la introducción que ha puesto el Dr. Rengger. . ." In *Museo Mitre. Documentos del Archivo de Belgrano.* 7 vols. Buenos Aires, 1913-1919, III, 313-340.

Tanzi, Héctor José. "Estudio sobre la población del Virreinato del Río de la Plata en 1790." *Revista de Indias* 27, nos. 107-108 (1967): 231-267.

Torre Revelo, José. "El fracaso de la expedición española preparada contra el Río de la Plata." *Boletín de la Academia Nacional de la Historia* (Buenos Aires) 33 (1962): 421-438.

Villamil, Manuel Peña. "Breve historia de la ganadería paraguaya." *Historia paraguaya. Anuario* (1969-1970), pp. 83-98.

Vittone, Luis. "El Mariscal Francisco Solano López." *Revista de las FF AA de la Nación* (Asunción) 179 (August 1961): 164-168.

Warren, Harris G. "Brazil's Paraguayan Policy, 1869-1876." *The Americas* 28, no. 4 (April 1972): 3-24.

_____. "The Hopkins Claim against Paraguay and the 'Case of the Missing Jewels.'" *Inter-American Economic Affairs* 22, no. 1 (Summer 1968): 24-44

Williams, John Hoyt. "The Conspiracy of 1820 and the Destruction of the Paraguayan Aristocracy." *Revista de Historia de América* nos. 75-76 (January-December 1973): 141-156.

_____. "Dictatorship and the Church: Dr. Francia in Paraguay." *Journal of Church and State* 15, no. 3 (Fall 1973): 419-436.

_____. "Esclavos y pobladores: Observaciones sobre la historia parda del Paraguay en el siglo XIX." *Revista Paraguaya de la Sociología* no. 31 (September-December 1974): 7-29.

_____. "From the Barrel of a Gun: Some Notes on Dr. Francia and Paraguayan Militarism." *Proceedings of the American Philosophical Society* 119, no. 1 (February 1975): 73-86.

_____. "Governor Velasco, the Portuguese and the Paraguayan Revolution of 1811." *The Americas* 28, no. 4 (April 1972): 442-450.

_____. "La guerra no-declarada entre el Paraguay y Corrientes." *Estudios paraguayos* 1, no. 1 (November 1973): 35-43.

_____. "Observations on the Paraguayan Census of 1846." *Hispanic American Historical Review* 56, no. 3 (August 1976): 424-437.

_____. "Paraguayan Isolation under Dr. Francia—A Reevaluation." *Hispanic American Historical Review* 52, no. 1 (February 1972): 102-122.

_____. "Paraguay's 19th Century Estancias de la República." *Agricultural History* 46, no. 3 (July 1973): 206-216.

_____. "Race, Threat and Geography: The Paraguayan Experience of Nationalism." *Canadian Review of Studies in Nationalism* 1, no. 2

(Spring 1974): 173-191.

———— . "Tevegó on the Paraguayan Frontier: A Chapter in the Black History of the Americas." *Journal of Negro History* 56, no. 4 (October 1971): 72-84.

———— . "Woodbine Parish and the 'Opening' of Paraguay." *Proceedings of the American Philosophical Society* 116, no. 4 (August 1972): 343-350.

Index

Abad Oro, Colonel Pedro, 143
Aberdeen, Earl of, 76
Abipón Indians, 4, 5
Abreu, Lieutenant José de, mission
    to Paraguay, 28-29
Acá Carajá, regiment, 204
Acaraí, 122
Acosta family, 51
Agüero, Romualdo, 87
Aguirre, Atanasio, 201
Ahó poí, 174
Alberti, Manuel, 24
Alliance, Triple, War of the. See
    Paraguayan War
Allies, 190, 208, 209, 211-212, 222-
    225. See also Paraguayan War
Almagro, José Ignacio, 50
Alós y Brú, Governor Joaquín, 22
Altos, 122, 132
Alvarez, Juan Manuel, 85
Antonelli, Cardinal, 161
Antonini, Andrés, 188
Apa, Río, 6, 19; as boundary, 44, 76,
    87, 99, 116, 123; fortification of,
    152, 153-154, 157; clashes with
    Brazil, 158, 159; land grants near,
    175
Apipé, Island, 77, 140; Paraguayan
    control of, 147, 166
Aquino, Cayetano, 138
Aramburú, Martín José de, 20

Araña, Felipe, 150
Archive, Asunción, 133
Areguá, 118, 188
Argentina: United Provinces, 46, 66,
    68-69, 72, 76-77; Argentine Con-
    federation, 149-150, 157, 200;
    as threat to Paraguay, 63, 75, 76-
    77, 150, 151, 154-155; internal
    strife, 105-106; commerce with
    Paraguay, 66, 72-74, 129-131,
    171, 178; intervention in Uruguay,
    197, 198, 199-201; Paraguayan
    War, 206-207. See also Buenos
    Aires; Candelaria; Corrientes;
    Litoral
Argos de Buenos Ayres, El, 51
Arias, José Manuel, 96
Arístegui family, 51
Arístegui, Dr. Juan, 53
Arrecife, Fort, 152
Arroyo, Gavino, 102
Arroyos y Esteros, 16, 55
Arsenal, Asunción, 120, 181, 183,
    185; moved to Caacupé, 190,
    216. See also Foreigners
Artigas, José, 32, 35; relations with
    Paraguay, 36, 39, 46, 48, 50, 52;
    enters Paraguay, 52; Ramírez
    threat, 67, 72, 75-76; in Para-
    guayan exile, 78, 85, 97, 102;
    offered military post, 180

Asunción, 5, 7; colonial description
of, 11, 13, 14-15; population of,
15, 113, 119; political tensions in,
53-54, 59; as garrison city, 60-61,
204; description of, 83-84, 90-91,
94, 113-115, 224-225; land rents,
133; and estancias de la República,
136; Gordon visit, 141; Hopkins
visit, 164; Page visit, 165, 179;
trade activity, 168, 171; Francisco
Solano's return, 170; Madame Lynch
arrives, 173; foreigners in, 179-180,
185, 186, 187, 188-189, 193; development of, 181; political repression,
195-196; Brazilian diplomacy, 199,
201; at start of war, 202; shipyard
production, 205; in the war, 208,
212, 221; cholera in, 215; under
occupation, 223, 225-226
Asylum, right of, 78-79, 99, 139,
238 n. 5
Atajo island, 147
Atirá, 82, 89, 122, 132; manpower
shortage, 222
Audiencia, 8
Aurora, La, 170
Avaí, battle, 223
Aviles, Viceroy, 23
Azara, Félix de, 177

Báez, Cecilio, 99
Báez, Manuel José, 23, 27
Bahia, 106
Bahia Negra, 160
Banda Oriental: internal disorders,
25, 27, 63; plan of federation
with Paraguay, 36; Portuguese
occupation of, 46, 75, 76; in
Cisplatine War, 66, 68. See also
Montevideo; Uruguay
Bandeirantes, 6, 75
Bareiro, Cándido, 187
Barrios, Vicente, 108, 160
Barton, Dr. George, 183

Bechmann, John George, 180
Bedoya, Francisco de, 85
Bedoya, Saturnino, 108
Belén, 132
Belgrano, Manuel: invasion of Para-
guay, 25-26, 27; mission to Para-
guay, 30-31, 35, 235 n. 65
Bella Vista, 152, 159
Bellegarde, Pedro Alcántara, 153-154
Benítez, Gregorio, 97
Benítez, José Gabriel, 81, 85, 102
Berges, José, 159, 167
Bermejo, Ildefonso, 107; notes on
social life, 109, 115, 125, 126,
127, 172; intellectual impact on
Paraguay, 186-187
Bermejo, Río, 56
Blanco, Juan José, 72
Blancos (Uruguay), 199, 201-202
Bliss, Cornelius Porter, 220
Blyth & Co., 161; as recruiter of techni-
cians, 162, 180, 181, 183, 184; con-
tact with Europe, 168; as trainer of
Paraguayan youth, 186; as purchaser
of materiel, 189; as shipbuilder, 205
Bobi, 119
Bogarín, Francisco Xavier, 21-22
Bogarín, Juan, 42; as member of
junta, 29-30; as conspirator, 51
Bolívar, Simón, 64; as threat to Para-
guay, 76
Bolivia, 64, 142; trade with Para-
guay, 219
Bonpland, Aimé, 53; in captivity,
64-65, 67, 76, 85
Boquerón, battle, 212
Bordeaux, 162
Bowlin, James B., 167
Brazil, 32; relations with Paraguay,
32-34, 44, 63, 130, 147, 149-150,
157-160, 189, 190, 195, 197;
trade with Paraguay, 53-55, 67-71,
131-132, 171; intervention in
Uruguay, 66, 68, 198-202; in

Paraguayan War, 206-224 passim; as threat to Paraguay, 226-227

Brent, William, Jr., 146

Britain, 33; merchant community at Buenos Aires, 65; merchants detained in Paraguay, 65-66, 69; trade with Paraguay, 76, 101; relations with Paraguay, 140-141, 144-145, 150, 152, 155, 178; blockade of Buenos Aires, 142-143, 145; Francisco Solano in, 161; Canstatt affair, 168-170

British invasions (Río de la Plata), 16-17; response in Paraguay, 17

Bruce, David, 171

Bryson, Andrew, 185

Buchanan, President James, 146, 167

Buenos Aires: colonial era, 7, 8, 9; British invasions of, 16-17; Revolución de Mayo, 24-25; attempt to conquer Paraguay, 25-26, 27; Belgrano-Echevarría mission, 30-31; Herrera mission, 34-36; relations with Paraguay, 39; commerce with Paraguay, 72-74; as threat to Paraguay, 75; repression of Corrientes, 139-140, 143-144; in control of the rivers, 141-144; claims to Candelaria, 147-149; detention of *Tacuarí* at, 169-170; British merchants in, 177-178; Paraguayan exiles in, 196; intervention in Uruguay, 200-201; Treaty of the Triple Alliance signed in, 208. *See also* Argentina

Buenos Aires (ship), 169

Burrell, Percy, 183

Buzzard (ship), 169

Caacupé, 7; as site of arsenal, 190

Caaguazú, 122, 188, 189

Caapucú, 181, 182; pardo community, 119; militia census, 221

Caazapá, 116, 132; militia census, 222

Caballero, Pedro Juan, 40, 41; in revolution, 27-28; as member of junta, 29, 34, 37, 39; as conspirator, 51, 52; suicide, 53

Cabeza de Vaca, Alfar Núñez, 13

Cabichuí, 220

Cabildos, 11; Asunción, 22-26, 28-30, 31-32, 34, 41, 50, 59, 132; Villa Rica, 59; in interior, 8, 11, 59-60

Cacique Lambaré, 220

Calvo, Carlos, 170

Campbell, Peter, 54, 78

Campo Grande (Ñu Guazú), 58

Campos, José Domingo, 103

Candelaria, 8, 32, 35; in 1812 treaty, 31; Artigas in, 46, 48; commerce through, 67-71; Bonpland expedition, 53, 64, 76, 77; struggle for control of, 78, 81, 99, 122, 130, 140; Paraguayan control of, 147-149; hostilities in, 150; fortification of, 152; claims to, 154, 199. *See also* Argentina; Buenos Aires; Corrientes; Ytapúa

Cañete, Agustín, 102

Canstatt, Santiago, 169-170

Capiatá, 89

Caraguatay, 7, 88, 133, 189

Caraí. *See* Francia, José Gaspar de

Carapeguá, 134; militia census, 214

Cardozo, Efraím, 30

Carlota Joaquina, 28

Carlyle, Thomas, 101, 106

Carmen, El, 87, 132

Carneiro de Campos, Colonel Federico, 202

Castelli, Juan José, 21; in Buenos Aires junta, 24, 27

Castro, Miguel, 77

Catedral (Asunción barrio), 114; merchants in, 115; population of, 119; foreigners in, 180

Cateté, 150, 151
Cathedral (Asunción), 119
Catiguaá, 133
Cavañas, Manuel Atanacio, 16; in defeat of Belgrano, 26, 27; as conspirator, 54, 55
Cavour (ship), 205
Caxias, Duke of, 222, 224
Centinela, El, 215, 220
Centurión, Carlos, 95
Centurión, Juan Crisóstomo, 187, 220
Cerda, Gregorio de la, 37, 42
Cerro Corá, 224
Cerro León: as military camp, 136; as railway terminus, 183, 186; as training base, 202; disease at, 215, 221
Céspedes, Roque Antonio Xeria; assumes control of Church, 57; acquires wealth, 86
Chaco: hostile Indians in, 5, 116, 123, 230 n. 8; as invasion route, 77; insufferable climate of, 107, 220; military patrols in, 147; Madame Lynch's lands in, 175; sawmill in, 189; Nueva Burdeos colony, 192-194; agricultural production of, 218
Charles III (Spain), 9
Charles IV (Spain), 12; concerning encomiendas, 20
Chaves, Julio César, 108, 110, 111, 143
Chile, 8, 142
Christie, W. D., 168-169
Church, 9, 10, 14, 49, 93, 118, 124; Jesuit order, 6, 8-9, 10, 13, 15, 108, 118; Franciscan order, 10, 14, 20, 57; Dominican order, 10; Mercedarian order, 10; controlled by Francia, 49, 56-59, 97, 119, 161; taxes, 57; as slaveholder, 119-120. *See also* Céspedes; Panés;

Seminary; Vatican
Cisplatine War, 63, 64, 74, 76, 198
Clamor de los Libres, El, 170
Club Nacional, 108, 174, 188
Colonization, 192-194. *See also* Nuevo Burdeos
Colorados (Uruguay), 199, 201-202
Comuneros revolt, 8, 9
Concepción, 11, 12, 82, 120, 214; as place of exile, 56, 67, 77; garrison at, 60; jurisdiction of, 87; estancias de la República at, 93; military units, 204; yerba production, 217; militia census, 222; executions at, 224
Congresses: 1811, 28-29; 1813, 36, 37-38; 1814, 40, 237 n. 112; 1816, 48-49; 1842, 111, 118, 141; 1844, 111, 142-143; 1849, 111; 1858, 172-173; 1862, 195-196; 1865, 206; Congress of the Provinces, 1813, 35, 37
Conspiracies: against Spain, 26-29; royalist, 30-31; 1820, 50-54, 64, 240 n. 70; 250 n. 13; Pilar, 54-55, 56; Rengger, 56, 65; 1841, 103-104; against Carlos Antonio, 169-170; San Fernando, 191, 196, 223-225
Constitutions: 1813, 37-38; 1844, 111, 142-143, 195; 1870, 225
Contraband: at Pilar, 55, 73-74, 86; at Ytapúa, 71, 90
Cordillera, 55
Córdoba, University of, 10, 14-15; Francia at, 20-21
Correa da Cámara, Antonio Manuel, 68-70, 151
Correa Madruga, Francisco, 120
Correntinos: at Pilar, 54; in Candelaria, 77-79, 130, 147, 149; revolt of, 139, 140, 144
Correo, El (ship), 182, 206
Corrientes: city, 7, 25, 27, 54, 113,

144; province, 5, 27; under Artigas,
46, 48; strife in, 69-70; commerce
with Paraguay, 72-74, 77, 131;
yerba production, 130; population
of, 139; in revolt, 139-149, 197;
treaty with Paraguay, 139; *Water
Witch* incident, 158, 165-167;
Paraguayan invasion of, 208, 214,
217, 223; as Allied base, 211-212;
cholera epidemic, 212
Corumbá, 202
Cotton: production of, 92, 122, 192;
during war, 218
Crecer, Lucas, 56, 67
"Creole problem," 21-23
Crimean War, 183
Cuarepotí, 12
Cuiabá, 6
Curuguatí, 11, 13; Artigas at, 52;
government of, 88; population
characteristics, 116-117; road
construction to, 122; militia
census, 219
Curupaití, 73; as military post, 148;
terminus of telegraph, 186; during
war, 211; battle of, 196, 212
Curuzú, battle of, 212

Decoud, Juan, 56
Decoud, Pedro Miguel, 85
Demersay, Alfred, 108, 110
Derqui, Santiago, 150
Descalzi, Nicolás, 56, 67
Dobrizhoffer, Martín, 5
Duprat, Dorotea, 187
Dupuis, Ana, 187
Dupuis, Francisco Sauvegeod de, 187
Dupuis, Pedro, 187
Duré, Ramón, 103

Echevarría, Vicente Anastacio: mission
to Paraguay, 30-31, 35; instructions
to, 235 n. 65
Eco del Paraguay, El, 170, 186

Education, 9; seminary, 10, 14, 21-22,
33, 118, 124; University of Córdoba,
10, 14-15; of Dr. Francia, 20-21;
during Francia years, 33, 37, 58,
95, 96; of Francisco Solano López,
107-108; during Carlos Antonio's
rule, 122, 124-126; foreign teachers,
186, 187; during Francisco Solano's
rule, 203; remuneration of, 246
n. 65
Emboscada, 118, 119
Encarnación (Asunción barrio), 114,
189
Encarnación, Church of the, 97
Encarnación, 204, 211. *See also*
Ytapúa
Encomienda, 12, 33
England. *See* Britain
Entre Ríos, 77, 148; under Urquiza,
149, 200. *See also* Litoral
Epidemics, 135, 137, 141, 172,
214, 223, 225; cholera, 190,
212, 215, 216, 223, 224; small-
pox, 123, 172, 215, 219, 260 n. 4;
venereal, 172
Epoca, La, 170
Escalada, Pedro, 95, 108
Espinillo, 123
Espínola, Colonel José de, 22-23;
mission to Paraguay, 24-25
Estero Bellaco, battle of, 212
Estigarribia, Colonel, 209
Estigarribia, Dr. Vicente, 85-86; as
confidant of Francia, 96-97, 102
Estrella, La, 220
Exiles, Paraguayan, 110; at Buenos
Aires, 159-160, 169, 170, 196;
Paraguayan Legion, 208

Farrapos, Guerra dos, 106, 255 n. 3
Federalism, 30, 31
Fermín, José, 26
Fernández, Pedro Nolasco, 123
Ferré, Pedro, 77, 140

Ferreira, Pablo, 102
Ferreira de Oliveira, Admiral Pedro, 158-159
Flores, José, 200, 201, 208
Flota, Manuel, 71
Foreign Office, British, 65, 140, 144; Canstatt affair, 168-169, 170; view of free navigation issue, 177
Foreigners in Paraguay: as technicians, 111, 115, 120, 143, 153, 163, 168, 170, 171, 172-173, 177, 178-193; in commerce, 72-74, 129-131, 179, 188-189; in medicine, 179, 183-184, 191, 204; during the war, 205, 211
Fox, Dr. John, 183; under arrest, 191
France, 125; relations with Paraguay, 145, 168, 193; blockade of Buenos Aires, 142-143, 146
Francia, García Rodríguez de, 13, 15; military career, 19-20
Francia, José Gaspar de, 14, 15, 17, 19-110 passim; youth, 19-20; in junta, 28-38; as consul, 38-41; and 1820 conspiracy, 50-55; control of Church, 56-59; creation of army, 59-61; and the true Paraguayan revolution, 61-62; directing commerce, 70-73, 74-75; personal lifestyle, 82-85; foreign policy, 44, 78; death, 96-97; concept of indispensability, 48, 81-82, 98-99; heritage, 111, 118, 120-121, 125, 129, 130, 132, 134, 136, 139, 143, 147, 171, 179, 186, 198, 203, 226
Francia, Petrona Regalada, 84, 104
Free Womb, Law of, 118, 121, 141; consequences of, 135. See also Pardos; Slavery
Fulton (ship), 145

Gamarra, Juan Manuel, 26, 40
Garibaldi, Giuseppe, 198
Garton, Frederick, 183
Gasorí, 215
Gelly, Juan Andrés, 101; as diplomat, 152-153, 160; as recruiter of foreign technicians, 179-180; as author of El Paraguay. Lo que fué, lo que es y lo que será, 153, 253 n. 54
Gill, Andrés, 141-142
Gill, José Tomás, 54-55
Godwin, Henry, 153, 180, 181
González, Anastacio, 145
González, Mariano, 148
Gordon, George R., 140-141
Gracia, Colonel Pedro, 25
Graf, Henry, 180
Grandsire, Richard de, 48
Grant, Alex, 183
Grappler (ship), 169
Green, Benjamin, 168
Grito Paraguayo, El, 170
Grivel, Admiral, 64
Guaicurú Indians, 4, 6, 51, 104, 116, 123, 218
Guairá, 6
Gualeguay (ship), 205
Guarambaré, 118, 132
Guaraní Indians, 6, 7, 9
Guaraní language, 8, 40, 61; bond with Corrientes, 139, 144; as lingua franca, 172, 197; in war journalism, 217, 220, 221; as vehicle of nationalism, 225
Guerra aduanera, 32, 33
Guido, General J., 146, 152, 154
Guillemot, Jeanne, 164-165

Henderson, Charles A., 168, 169
Herrera, Luis Alberto de, 200
Herrera, Nicolás de: mission to Paraguay, 34, 35-37, 68
Hope, Mr., 94

Hopkins, Clement, 163, 164
Hopkins, Edward Augustus: as
    diplomatic agent, 145-147, 158,
    162-167; as entrepreneur, 162-
    167, 255 n. 43; expelled from
    Paraguay, 166-167
Horqueta, 224
Hotham, Charles, 168
Hughes, W. R. B., 101-102
Humaitá, 111; as fortress complex,
    167, 179; telegraph to, 186; role
    in Paraguayan War, 204-206, 208,
    211-212, 215, 222-223
Humboldt, Alexander von, 64

Ibáñez, José Miguel, 41, 48, 50
Ibicuy, 119, 120, 127; as site of
    iron foundry, 181, 186, 190,
    214, 216
Ibitimí, 119
Igatimí, 7, 224
Immigration, 162, 164. See also
    Nueva Burdeos
Independencia (ship), 160
Indian wars, 39, 44, 153, 230 n. 8
Indians, 12; pueblos de, 5, 11, 13,
    122, 132-133. See also Abipón;
    Guaicurú; Guaraní; Payaguá
Isabella II (Spain), 161
Itamaratí, 150
Itapirú: in Water Witch affair, 166,
    167; site of Allied invasion, 211
Itatí, 139, 149
Itatín, 6
Itá-Ybaté, battle of, 223, 224
Iturbe family, 16
Iturbe, Lieutenant Manuel, 41
Iturbe, Captain Vicente, 49, 50

Jeffers, Lieutenant Williams, 166-
    167
Jejuy, Río, 87
Jesús, 87, 122, 132, 133
Johnston, Dr. John H., 183

Jovellanos, Bernardo, 145
Juarú, Río, 6

Lambaré, 16, 215
Lápido, José, 200-201
Legal, Gerónimo, 115
Lescano, Pedro, 196
Libertos. See Slaves
Library, public, 96, 103, 134
Limehouse. See Blyth
Limpio, 119, 121
Liniers, Viceroy Santiago, 16
Lisbon, 162
Literary academy, 124
Litoral, Argentine provinces of:
    harassment of Paraguay, 32, 33,
    46, 69, 72, 76; internal disorders
    in, 131, 142, 145; under Urquiza,
    200. See also Candelaria; Corrien-
    tes; Entre Ríos; Santa Fe
Lobato, 137, 138
London, 168, 169, 170, 173, 178,
    181, 205
Longchamp, Marcel, 65, 83, 85, 91
López, Basilio, 161
López, Benigno, 108, 133, 160,
    173; executed, 196
López, Carlos Antonio, 14, 54, 65,
    91, 95, 96; rise to power, 103-105;
    as consul, 106; lifestyle, 106-109;
    family life, 108-109; in power,
    110-195 passim; heritage, 197,
    198, 203, 226
López, Enrique Venancio, 174
López, Estanislao, 53
López, Federico Lloyd, 174
López, Francisco Solano, 95, 105;
    education, 107-108; as young
    officer, 124-125, 143-144, 148;
    on European trip, 160-163, 168;
    as mediator in Buenos Aires, 169;
    detained by British, 169-170; with
    Madame Lynch and sons, 173, 174,
    175; contact with Blyth & Co.,

180, 185, 189; San Fernando
"purge," 191, 223-224; in power,
195-227 passim; physical description, 196-197; conception of
diplomacy, 197-199; activity
during the Paraguayan War, 210-
224; death, 224
López, Inocencia, 108, 109
López, Juan Francisco, 173, 174,
224
López, Pascual, 214
López, Rafaela, 108
López, Venancio, 108, 133, 148;
execution, 224
López Carillo, Juana Paula, 105;
physical description, 107, 108,
109
Luque, 133, 186; as capital, 223;
postwar, 225
Lynch, Eliza Alicia, 109, 133, 162;
lifestyle, 173-175; landholdings,
175, 225; with López at Cerro
Corá, 224
Lynch, John Pablo, 189

Machado, Pablo, 68
Machaín family, 51
Mackenson, Gustavo, 187
McMahon, General Martin, 175, 223
Maíz, Antonio, 124-125
Maíz, Fidel, 196
Maíz, Marco Antonio, 48
Maldonado, Miguel, 102
Mandeville, R., 101
Manlove, James, 191
Marecos, Ramón, 222
María, José (servant), 84; arrested,
120, 121
María, José de, 26-27
Mariscal, El. See López, Francisco
Solano
Marquez de Olinda (ship): seized by
López, 202, 203, 206, 217; as
Paraguayan warship, 205

Marshall, William, 183
Martínez, Captain Toribio, 159
Masterman, George, 185, 191
Matiaúda, Vicente Antonio, 39
Mato Grosso: border questions, 6, 16,
68, 151, 160, 199; commerce
with Paraguay, 44, 67; hostilities
in, 158, 160; Paraguayan invasion
of, 206, 209; warfare in, 216, 217,
219
M'Bayá Indians, 16, 67, 75, 116, 123;
capture Fort Borbón, 33, 44
Mbuyapeí, 119, 181
Meister, Dr. Jorge Frederick: recruited,
153, 179, 180; leaves Paraguay, 183
Melgarejo, Sergeant, 181-182
Melo de Portugal, Pedro, 15
Mendoza, Prudencio de la C., 20
Mestizaje: as characteristic of Para-
guay, 7, 9, 13, 39, 98, 116, 120,
139
Meza, Pedro Ignacio, 205
Miranda, 157, 158
Misões, Brazilian, 28, 53, 79
Misiones, 11, 25. See also Candela-
ria
Mitre, Bartolomé, 199, 200, 206;
as Allied commander-in-chief,
208, 211
Mocobí Indians, 4, 5
Molas, Mariano Antonio, 40, 48,
54, 96; in 1811 congress, 29;
arrested, 96; author of Descrip-
ción histórica de la antigua pro-
vincia del Paraguay, 96, 235 n.
57
Monroe Doctrine, 146
Monteses Indians, 5
Montevideo, 69, 101, 145, 146, 149,
162, 163; in British invasions, 16-
17
Montiel, Captain Vicente, 16, 51;
arrested, 51; executed, 53
Mora, Fernando de la, 42; member

of junta, 29-30; arrested, 37
Morice, George Francis, 162, 169
Moynihan, John Owen, 188
Munck, Eberhard, 122; arrives Pilar, 129, 178; as physician, 180, 191; as tax collector, 134; executed, 221

Ñanducuá, 137, 138
Napoleon, 84
Napoleon III, 161
Newton, William, 183
Noceda family, 51
Ñu Guazú. *See* Campo Grande
Nueva Burdeos, 192-193

Obligado, battle of, 145
Observación, 152
Olimpo (ship), 205
Olivares, 105, 107
Orange, Fort, 82
Orrego, 34
Ortellado, Norberto, 87, 104
Ortiz, Manuel Antonio, 102
Ortiz, Miguel, 138
Ouseley, W. E., 144-145, 178

Paddison, George, 183
Page, Captain Thomas Jefferson, 158, 165-166, 179, 193. *See also Water Witch*
Palacios, Bishop, 223
Palacios, José Joaquín, 125
Palleja, Colonel León de, 216
Panadero, 224
Panés, Bishop, 52, 57, 96
Pão de Açucar, 154
Paraguarí, 27; battle of 25-26
Paraguarí (ship), 205
Paraguay: agriculture, 9, 92-99, 188-189; colonial description of, 3-14, 23, 27-28; commerce, 53-55, 66-74, 129-132, 171-172; crime and punishment, 39, 44, 51-53,

55, 59, 90-91, 99, 102, 113-114, 121, 124, 126-128, 137-138, 140, 185, 186, 196, 216; government of, 11-12, 27-29, 30-34, 85-87, 89-90, 116-118, 119, 123, 124, 131, 175, 204, 216, 225; relations with Brazil, 67-71, 78-79, 147, 149-150, 150-155, 157-160; with Buenos Aires and Argentina, 29, 66, 72-74, 76-78, 139-142, 143-149, 150, 152, 206-207; with Corrientes, 139-140, 141, 143-144; with France, 63-64, 152, 155, 159, 161; with Great Britain, 64-66, 101-103, 140-141, 144-145, 150, 152, 155, 161, 168-170, 178; with United States, 141, 145-147, 150, 152, 155, 157, 158-159, 162-168; industry, 92, 180-182, 186, 217, 219, 220; internal improvements, 33, 34, 122, 178-193; military, forti-fications, 6, 15, 16, 19, 26-27, 31, 33, 44, 123, 179, 183, 192; military, militia, 7, 9, 13, 15-16, 17, 19-20, 25-27, 28, 46-49, 60, 120, 123, 124, 144, 148, 206, 211, 214, 222-223, 225; military, navy, 108, 111, 127, 143-144, 147-149, 160, 166, 182-183, 184, 187, 189, 190, 205-206, 208; military, regular army, 35, 39, 41, 49-50, 52, 59-61, 69-70, 123, 143-145, 147-149, 154, 158, 171, 179, 182-184, 192, 202-206; population, 8, 13, 115-122, 214-215; racial nationalism, 7, 38, 43, 61, 99, 111, 197, 217, 223, 225, 226-227; state socialism, origins, 54, 58, 73, 82, 92-95, 130, 132-138; state socialism, estancias de la República, 71, 73, 82, 93-94, 118-119, 120-123, 127, 133, 134, 152, 192, 215, 219; state socialism,

state lands, 93-94, 132-133, 218,
219; state socialism, state stores,
94; state socialism, trade monopolies, 73, 94, 132, 133-134, 171-
172; state socialism, slavery, 118-
121
Paraguay, Río, 7, 87, 123, 158
Paraguay (ship), 163
Paraguayan Legion, 208
Paraguayan War, 116-117, 183-184,
189-191, 202, 206-224; outbreak,
206-207; demographic base, 214-
215; disease, 215; life on the
homefront, 216-222; Allied occupation, 225-226; casualties, 260
n. 7
Paraná, Río, 33, 77, 78, 177, 180,
204, 208, 209, 211, 217; control
of, by Buenos Aires and Litoral
provinces, 139, 145, 147, 148,
163; free navigation of, 66, 67,
75, 87
Paraná, Río Alto, 5, 6; as barrier,
46, 116, 122; control of, 131,
139, 147, 166
Paraná (ship), 205
Paraná state (Brazil), 7, 130
Pardos (Blacks), 11, 13, 15, 33-34,
39, 58, 79, 82, 84, 90, 93, 98,
110; community characteristics,
115-121; in army, 120, 206; as
criminals, 126-127; on state estancias, 134-138; as Chaco settlers,
192; during Paraguayan War, 220-
222. *See also* Slavery
Paris, 173, 174
Parish, Woodbine, 64-66, 68, 73, 76
Paso, Juan José, 21, 24
Paso Laguna, 137, 138
Paso de Patria, 140, 147, 148; Allied
invasion route, 211
Paso Pucú, 220, 221
Pastore, Carlos, 133
Patiño, Policarpo, 81, 83, 85-86, 97;

attempt to seize power, 102-103;
suicide, 103
Patriotic Literary Society, 33
Payaguá Indians, 4, 5
Paz, General José María, 143-144
Pedro II (Brazil), 151-153, 197,
200, 201, 208
Peel, Sir Robert, 177
Peña, Manuel de la, 55, 108, 142
Peninsulares, 38, 39; restrictions
against, 39, 49, 50, 98; mass
arrest of, 52-53, 91, 95; depor-
tation of, 77; at Pilar, 54-55,
65; as shopkeepers, 114
Pereira Leal, Felipe José, 158
Pérez, Manuel Antonio, 81, 97
Peru, 8
Piers, Claudius B., 184-185
Pikysyry, battle of, 223, 224
Pilar (del Ñeembucú), 12; Espínola
mission, 24-26; conspiracy at,
54-56; commerce at, 54-55, 60,
67, 72-74, 77-78, 93-94, 104,
129, 130-132, 140, 168, 171,
177-179, 217; Argentine threat
to, 147, 148; as seat of sub-
delegado, 87-88; garrison of,
204
Pilar (servant), 84
Pilcomayo, Río, 123
Pimenta Bueno, José Antonio, 151
Pirayú, 119, 186
Piribebuy, 88, 116, 220; as capital,
223
Pla, Josefina, 189
Porteñismo, 18-31, 37, 38, 50
Porteños. *See* Buenos Aires
Prickett, James, 183
Provincia Gigante. *See* Paraguay

Quatrefages, Jean Luis Armand de,
173
Quién Vive, 152
Quiindí, 119, 125; census of libertos,

221
Quiquió, 7, 40, 50, 53, 88; pardo
    community in, 119-120; land
    rents, 133; war donations, 219;
    census of libertos, 221

Railroad, 110, 136, 181, 183, 185-
    186, 188-189; fare schedule, 202
Ramírez, Francisco, 52, 64; as threat
    to Paraguay, 72, 76, 78
Ramírez, José León, 94
Ranching, 12, 92, 133; during war,
    219. *See also* Paraguay, estancias
    de la República
Ranger (ship), 205
Ravizza, Alejandro, 188, 203
Recoleta (Asunción barrio), 105,
    113, 114, 117; auctions in, 134
Recopilación, 89
Regency Council (Spain), 25, 29
Registro Oficial, 225
Remolinos, 16, 19
Rengger, Johann Rudolf, 56; in
    captivity, 65, 83, 85, 91; anti-
    Francia plot, 84
Resquín, General Isidoro, 209
Rhynd, Dr., 191
Riachuelo, battle of, 190, 191, 208
Ribera, Governor Lázaro de, 22-23
Rice crop, 92
Richardson, William, 181, 183
Rinconada, 123, 152
Río Apa (ship), 182, 206
Río Blanco, 154; as boundary, 157,
    158, 160
Río Blanco (ship), 182, 205, 206
Rio de Janeiro, 19, 68, 69, 106, 140,
    146, 150, 151, 152, 154, 159,
    162, 179, 180
Río de la Plata: as region, 7-8, 140-
    141, 182, 189, 197, 198; control
    of, 169, 189
Rio Grande do Sul (Brazil), 7, 28,
    200, 201, 206

Río Jejuí (ship), 182, 206
Río Negro (ship), 205
Río Ygureí (ship), 205
Rivadavia, Bernardino, 72
Rivera, Fructuoso, 76, 77
Riviere, Carlos, 187-188
Robertson, John Parish, 33, 46, 85
Roca, Tristán, 220
Rodríguez, Martín, 72
Rojas, Blas, 27
Rome, 161
Roque Alonso, Mariano, 103-104; as
    consul, 105, 142
Rosas, Juan Manuel: hostility to Para-
    guay, 106, 131, 139, 141-142, 146,
    147-149, 150, 151-152, 154-155,
    177, 178, 198; in Corrientes revolt,
    140-141, 143, 144; fall of, 157,
    158

Saladillo, 82
Salinas, 158
Salta (Argentina), 56, 77
Salter, Commodore, 166
Salto (ship), 205
Salto de Guairá (ship), 182, 206
San Antonio, 16, 133, 163
Sánchez, Domingo, 218; death, 224
San Cosme, 12, 71, 87, 132
San Estanislao, 7, 87, 88, 125, 132;
    executions at, 224
San Fernando, 186; executions at,
    191, 223, 224
San Joaquín, 116, 122, 132, 133,
    222
San José, 123
San José de los Arroyos, 117
San Juan Nepomuceno, 219
San Miguel, 59, 181
San Miguel (Corrientes), 67, 69, 148
San Roque (Asunción barrio), 114,
    119
San Salvador, 216
San Ygnacio Guazú, 132, 133

San Ygnacio Miní, 15
San Ysidro Labrador, 193
Santa Catarina (Brazil), 7
Santa Cruz de la Sierra (Bolivia), 7
Santa Fe (Argentina), 53-54, 77, 91,
    170
Santa Fe y Animas (ship), 72
Santa María de Fe, 12, 64, 132
Santa Rosa, 132, 147
Santiago, 5, 11, 50, 87, 88, 122,
    132
Santo Thomé, 149
São Borja, 32, 53; as commercial
    center, 65, 67-68, 129, 131, 154
São Paulo, 6
Sardinia, 161, 168
Savie, Pascual, 171
Semanario, El, 111, 164, 170, 186,
    220
Seminary, 10, 14, 21-23, 58, 118,
    124
Seven Missions, War of, 9, 231 n. 17
Shipyard, Asunción, 120; British
    guidance of, 181-186
Shubrick, Commodore William B.,
    167
Silva Paranhos, José Maria de, 160
Skinner, Dr., 216
Slavery, 5, 11, 13, 15, 33, 34, 39, 54,
    58, 93, 110; characteristics of,
    117-121; prices, 121; self-purchase,
    121; as labor on estancias de la
    República, 126, 134-138; as
    military resource, 164, 187, 214,
    215, 221-222; abolished, 225
Smith, Thomas Norton, 182
Somellera, Pedro Alcántara, 23, 27-
    29, 31, 82, 97
Soria, Pablo, 56, 67
Spain, 33, 46
State socialism. *See* Paraguay, state
    socialism
Stewart, Dr. William, 183, 216
Sugarcane crop, 92

Supremo, El. *See* Francia, José Gaspar
    de
Surubí, 134-138

Tabapí, 33, 93; as pardo community,
    118, 119, 120; as estancia de
    la República, 134-136; slave
    community during war, 215,
    221
Tacuacorá, 121
Tacuarás, 87
Tacuarí, Río, 26
Tacuarí (ship), 162, 166, 169, 170,
    180, 182, 202, 206
Tacumbú, 109
Talavera, Natalicio, 187, 203, 220
Tapé Indians, 5
Tapúa, 10
Taylor, Alonzo, 183, 188
Tebicuari, Río, 5, 87, 92, 93, 134,
    186, 189, 211; as area of pardo
    settlement, 116, 119
Tebicuari-Guazú, Río, 87
Telegraph, 181, 185-186, 189
Téllez, José Gabriel, 95
Téllez, José M., 184-185
Tembetarí, 90
Temple of Mercy, 37, 40-41
Tevegó, 33-34, 44, 99, 118, 123,
    127. *See also* San Salvador
Theater, National, 109, 115, 187-
    188, 203, 220-221, 222
Thompson, George, 183
Thornton, Edward, 196
Tobacco crop, 19, 44, 71, 72, 92,
    93, 171, 192, 218
Tobatí, 119, 132
Torres, Juana Ysabel Francisca de,
    84
Tranquera de Loreto, 68, 148. *See
    also* Candelaria
Trayo, Jordan Luis de, 130
Treaties, 161-162, 167, 168, 171;
    Madrid, 7; San Ildefonso, 7, 151;

of October, 1812, 31-33, 37, 38;
with Corrientes, 139-140, 143-
144; with Brazil, 149, 151, 152,
154, 157; of the Triple Alliance,
208, 211, 226
Treuenfelt, Robert von Fischer, 186
Trinidad, 87, 132
Trinidad (Asunción suburb), 107,
225
Triple Alliance, War of the. *See* Paraguayan War
Tuyú, 123
Tuyutí, battle of, 212, 214; second
battle of, 222
Twiddell, John, 185

United States: and Paraguay Naviga-
tion Co., 163, 167
Urbieta, Bishop, 161
Urquiza, Justo José, 149, 167, 169,
199; as potential ally of Paraguay,
200, 206
Uruguaiana, battle of, 209, 214
Uruguay, 70, 78; commerce with
Paraguay, 131; hostilities with
Rosas, 143, 149, 150, 151, 154;
recognizes Paraguayan indepen-
dence, 145; Brazilian meddling in,
160, 197-200; political upheavals in,
197-200; signs Treaty of the Triple
Alliance, 208. *See also* Banda
Oriental
Uruguay, Río, 6, 78, 147-148

Valdovinos, Marcos, 21, 51
Valle, Francisco del, 49
Valpy, Henry, 183
Varela, Benito, 154
Varela, Florencio, 196
Vatican, 56, 161
25 de Mayo (ship), 205
Velasco, Governor Bernardo de, 3,
11, 23, 24; in defense against
British, 16-17; response to

Espínola mission, 24-25; mobilization of Paraguay, 25-27; during
1811 coup, 27-28, 29; in royalist
plot, 30; dies, 52
Versen, Max von, 216
Villa del Rosario, 204
Villa Franca, 87, 148
Villamayor, Bernardino, 56, 66, 73,
85, 86, 99
Villa Occidental, 218
Villa Oliva, 148
Villa Rica, 10, 11, 13, 59, 82, 86, 97,
189; political jurisdiction, 88;
estancias de la República at, 93;
as population center, 116; linked
by road to capital, 122; projected
railroad to, 183; telegraph link to,
186; police unit from, 204; contribution to war effort, 214, 215,
219; militia census of, 222
Villeta, 58, 117, 119, 136-137, 223

War of the Triple Alliance. *See* Para-
guayan War
Warren, Harris Gaylord, 133
Washburn, Charles Ames, 162
Washington, D.C., 146, 165, 167
Water Witch (ship), 165; incident
involving, 158-159, 166
Watts, John, 190, 191
Wells, Dr. Henry, 185
Westgarth, Cuthbert, 190
Wheat, crop, 92, 93
Whytehead, William K.: coordinates
Paraguayan modernization, 180-
182, 183, 186, 189; suicide, 190
Wise, Henry A., 146
Wisner, Francisco, 95; leads Corrien-
tes expedition, 143-144, 252 n.
13; leads Candelaria expedition,
147-148; as military advisor, 179,
184

Yabebirí, 139

Yacaguazú, 214

Yaci-Retá Island, 147

Yaguarón, 13, 20, 132; as Velasco's headquarters, 25-26

Yataí, battle of, 208

Yatayty Corá, battle of, 212

Ybiraí, 113; Francia's retirement to, 22, 29, 31, 34, 37, 83

Ybitimí, 7, 215

Ycuamandiyú (San Pedro), 12, 16, 88, 121, 125

Yegros family, 16

Yegros, Antonio Tomás, 29; as barracks chief, 34; arrested, 53; old age, 133

Yegros, Fulgencio, 16, 105; in 1811 coup, 27-28; as junta member, 29, 34, 37; as consul, 38-39, 40, 41, 42, 50-51; executed, 53

Yegros y Ledesma, María Josefa, 20

Yerba mate: commerce in, 4, 7, 8, 33, 44, 46, 71-72, 84, 86, 92, 130, 160, 171; as crop, 8, 93, 122, 132, 133, 134, 147, 153, 217-218

Ygarapé, 137

Yhú, 59, 93

Ypacaraí, 204

Ypané, 132, 220

Ypané, Río, 116, 159

Yporá (ship), 182, 206, 215

Ysasi, José Tomás, 40, 55, 72, 73, 86

Ytá, 7, 27, 132

Ytapé, 132

Ytapúa, 11, 25, 27, 28, 53, 60, 65, 76, 87, 88, 94, 220; as commercial center, 66, 67-71, 72, 74, 77, 78, 82, 93, 97, 104, 130-131, 177, 178

Ytaquí, 152

Ytauguá, 219

Ytororó, battle of, 223

Yutí, 71, 87, 132, 222

Zevallos, Colonel Juan Valeriano de, 28, 34